A Defiant Brush

A Defiant Brush

Su Renshan and the Politics of Painting in Early 19th-Century Guangdong

Yeewan Koon

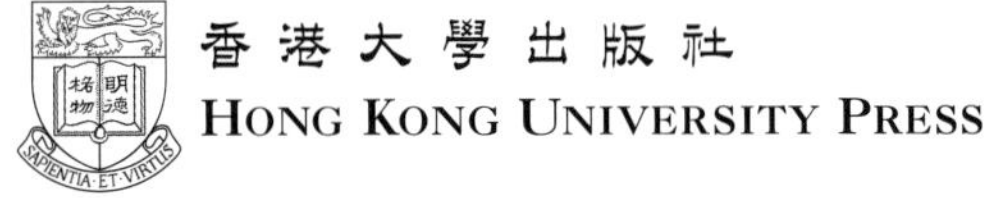

香港大學出版社
HONG KONG UNIVERSITY PRESS

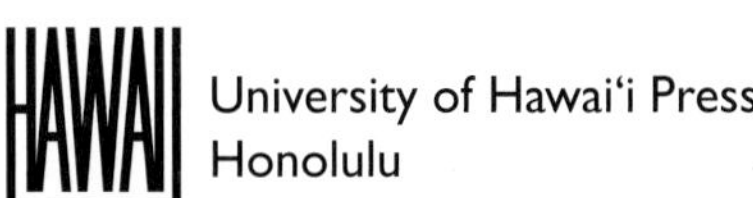

University of Hawai'i Press
Honolulu

This publication has been generously supported by the Hsu Long-sing Research Fund at the University of Hong Kong.

For distribution in Asia, Australia and New Zealand:
Hong Kong University Press
The University of Hong Kong
Pokfulam Road
Hong Kong
www.hkupress.org
ISBN 978-988-8139-61-3

For distribution outside Asia, Australia and New Zealand:
University of Hawai'i Press
2840 Kolowalu Street
Honolulu, Hawai'i 96822 USA
www.uhpress.hawaii.edu
ISBN 978-0-8248-4103-4

Library of Congress Cataloging-in-Publication Data

Koon, Yeewan, author.
  A defiant brush : Su Renshan and the politics of painting in early 19th-century Guangdong / Yeewan Koon.
    pages cm
  Includes bibliographical references and index.
  ISBN 978-0-8248-4103-4 (cloth : alk. paper) 1. Su, Renshan, 1813–1849?—Criticism and interpretation. I. Title.
  ND1049.S894K66 2014
  759.951—dc23
                    2014005774

10   9   8   7   6   5   4   3   2   1

Printed and bound by Paramount Printing Co., Ltd. in Hong Kong, China

To my father

Contents

Chapter Two

Chapter Three

Maps and Charts

Acknowledgments

This book is a labor of love and pain. I was first introduced to Su Renshan in a class held by my advisor, Jonathan Hay. He is a dedicated scholar who asks tough questions and tolerates no fools. So it was that my research on Su Renshan began with a challenge from him. I could not understand how an artist would make paintings that flaunted the boundaries of good taste. When I casually voiced my ponderings, I was asked more seriously in return what I knew about Daoguang paintings. That question led to searches through libraries, archives, museums and private collections. This book is a small measure of a long journey during which time I was fortunate to have had many helping hands directing me to the right course.

From the Institute of Fine Arts, Nixi Cura, Philip Hu, Joan Kee, Francesca Dal Lago, Liu Lihong, Michele Matteini, and Miriam Wattles bounced ideas and prodded thoughts, giving me much-needed feedback with this project. Danny taught me the Irish jig under the Institute's chandeliers because it kept the Qing demons at bay. Roberta Wue was a beacon of light and I could not imagine surviving this journey without her guidance and her grace. Outside the IFA, Dorothy Ko, Jenny Purtle, Mike Hearn, Matthew McKelway, and Stephen Miles were among the many scholars whose words have left their marks. Kao Mayching is a model of scholarly camaraderie, generously sharing her work when a young scholar came knocking on her door.

Mei Chin, Chris Thomas, and Peter Carroll are the dearest of friends who encouraged me by reading various bits of my work as it plodded its way to the finishing line. They are the best of readers and the sharpest of writers, setting a bar that I only dream of reaching. Michael Ouyang provided levity and lightness, often alongside support of the decadent bottled variety. Jonathan, Annping, and Maddie gave me a home whenever I needed an escape and a good meal. But it is their quiet and steadfast support that mattered the most. They taught me what it meant to "just get on with it" by their own exemplary dedication to Chinese history. And my Qing Art Workshop friends, affectionately known as the Qing'sters—Chen Kaijun, Lisa Claypool, John Finlay, Kristina Kleutghen, Lai Yu-chih, Wang Cheng-hua, and Stephen Whiteman, together with Nixi, Roberta, Michele and Liuhong, are the most ardent of supporters of all things Qing. They are my fellow travelers and I am in good company.

At the University of Hong Kong, I am fortunate to have a supportive department with Roslyn (Roz) Hammers, Carolyn Muir, David Clarke, Greg Thomas, and Opher Mansour, alongside my head Daniel Chua, and Dean, Kam Louie. I am especially grateful to Roz who has been a true rock throughout. My students Alice Wong, Candy Leung, Nicole Fung, and Michelle Lau, together with our department's wonderful team (Grace Wong, Karen Leung, and Mr. Yan Pui Ling) helped with the final leg of the journey. Other HKU colleagues were unstinting in their support: Wendy Gan and Tina Pang gave more than required, John Carroll was also ready to share his own works and findings, while Douglas Kerr, Elaine Ho, and Chris Hutton dished out wisdom and apple pies. Liz Puhl, a friend and a cartographer, helped me with my map. Outside the University walls, Penny Tang, Regina de Luna, Yuen Chan, Chris Lalogiannis & Chao He, David & Rachel Schlesinger, Tai Lam & Michael Burke, Alexandra Seno, Kelvin Au, and Louise Wong were always ready to pull me back into the twenty-first century.

This project could not have happened without generous help from numerous institutions. A General Research Fund fellowship from The Research Grants Council, Hong Kong, assisted my fieldwork and writing. The University of Hong Kong provided funding with a Small Projects grant and the Hsu Long-Sing Research Fund generously supported the publication of this book. There are also many curators, collectors, and librarians who opened their doors: Nishigami Minoru and Kure Motoyuki at the Kyoto National Museum; Jenny So, Peter Lam, and Lee Chi-Kwong at the Chinese University of Hong Kong and the Art Museum there; Zhu Wanzhang at the Guangdong Museum; Szeto Yuen Kit, Raymond Tang, and Maria Mok at the Hong Kong Museum of Art; Zhang Hongxing at the V&A Museum; Richard Fabian, the Fok family, and Cary Liu at Princeton Museum; and the librarians at the Sun Yat-sen Library of Guangdong Province, the Philips Library at the Peabody Essex Museum, and the National Archives in Kew, London. Chris T. with his sharp copyediting eye made this a better book—though all erroneous remnants are my own. The HKU Press team headed by Sherlon Ip steered the publication process. Michael Duckworth, the publisher, is a constant force whose unwavering support for scholarly art publications is a splendid, and far too rare, thing.

Over the years, I have tested the patience of my parents and my siblings, and have been aided in no small parts by my beautiful nieces, Chloe, Emily, Sophie, Abigail, and Kayley. My family have supported my many endeavors, even when they were never quite sure what I was doing. They were gentle when needed, tough when required, and always there. They have been waiting for this book, which in their minds was a tangible object that may explain in some small part my insanely long Ph.D., the constant travel, my luddite computer skills that never improved, and the need for coffee. This book is for, especially, my dad, who never saw the project complete, but if he did, I know he would nod and sit me down in front of a bowl of soup, because he never gave up his attempts to wean me off caffeine. He might pat my back, and possibly even be proud.

An Introduction

I began this book as a monograph of an unusual Cantonese artist, Su Renshan (蘇仁山, 1814–ca.1850), who worked at the time of the Opium War. He was from Shunde, a provincial town in the Pearl River Delta area in south China, known more for its silk production and powerful lineage clans than for its great painters. In the mid-nineteenth century, Shunde and its surrounding area, including Guangzhou City (more popularly known as Canton),[1] were subjected to attacks first by the British army and then by local bandits and rebels. Against this rough, volatile background, Su Renshan made paintings that were uncompromising and brassy. Large hanging scrolls abound with unexpected juxtapositions and bear provocative inscriptions criticizing Confucius as someone who "poisoned the people" and otherwise scolding those who mindlessly followed him. His tradition-flouting paintings and transgressive inscriptions make him an ideal candidate for a discussion of the emergence of the modern political artist in Guangdong in the nineteenth century.

His art, however, prompts more questions than answers. To take an example, in his large hanging scroll, *A Celebration of Myriad Birds* (Fig. 1),[2] a subject matter that commonly offers a message of peace and prosperity, Su Renshan has depicted some of the strangest-looking birds in Chinese art. At the bottom of the scroll and painted in the *baimiao* (白描 plain drawing) style of ink outlines is a crane with a misshaped beak bent into a strange hook. Next to this crane is an unusually timid eagle staring at the ground. In the top half of the painting is a group of dagger-tailed swallows flying into one another, creating a cluster of short, fast strokes of black ink. How do we read this painting of odd birds? The damaged title offers little information. Given Su Renshan's contrary personality, do we read the painting as a subversion and inversion of traditional iconography? Do we consider the cluster of swallows as a form of befuddled chaos of human behavior? If we conduct an iconological examination and consider that the image is ideologically informed and relies on the social context for its force even as it shapes that context, what were the cultural and social values that were at stake? As it was likely to have been painted in post-Opium War Guangdong, is it possible to push for a sociopolitical reading of the painting as a manifestation of the collapse of local society, or argue that it reveals a collective expression of frustrations with the government and an emperor oblivious to the situation in Guangdong as foreign traders claimed possession of land that was once theirs. The painting also raises the question of whether other artists were making similar types of painting or whether they shared Su's sociopolitical concerns. Furthermore, the painting is satirical in scope and angry in effect. How does anger find its way into ink painting? How do we evaluate this type of painterly process in relation to a social history of nineteenth-century painting? If Su subverted the traditional meaning of the genre, is a similar type of transgression reflected in the formal

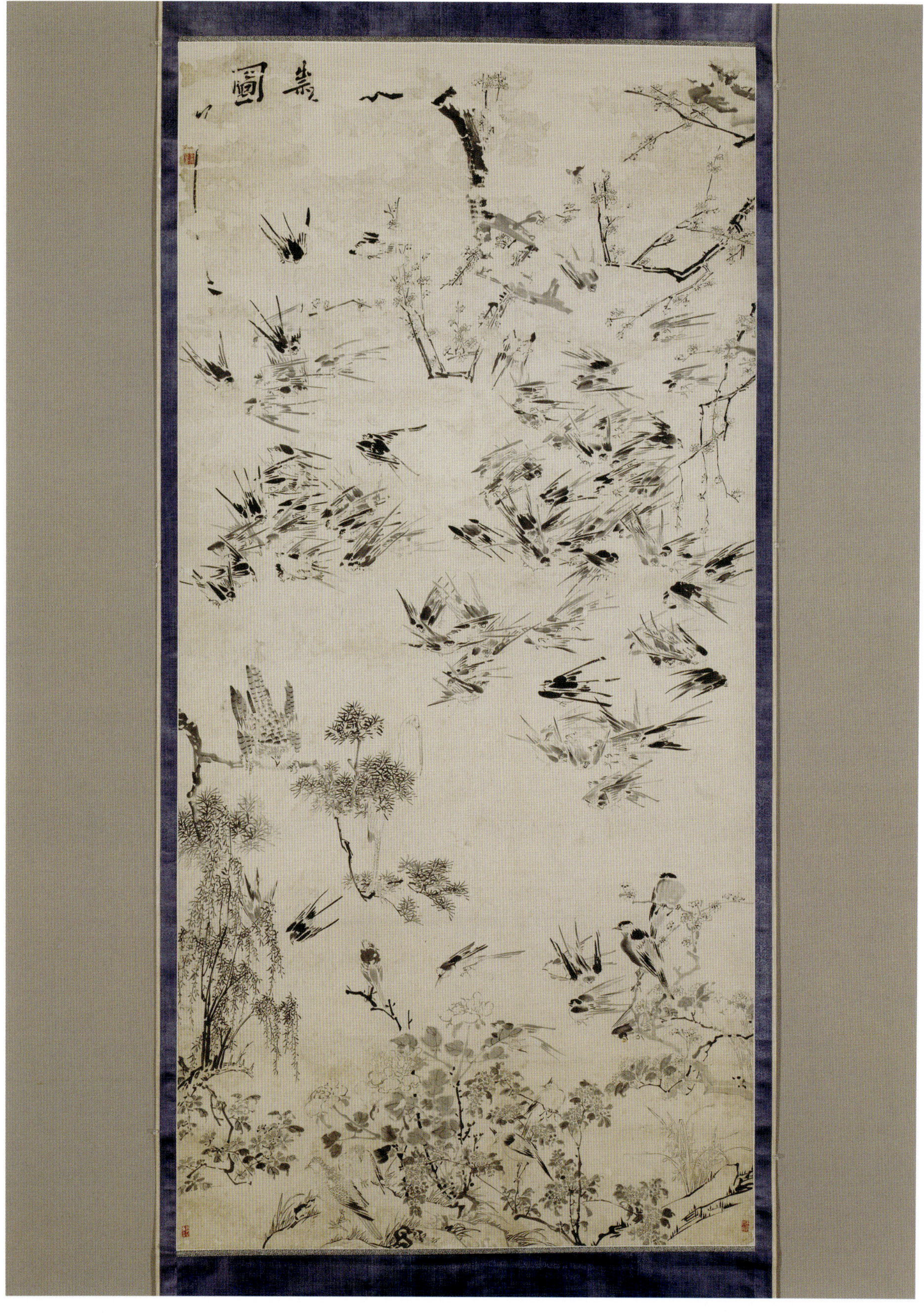

Figure 1 Su Renshan, *A Celebration of Myriad Birds*. Hanging scroll, undated, ink on paper, 243 × 123 cm. Kyoto National Museum.

properties such as the brush mode or the composition? How far does he go?

I wanted to write a monograph that could make sense of Su Renshan's *A Celebration of Myriad Birds* and consider (among other questions) how a painterly process may impact (and vice versa) the sociopolitical landscape of a postwar Guangdong, and how shifts in painting practices and styles also corresponded to changes in values and ethics in ink painting during the early nineteenth century. It quickly became clear that this task had some major obstacles, at least two of which are related to Chinese art historiography. First, Su did not operate within the familiar art circles of Guangzhou City, whose participants were the primary record keepers and tastemakers in the region. Since he is missing from the records and texts, and absent from literary art activities, it is impossible to anchor Su Renshan using the standard primary sources (e.g. collected writings, poems, and gazetteers) to investigate his role and position in relation to his peers, which in turn makes a broader study difficult if it was solely based on relational coding (where social connections such as friendships, or client-patron relationships follow certain codes such as inscriptional formalities or placement of figures). If I maintained the canonical tradition of situating those who stray outside the norm as oddballs and misfits, then a monograph would inevitably cast Su Renshan's work as an exception rather than as an example of early nineteenth-century art. The resulting danger would be an intimate picture using only his biography to explain his art, and unwittingly replicating the monograph's tendency to celebrate the "genius" of an artist.

The second obstacle is that the early nineteenth century is an under-researched area, referred to, often frustratingly, as the "black hole" of Chinese art history. Added to this, the study of Guangdong art has been the casualty of the parochialism of a literati-biased canon that favored the cultural centers of Beijing and Jiangnan (the Lower Yangtze region) and saw the 1800–50 period as either too late (past the Qing Dynasty's peak), or too early (not yet modern).[3] Pivotal in this narrative of decline is the Opium War that demarcates the mid-nineteenth century as a time when China was weak and needed the West in order to modernize. While historians of China and international relations have revisited and interrogated this assumption with numerous tomes, the smaller community of art historians has yet to make substantial arguments by looking at the mid-nineteenth century. The current art history canon links eighteenth-century Yangzhou to late nineteenth-century Shanghai with only whispers of what happened in between. There are a few exceptions. In Zhuang Shen's study of collecting in Guangdong, *Cong baizhi dao baiyin: Qing mo Guangdong shuhua chuangzuo yu shoucang shi* (從白紙到白銀：清末廣東書畫創作與收藏史 From paper to gold: A history of collecting painting and calligraphy in late Qing Guangdong), he examines five major local collections and related painting movements.[4] Another rare exception is Wan Qingli's book *Bing fei shuai luo de bainian: 19 shiji Zhongguo huihua shi* (並非衰落的百年：十九世紀中國繪畫史 The century was not declining: A history of Chinese painting in the nineteenth century), whose title says it all.[5] However, the reluctance, if it is such, to acknowledge the early nineteenth century pales in comparison to the bias against the possibility that mid-nineteenth century Guangdong was an art center of consequence.

This book attempts to address the current gap in the field, by connecting different spheres of artistic production into a broader historical context that includes the much-maligned Opium War. But it also leaves areas that cannot be covered. For example, I have neglected works by female artists, an area of Chinese art history that is still under-studied because of the lack of textual sources. Some Guangdong female artists worked alongside the male artists discussed in this chapter, including Yu Ling (余菱, mid-nineteenth century), who was the concubine of Su Liupeng (蘇六朋, ca.1814–60), a professional artist who I discuss in Chapter One. Yu Ling worked at the Su family workshop in the old part of the city and made paintings that deftly followed the style of Su Liupeng. Another female artist is Ju Qing (居慶, ca. nineteenth century), who was the daughter of Ju Chao (居巢, 1811–65), a notable bird and flower painter in Guangxi. I have also sidelined the finger painters of Guangdong, a type of art-making popular in the late eighteenth century by scholarly artists and continued by professional workshop artists in the nineteenth century. Finger painting is more commonly associated with Bannerman artists and in particular the seventeenth-century painter Han Bannerman Gao Qipei (高其佩, 1660–1734) in Beijing. There are, however, two reasons that may account for the flourishing of this type of art-making in Guangdong: The largest concentration of Bannermen outside of Beijing was in Guangzhou; and Gao Qipei's grandson, Gao Bing (高秉, act. ca. late eighteenth century), who, in 1771, published his grandfather's treatise *Zhitou huashuo* 指頭畫說 (On finger painting) in Guangdong while he was working in the region, wanted to take advantage of the low cost of printing.[6] The publication of a finger-painting manual associated with known artists who served the Qing court may have also contributed to an interest in this type of painting in Guangdong. Overall, the presence of these artists would have enriched the story of Guangdong art, and, in the case of female painters, may intersect with Su Renshan's interest in depictions of women; but without further resources, I must put their achievements and contributions aside.

I do, however, address other gaps and biases—against early nineteenth-century art in general, and Guangdong and Su Renshan specifically—in order to answer a slew of questions: What type of art

circulated in early nineteenth-century Guangdong? What is the significance of Su Renshan? Is it possible to integrate the mainstream with the regional (such as Guangdong) and the misfits (such as Su Renshan)? And how might the answers to these questions alter the contours of the current Chinese art narrative?

In *A Defiant Brush*, the story begins with an examination of artistic practices and political engagement in Guangzhou City that act as indices for a critical assessment of Su's paintings and ends with a second narrative of what happened to these structures after the Opium War. The result is not a seamless narrative but one that sets up two related contexts in which Su Renshan's works are evaluated and results in Su coming in and out of the overall story. What I may have lost by giving up the coherence of a linear narrative that follows the career of a single artist I have gained in a more trenchant mode of assessing a complex figure who can only be approached through refractions like mirrors of a kaleidoscope that show the material at the core of the device and that can be incorporated in different fields. It allows for a better understanding of Guangdong during its transition from a trading hub to a place of war, and of an artist caught in the midst of that change. With each of the contextual narratives, the politics are different: The first of a mercantile world demonstrates the sociopolitics of art at a time when the negotiation and competition of local identity took on different rhetoric and form. The second is the politics of war where violence and chaos prompted complex responses to a world that was both changed and still changing. The themes of transformation and of temporal disconnect reflect the anxieties of a region afflicted by war, and the social differences that were evident as dominant forces shifted, especially as elite members took on grassroots themes and narratives as modes of defiance.

Interwoven within the different contexts are a biography of Su Renshan and my close readings of his paintings. I am aware that my reliance on biography strays back to earlier art historical practices (which I have been critical of) and veers away from the current art history preference for using social matrices, and urban relations, and similar issues to extrapolate art's meaning (which I do make use of). But I cannot conceive of this book without a nuanced reading of Su Renshan's biography. Reading his inscriptions (the only textual source available), his social awkwardness, his frustrations with conventions, and his difficult relationship with his father seep out of the surface of his paintings, at times so palpably that it is impossible not to consider his personal circumstances. My close reading of his artworks also shifts from a purely social history of art to an argument based on visual analysis that allows me to better situate Su's work against a network of ideas and reflections. It is a process that can be speculative (in that it is not reliant on external sources), but it is also an explorative approach that can expose points of view that are never explicitly revealed in texts and social relations. It is only with this serpentine mapping of people and places, and a deliberate variety of approaches, that I am able to show how Su Renshan's paintings are prototypical and representative rather than singular and unique. The biography anchors my close readings of Su Renshan's painting as much as the social context explains his reasons to paint.

The chronological and methodological structures of the book are grounded by my interest in the representation (and misrepresentation) of multiple identities—a feature of nineteenth-century Guangdong and arguably of Qing Dynasty in general. Recent scholarship on the multiple identities of the Qing has focused on the imperial family and the capital. Notable works include Patricia Berger's *Empire of Brightness: Buddhist Art and Political Authority in Qing China*[7] and Susan Naquin's *Peking: Temples and City Life (1400–1900)*.[8] Two earlier publications continue to exert influence in the field: Richard Vinograd's *Boundaries of the Self: Chinese Portraits 1600–1900*[9] investigates the negotiation of identity as a core element of representation, and Jonathan Hay's dense *Shitao: Painting and Modernity in Early Qing China*[10] discusses, among many other themes, the nuances of art as a mediator and agent of an artist's subjectivity. The works of these scholars have directed my own undertaking as I looked at the multiple identities that were handily adopted by the people, places, and art discussed, as well as what was at stake in the aftermath of war. As the chapters unfold, we will see that differences and multiplicity (e.g. serial images or local versus metropolitan settings) were necessary to forge relations between different communities. In contrast to the multiplicities, the singular identity stands as a performance rather than an actuality, even if it appears to be concrete and abiding.

Multiple identities were an important part of forming networks, in which a wealthy merchant could command the identity of a Fujian migrant, a Guangzhou scholarly elite, or an international entrepreneur, depending on the situation. This mobility of identity extends to place: Guangzhou was alternately a synecdoche of China, a place of strange customs, and a site steeped in local history. Each of these roles relied on the dialogue between the viewer, the artist, and the object viewed, so that an image of the thirteen factories could mean Guangdong as China, as a tourist site, or as a symbol of ownership. Similarly, there are dialogues that contested the invisible boundaries designed to segregate social and cultural spaces by crisscrossing the high and low, and in Su Renshan's *A Celebration of Myriad Birds*, the painting and the satire.

To untangle the tight-knit communities and identities in Guangdong's art world, broad strokes are used in the first chapter to determine how value and meaning of works of art were formed and assessed when export trade was thriving in the city. The first broad stroke in the opening chapter looks at the circulation of images. Taking on Carlo Ginzburg's idea of iconic circuits and Deborah Poole's work on the visual economy of the Andes, I examine the relationship between different types of art forms, audience, and value systems.[11] The conventional mode of defining "high" and "low" in Chinese art tends to group artists, audiences, and modes of making into distinct social groups: literati ink painting and the elite in one group, and popular arts in colorful palette in the second group. In general, scholars have debunked the simplicity of this model, and I follow this path but would add that the model of literati versus non-literati works was used in the early nineteenth century as a way of constructing social exclusion and is therefore still relevant to our understanding of art of this period. In particular, the closed circuit operated to define relationships between patrons and artists, viewers and makers that determined certain types of art as being appropriate. In contrast, the open circuit allowed for a greater blurring of social and cultural audiences, multiple meanings and readings of certain types of images, and determined meanings for more popular imagery that could be understood by a broad range of viewers. Similarly, these relationships between audience, artworks and artists also established different ranges of costs, and modes of transactions.

To make my argument of a closed circuit in Guangzhou City, I scrutinize the making of a regional literary identity among the elite and the relationship between the center and the periphery (or the capital and the local) where the center was being co-opted into the local (and vice versa). I argue that the early nineteenth century marked the beginnings of a Guangzhou literati art canon with artists and patrons participating in the construction of a regional identity that fits into a national narrative.

Recent scholarship that focuses on the local has looked at the significance of diverse human activities as opposing agents in the construction of place and identity.[12] For example, William Rowe has looked at local elite cultures through a number of different lenses, including the importance of lineage corporations, different associational forms, elite activism, and local competition.[13] These studies shift the discussions of the elite class from outside a state-sanctioned hierarchy and the core-periphery model. I follow this approach of local history by framing the making of regional art as a construction rather than as an accident of geography. Guangdong was, after all, made up of migrants, sojourners, and lineage clans who were competing for cultural clout by appropriating icons, histories, and local affairs.

One of the key players in the construction of a Guangdong identity was the nationally renowned Yangzhou official Ruan Yuan (阮元, 1764–1849), who arrived as the new Governor-General of Guangdong and Guangxi in 1817 and within three years had set up Xuehaitang Academy, an institution supervised by the local leading scholarly elite. Ruan's interest in Han scholarship and evidential research set the academic tone of his institution. Previously, in Yangzhou, Ruan had founded academies, published gazetteers, and promoted the rigorous study of *jinshixue* (金石學 the study of bronzes and stone inscriptions) that contributed to the city's intellectual reputation.[14] Ruan Yuan's Yangzhou provided a template for Guangzhou's transformation into a scholastic city of literary significance. By mapping a connection between Yangzhou and Guangdong, I add to the current discussions of the making of urban cosmopolitanism that view eighteenth-century Yangzhou as the precursor to late nineteenth-century Shanghai.[15] As with their Jiangnan counterparts, the Xuehaitang scholars honed their skills by collecting and transcribing inscriptions, compiling anthologies of Guangdong poets, and publishing studies on local products and other investigative compilations of works. The high volume of published books printed on the premises added to the academy's scholastic aura.

The Xuehaitang scholars formed a community outside of kinship and native ties, structured according to empire-wide models of intellectual brotherhoods. Shared intellectual interests not only brought together scholars and officials with similar pedagogical concerns but created a network of patrons that financially supported the academy's projects and related interests, such as bookshops, publishing, and libraries. The pedagogical agenda, linked to the Jiangnan tradition, also appealed to Guangdong's community of sojourners and migrants, who had tenuous ties to the dominant lineages from the Delta region.[16] This is evident in the financial support given by the Fujian entrepreneurs who had made Guangdong their home and who used their attachment to the academy and its community of scholars as a means of gaining local cultural cachet.

Similar activities can be seen in the Guangdong art worlds. Between 1840 and 1865, eminent Guangzhou-based collectors were publishing catalogues of their collections on an unprecedented scale, thereby making known what they owned, and in one case, how much they paid for it.[17] On one level, catalogues were effective mechanisms for transforming economic power into cultural power by reinforcing one's reputation within and beyond one's immediate space and time. On another level, catalogues were a means to connect previously marginal localities to broader networks of cultural power. Pan Zhengwei (潘正煒, 1796–1850), belonging to the third Guangzhou-based generation of a Fujian merchant family that settled in Panyu, had one of the largest collections of paintings documented with a price list attached, *Tingfanlou shuhua ji* (聽颿樓書畫記 Record of calligraphy and painting at the Tower of Listening to the Sails). Close scrutiny of this catalogue reveals networks formed by marriages, mentorship, patronage, and friendship, as well as the relationship between social identity of collector and possession of objects in the collection. The price list is also a valuable indicator of what type of art and what art objects were more prized, contributing insights into elite taste in the region.

I conclude my discussion of the making of a Cantonese literati canon by focusing on Xie Lansheng (謝蘭生, 1760–1831), the leading scholar-artist of the early nineteenth century. Xie was closely linked to the Pan family, participating in gatherings and other literary activities hosted by the *cohong* merchants (a state-sanctioned guild of merchants responsible for trade with Europe and America) and other members of this elite group of men. Xie attempted to create a lineage of Cantonese literati painters that could trace their roots to Shitao (石濤, 1642–1707), the Ming loyalist who had close ties with poets and families in Guangdong. He also adapted the style of Wu school artists to depict Guangdong landscape. I examine how Xie adopted and adapted the traditional forms of iconography and canonical styles of "literati" painting into Guangdong, and more specifically into Guangzhou City.

My investigation of an open circuit narrows to focus and expand on current scholarship on pre-modern non-literati Guangdong art, namely, export art made at workshops for a Euro-American audience and that had little or no engagement with "real" Chinese ink paintings. I will show how the categories differentiating art practices—Chinese and Western, scholarly and non-scholarly—were crossed, mixed, and separated. Although arguments that stress the fluid boundaries between China and the West, or scholarly and non-scholarly, are so common in modern art history as to be almost trivial, these categories were used by nineteenth-century practitioners, sometimes as rhetorical devices, to form an image of an urban cosmopolitan.

An example of the complex interactions between the cognitive nature of an image (what it purports to represent) and its social usages (how the object or image is used) is a 1761 album of different types of street workers commissioned by a local official and presented to the Qianlong Emperor (乾隆帝, r. 1739–96) as a birthday gift. The album, showcasing local street customs, products, and characters, was also a representation of the variety of life that prospered under the emperor's rule. By the end of the eighteenth century, the album, or a variation of it, found its way to Guangdong, where it was used as a template for export art made by local artisans for a Western audience who understood them as quintessential images of China. What we see is that the ethnographic art of the export world shares properties with local art practices, thus complicating the current narrative that divides the two practices as separate arenas. Overall, Guangzhou emerges as a city of active borrowing, creative imitation and diverse appropriation.[18]

Chapter Two turns away from Guangzhou into the outlying areas of the Guangdong region and the West River Basin area. Focusing on Su Renshan, I turn to his biography and examine an artist who straddled the world of scholarly ink painting and the popular arts in an area that competed with the cultural center of Guangzhou. Su was very aware of the urban dynamics and intellectual and artistic interests current in the city, but he left no mark on Guangzhou's cultural production. This was not unusual, as there is a general dearth of textual information about artistic production outside the city. The lacuna does not imply that there was no artistic practice outside the city. For example, a rare entry in the *Foshan Gazetteer* recorded that a young Su Renshan worked briefly as an artist in residence for Liang Jiutu, a scholar-official who was active in local community projects and known for his collection of rocks.[19] The record suggests that elite art practices in Delta towns were not unusual. In fact, it is more likely that their absence in documents reflects the lack of compulsion to catalogue cultural production to gain social cachet in an area

where lineage connections formed the most important power structure. A parallel situation existed in other forms of elite cultural practices. Steven Miles's research on Guangdong's academies has shown a conscious differentiation and competition between the outer regions and a city that separated literary practices.[20] Furthermore, the textual production of compilations and anthologies of local traditions, which was once under the purview of the Delta hinterlands, was co-opted by Xuehaitang scholars who redirected the focus from Guangdong's outskirts to the city center. While it is always dangerous to use historical absences as evidence, in this instance, it is possible to suggest that elite art circuits may have existed in the hinterlands, but as with scholarly textual practices, much of the center of production shifted to the city. Scholar-artists such as Su Renshan, who did not venture into the city to find work but remained in distant regions such as Cangwu (which bordered the provinces of Guangdong and Guangxi), faced the challenge of being very peripheral members of a scholarly world dominated by those in the city. However, Su's outsider status was partly of his own doing; after failing his exams for the second time, he decided he would never sit for them again despite his father's wishes, and secretly wandered elsewhere rather than study. As a result, he was forced to leave home. Su, who recognized that his life was about to change, wrote three autobiographical chronicles (in inscriptions) charting his life from the age of two until this moment. His accounts trace the journey of a person who felt restricted by the social confines and familial responsibilities of being the elder son of a large clan family. In the absence of anything more reliable, Su's own words provide the best insight into his paintings and life as an artist in the Delta hinterlands and offer a rare insight to a third type of artistic production. It is in light of this that I have chosen to split the analysis of Su Renshan into two parts: a biographical account with an analysis of his approaches, to a consideration of his works after the Opium War. It is as important to recognize where to place Su in a broader context of Guangdong art world, as it is to consider how a historical event can shape the direction of art.

Su Renshan's personal circumstances and his willful character explain in part his pictorial experiments, which often navigated the tension between the vernacular and the elite world of learning. Su's artistic experiments form what I call a "literary vernacular." He created ink paintings with long textual inscriptions that were often self-referential and typical of elite practices. He drew on his own literatus background and often cited canonical texts such as the Classics, histories, and biographies of famous paragons. However, his ink paintings also refer to the religious and mythical worlds favored by popular artists and local Cantonese language and rituals. His paintings have been described as intellectualized folk art, which is a fitting description, although it omits his paintings of ordinary mothers, earlier scholarly exemplars, as well as literary women. Hence, I use the term "literary vernacular" to capture the breadth of his themes and the juxtapositions that he favored. As an artistic conceit unfettered by literati and vernacular expectations, this approach led to some of his most experimental works.[21]

Su's five-year exile from home also coincided with the end of the Opium War. Stepping back to look at the larger context of what the war meant to the people who witnessed the event, Chapter Three attempts to interpret the Opium War not as a marker of China's modernity but as a local war. The consequences of war affected those who experienced and witnessed the violent skirmishes on the streets, the increased banditry in the suburbs, and the growing xenophobia that extended to anyone considered an outsider. As a result of the waning of the state's presence, local power grew with each militia organization, street watch campaign, and fight against angry mobs. Despite the signing of the treaties, various communities, sometimes organized by shops on a street overseen by the wealthiest merchant, joined forces to prevent the British from entering the Old City. The Manchu plenipotentiary Qiying (耆英, 1787–1858), who was responsible for placating his foreign counterparts while maintaining the interests of the emperor, failed to appease an increasingly angry Guangdong. His diplomatic gestures, while seemingly successful to the court and those outside south China, did not achieve any semblance of peace in Guangdong.

If art can be considered a mediated form of ethos, what type of art emerged at this critical junction of Guangdong history? A surfeit of attention towards the intricacies and exigencies of pictorial responses to war in Chinese art means that Chapter Three is partly a recovery of this history. Some of the responses to the Opium War followed traditional narrative strategies, including referencing famous stories of the past to talk of contemporary events. This indirect, but common, form of storytelling could simultaneously combine poignancy and emotional distance by tapping into a ready body of works with established sets of emotional sensibilities and aesthetics; it provided a familiar shortcut to intelligibly relay experiences and emotions. The historical circumstances are what give the strategies specificity, but also pose different problems. For example, the differences in circumstances between the Opium War (which primarily affected the southeast) and earlier dynastic wars and changes (affecting the whole country) may have led to a type of narrative rupture.

From a methodological perspective, there are two impediments that make my analysis more challenging. First, in painting, the lack of a schema or structure to depict violence made any attempts to do so seem strange or at times overly transgressive, so any attempts to depict violence had to demonstrate a certain restraint (unless the goal was to be openly and politically transgressive). Second (and here I draw on work by trauma studies specialists), the experience of violence is often mitigated by the tension between the compulsion and the inability to tell. I would argue that these two elements (a struggle with pictorial conventions and an inability to directly articulate events and emotions) came together in the shadowy worlds of mists, dreams, and ghosts, and that precedents for the use of this type of space in text and images allowed a means of speaking of contemporary anxieties and fear, and at the same time, the ambiguity allowed artists to better negotiate the gap between experience and narrative. I will argue that it was in this ill-defined space that rebirth (of power, of city, of country) was deemed possible, and stories of defiance were told, even though the war had been fought and lost. This delayed response imbued the limbo state of dreams and mists with a foreboding as much as it exerted the need to fight. At the same time, the circulation of stories about individual acts of defiance cultivated a collective sense of loyalty and regional pride that reached outside the social networks of individuals and contributed to a repository of images that potentially spoke of the nation.

As outlined in Chapter Three, the connections between art and specific social attitudes towards acts of violence are often too amorphous to construct any systematic examination of pictorial expressions, and in order to excavate richer meanings I delve deeper, rather than wider, with close readings of works by a single artist.[22] Refocusing on Su Renshan and turning to his virulent attacks on the hypocrisy of Confucian institutions and learning, my final two chapters look at the darker facets of history and psyche by examining the "violence" in his painting. Both chapters use close readings and, when placed side by side, return my analysis to the theme of the literary vernacular discussed in Chapter Two.

The first focuses on how Su politicized vernacular images of gods and fables to attack Confucius

and certain types of learning. Here, violence is understood not as a motif (as in images of violence) but as an outward gesture of anger. Su's literary vernacular approach allowed for satire, interventions, and destructions to take place by drawing on the conflict between differences. Unlike the depiction of absence, which acts as a form of limbo where rebirth is possible, discussed in Chapter Three, Su's angry, disruptive gestures spill forth excessively, crowding his paintings with words and markings that have the visceral presence of someone shouting out words at the viewer. There is no room for a response from the reader, for reflection, but only confrontation.

The final chapter continues the argument, but my line of reasoning follows Su's depiction of women. This chapter also returns full circle to the root of the literary vernacular: the world of novels. I have borrowed this term not only for its usefulness but also to highlight an aspect of being an artist in imperial China. Scholar-artists were trained as and perceived themselves to be educated men who painted, composed poetry, wrote calligraphy, and, later, some penned books. In the eighteenth century, the literary novel was an established genre, and notable works include *Rulin waishi* (儒林外史 The scholars, 1750, by Wu Jingzi 吳敬梓), *Honglou meng* (紅樓夢 Dream of the red chamber, ca.1791, by Cao Xueqin 曹雪芹), and *Jinghuayuan* (鏡花緣 Flowers in the mirror, 1821–28, by Li Ruzhen 李汝珍). At the core of these novels is the nature and value of the more traditional *ru* (儒 Confucian) scholarship. The paragon sage embodied not only benevolence, righteousness, and virtue but also textual and ritual competence. However, in the seventeenth and eighteenth centuries, there were many debates between those who followed Song learning and those who favored classical Han learning as to which provided the greater example of learning for the career official, and what sort of literary values were fundamental for the moral and intellectual well-being of the scholar. As writers placed these values under scrutiny, and they themselves received the training that forged these values, what was increasingly at stake was the very core of their identity: the purpose of scholarship. If the novels used various narrative devices that teased out this identity crisis, by the mid-nineteenth century, Su Renshan, with an arguably heavier hand, pushed these issues to the forefront with his political paintings that berate the failure of Confucius and the state academies. Su's many portraits of female scholarly communities have to be considered side by side with his belligerent attacks on Confucius and the hypocrisy of systems that primed male scholars to become the moral and intellectual backbone of China.

In the course of my research, I came to realize how the Qing literary novel was more than a source of inspiration for Su Renshan. Su was at his most daring when he interwove histories, recalled anecdotes with puns and passion, and placed himself within his accounts as a storyteller chronicling the twists and turns of a world turned upside down. To understand Su as a storyteller is to understand him as someone who took on the role of a cultural critic, who crossed the past with the present and blurred reality with fiction, as literary novelists have done for so long. In this broader picture, far from an anachronism, Su Renshan emerges as an example of a scholar who painted, and his paintings are testimonies urging for change.

Collecting and Writing Su Renshan

The writings of Su Renshan and Guangdong art have their own particular historical path. As Su Renshan was not part of Guangzhou's urban elite, his life and works received little attention prior to the 1940s. The Su family genealogy, the preface dating to 1856, provides rudimentary information. An inscription of 1904 by Su Ruohu (蘇若瑚, 1856–1917), a clan member, is one of the earliest writings on Su Renshan and his life as an artist.[23] As mentioned, several anecdotes recorded in the *Foshan Zhongyi xiangzhi*, a local gazetteer compiled by Xian Baogan (冼寶幹) and others in 1923, provide a rare record of Su working for one of his few known patrons, Liang Jiutu (梁九圖, act. nineteenth century), a Shunde native based in Foshan. However, Su escaped the attention of Wang Zhaoyong (汪兆鏞, 1861–1939), who compiled the first comprehensive collection of biographies of Cantonese artists, *Lingnan hua zhenglue*, in 1927.[24]

Academic interest in Su Renshan has been closely linked to the sociopolitical situations of Guangdong and the interests of collectors. The first major collector to systematically accumulate Su Renshan's works was an outsider: Suma Yakichiro (須磨彌吉郎, 1892–1970), a Japanese consul serving in Guangzhou from 1924 to 1928. He collected many of Su Renshan's paintings and may have stimulated a cottage industry in forgeries.[25] Interest among local scholars and collectors occurred soon after with the Cantonese scholar Jian Youwen (簡又文, 1896–1978), known best for his work on the Taiping Rebellion, who began collecting in the 1930s, compiling a large collection that was later given to the Art Gallery, The Chinese University of Hong Kong. Jian was an ardent promoter of Cantonese historical and cultural studies. In 1940, he organized the exhibition "Cultural Relics of Guangdong Province" held at the Fung Ping Shan Museum (February 22–26) in Hong Kong. The exhibition produced a three-volume work on Guangzhou culture, society, and the arts, including several short studies on Su Renshan. However, the Japanese invasion of Hong Kong following their attack on Pearl Harbor interrupted further scholarship. Jian fled to Guangzhou, and this became his new base of activities. In May 1948, he organized an exhibition at the Guangdong Archives, supported by the Committee for the Cultural Treasures of Guangdong, featuring 120 paintings from his collection. However, political tensions in Guangdong led to Jian's return to Hong Kong, along with his collection.

Jian's interest in Su Renshan intersected with other Hong Kong-based collectors and scholars, and collectively they have been crucial in advocating for studies on Cantonese arts and culture, with regular newspapers and journals contributing to a mass dissemination of Cantonese identity that has had a national impact. Su Renshan's paintings have been represented in several exhibitions, including the 1958 exhibition held in Beijing entitled "The Last One Hundred Years of Chinese Painting."

The next two waves of studies on Su Renshan occurred at times when identity politics was at its most vocal. In May 1967, Hong Kong pro-communists turned a labor dispute into large-scale unrest against British colonial rule. Massive strikes, organized demonstrations, and bombings continued throughout that year. Some members of the media who voiced opinions against these actions were murdered. By the time the riots finally subsided, 51 people had been killed, and over 800 had been wounded. The leftist plans backfired, as the indiscriminate violence interrupted and threatened the lives of ordinary citizens. Indeed, it was during this period that a Hong Kong identity emerged. From this intense period to the early 1970s, there was widespread interest in a romanticized notion of subverting the established order and fighting for the rights of the underdog, particularly within the film industry. Rebellion and the challenge of social norms were two of the defining aspects of Hong Kong's cultural identity during this period. Not surprisingly, Su Renshan's rebellious nature found a place within this milieu. In 1966, an exhibition of his work was shown in the City Hall Museum, Hong Kong. His work was also part of another major exhibition again held in City Hall in 1974 entitled "Kwangtung

Painting." Bridging these two exhibitions, in 1970, there were three major publications on Su Renshan looking to place him, and by extension Hong Kong, on the international map: Chu-Tsing Li's article, "Su Jen-shan (1814–1849), The Rediscovery and Reappraisal of a Tragic Cantonese Genius"; Pierre Ryckmans's *The Life and Work of Su Renshan: Rebel, Painter and Madman, 1814–1849*; and Jian Youwen's *Huatan guaijie Su Renshan* (畫壇怪傑蘇仁山), which is also entitled *Su Jen-shan: Eccentric Genius of Kwangtung: His Life and Art.*[26]

Chu-Tsing Li identifies Su Renshan as an anachronism, a genius born out of his time; Pierre Ryckmans has written a lively account based on anecdotes that speak of the radical perversity of an artist who may have been mad and was certainly different from his peers. Jian Youwen is more tentative in presenting Su Renshan's psychological profile, although he, too, suggests that the personal eccentricities of this artist indicate his possible insanity. Jian, as an intellectual historian, focuses on the philosophical ruminations in Su Renshan's colophons to paintings in his own collection.[27] Nonetheless, what all three scholars share is a sympathetic picture of Su Renshan as a tragic artist, even drawing comparisons with Vincent van Gogh.[28]

The next wave of interest occurred in the late 1980s and early 1990s, and again appears to coincide with the political situation in south China. On December 19, 1984, the Joint Declaration was signed between China and the United Kingdom, whereby China was to resume sovereignty over Hong Kong in 1997. The anxiety generated before and after this political watershed may have been the impetus for two important exhibitions. The first, "Paintings of Su Liupeng and Su Renshan," was held in May 1988, at the Guangzhou Art Gallery. This exhibition became the occasion to invite many prestigious scholars from China as a means of highlighting Guangdong as a national cultural center. The second exhibition, which was the first of a series on Cantonese art planned by The Chinese University of Hong Kong and Guangzhou Art Gallery, was held in 1990, as an exercise in co-operation between these leading institutions of adjoining regions. The catalogue of the latter exhibition by Kao Mayching is the most informative study on Su Renshan's style to date and divides the development of Su's styles into early, mid, and late periods.[29] It also investigates issues of authenticity and traces the origins of various anecdotes that had hampered previous scholarship.

Issues of Authenticity

In the field of Chinese painting, authenticity is often a thorny issue, and scholars are in frequent disagreement, partly because the criteria and methods for assessing paintings vary so widely. While some scholars prefer a close microscopic reading of seals and brush strokes, others look for verification in compositions, stylistic quirks, and inconsistencies. Pierre Ryckmans has contributed the most in this area in relation to Su Renshan. He assesses the authenticity of Su's paintings in his catalogue with short commentaries on individual paintings. Furthermore, he attempts to identify different "forgery hands" as well as different methods of forgery that include reversing set compositions and using the same figures in different paintings. Jian Youwen approached the issue of forgery by noting contradictory information found in inscriptions, while Kao Mayching's exhibition catalogue selects works that best exemplify Su Renshan.

Given the large quantity of works attributed to Su Renshan, it is necessary to establish benchmarks by which to assess the authenticity of his paintings. At opposite ends of the spectrum are paintings that are striking in their originality of composition coupled with confident brushwork, and those that are weak in composition and brushwork. Distinctive works that are the most original, such as his 1848 *Riding Dragons*

and *Leading the Phoenixes by Playing the Flute* (Figs. 2 and 3), can be generally accepted as genuine because of the sheer bold statements of their originality.[30] Bad fakes are identified by the crudeness of execution that bears no resemblance to Su's own high standard and by styles unrelated to Su Renshan.

It is the gray area of good copies and high-quality fakes that is the hardest to elucidate.[31] One of the concerns in recent connoisseurship practices is the need to distinguish between the authenticity of the artifact and the authenticity of the composition.[32] The former involves identifying seals, inscriptions and brush styles, and habits of the artist. This practice entails close examination of the details of the painting. The study of the authenticity of the composition looks at the overall manner of the painting and whether it fits in the conceptual craft of this artist. It allows for paintings that compositionally may fit into an artist's metier, but there are one or two details, such as certain hooks of his brushwork, that may appear problematic, to be categorized as "close copy at worst."[33] This would permit certain paintings to be considered as part of understanding an artist's work but with the knowledge that any information gathered should be used cautiously.

Given that Su Renshan's painting style deliberately overturns traditional methods of representations, using conventional modes of assessing authenticity such as a microscopic reading of brush trace is not enough in itself. Using an additional method of identifying the conceptual craft of Su Renshan can ensure, to the best of my abilities, I am consulting works that I consider to be authentic or have authentic value. I have identified Su Renshan's conceptual craft as different types of pictorial strategies, where when combined they generate the pictures to which they are applied. These are as follows: graphic brushwork in relation to spatial systems such as geometric forms, organization of thematic units including the bringing together of disparate historical figures or themes, and

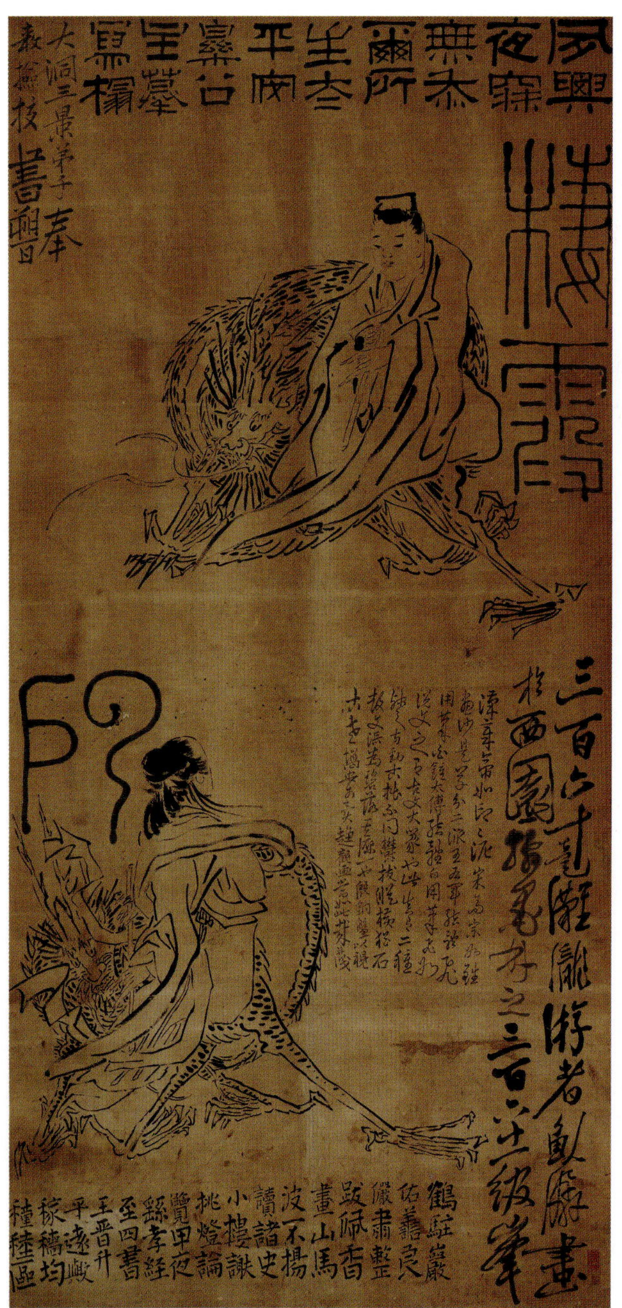

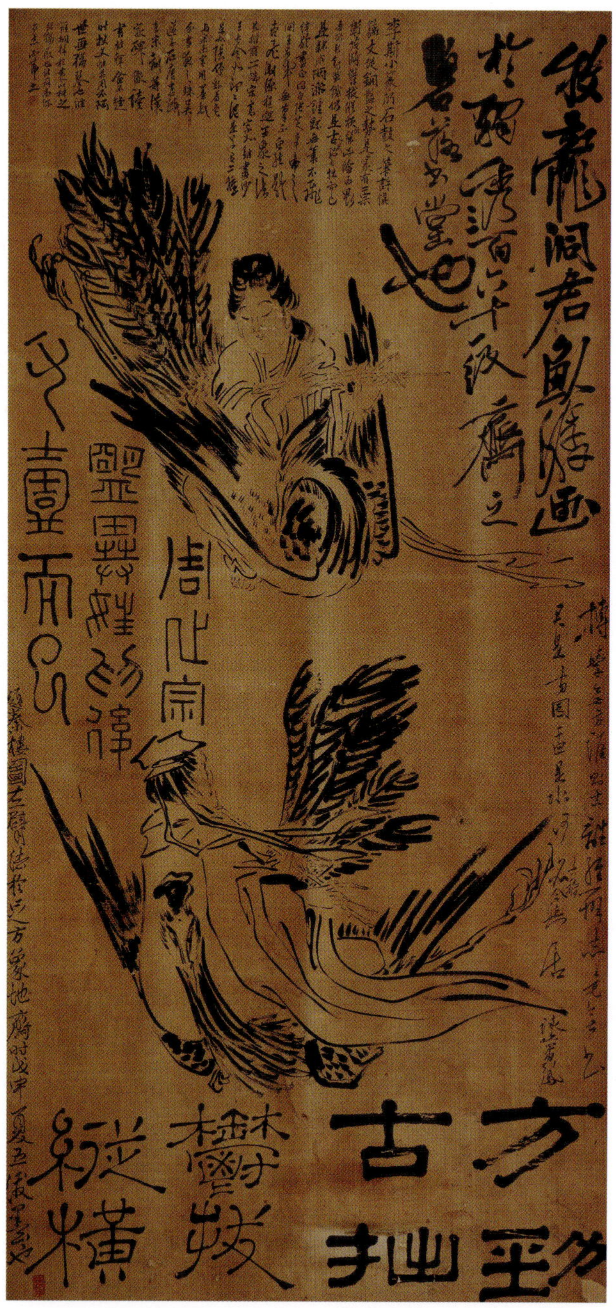

Figure 2 *(left)*   Su Renshan, *Riding Dragons*. Hanging scroll, undated, ink on paper, 254 × 118 cm. Reproduced by permission of the Art Museum of the Chinese University of Hong Kong from the collection of the Art Museum.

Figure 3 *(right)*   Su Renshan, *Leading the Phoenixes by Playing the Flute*. Hanging scroll, dated 1848, ink on paper, 278 × 120 cm. Reproduced by permission of the Art Museum of the Chinese University of Hong Kong from the collection of the Art Museum.

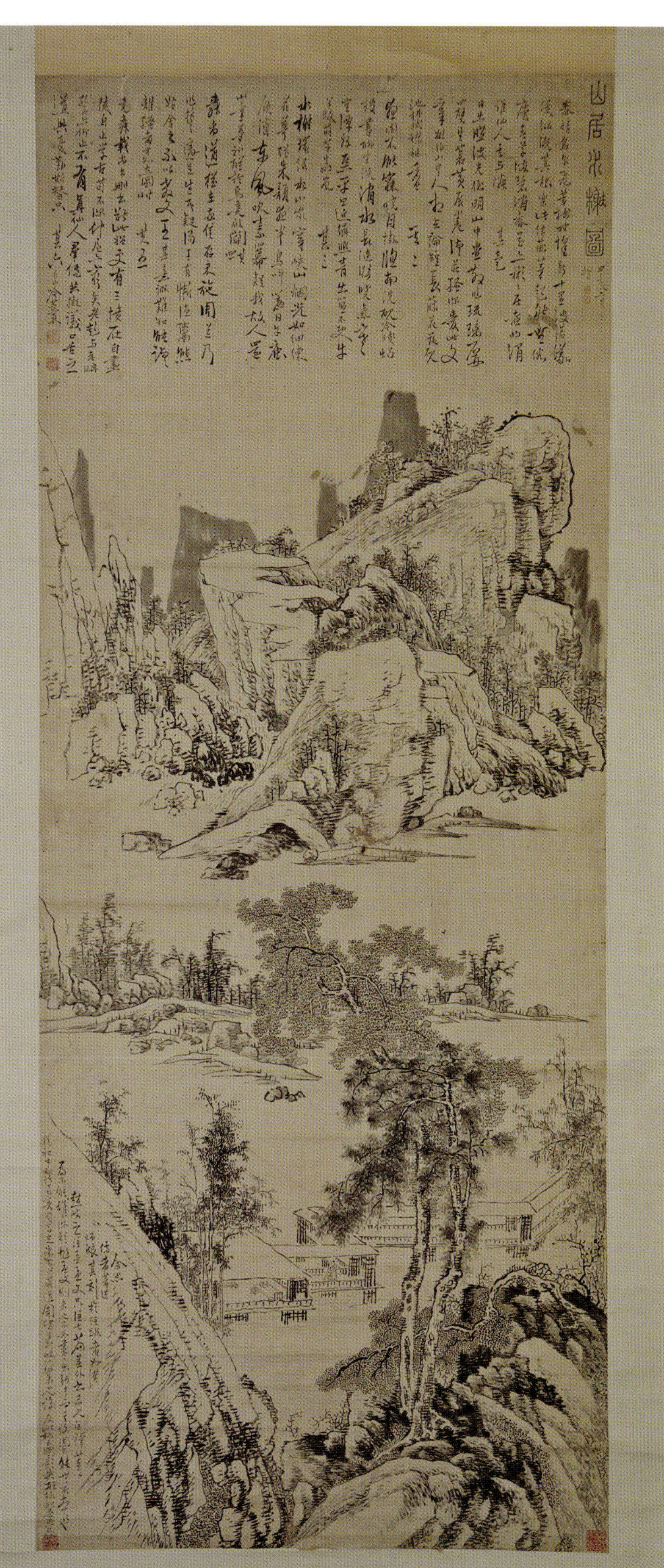

Figure 4 Su Renshan, *Landscape*. Hanging scroll, dated 1844, ink on paper, 147.9 × 76 cm. Guangdong Museum (廣東省博物館).

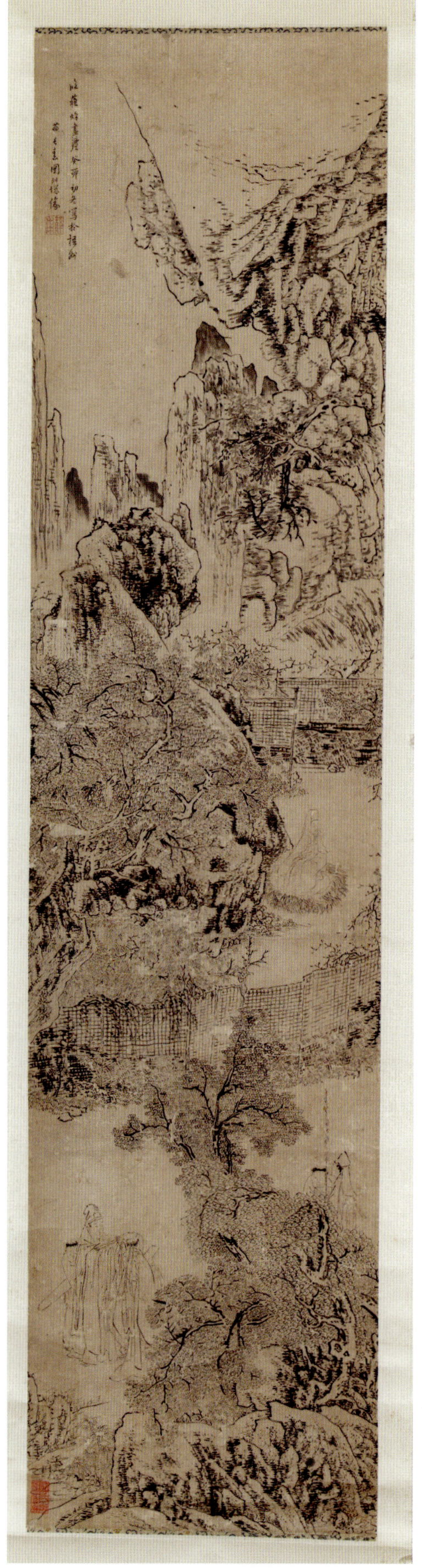

Figure 5 Su Renshan, *Liezi in a Landscape*. Hanging scroll, dated 1843, ink on paper, 192 × 46.5 cm. Reproduced by permission of the Art Museum of the Chinese University of Hong Kong from the collection of the Art Museum.

internal dynamics of compositions such as an organic mass offset by a circuit of disconnected gazes. These pictorial systems are identified and assessed in my various chapters as a means of understanding how he constructed his pictorial arguments.

This type of assessment involves a double-layered approach: to identify Su Renshan's systems of depiction—following the premise that all artists favored certain strategies of representations—and to use these systems as a gauge to measure whether the paintings in question are more likely to be a fake or a copy. There is another element that needs to be addressed, and that is the question of workshop production and whether Su Renshan worked with other artists. Given his itinerant lifestyle, his abrasive personality, and obsessive presentation of self, there is little to indicate that he had a student or workshop partner. This reasoning, while debatable, is the best conclusion that can be drawn given present information.

Typical forged images of his works favor certain motifs, which can either be a trait of the workshop or reveal how Su Renshan was understood. We see the forgers take certain motifs in genuine works and reduce them to types that get repeated time and again in their fakes. One of these motifs is the overhanging cliff or mountain base depicted as an inverted U-shape, one of its sides depicted with gradations of short strokes that can also be used to depict a series of rocky edges creating a vertical patterning. In his 1844 *Landscape* (Fig. 4), a beautifully rendered large hanging scroll, the complexity and variety of this structural approach is evident. It is a form that is seen time and again as in his 1843 painting, *Liezi in a Landscape* (Fig. 5), suggesting the possibility that he was exploring this form for large landscape paintings at this time. In an 1847 painting, *Landscape after Wang Wei* (Fig. 6), the U-structure at the bottom of cliff faces is made up of weak lines that render the rocks as pillowy forms that collapse into the houses at the

front. Denser lines are used for the mountain shapes in the distant ground, but these are also loose definitions turning into weak blocks of ink. Aside from the weakness of the lines that fail to create structural forms, there are too many lines that overwork the compositions. This type of overworking is a typical flaw seen in dubious landscapes and figure paintings (especially in the excessive zigzag strokes at the end of the robes where it no longer describes form).

Another way of assessing whether a painting is real, a copy, or an out-and-out forgery is to examine the structure of his inscriptions. Su Renshan's own inscriptions are usually highly complex and have unexpected associations that reveal his circuitous train of thought. One of the compositional traits of his longer inscriptions is that they are often made up of parts. The opening paragraph will suggest a theme for the painting, usually bringing figures from different periods together and seeing connections that emphasize the theme. The last paragraph is often a personal statement, sometimes beginning with "Renshan says," in which he further elaborates a point and thereby places himself in line with any famous historical figures cited. Overall, it creates an elaborate web of relations crossing time and space, and this idiosyncratic way of positioning himself is a trait that cannot be easily mimicked. However, generic inscriptions can be copied, and as such, paintings falling into this category can be used cautiously.

There exists an intriguing album of calligraphy attributed to Su Renshan in the Kyoto National Museum, to support my argument that inscriptions by Su Renshan were copied. One of the leaves is dated to 1847 in Cangwu, and several inscriptions are written on the same page (Fig. 7). It is difficult to determine the authenticity of this album, as it appears to have been a motley collection of ideas and writings. In 1848, Su was in Cangwu, so the date of the work makes it appear feasible. The quality of the writing varied, but if this was indeed a collection of

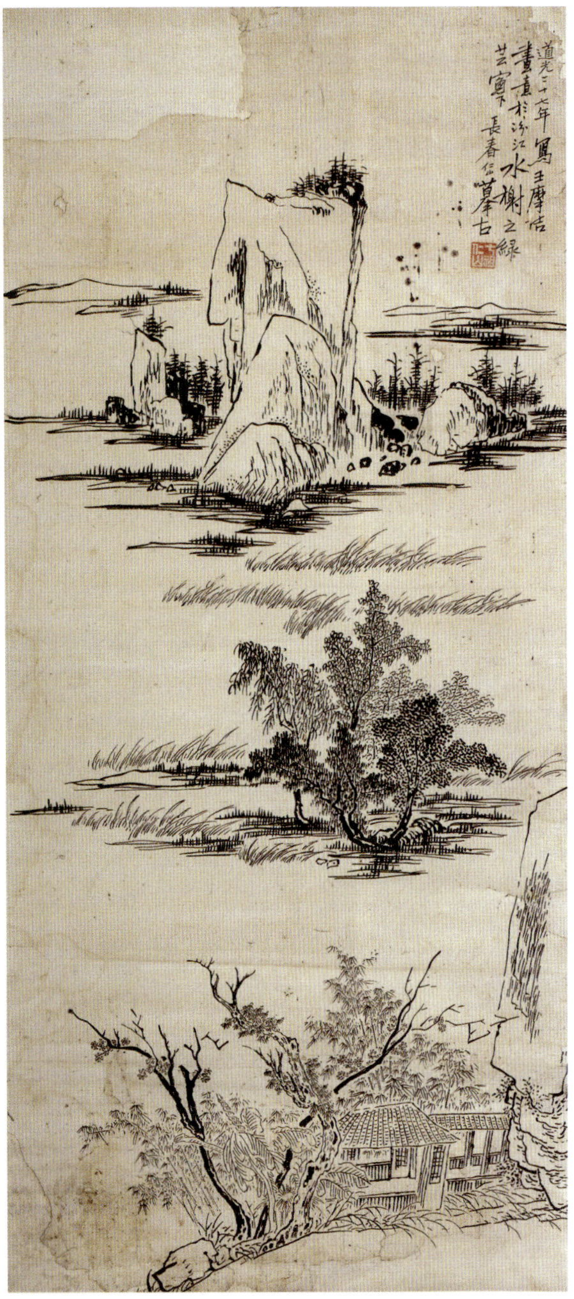

Figure 6
Su Renshan, *Landscape after Wang Wei*. Hanging scroll, dated 1847, ink on paper, dimensions unknown. Guangdong Museum.

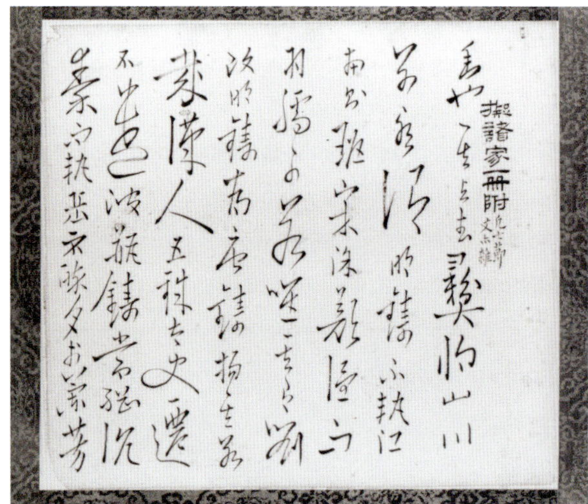

Figure 7   Su Renshan, Leaf 2 from *Album of Paintings and Calligraphy*. 20 leaves (14 calligraphy, 6 paintings), one leaf is dated 1847, ink on paper, 121 × 35 cm each. Kyoto National Museum.

notes and sketches of ideas, it is harder to make an argument for it being a forgery. What is interesting about this album, however, is that the inscriptions are arranged on the album leaf as one would expect them to be part of a painting. The question is why? If this is a genuine work, Su may have included some of his inscriptions not only to keep a record of what he had written but also how he wrote various inscriptions. If this album is not by Su Renshan, then it may be a facsimile of real inscriptions later used by forgers to create imitations of his works; alternatively, it may preserve drafts of copies that were later sold as genuine.

Along different lines, there exists a group of landscape paintings, each of which follows a similar composition: a cluster of trees at the front, a mid ground of low cliffs, and a distant horizon line. The mountain forms are usually made up of stretched triangular forms or the U-shaped cliffs. Occasionally a boat or two is drifting between the mid and far distances, and sometimes small figures are gathered at the front (Figs. 8 and 9). In many ways, these are typical of Chinese landscape paintings but rendered with "qualities" considered to be characteristic of Su Renshan, such as the U-shaped cliff textured with excessive horizontal short, dry brushwork, a mixture of calligraphy styles, and contrasts of ink tones. Some

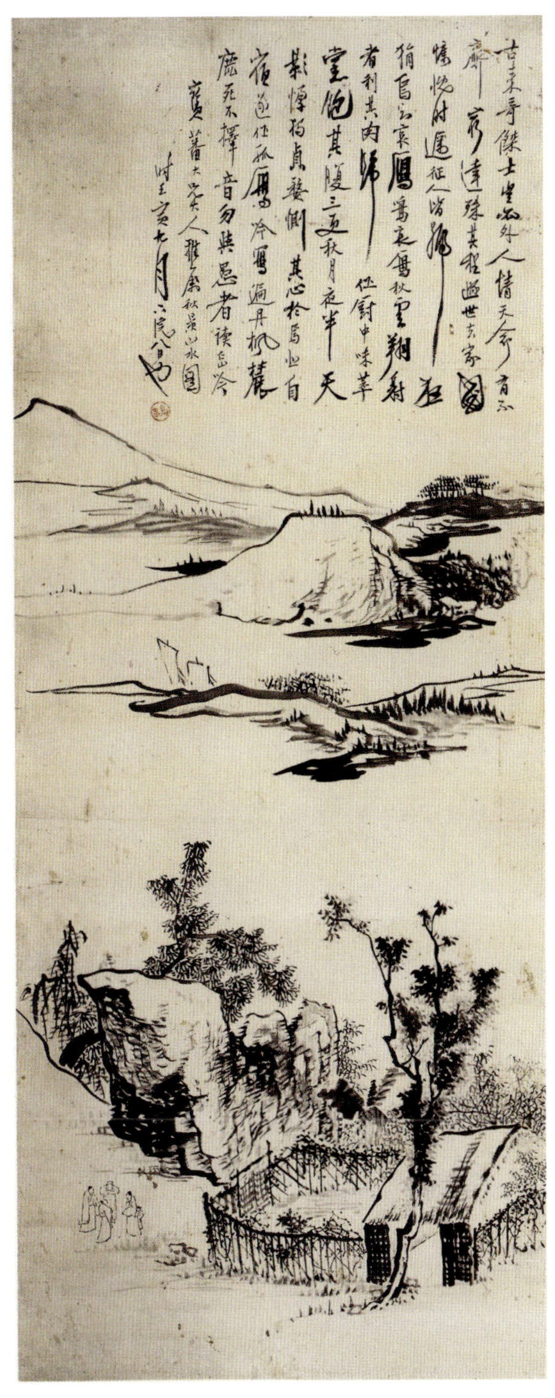

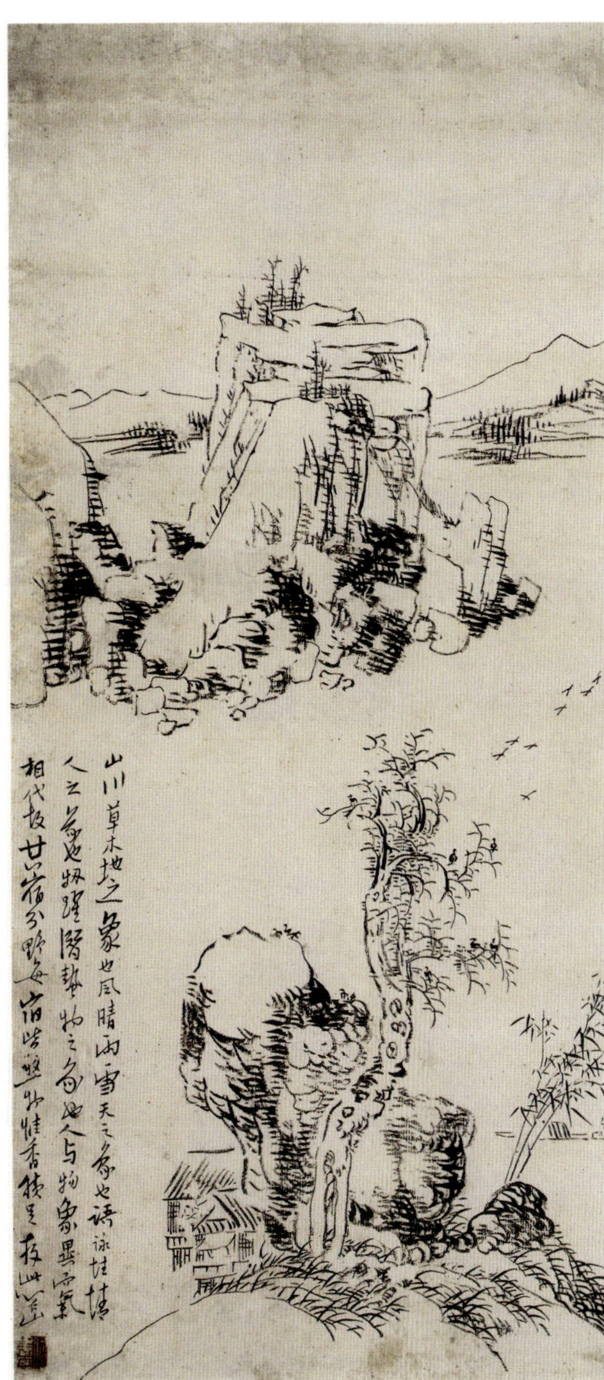

Figure 8 *(left)*   Attributed to Su Renshan, *Autumn Landscape*. Hanging scroll, dated 1842, ink on paper, 142.5 × 55.5 cm. Guangdong Museum.

Figure 9 *(right)*   Attributed to Su Renshan, *Landscape*. Hanging scroll, undated, ink on paper, 120.3 × 59.7 cm. Guangdong Museum.

of these landscapes are painted with heavy ink and "spontaneous" style brushwork; others are more detailed with careful rendering of forms. What is of interest, aside from the quality of brushwork, is the lack of compositional and inscriptional inventiveness. One could argue that Su Renshan made many variations of this type of landscape, but given his unusually aloof character, it seems unlikely that he made this type of image, one that would be more probable in a workshop environment. It may be possible to suggest that this set of landscape paintings uses small components considered to be representative of Su Renshan—the small houses and strange cliffs—but depicted within a conventional format. In creating so many paintings of this variety, the forgers were able to create an identity for Su Renshan in a newly emerging market when collectors were buying large number of works of this hitherto under-appreciated artist.[34]

Admittedly, the potential risk of my connoisseurship approach is that it can be considered as inherently self-fulfilling, as I am identifying these systems also as ways of understanding Su Renshan's originality. In order to maintain validity, it is still necessary to use standard measurements of authenticity, such as assessing the quality of execution. For example, Su's brushwork is very bold, often employing a long stroke with little variations of ink tone, almost a burnt-ink stroke. Interestingly, when he is using this long brushstroke, he juxtaposes it with a play on space: a blank torso, a tall rock with geometrically arranged holes, or a simple cliff face. He never, however, overworks this juxtaposition; there are never too many lines at the edge of the torso or plant details between the rocks and tiny stones lining the edges of the cliff. Attention to details such as these has been crucial to my selection of paintings discussed in this book.

♦♦♦

To summarize, although this book is as much about art in Guangdong and early nineteenth-century painting, Su Renshan is its heart. Biography is important in our understanding of an artist, if only because it reminds us how elusive meanings of paintings can be. His transgressive works have allowed us to identify early nineteenth-century norms and to consider the rich ideas and images circulating in the region. But more than anything, his paintings daringly embody frustration with the prevailing system of learning and governing. His life story has attracted audiences, cultivating a plethora of romantic anecdotes about a man born out of his time. The anecdotes help to give a human presence in paintings that are otherwise often too unusual and too difficult. Social history plays a strong role too, providing the threads to tie together themes of trade, issues of taste, and anxieties of war. I end with close readings of a small handful of paintings, to determine with greater depth interpretations that can provide more nuanced logic to the issues and themes laid out in earlier chapters. Although some scholars may not agree with the connections that I see between the artworks discussed, and perhaps even less with my interpretations of them, I place my efforts in the spirit of the oft-quoted comment by Clifford Geertz, that "progress is marked less by a perfection of consensus than by a refinement of debate. What gets better is the precision with which we vex one another."[35] Let this be my vexation.

Chapter One

Art and Trade in Guangzhou

In 1792, Shen Fu (沈復, 1763–ca.1810), an educated man who left his government clerk post as *yamen* secretary, was persuaded to travel to Guangzhou City for a quick money-making trip, because, in his wife's words, "rather than constantly scrimping and saving, it would be better to ensure our happiness at one stroke."[1] Cautiously reluctant, Shen Fu borrowed some money, purchased Suzhou embroidery, and crabs soaked in liquor (a local delicacy), and traveled to Guangzhou. Within ten days of arriving in the city, he sold all his wares for barbarian silver.[2] However, captivated by the unfamiliar sights and late-night revelry of the city, he decided to stay rather than return home with his earnings.

Anyone with even a modest income could afford a variety of leisure activities there: A night on a "flower-boat" with Yangzhou singing-girls cost four pieces of silver, for example.[3] Shen Fu's four months indulging in women, opium, sightseeing, and lychees (a Guangdong delicacy) cost little more than one hundred gold pieces. Reflecting a common northern prejudice against the south, he found some of the strangeness ugly and overbearing but discovered much of interest, including theaters, boat-girls, and a market full of things he had never seen before. He wrote of the unusual clatter of Cantonese, which, despite imperial efforts to standardize the language, remains to this day the dominant dialect in Guangzhou. He observed the numerous bizarre religious festivals, the Western imports, and local imitative production, including automated clocks and Western-style glass. Guangzhou was the city of *yang* things (洋物 things from across the sea), which piqued curiosity and offered strangeness as a commodity. On this short trip, Shen Fu experienced the sometimes disorderly intermingling of city dwellers and visitors. It was a place where money and goods openly circulated, where one could make or lose a fortune quickly.

In 1757, Guangzhou City was officially designated the sole trading port for Western goods.[4] The concentration of international and domestic trade led to dramatic changes in the physical and economic geography of this region.[5] Prosperity and work opportunities produced large-scale migration in the seventeenth and eighteenth centuries: Hakka farmers moved out of the hills into northeast Guangdong, and Tanka boat people of aboriginal heritage dominated the coastal edges. Fujianese merchants shifted their base to Guangzhou City to capitalize on the more lucrative Euro-American trade. Select members of these Fujian clans became leaders of *hongs*, collectively known as *cohong*, organizations licensed by the state to monopolize foreign trade. There was also a large population of northern Zhejiang migrants, particularly from Shaoxing and Hangzhou, whose ancestors had settled in Guangdong.[6] Government presence overseeing the domestic and international trade included the largest Bannermen military company in a frontier town and a constant stream of high-ranking officials. Nineteenth-century Guangzhou has been described as a city of newcomers.[7]

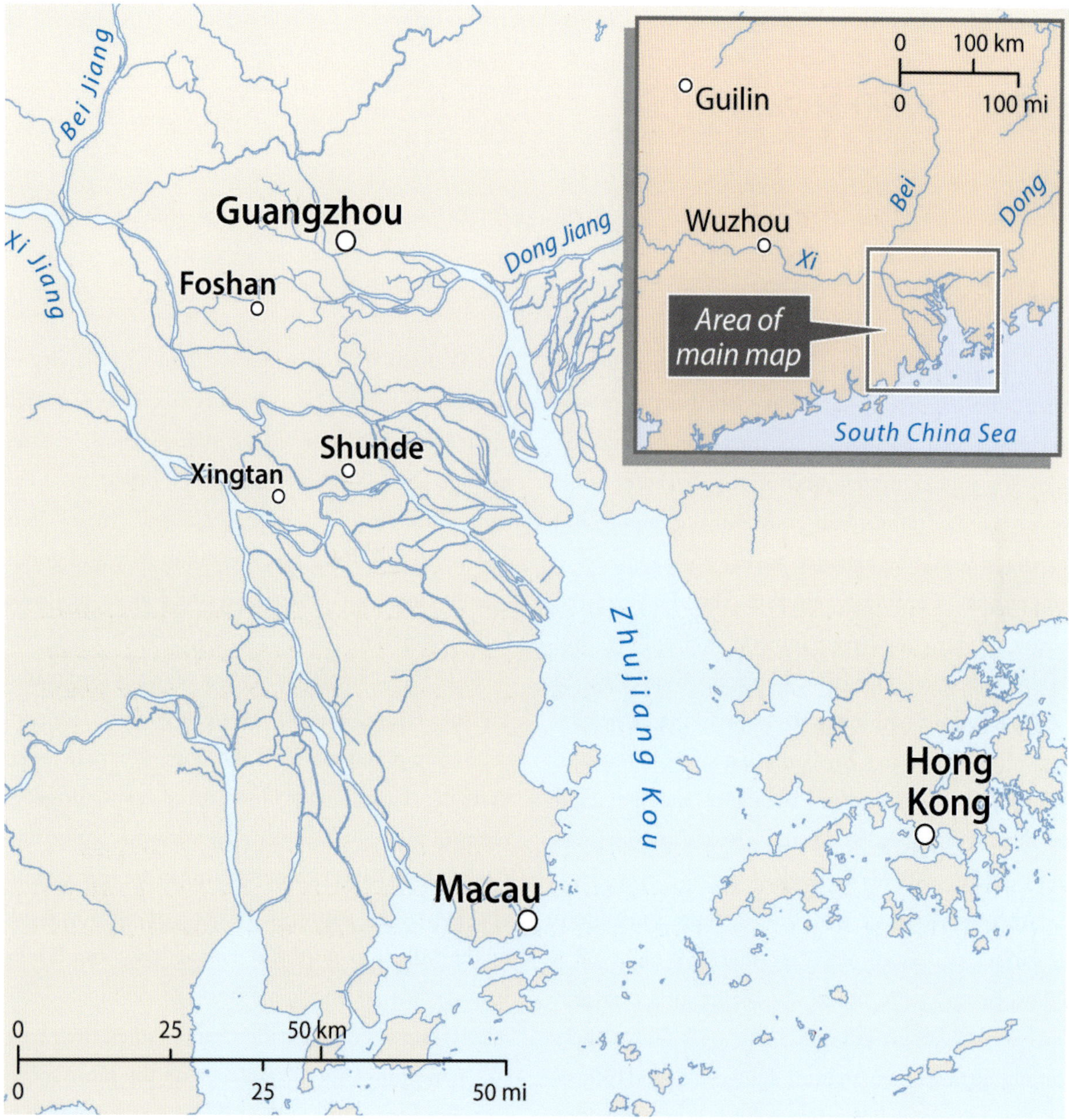

Figure a   Map of Pearl River Delta Area

Guangzhou was a cosmopolitan Qing city with a thriving economy and trade networks that connected the region to the outer world and other Chinese cities. It was, along with key Jiangnan cities (Suzhou, Hangzhou, Yangzhou, and Nanjing), one of the major cultural centers within the Qing Empire and outside the capital.[8] My measurement of cultural success is based on the quantity of a city's cultural production and exchange. For example, all these cities were centers for book publishers, private libraries, and academies, some of which were nationally renowned. They were also bases for wealthy merchants who appropriated literati tastes by hosting literary gatherings in grand gardens and cultivating art collections and libraries. These cities all had vibrant art markets and workshops that nurtured craft technologies.

Guangzhou's cosmopolitan urban identity, however, was also mitigated by a strong sense of the local that differentiated it from the other Chinese cities. Guangdong's historical reputation as a strange and exotic frontier, with its odd fruits, beasts, and religious practices, continued to ignite the imaginations (and at times stereotypical views) of visitors, this time directed by its engagement with Western trade.[9] It was perceived as a curious, exciting place by Jiangnan outsiders like Shen Fu and as a synecdoche of China in the eyes of foreign maritime traders. How did Guangzhou City dwellers see themselves, and how did the outsiders' views intersect with their own perceptions? In this melting pot of large clans, in-migrant families, sojourning merchants, foreign traders, and local scholars, was it even possible to define a Guangdong identity in the arts?

To help answer some of these questions, I have turned to the work of anthropologist Deborah Poole, who proposes a "visual economy" where images accrued economic, symbolic, social, or political values.[10] She moves away from the broader rubric of visual culture to examine three important systems of engagement: production, circulation, and the cultural systems that assessed the meanings of the image. Poole is interested in the intricacies of how different values were accrued by the same image, and how at the same time boundaries were developed to cement these values as truths. What I have taken from her work is the untidiness of images as historical records and narrative forms and, more importantly, the significance of attempts to "tidy" them. Her approach is particularly useful, because images are not treated as discrete signs (even if the artist proposes such an ambition), and while iconographic readings remain important, they are not the primary mode of understanding of how images were valued in their time and place.

Carlo Ginzburg's work on Venetian painting further buttresses this idea of a visual economy. Ginzburg speaks of two distinct "iconic circuits" in a visual economy, distinguished largely by differences in their audiences.[11] Ginzburg uses the terms "private" and "public" to distinguish the different circuits, but these terms do not readily translate into a Chinese context. Therefore, I follow Craig Clunas's example of using the more neutral terms "closed" and "open" to describe the iconic circuits of early nineteenth-century Guangzhou.[12] A closed circuit was one with a limited circulation, where the use of cultural goods was socially circumscribed to establish boundaries (however flawed and inconsistent the demarcation may have been). An open circuit, in contrast, allowed for a greater circulation of images and production and for a much wider social, and I would argue cultural, audience. Ginzburg's approach suggests that an individual icon or object could indicate a social circuit of cultural relations within a specific historical moment. The appeal of using this model is that it allows us to look closely at individual images within a visual economy and encourages the crisscrossing of the entrenched boundaries in our discipline, such as China and the West, and artist and artisan. Each circuit drew on different systems of value and interpretation, so it was possible for a viewer to participate in both without conflict. Moreover, "value" is taken literally as I assess how much paintings cost in each circuit, adding another layer to the discussion.

The wealth of visual source material on nineteenth-century Guangdong requires filtering, so I focus on examples that best illustrate my argument for a local cosmopolitanism. I begin my examination with an analysis of the closed circuit supported by the elite city dwellers of Guangzhou, many of whom had native roots outside the city but who promoted and pursued a Guangdong identity. It was also a means of gaining cultural standing for rich merchants who sought friendships and ties with eminent scholars and officials from both in and outside the city. My focus is twofold; first, I examine the art catalogue of the *hong* merchant Pan Zhengwei (潘正煒, 1796–1850, also known as Puankhequa III), and, by looking at issues of taste and social networks, I demonstrate how interregional and local ties operated in Guangdong. Second, I look at paintings by the Cantonese scholar-artist Xie Lansheng (謝蘭生, 1760–1831), who was among Pan Zhengwei's coterie of friends. My argument focuses on how Xie created a canon of Guangdong art that aligned Cantonese ink painting with a master narrative of Chinese art history while maintaining a regional identity. Juxtaposing these two men, the collector and the artist, clarifies how the production, circulation, and interpretative systems of a closed circuit operated.

The second section of the chapter examines the open circuit of images of street life. It begins with a brief overview of narratives of the city by both Chinese and foreign visitors. Guangdong is exceptional because we see, increasingly, the coming together of parallel forms of descriptive narratives. Within this large corpus of work, the street is exploited as a connective space that provided spectacles for consumption. The street was a place where one did things, whether to sell, to buy, to perform in, or to watch. It is always tempting to read export art versions of street life as a form tailored for a Western audience, but, while there is some truth to this, widening the scope of analysis to include this circuit's domestic market would break preconceptions of two completely separate worlds. The final part of

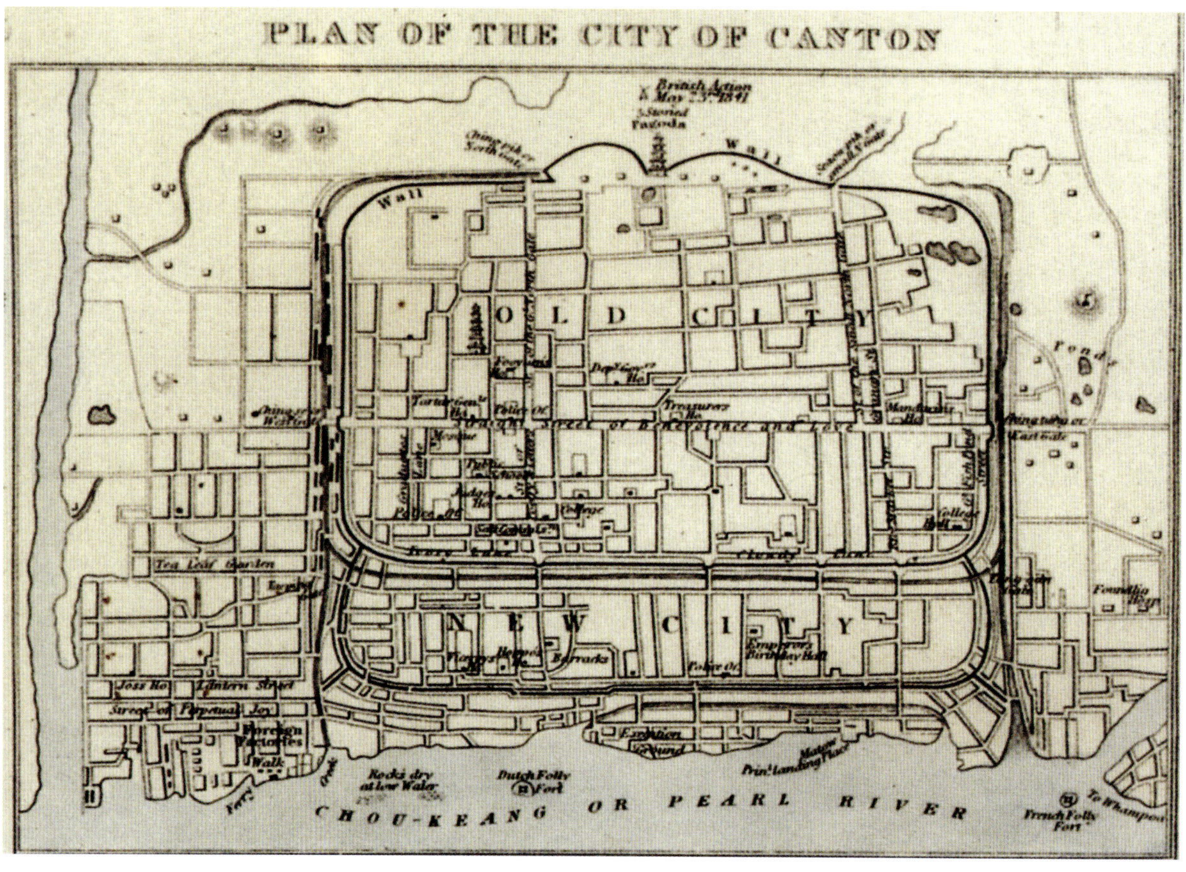

Figure b   Plan of the City of Canton from The Canton River Map by James Wyld, 1841

this section lengthens the scope of my examination by situating export art versions of social types within a broader history of Chinese genre paintings, thus providing a historical mapping that speaks to the changing focus of genre painting. What unfolds is less an image of the city as an experience of modernity, although that too is evident, but more how the appropriation of existing models, and the blurring of cultural boundaries, contributed to the polysemic nature of urban imaginations.

A Closed Circuit in Guangzhou

In Guangzhou, cultural production became an important component of the city's growth, led by the region's elites who sponsored the building of academies and their literary projects. Academies were places where people gathered, inside and outside, and more importantly where connections were forged, creating a community outside of kinship and native ties, and structured according to national models of intellectual brotherhood. The early sponsorship of academies was largely made out of necessity: Yuehua Academy was initially set up in the early eighteenth century as a training ground for sons of in-migrant merchants, who could then gain schooling in their relocated home and sit for examinations without having to travel back to their native provinces.[13] Another important academic institution was Yuexiu Academy, located in the south of the Old City. As an examination-based institution, it adhered to the Song dynastic Cheng-Zhu tradition. Yuexiu Academy also attracted many entrepreneurs and business ventures capitalizing on the popularity of the institute with stalls and shops offering study guides, books, and printed manuals, as well as restaurants and markets feeding the students and their families (and with the local *yamen* nearby).[14]

The most important addition to Guangdong's intellectual landscape was Ruan Yuan and his Xuehaitang. Although he was not the first influential scholar from Jiangnan or Beijing to serve in an official position in Guangdong, his academy provided both a hub for ambitious local elites and a legacy that continued into the twentieth century. Ruan's interest in Han scholarship and evidential research set the academic tone of his institution and reflected the shift of scholarly interest transpiring in Jiangnan cities and the capital as well as Guangzhou. From the sixteenth century onwards, evidential studies advocated a return to the original early texts, veering from the normative practice of using the commentaries on texts by Song Dynasty scholars. Philologists objected to what they believed to be careless interpretations of the Classics and insisted on more concrete analyses of the texts. Ruan Yuan, during his term as Governor-General of Guangdong and Guangxi, published *Huang Qing jing jie* 皇清經解 (Qing exegesis of the classics). This was a Confucian collectanea, designed as a sourcebook for philologists, that received great acclaim and further cemented the importance of Han learning in Guangdong.

Ruan Yuan had headed similar projects in Yangzhou prior to serving in Guangdong. He also founded academies, published gazetteers, promoted rigorous evidential studies that contributed to the city's intellectual reputation, and initiated projects that documented Yangzhou's regional history.[15] This was possible because of Yangzhou's complicated history in the previous century. In 1645, the newly anointed Qing Empire had conducted a ten-day massacre, using Yangzhou as an example for others actively supporting the fallen Southern Ming emperor. By the eighteenth century, with monetary support from the state, Yangzhou rose from the ashes and quickly emerged as a commercial hub, particularly with its concentration of rich salt merchants. The renewed wealth in the region attracted artists and scholars seeking patrons and contributed to a vibrant literary and cultural scene that made it one of the key cities in eighteenth-century China. However, scandals led to the demise of the Yangzhou salt merchants; Guangdong, meanwhile, as a port city, became increasingly important as a commercial nucleus. Especially with the arrival of Ruan Yuan, Yangzhou provided Guangdong with a template of how to make a city a place of literary significance.

As with their Jiangnan counterparts, the Xuehaitang scholars honed their skills by collecting and transcribing inscriptions, compiling anthologies of Guangdong poets, and publishing studies on native products and other investigative compilations. Many of these projects involved compiling works of Cantonese scholars, writing regional histories, and publishing themes that had a distinct local character. One of Ruan Yuan's first commissions was to compile a gazetteer (a genre of local history that has existed since ancient times), which brought to light many figures and sites that had been previously neglected in history. As Steven Miles's study on the academy and its role in shaping cultural identity has shown, Xuehaitang's pedagogical agenda, linked to the Jiangnan tradition, appealed to Guangdong's community of sojourners and in-migrants, who had tenuous ties to the dominant lineages from the Delta region.[16] This is evident in the financial support given by Fujian entrepreneurs who had made Guangdong their home and who used their attachment to the academy and ties with local scholars to gain cultural cachet. They sponsored major publication projects that involved compiling, collating, and printing texts, adding to the scholastic aura of a flourishing Cantonese culture. It is against this constellation of literary activities, which also saw ties strengthened between Jiangnan/Zhejiang and Guangzhou, that a Cantonese literary art identity was being formed.

Pan Zhengwei and the Tingfanlau Art Collection

Art catalogues were effective mechanisms for transforming economic power into cultural cachet by reinforcing the reputation of the collector within and beyond their immediate space and time. What was recorded (and omitted) was carefully chosen to connect the owner to a broader network and heritage of tastemakers. This is perhaps the most obvious mechanism for assigning value to a work of art and offers glimpses into the art market and cultural competition among art collectors, who displayed their aesthetic ambitions and sophistication through texts. It also provides textual information about which genres or artists were the most highly prized, as well as who sold or viewed the paintings, providing a social history of networks. In the late eighteenth and early nineteenth centuries, many Guangdong collectors began making catalogues, showing evidence of the rich repository of old and new paintings in the city. I will narrow my focus by concentrating on the art catalogue of the *hong* merchant Pan Zhengwei and demonstrate how a closed circuit was formed (Chart 1). This chart maps relationships that were crucial in the elite world and shows the connections formed between merchants, scholars, officials and artists, as well as the connections formed between Guangdong, Fujian, Yangzhou, and other parts of the country.

Pan Zhengwei was part of an influential Fujianese clan of *hong* merchants, salt merchants, officials, collectors, patrons, and even pseudo-diplomats. His family had originally been engaged in the Southeast Asia boat trade before resettling in Panyu, Guangzhou. His grandfather was Pan Zhencheng (潘振承, 1714–88), who began his career as a clerk at a foreign trading house in Guangdong and later set up his own company, Tongwen Hang (同文行).[17] The elder Pan's knowledge of Western languages and business acumen made him a leading security merchant in the incipient Canton trade system in the eighteenth century.[18] Tongwen Hang was a successful enterprise passed down many generations from Pan Zhencheng to his son, Pan Youdu (潘有度, d.1821), and later Youdu's nephew Pan Zhengwei, who eventually changed the company name to Tongfu Hang (同孚行).[19]

By Pan Zhengwei's time, the family was well established and participated in literary and official worlds, as well as in trade. Many members of the family also became known for their literary talents: Pan Zhengwei's father, Pan Youwei (潘有為, 1743–1821), and his uncle, Pan Youdu, published a collection of poems by Pan family members.[20] The third generation of Pans, Zhengwei and his cousins, received a classical education, studying with many of the leading scholars in Guangdong, including Zhang Bingwen (張炳文, 1753–1826), father of Zhang Weiping (張維屏, 1780–1859), who later became a literati leader and famed poet in Guangzhou. In 1829 and again in 1838, Zhang Weiping became a supervisor of Xuehaitang Academy. Thus, the young Zhengwei was already well placed in Guangzhou's emerging literary world.

Pan Zhengwei was a keen art collector. As is typical of other important collectors in nineteenth-century Guangzhou, he published records of his collection in a catalogue named after his studio, Tingfanlou (聽颿樓 Tower of Listening to the Sails). It was one of the richest collections of art in China, significantly outstripping, in volume, those of his peers. But what is distinctive about this catalogue is that it came with a price index that boldly attests to the commercialization of culture, a disclosure many collectors would have shunned. Pan offers no explanations for this unusual divulgence; in the past, patrons or artists referenced the monetary value of their artworks in a discreet manner, or, if they openly revealed the costs of art, they did so as a transgressive act, highlighting their individuality by going against social mores.[21] Pan, however, was not a transgressive individual. It

has been suggested that his price list may have been the natural response of a merchant who liked to have his accounts on record and to display his wealth.[22] However, this perspective may derive from a bias that views merchants as coarse cultural pretenders. The Pan family had several members who were literary scholars known for their poems and paintings. The literary entrenchment of the Pan family, who had continuously supported and maintained the traditional roles of patron and artists, makes it unlikely that Pan Zhengwei included the price list as the uncouth act of a merchant.

Historical circumstances may account for the inclusion of the price list. Pan's two catalogues were written at a time when the country was facing major changes: some violent, many disruptive, and all propelling China forward into a modern world, with global repercussions. In 1842, as part of the Nanjing Treaty, the *hong* mechanism was abolished, and Pan Zhengwei lost his monopoly on Western trade. It is telling that Pan's catalogues were written after the negotiation of the peace treaty, when he was no longer a *hong* merchant. Perhaps he published the catalogues and recorded the costs of his collection as insurance against loss, driven by an anxiety to have records that could bear witness to an art collection housed in a city with a precarious future.

Pan's catalogue was arranged in two volumes: *Tingfanlou shuhua ji*, 5 *juan*, preface date 1843) and an addendum, *Tingfanlou shuhua xuji* (聽颿樓書畫續記, preface date 1849). There were over 1,400 paintings and calligraphy pieces, ranging from the ninth century to the eighteenth. The most expensive artwork in his collection was 500 taels; his entire collection was valued at 17,463 taels. The so-called "Daoguang Depression"[23] saw huge fluctuations in the copper-silver ratio between 1000:1 and 2000:1, making it difficult to assess it in copper currency and therefore provide a meaningful value of 500 taels in 1843. Looking at grain values, however, and

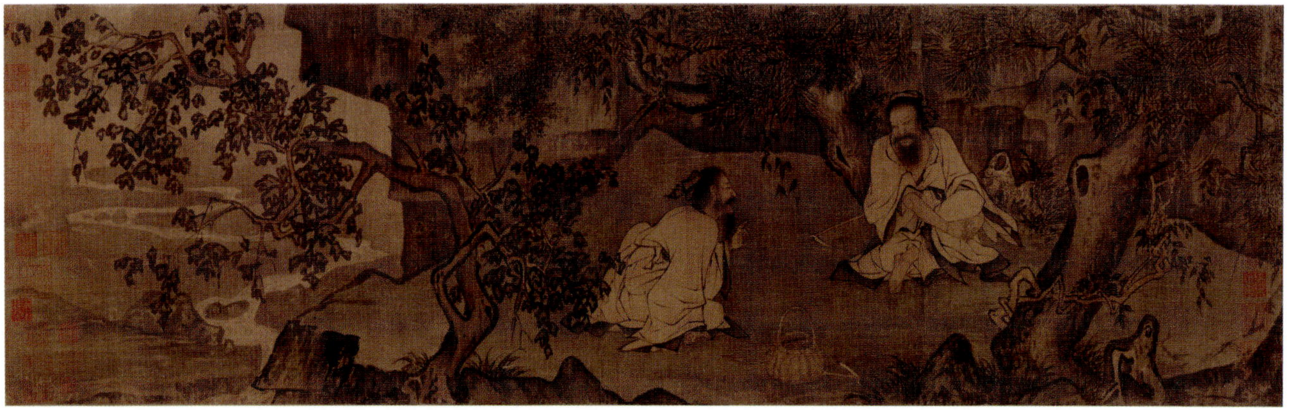

Figure 10	Li Tang, *Gathering Herbs*. Handscroll, undated, ink and colors on silk, 27.2 × 90.5 cm. Palace Museum, Beijing.

estimating the cost of rice in 1843 at approximately 2.0 taels per *shi*,[24] 500 taels could purchase just a little under 250 *shi* of rice. Given that an average man would consume 2.17 *shi* a year,[25] this one painting could feed a man for approximately 116 years.

Pan purchased his paintings primarily from two Guangzhou-based collectors. The first was Wu Rongguang (吳榮光, 1773–1843), a Nanhai native of salt-merchant stock, who passed the civil examinations to become a Hanlin academician. His official post meant he spent significant periods outside Guangdong, and many of his art-connoisseur skills and cultural ambitions were informed by teachers and friends from his sojourns.[26] He returned to Guangzhou after his retirement and quickly gained a reputation as one of the leading connoisseurs in the region. Because of the encroachment of British troops, Wu returned to the provincial regions of Nanhai, fleeing the uneasy environment of Guangzhou and selling off his paintings. However, prior to leaving, he penned a catalogue of his art collection (following the standards set by leading Beijing and Jiangnan collectors), which became the template for Pan Zhengwei.[27]

Wu was deeply influenced by two leading scholars of the late eighteenth century who had served government posts in Guangzhou: the Yangzhou scholar-official Ruan Yuan and Weng Fanggang (翁方綱, 1733–1813), also an eminent poet, calligrapher, and Beijing official. Both men were leaders in their areas of interest: Ruan, as aforementioned, was a proponent of evidential research that emphasized Han and earlier texts as fundamental tools of investigation. Weng's pursuit of epigraphy had similar pedagogical ambitions of returning to original sources and stimulated a revival in ancient scripts. Both these gentlemen were very influential and left a deep and long-lasting effect on Guangdong's intellectual and cultural environment, even after their departure from the city. Wu's personal relations with these two gentlemen secured his place as a leading cultural arbiter in Guangzhou. According to his *nianpu* (年譜 a chronicle account of one's life by ages), Ruan was Wu's examiner during his metropolitan exams, and the examiner-examinee relationship was extended to one of mentor-student when Wu studied the Classics and arts with Ruan in 1809.[28] Wu's penchant for textual research followed Ruan's scholarship; his catalogue was written in a specific and unadorned manner that listed all the various inscriptions, sizes, and formats of the artwork, followed by his considered opinions. Between 1764 and 1771, Wu's other

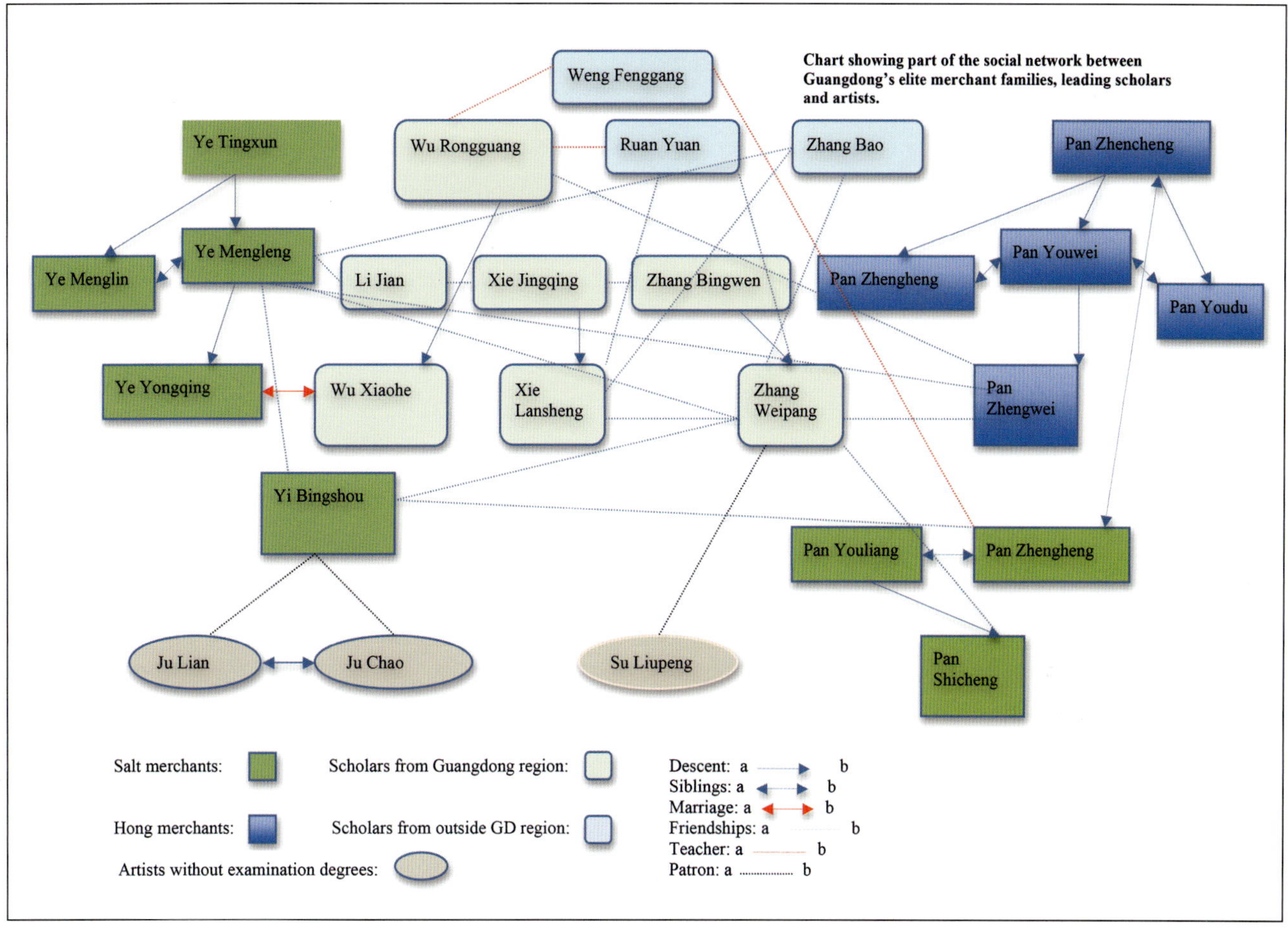

Figure c   Chart of social network of Guangdong elite

mentor, Weng Fanggang, was Inspector of Education in Guangzhou, befriending Wu's teachers at Yuexiu Academy (the key academy prior to the building of Xuehaitang). Later, when Wu gained entry into Hanlin Academy in Beijing, he further cemented his relationship with Weng by studying epigraphy with the elder scholar.

Wu Rongguang's prestigious academic achievements and his connections with the leading scholar-officials of the day made him a sought-after connoisseur when he retired to Guangdong. His own art collection and cataloguing style became a model for other collectors in this region. More importantly, in his retirement, Wu acted as a dealer of artworks,

setting the standard for pre-Qing art in Guangdong. His taste was very orthodox, favoring landscape paintings that had been verified by esteemed connoisseurs and that were by artists firmly placed within the canon. Wu's scholarly conceit can be seen in his exacting taste for paintings conventionally recognized as "good" and his disregard for those that were more flamboyant, flashy, or made by marginal art-makers. Almost all the works listed in his catalogue were by non-Cantonese artists (with the exception of four calligraphy works), and there are no artworks by female artists. This was the niche that he carved out for himself, a conservative collector with a discerning eye for works by established artists. Among his treasure trove of early paintings, his most cherished was *Gathering Herbs*, by the Southern Song artist Li Tang (李唐, 1050–1130), which is currently in the Palace Museum in Beijing (Fig. 10). When Wu fled Guangzhou, Pan Zhengwei paid 200 taels of silver (or approximately 100 *shi* of rice) for the handscroll painting.

Pan also bought paintings from Ye Menglong (葉夢龍, 1778–1832), a contemporary and friend of Wu Rongguang. Ye, like Wu, came from a well-established salt-business family and pursued a minor official career. His duties occasionally took him to Beijing for short periods, but he spent the majority of his life in Guangzhou. Ye was also an art collector and documented his collection in his catalogue *Fengmanlou shuhua ji* 風滿樓書畫記 (A record of paintings and calligraphy in the Breezy Tower), which had a preface by Xie Lansheng, an academician and one of the most influential Guangdong literati in the early nineteenth century.[29] Ye Menglong was a friend of Wu Rongguang, but the two men were also connected by the marriage between Ye's son, Ye Yingqi (葉應祺, ca. nineteenth century) and Wu's daughter, Wu Xiaohe (吳小荷, nineteenth century).[30]

Ye Menglong was very active within the region's literary circles: His father was a friend of Li Jian (黎簡, 1747–99), a local poet and painter. This was an important relationship that would later help to forge a distinctive Cantonese literati style. Ye Menglong often held gatherings with local artists and art collectors, including Pan Zhengheng (潘正亨, 1779–1837, Pan Zhengwei's uncle) and Yi Bingshou (伊秉綬, 1745–1815). Yi's family was in the salt business and had moved to Guangxi from Fujian. He also had connections with Yangzhou, in part because of the family business, but also because he served there as an official. In his move to the south, Yi also brought with him two Jiangnan bird and flower painters as artists in residence, who then trained local artists, including the cousins Ju Chao (居巢, 1811–65)

and Ju Lian (居廉, 1828–1904). Artists in residence were important additions to a wealthy household, providing training, making paintings for gatherings, and helping maintain one's collection. Ye Menglong often called on the services of local professional artists to help mend damaged paintings or make copies of famous ones. This social network between patrons and artists in Guangxi and Guangdong and connected by an interest in colorful bird and flower tradition requires further research. A cursory investigation shows that the network continued to thrive into the next generation. For example, Li Bingshou (李秉綬, act. ca. 1840s), a Jiangxi official based in Guilin hosted many gatherings in his famous garden including Zhang Weiping and the Ju cousins.

The price index and catalogue details in Pan Zhengwei's collection reveal two distinct aesthetics. The first is a preference for works that followed canonical tastes of landscape painting, including works by Yuan artist Ni Zan (倪瓚, 1301–74), Ming paintings by the Wu school artists including Shen Zhou (沈周, 1427–1509), Tang Yin (唐寅, 1470–1524), and Wen Zhengming (文徵明, 1470–1559), and early Qing landscapes by artists better known today as the Orthodox school. Pan Zhengwei's landscape painting collection demonstrates the currency of a literati painting canon. By housing a history of recognized masters in his library, the collection acted as a testament to his taste and learning that could easily be understood by those who belonged in a similar scholarly circuit. It was not, however, a testament to his connoisseurship skills, as his collection included paintings of dubious authenticity. Nonetheless, there were times when his less discriminate approach bore surprising fruits. Pan was one of the few Guangdong collectors to possess artworks by Dong Qichang (董其昌, 1555–1636) and his early Qing followers, the Four Wangs, whose monumental landscapes were co-opted by the Qing emperors to establish a Han aesthetic orthodoxy

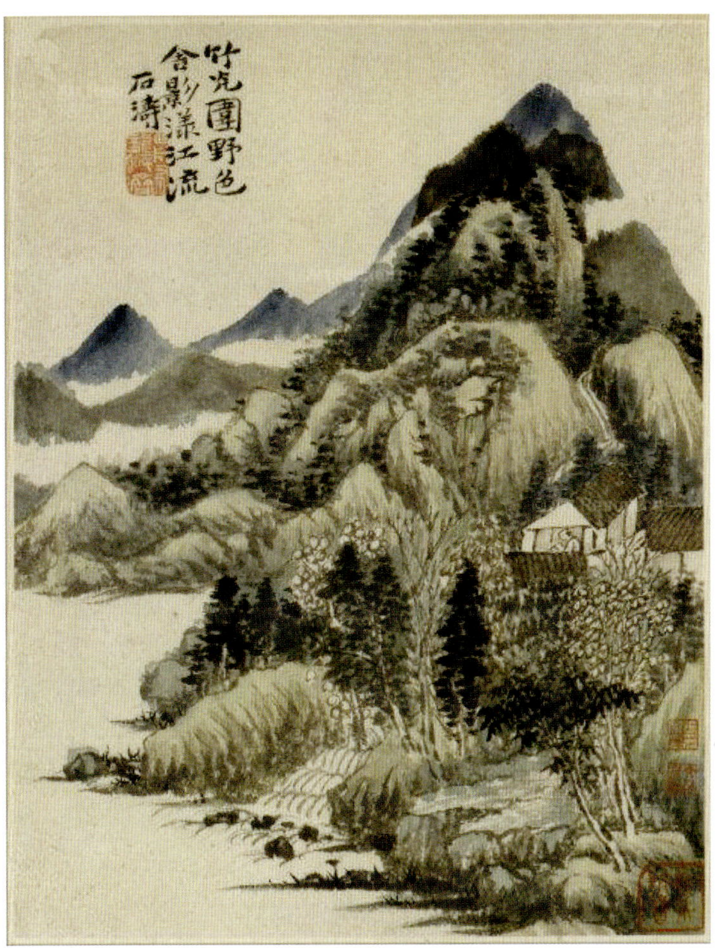

Figure 11 Shitao, *Wilderness Cottage.* Leaf G from *Wilderness Colors* album of 12 leaves, dated ca. 1700s, ink and color on paper, 26.7 × 21.6 cm. The Metropolitan Museum of Art, The Sackler Fund, 1972 (1972.122a-1). Image © The Metropolitan Museum of Art

during the early eighteenth century. Paintings by these gentlemen were highly desired in Beijing and Jiangnan but less so in the south, where the Ming Wu school of Shen Zhou and Wen Zhengming dominated. According to Pan's price index, he paid large amounts of money for major works by these men, in comparison to more minor works by artists such as the Ming loyalist painters Bada Shanren (八大山人, 1626–1705) and Gong Xian (龔賢, 1618–89).

It is also possible to see how social relationships with local collectors such as Ye Menglong, and his strong family ties also influenced Pan's art collecting, and moreover, these deep connections may have directed his decision to collect works by artists from Fujian and Guangdong. This regional dimension—a feature that is never seen in Wu Rongguang's collection—illuminates how important local relationships were in Pan's cultural activities. I emphasize local relationships because Pan selected works by these Fujian and Guangdong artists that are relatively conservative, favoring only works that were deemed suitably "literary." For example, Pan Zhengwei's father, Pan Youwei, was known for his colorful bird and flower paintings. It seems feasible that the elder Pan's cherished collection of bird and flower paintings would have informed his son's knowledge and appreciation of this genre. There were many such paintings in Pan's collection, especially dating from the seventeenth century. There were ten sets of albums and paintings, totaling sixty individual works, by the early Qing artist Yun Shouping (惲壽平, 1633–90), the most famous early Qing painter of such subjects. Regarded as one of the Six Masters of Early Qing (along with the Four Wangs), Yun was well known for his delicate rendering of luscious foliage without ink outlines, and other artists and artisans often imitated his style on silk, paper, ceramics, and other media. Among his many followers was the Fujian artist Hua Yan (華喦, 1682–1762), who is often included as one of the eighteenth-century Yangzhou Eccentrics. Hua painted numerous genres and was known for his intimate depiction of genre scenes, including paintings of villagers, a portrait of himself as a *wuxia* (武俠 knight-errant) hero, and paintings of rural musicians that the later Cantonese artist Su Liupeng also favored. However, Pan Zhengwei was more interested in Hua Yan's delicate rendering of birds and flowers, made in the Yun Shouping mode. This was considered a more orthodox style, using a delicate palette and fine brushwork and washes. The most prized Hua Yan painting in Pan's collection was *Ink Orchid* (which includes an inscription by Ruan Yuan), a subject with literary connotations, especially if we consider this to belong in the genre of bird and flower painting. This is one of many examples that affirms Pan's desire to be remembered for his more scholarly tastes, even when he was purchasing works by artists from his home province who were not as readily collected and recorded in art catalogues in the mid-nineteenth century.

In all, Pan had twenty-four individual works by Fujian artists. Most cost under thirty-five taels, averaging about half the amount for works by the earlier seventeenth-century master Yun Shouping. While none of these works belonged in the high-price range, the quantity recorded in the catalogue testifies to their popularity. Hua Yan's Fujian roots may have also added to his appeal to a collector whose family was strongly attached to their native place. In Guangdong, Pan Zhengwei's grandfather had established an organization for merchants from his home province, and Pan Zhengwei's father was acutely aware of how native ties were important for sojourners and migrants like them. He observed how their street in Henan (the suburb to the south of the city) was full of "Fujian natives who have grown old with navigating the sea."[31] By as early as the 1730s, at least a thousand other merchants from Quanzhou and Zhangzhou, in Fujian Province, were trading and residing in Guangzhou.

Artists from Fujian most likely followed their patrons, producing artworks that would have suited their tastes and needs, including figure paintings of mythical gods and auspicious themes. One example is the seventeenth-century Fujian professional (non-literati) artist Shangguan Zhou (上官周, 1665–1749), who traveled to Guangzhou City and found work making portraits of mythical gods and historical figures that would be hung on propitious days in the public rooms of a merchant's home. However, despite the popularity of Shangguan Zhou, there are very few paintings by these artists in Pan Zhengwei's collection. Instead, Pan's Fujian ties are found primarily in bird and flower paintings by Hua Yan that can be linked to the works of the orthodox artist Yun Shouping, maintaining a standard of taste that fit more established conventions.

If Pan's collection provided an overview of a painting canon that fit into a grand narrative of Jiangnan taste (with strays into more marginal, but still conservative, tastes), there is a surprising inclusion: Li Jian, the only Cantonese artist included in his collection of 1,400 artworks. He declined to include the more famous Ming Cantonese artist Lin Liang (林良, ca.1416–80), who gained fame as a court artist. Pan Zhengwei's interest in Li Jian may reflect the taste of his elder clan brother Pan Zhengheng (潘正衡, 1787–1830), who was an ardent admirer of Li, collecting many of his paintings and calligraphies, and even naming his studio after the artist.[32]

Moreover, many of these paintings were purchased from Ye Menglong's father, a friend of Pan's uncle. Ye was also a good friend of Xie Jingqing (謝景卿, act. eighteenth century), a notable connoisseur who was also a dealer for Li Jian.[33] The intertwined lives of family, patrons, dealers, friends, and artists suggest something about the business of art and the making of this closed circuit. It is through these interactions that we find Li Jian promoted as the linchpin that held together the pictorial traditions of the Jiangnan region and Guangdong. During Li's lifetime, however, he was better known as a poet and was honored as a local literatus celebrity, a status conferred by visiting national figures such as Jiangnan officials Weng Fanggang and Yuan Mei (袁枚, 1716–98).[34] His literary background and connections undoubtedly contributed to his revised status among the Cantonese community in the early nineteenth century, when Li Jian was held up as a leading figure in a Cantonese literary painting lineage.

The Formation of a Guangdong Literati Painting Lineage

Paralleling the literary activities of scholars linked to the academies were the artistic experiments of scholarly painters. We have seen, in the above, how Li Jian's artistic reputation was cemented in Pan Zhengwei's Tingfanlou catalogue and how these merchant collectors were first introduced to Li Jian in the late eighteenth century by the local scholar Xie Jingqing. In the nineteenth century, Xie's close friendships with the merchant families and his role as a dealer were continued by his son, Xie Lansheng (謝蘭生, 1760–1831).[35] Xie Lansheng was one of the prominent literati elites in the early nineteenth century. He was a metropolitan graduate, poet, and skilled artist. His literary fame meant that he was part of a circle of men, the *hong* merchants, who were linked to Xuehaitang and other academies as well as other leading literati gentlemen in Guangdong.

The academies were very active in writing a history of Guangdong through the publication of literary projects, including compiling a gazetteer and holding poetry competitions. In painting, however, the means to create a Cantonese history with national cultural resonance was more complicated, as the region's art historical contributions rested largely on artists who gained renown as court artists or worked in styles akin to the Ming Dynasty's Zhe school of painting, which would have been regarded as too professional to fit into a grand literati narrative. Although these artists were appreciated, they were not considered suitable forebears of a Cantonese literati tradition.

Xie was instrumental in promoting two artists who would form the beginnings of a Cantonese literati painting tradition: the local artist Li Jian, and the seventeenth-century Jiangnan artist Shitao (石濤, 1642–1718). Since the ideal artist had to have literary skills, Li Jian, as a famed poet, was a good candidate despite the fact that he supported himself by painting, among many things, lanterns. Li was plagued by an unspecified sickness and was dependent on opium to help alleviate his pain, especially from the 1790s onwards, when his health deteriorated.[36] Zhang Weiping, a friend and notable scholar-official who was also friends with the Pan family, wryly noted that Li depended on opium to rouse his spirits so he could paint, and, in turn, relied on the sale of his paintings to purchase his opium.[37]

Li Jian's painting style followed the seventeenth-century individualistic artist Shitao. Shitao, now widely credited as the grandfather of modern Chinese art, was unusually popular in nineteenth-century Guangdong. Recognized as an artist and a talented scholar during his lifetime, his work was first actively collected in Guangdong, where it resonated with many artists and collectors. In Li Jian's late oeuvre, there are strong echoes of Shitao in his lush dots and strokes—both clumsy and deliberate— creating an atmospheric suffusion of light, depth, and

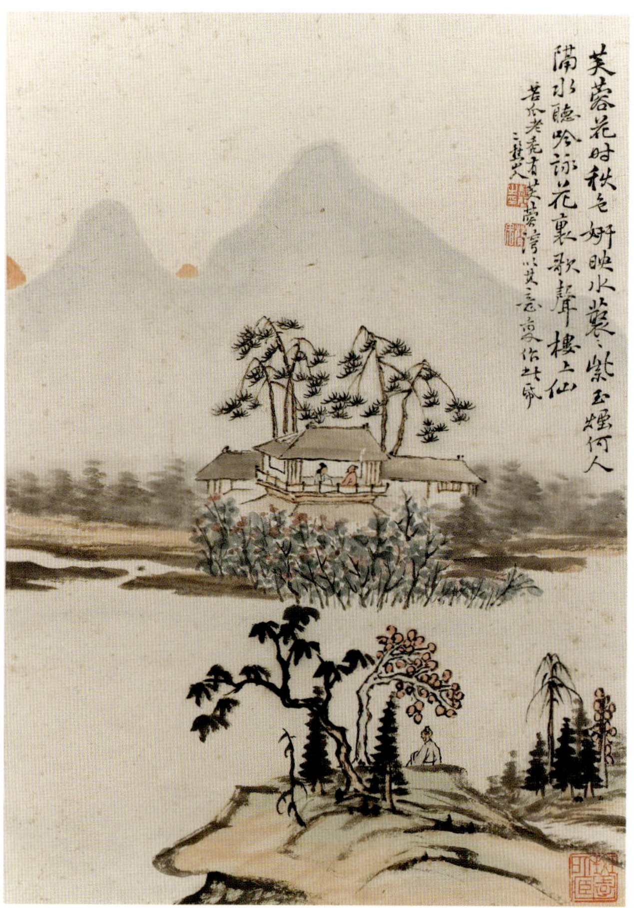

a

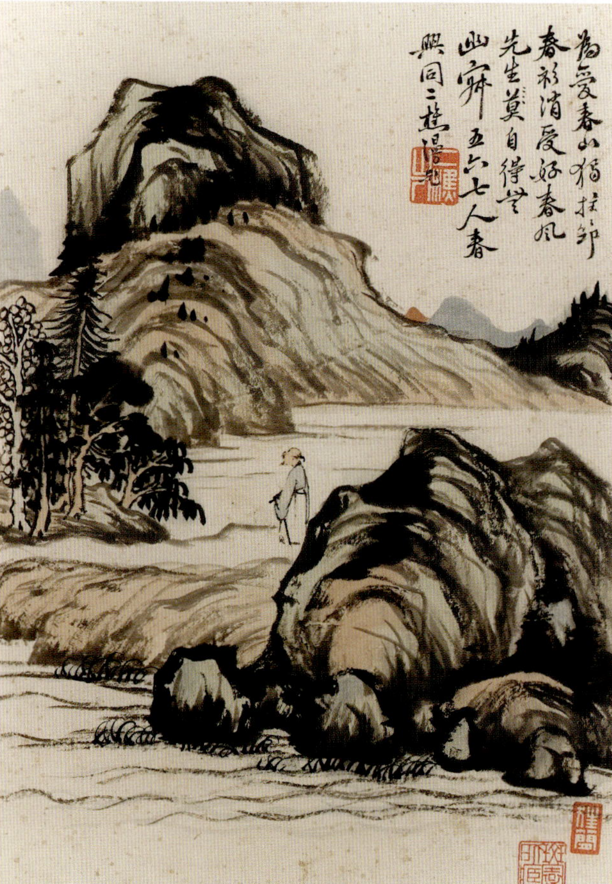

b

Figure 12 *(a-h)* Li Jian, *Album of Landscapes and Figures.*
Album of eight leaves, dated 1789, ink or ink and color on paper,
each leaf 35.5 × 25.5 cm. Reproduced by permission of the Art
Museum of the Chinese University of Hong Kong from the collection
of the Art Museum.

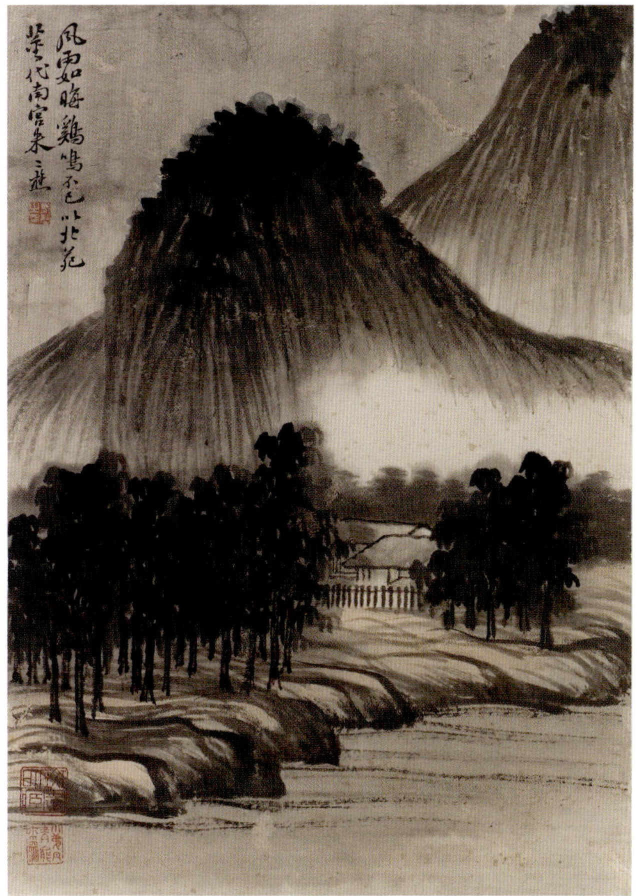

c

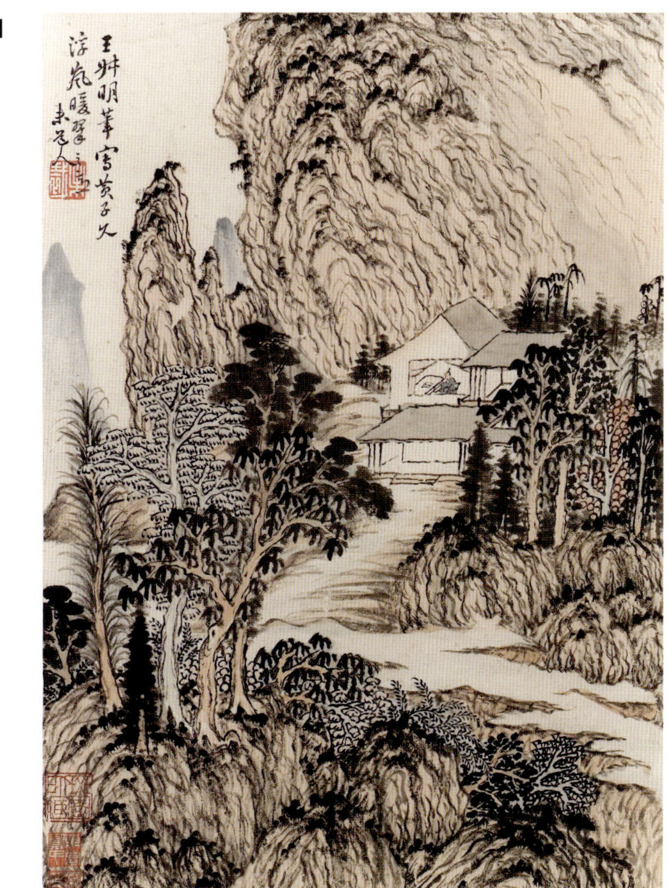

d

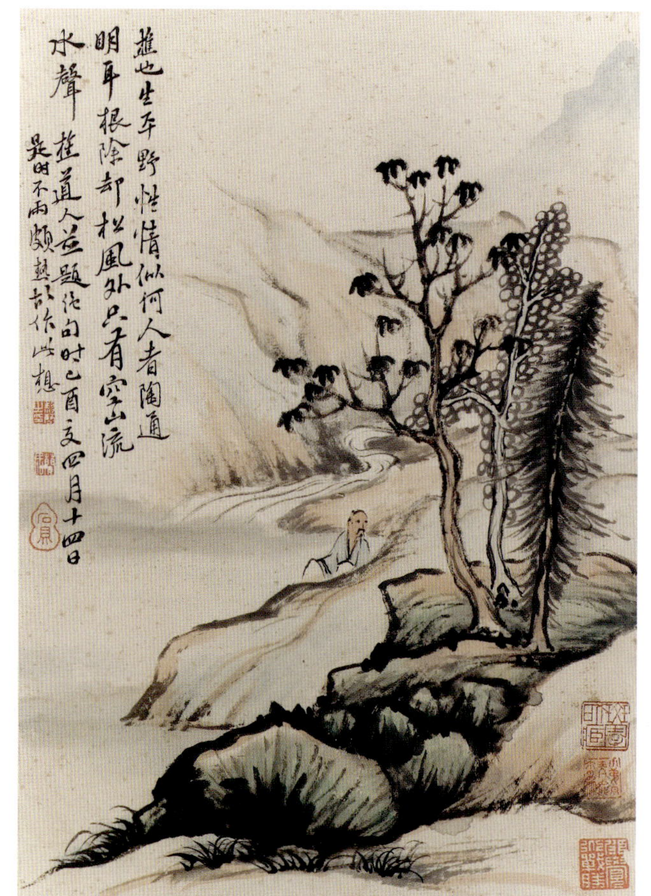
雖也生平野性情似何人者陶通
明耳根除卻松風外只有空山流
水聲　枉道人益題偶句時己酉夏四月十四日
是日不雨頗熱故作此想

e

f

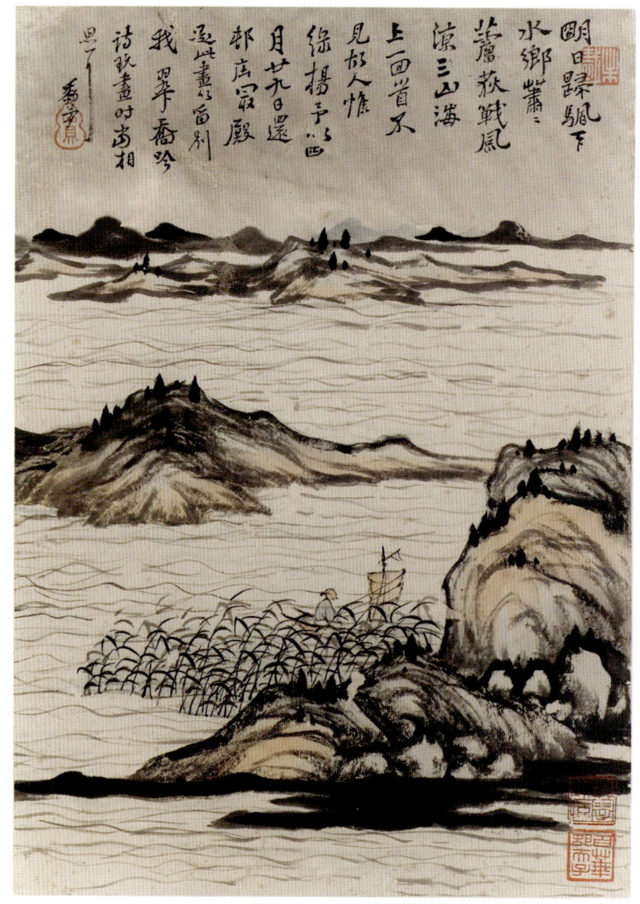
明日躁驄下
水鄉蕭蕭
蘆荻戰風
涼三山海
上畫當不
見故人懷
徐揚予以酉
月廿九日還
都庄寂寂殿
泛此畫竹留別
我翠喬吟
詩玩畫時尚相
思了　李雪原

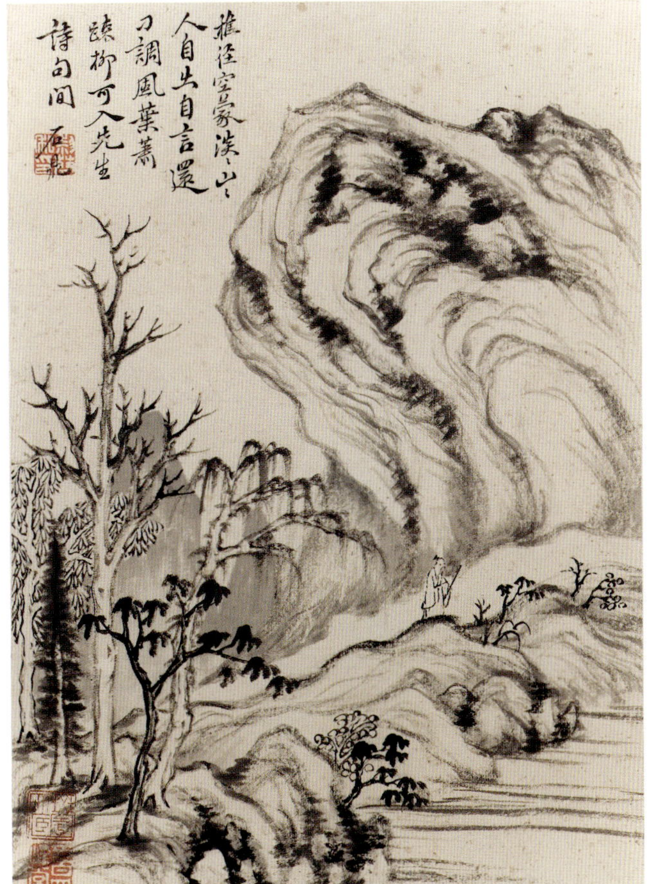

g

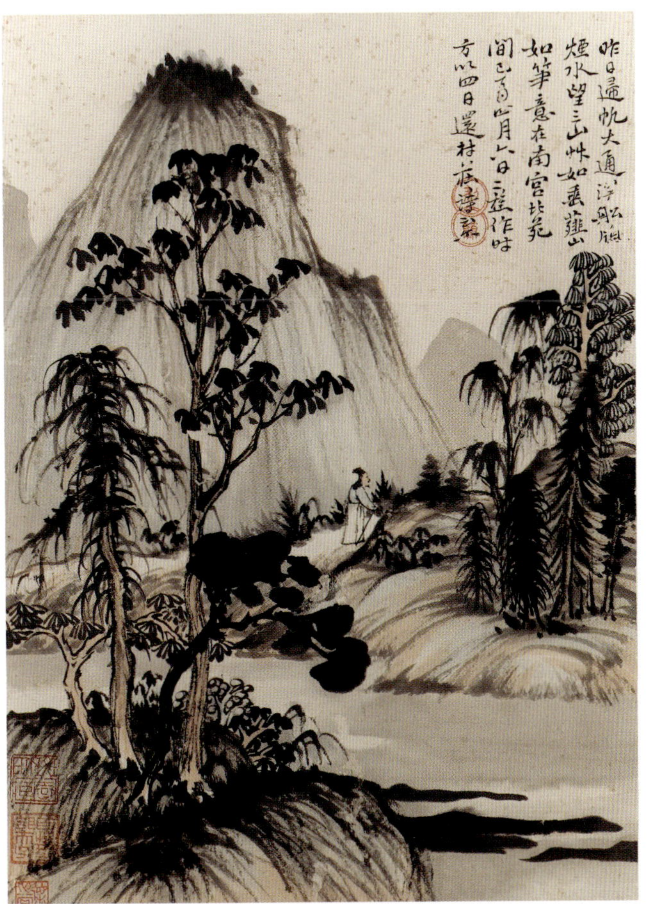

h

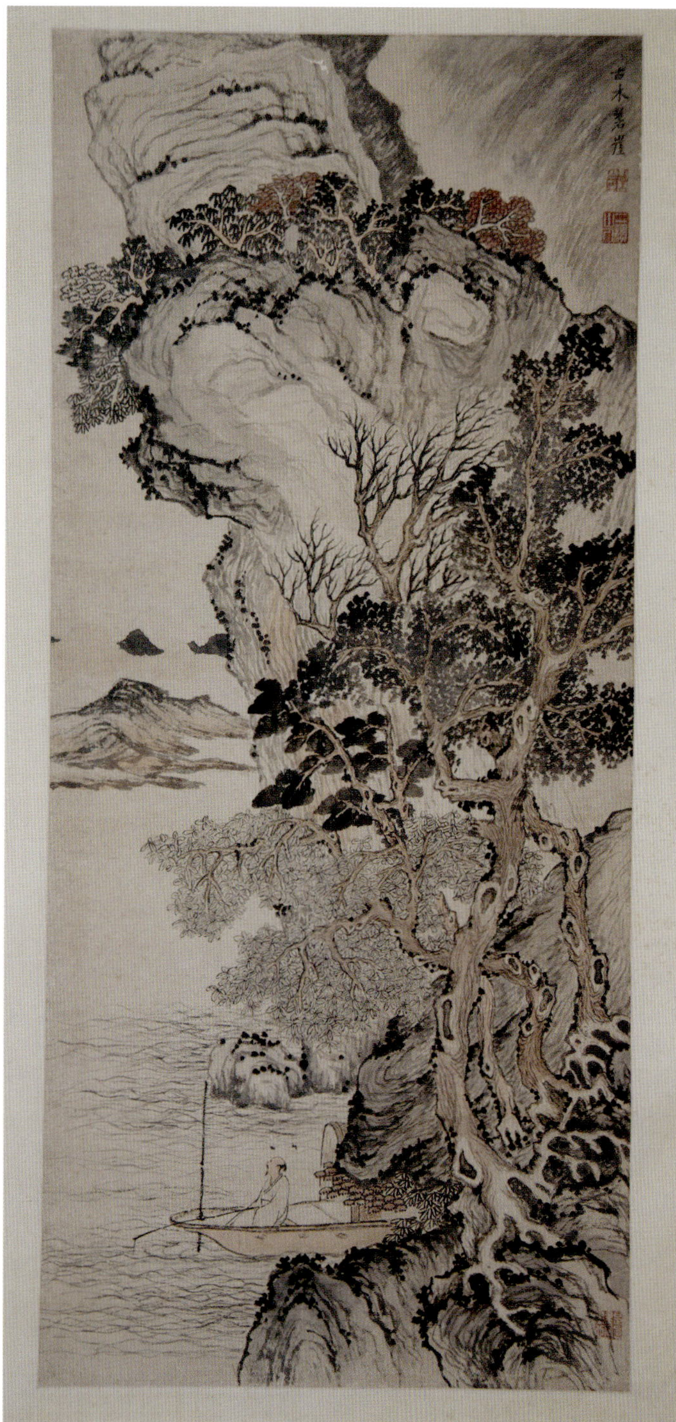 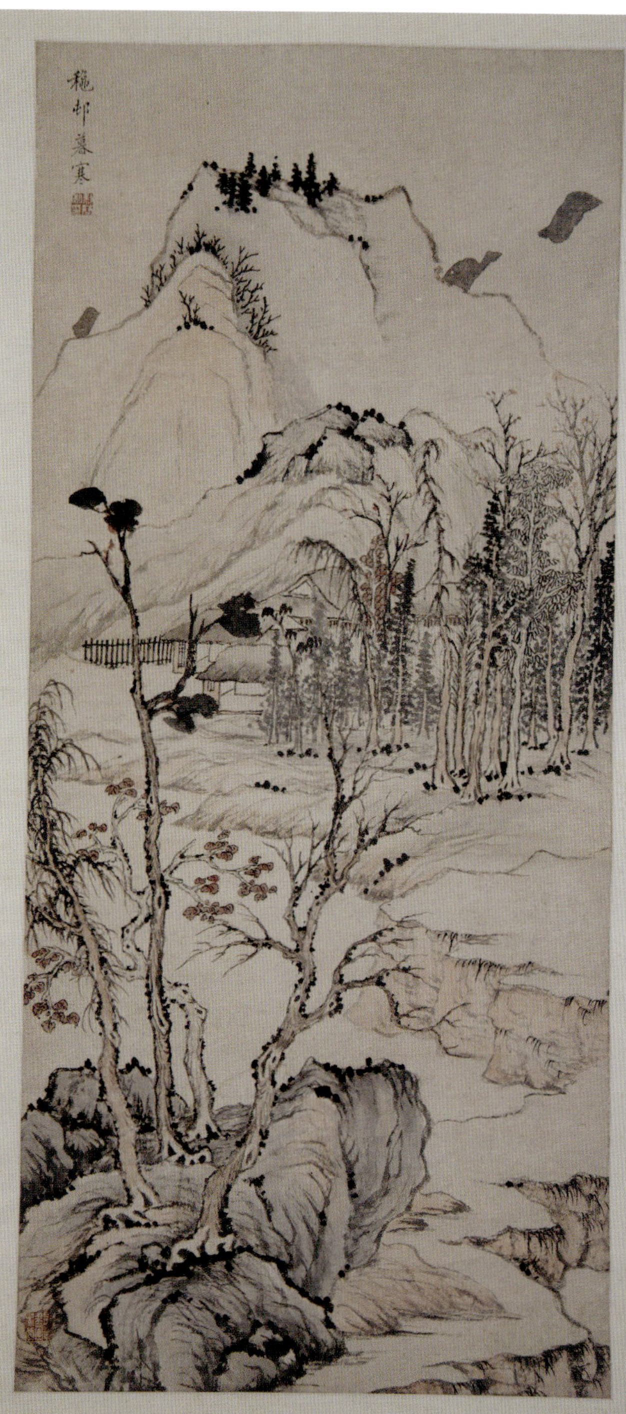

a b

Figure 13 *(a-d)* Li Jian, *Landscapes*: (a) *Cliff with Old Trees*, (b) *Furong Bay*, (c) *Hamlet in Autumn*, (d) *Searching for Plum Blossoms in Morning Snow*. Set of four hanging scrolls, dated 1797, ink and color on paper, 99 × 45 cm. Guangdong Museum.

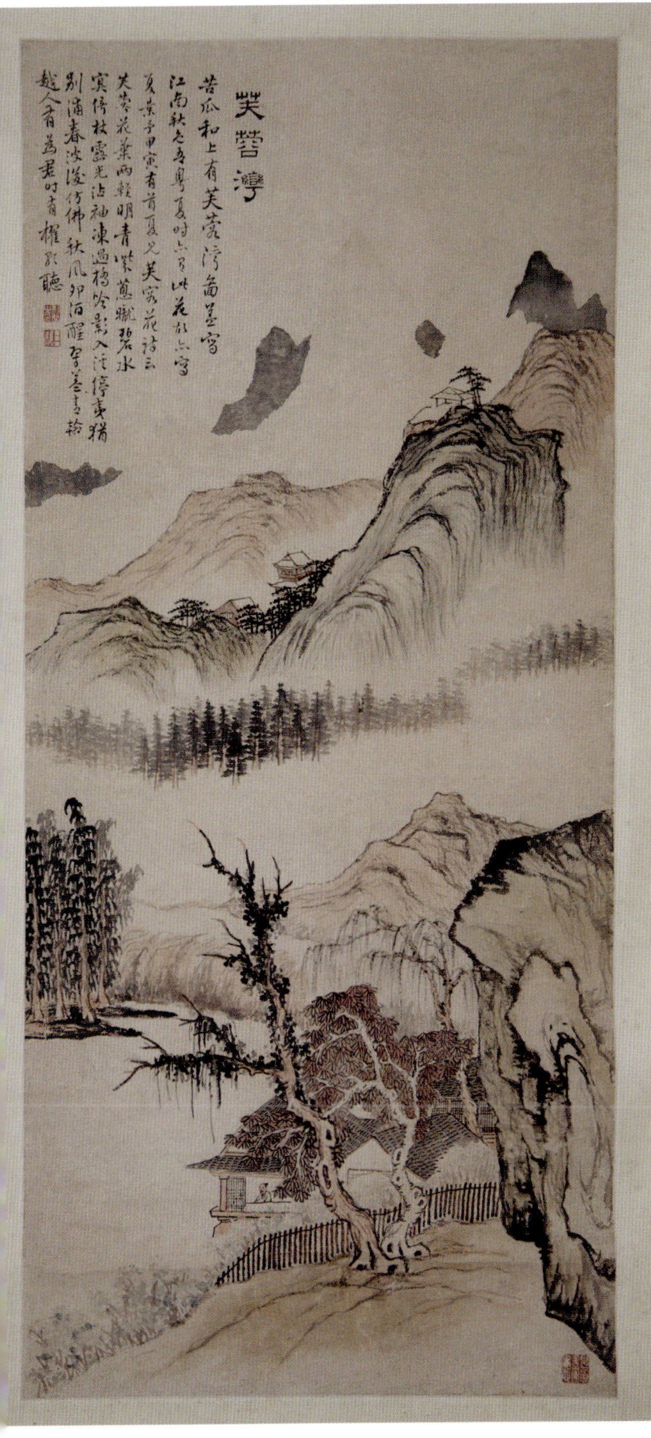

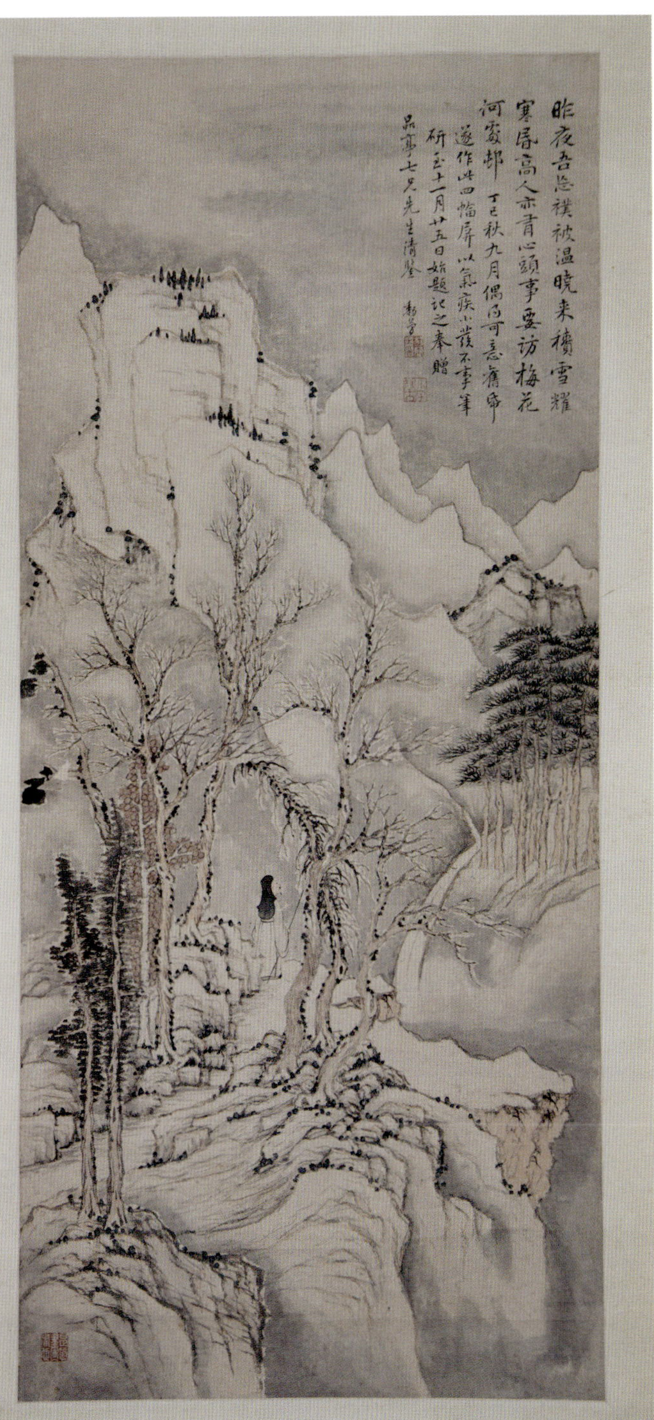

c d

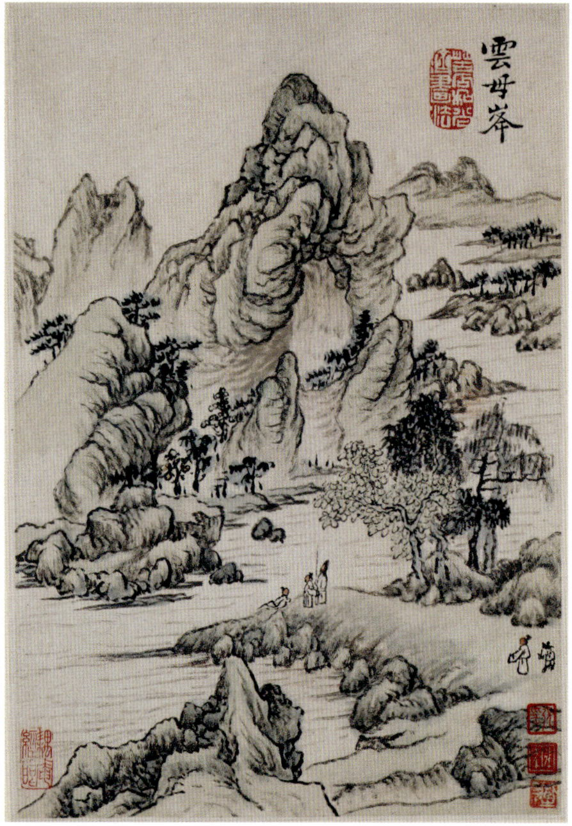

Figure 14   Shitao, *Mount Luofu, Calligraphy and Painting.* From an
album of eight leaves, undated, ink and color on paper, 28.2 × 19.8 cm.
Princeton University Art Museum/ Art Resource, NY.

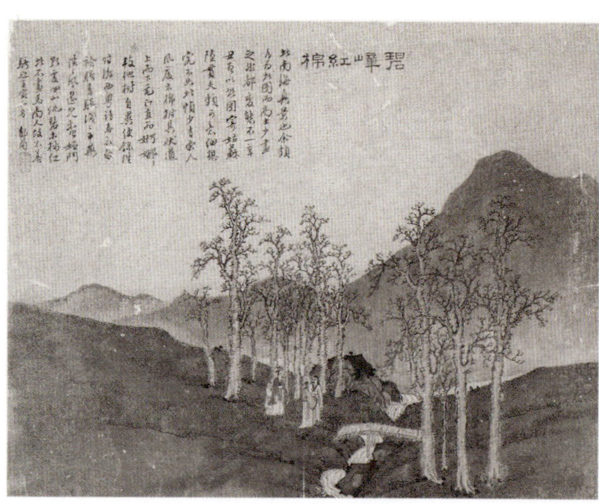

Figure 15   Li Jian, *Green Mountains with Kapok Trees* in *Album of
Landscapes after Great Masters Dedicated to Juhu.* From an album
of twelve leaves, dated 1782, ink and color on silk, 25 × 32 cm.
Guangzhou Art Gallery, Guangzhou Art Museum. After Kao Mayching, ed.,
The Art of Li Jian and Xie Lansheng. Hong Kong and Guangzhou: Art
Gallery, The Chinese University of Hong Kong and Guangzhou Art Gallery,
1993, 60.

color through ink and broken up with bands of mist.
Shitao's *Wilderness Cottage,* a leaf from his album
Wilderness Colors (Fig. 11) was formerly in the Pan
family, and it was likely that Li Jian had access to this
album and other similar works. In his 1789 *Album of
Landscapes and Figures,* Li's eight leaves bear remarkable similarity to works by Shitao (Fig. 12a–h). The
richness of Shitao-style brushwork lends itself well
to evocations of the moist, humid environment of
Guangdong, as in Li Jian's *Furong Bay* (Fig. 13), a
hanging scroll from a set of four. The word *furong* was
a popular epithet for the opiate drug, and Li Jian's
well-known addiction made his references to *Furong
Studio* both playfully and poignantly apt.

Xie Lansheng used this transregional art connection to anchor Cantonese literati painting into a larger
matrix of Jiangnan and Beijing culture. In a colophon
to a painting by Shitao, which had made its way to
Guangdong, the Cantonese scholar Luo Tianchi (羅
天池, b.1805) credited Xie for promoting Shitao, and
thereby Guangdong:

> Qingxiang's (Shitao) painting practice belongs
> to the Southern tradition. He stands out for his
> embodiment of strangeness (*qi* 奇). Those who
> dislike him see his works as wild and singular
> meditations, and lacking in cohesive theory...
> When Xie Lifu (Lansheng) with an indefati-
> gable obsession became an advocate of Shitao,
> the crowd of [non-believers] gradually under-
> stood. At a time when strange (high) prices were
> paid first and second for Song and Yuan works,

dealers of ancient paintings, when confronted with paintings that they considered strange, would send them from Jiangnan and the North to Guangdong. That is why we have more of such works in Guangdong [than elsewhere].[38]

Luo's telling inscription reveals Xie's success in promoting Shitao in a way that at once highlighted Guangdong's individuality and its connection to an important artist. There are many reasons why Shitao was an apposite choice for the southern region at a time when the orthodox style of Dong Qichang and the Four Wangs dominated the Jiangnan art world. First, Shitao was a scion of the Ming imperial family and was a young child when the Ming Dynasty collapsed. He initially pursued Buddhism, making himself an outsider to imperial politics as a *yimin* artist (遺民 leftover subject of the Ming), but he maintained close ties with leading scholars and officials who served the Qing. Shitao's *yimin* status resonated with Guangdong's own insurgent past, the region's Ming Loyalist ties, and resistance to Manchu power. Furthermore, although Shitao lived and worked predominantly in Jiangnan, he was born in Guangxi and was friends with several Lingnan poets.[39] Moreover, Shitao's ardent pursuit of individuality, admired by his Jiangnan friends, made him emulable for Lingnan artists who wanted to cast their geographic marginality as a form of artistic individuality that separated them from the Jiangnan center. Shitao's affection for his southern friends can be seen in an album of the most famous mountain range in the region, the Luofu Mountains (Fig. 14). In the album, he discusses his regret that he never visited the site and could only capture it in his imagination.

Xie Lansheng, like Li, made numerous copies after Shitao, but he pursued the relationship between Guangdong and Jiangnan-centric traditions by highlighting and developing regional aspects of Li Jian's art. For example, between 1782 and 1785, Li Jian often depicted different types of trees as representative of his friends and their moral character (thus

reflecting well on him). He was particularly fond of the kapok tree found only in the southern regions and executed paintings of this motif as gifts for those close to him. It came to symbolize integrity and strength, characteristics that he valued in the friends who supported him through his difficult periods of illness, mourning, and poverty. In a 1782 album leaf entitled *Green Mountains with Kapok Trees* (Fig. 15), he depicts the meeting of two companions on a mountain. In the inscription, he wrote, "The green mountains and red kapok. This is a *zhenjing* (真景 true scenery) of Nanhai. I like this image, though the people in the South do not often depict it . . . The kapok tree is upright; it never withers." It takes on the emblematic qualities of the pine tree or bamboo, traditional subject matter embodying righteousness and friendship in the literati canon.

Xie Lansheng later picked up on the same motif and executed a version of Li Jian's album painting of a true Nanhai scene in his undated *Landscape Album after Ancient Masters* (Fig. 16). Xie's painting differs by pushing the distant mountain to the left and adding a dwelling to the side, suggesting that this is now about a visit to a friend's place. The foreground scene, which follows Li Jian's version, shows two groups of kapok trees separated by a small path. In Li Jian's leaf, the men meet under the trees; in Xie's painting, a man is making his way across the path heading towards the dwelling. It is the meeting of trees across the path that evokes the theme of friendship and is picked up by Xie, but, as the inscription shows, this scene of kapok tree and friendship is now affiliated with Li Jian and Guangdong art. As he wrote elsewhere, "for us Yue artists, the theme of the kapok tree began with Li Jian."[40] The motif was seen as a signature of Li, laden with Yue pride and an originality that made him the artist Xie followed.

Since the Song Dynasty, the pine tree, bamboo, and plum blossom were often painted as the Three Friends of Winter and represented the lofty nature

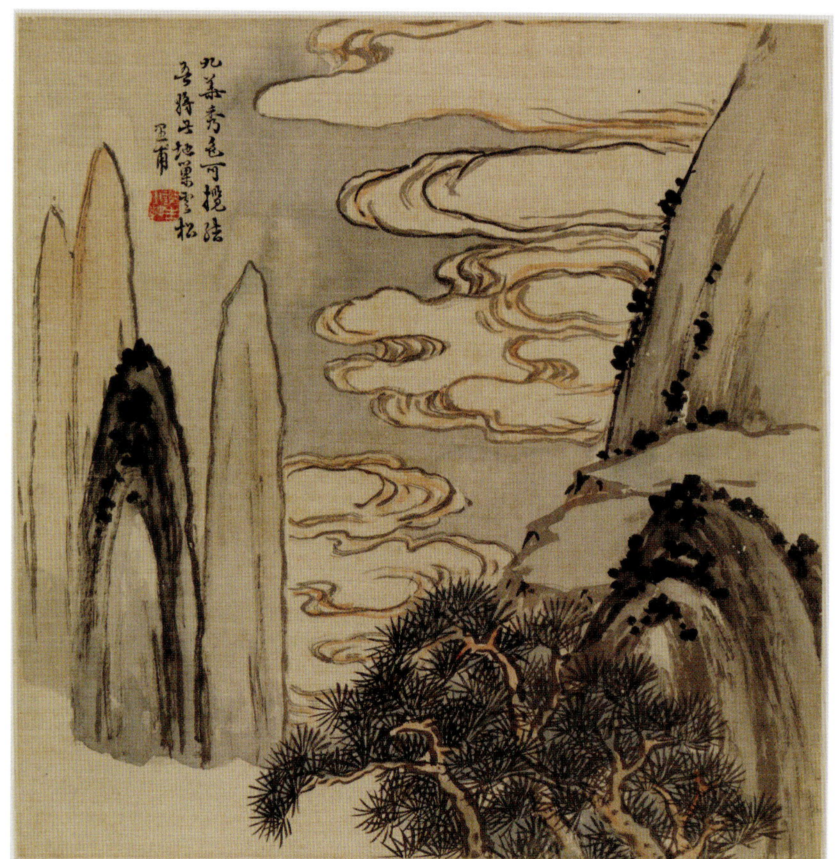

a

b

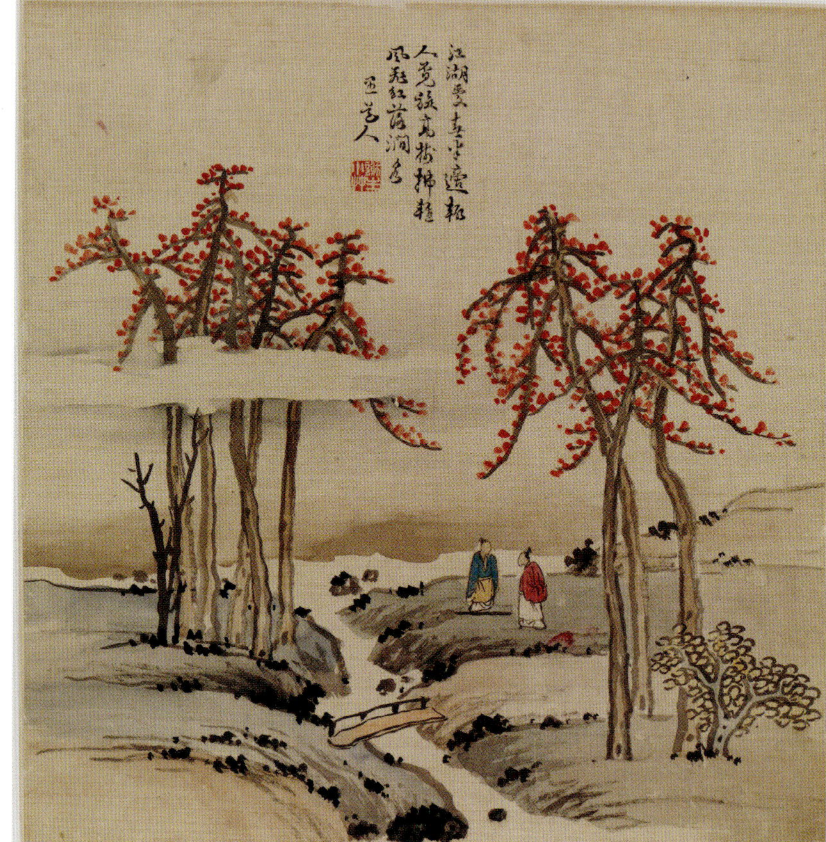

Figure 16 *(a-h)* Xie Lansheng, *Landscapes.* Album of 8 leaves, 1823, ink and color on silk or ink on gold-sprinkled paper, 35.2 × 34.5 cm (4 leaves); 31.6 × 29.8 cm (4 leaves). Hong Kong Museum of Art Collection.

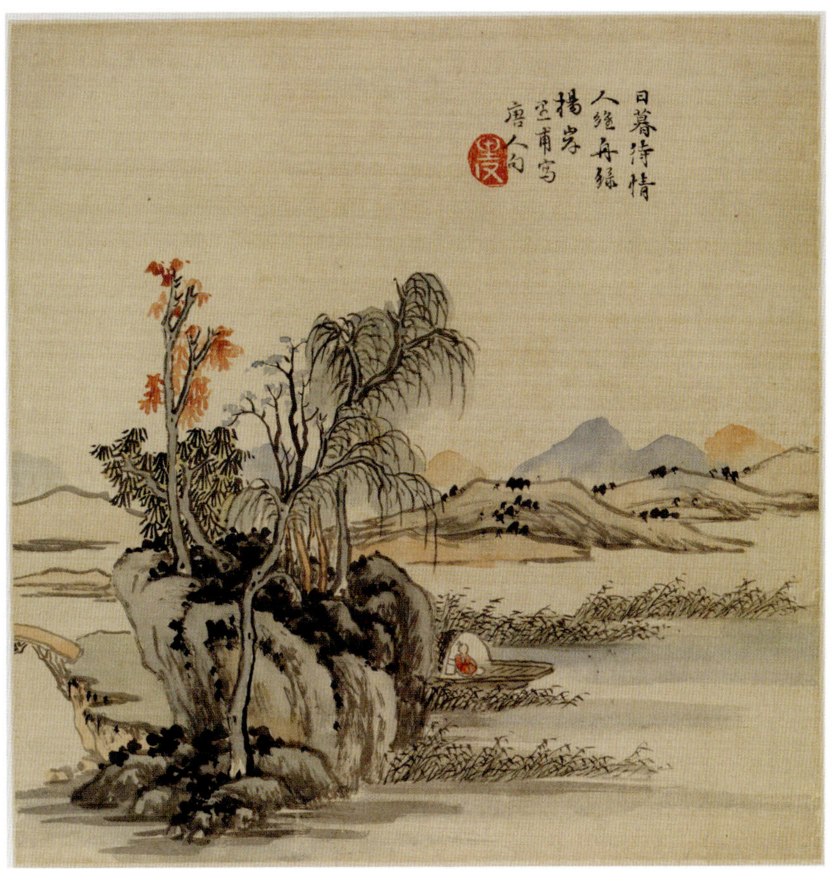

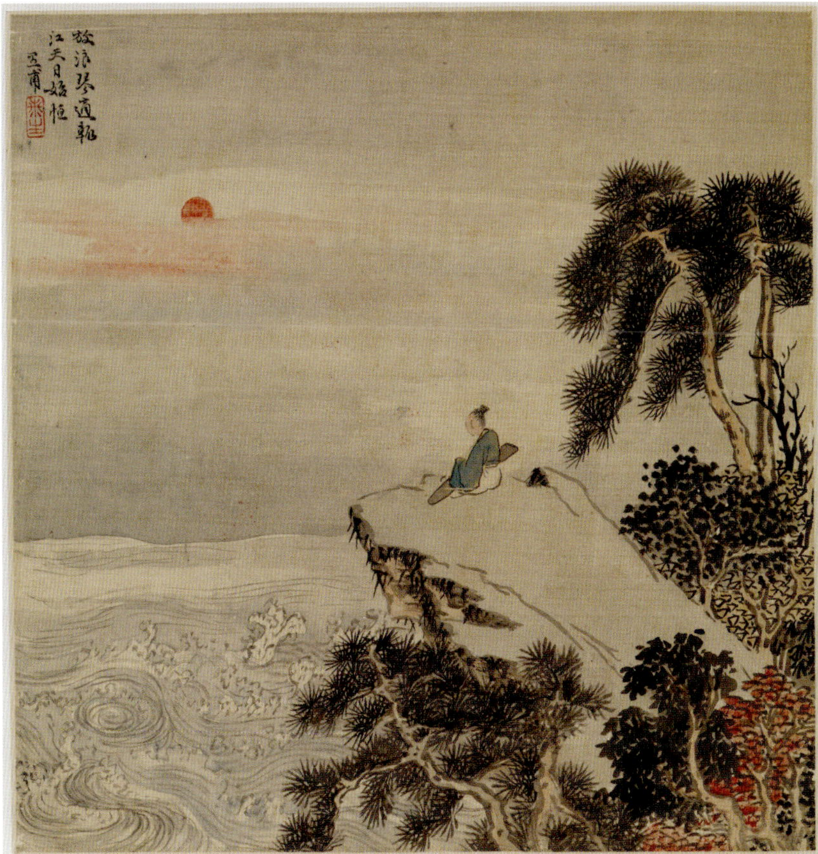

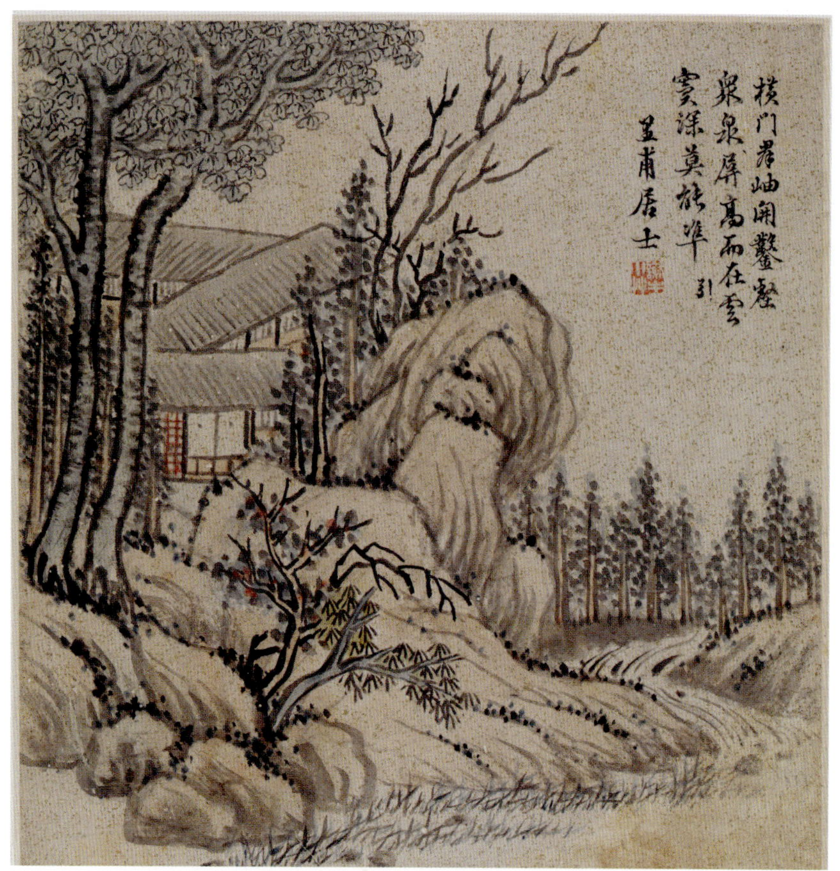

e

f

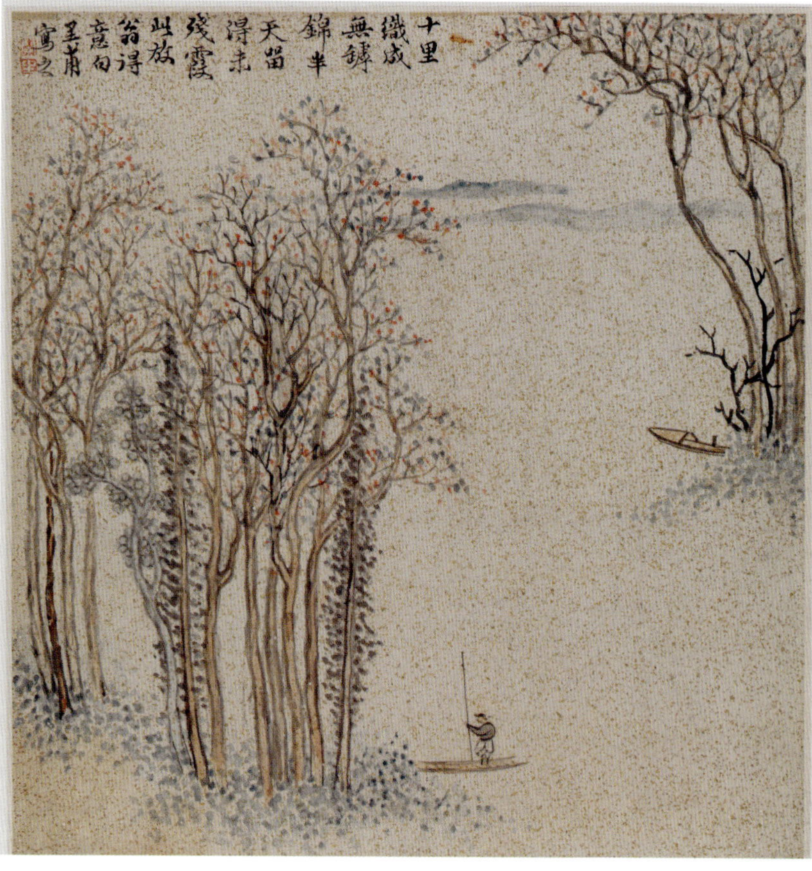

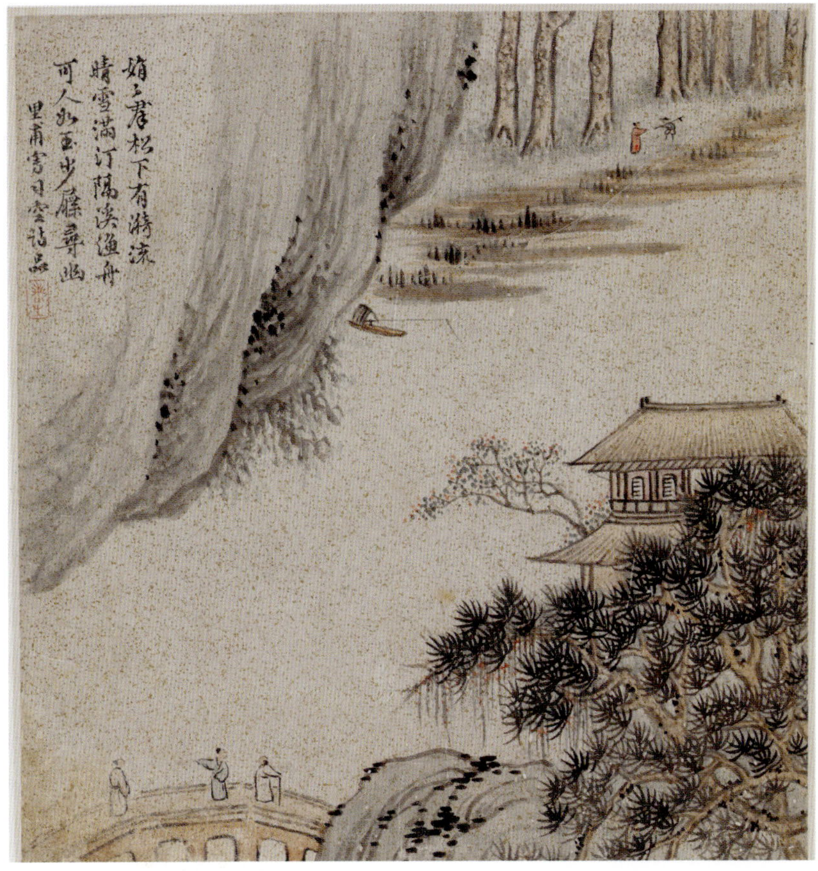

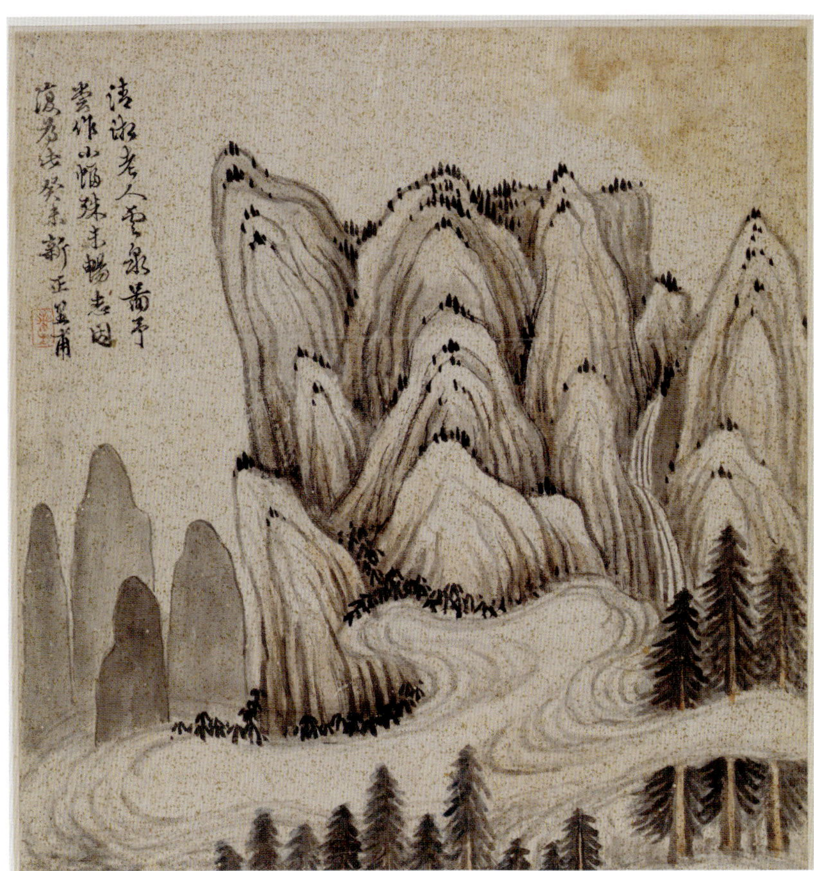

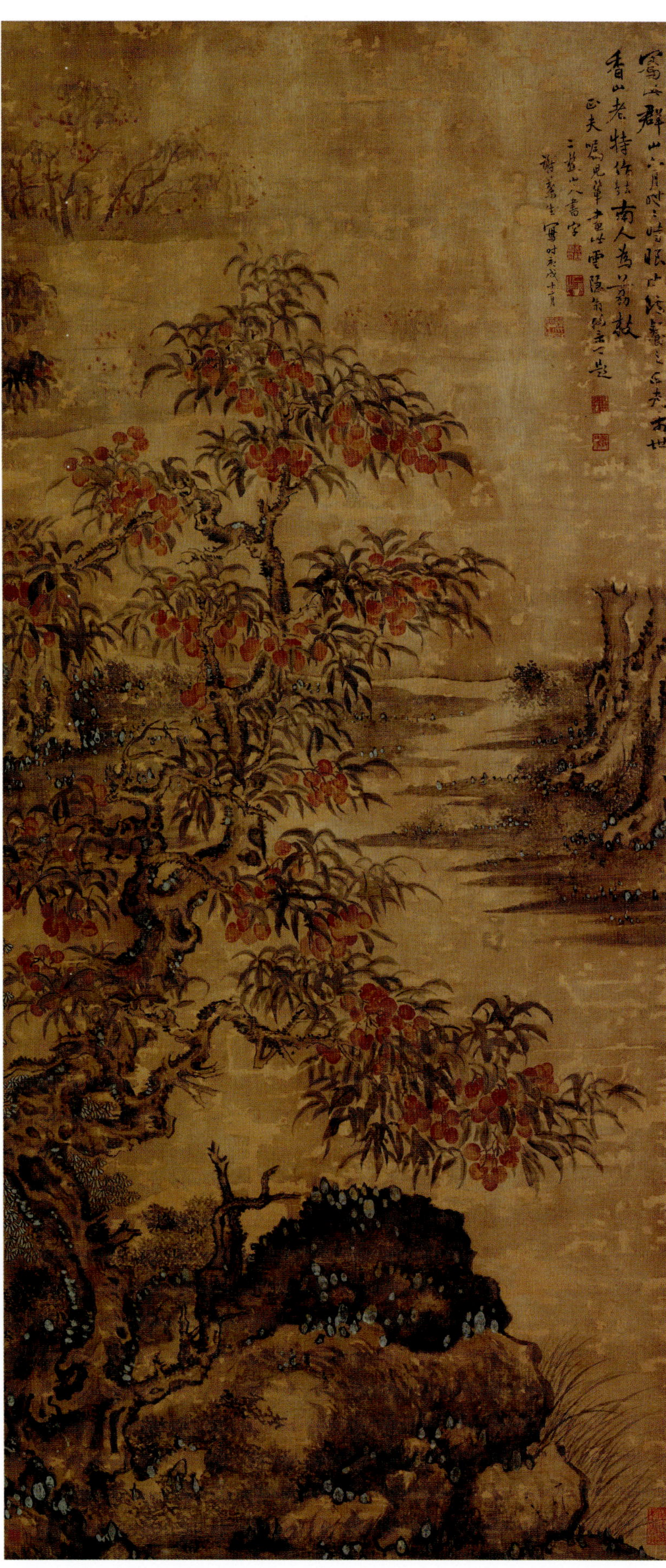

Figure 17 Xie Lansheng, *Lychee Tree.* Hanging scroll, dated 1791, ink and color on silk, 166 × 75 cm. Reproduced by permission of the Art Museum of the Chinese University of Hong Kong from the collection of the Art Museum.

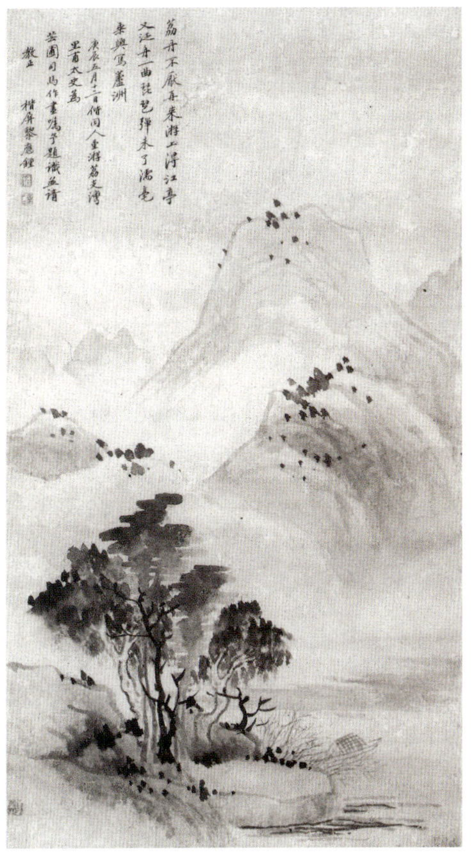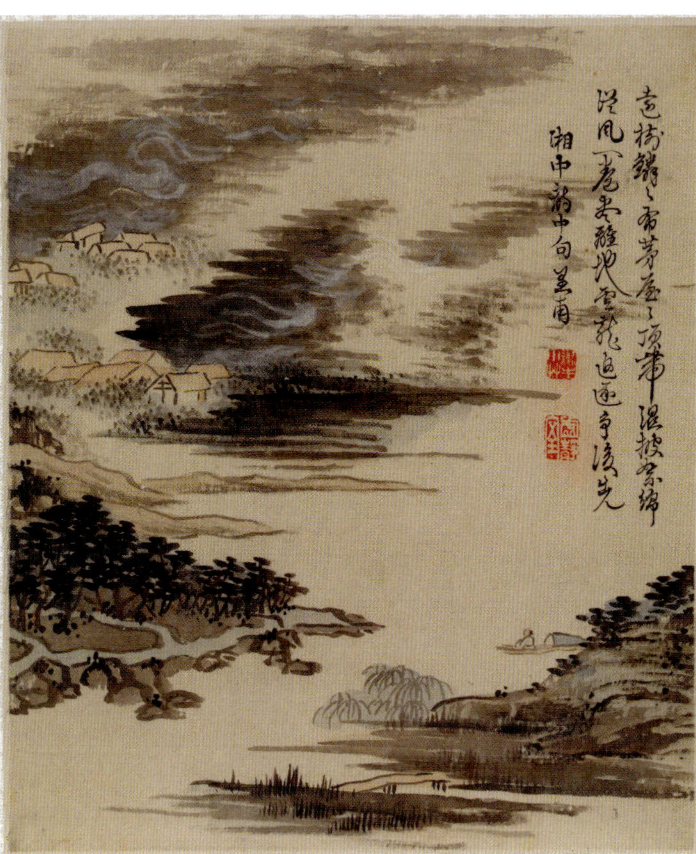

Figure 18 *(left)*   Xie Lansheng, *Lychee Grove*. Hanging scroll, dated 1820, ink and color on paper, 58 × 31.5 cm. Guangzhou Art Gallery, Guangzhou Art Museum. After Kao Mayching, ed., *The Art of Li Jian and Xie Lansheng*. Hong Kong and Guangzhou: Art Gallery, The Chinese University of Hong Kong and Guangzhou Art Gallery, 1993, 191.

Figure 19 *(right)*   Xie Lansheng, *Landscapes*. One leaf from album of 12 leaves, 1830, ink and color on paper, 35 × 30 cm. Hong Kong Museum of Art Collection.

of cultivated, emulable men. The kapok tree came to be imbued with iconographic values similar to the pine tree or bamboo, while the iconographic values of plum blossom were transferred to the lychee. The fruit was one of the most potent and ubiquitous motifs of the Cantonese literati community, their paintings, poems, and essays championing the lychee as a symbol of the south. A handbook of the fruit, *Lingnan lizhi pu* 嶺南荔枝譜 (Manual of Lingnan lychee), was devoted to discussing the varieties and its cultivation in Guangdong, claiming it as the best in the empire, outstripping those cultivated by their Fujian neighbors. This celebration of the local fruit is a far cry from its inclusion in early ancient texts that used it as a marker of the region's marginal exoticism.[41] Indeed, the Xuehaitang scholars used the Lingnan lychee as allusions to themselves in poignant rhapsodies, whether to praise their talent or to lament their lack of appreciation in the empire.[42] As the Guangdong literatus Lin Botong (林柏桐, 1778–1847) wrote, in comparing the Guangdong lychee to the northern plum:

> South-facing branches of the Great Yu Pass include the ancient plum,
>
> Yet among the fruits the fragrant lychee contends for greatness.
>
> Comparing [judging fruits] to recommending scholars, seeking a generation of renowned ones.

> From the distant past South of Heaven has never lacked talents.[43]

On one of the earliest dated paintings by Xie Lansheng, *Lychee Tree* (dated 1790) (Fig. 17), there is an inscription by Li Jian that reads:

> This [painting] was executed in the sixth month. Each time [one gazes at the painting] their eyes are filled, as one's appetite is sated. Zhengfu (Xie Lansheng) in his former life was an elder of Xiangshan, and I specifically depicted this to let it be known that the reputation of the people of the south is like that of the lychee. (Xie) Jingqing instructed his son to paint this scene of cloudy retreat.[44]

The painting and the poem attest to the proud marginality of the region, but, in so doing, they also reinscribe the importance of the center by placing the Jiangnan/Beijing region as the dominant cultural heartland. They also highlight one of the strategies of fostering a strong regional identity: exalting local produce and leisure sites. Entire chapters in books were dedicated to listing the varieties of flowers, insects, and produce available in Guangdong.[45] Examination questions at Xuehaitang would likewise be related to local themes, including food and marketplaces where these goods were available. This exhaustive collecting and celebration of native products was part of a larger interest in recording the physical world as a way to develop a regional identity that could compete with that of Jiangnan and Beijing. The literary elite chose plants and food that were part of their leisure activities: viewing lychee trees, or, as part of their social exchange, the gifting of mandarin oranges. Above all, their local references were to sites or products that were part of their physical environment and social interactions—a celebration of the here and now.

The attachment to the local produce of Guangdong, such as indigenous food and plants, extended to the celebration of leisure and commemorative sites. One of the favorite leisure sites was Lychee Bay, or Litchi Cove, on the border of the Western Suburbs, where many merchants had their homes and gardens. The site was a popular destination in May, when the fruit was in season. In 1820, the Nanhai merchant Qiu Xi (邱嬉, act. ca. early nineteenth century) built a garden, the Tang Lychee Garden, and invited Xie Lansheng and Li Yingzhong (黎應鍾, dates unknown), both Nanhai scholars, on a boat trip along the cove. Xie painted a landscape to commemorate the event, and his good friend Li Yingzhong penned an inscription (Fig. 18). The ink-sketch hanging scroll was typical of this type of occasional painting made for such an event: a small skiff hidden behind a bank with trees painted with variations of ink tones in the foreground and a mountain in the back that disappears into a ghostly whisper. There are no pictorial motifs that highlight the beauty of the site as a rich bank filled with lychee trees. Instead, the beauty is found in the calligraphic quality of the painterly technique, which conforms to the literati ideal of landscape documented by a poetic inscription.

Xie Lansheng's goal of capturing qualities and characteristics of Guangdong that still fit within the literati canon pushed some unexpected boundaries. In an album of joint works by Xie Lansheng and a younger friend, Huang Peifang (黃培芳, 1779–1859), Xie experimented with capturing the atmospheric quality of light and sky. Guangdong had long been perceived as a miasmic land where the humid atmosphere led to diseases, bestial natives, and strange wildlife. On a leaf in *An Album of Landscapes*, Xie used color pigments and washes to capture a red sky, suggesting the coming of rain (Fig. 19). This bold use of color may have been prompted by Western-style painting. Given the geographical proximity of foreign-merchant bases and Xie's relationship with *hong* merchants who also favored Western-style oil portraits as gifts to their foreign partners, Xie may have indeed looked at Western landscape paintings in which the sky is an important feature. Although Xie's attempt is not wholly successful, it does suggest, once again, overlaps between social groups and artistic genres.

Another example of famous sites in Guangdong being incorporated into a corpus of regional symbols was Shitao's painting of Mount Luofu, the tallest mountain in the Lingnan region. According to *Records of Mount Luofu*, this was a subsidiary island of Penglai Island, and its association with the Daoist mythical land imbued this range with numerous myths and stories. In the Eastern Jin Dynasty, the renowned Daoist Ge Hong (葛洪, 283–343) was said to have once concocted elixirs on the mountain and later to have cultivated his *dao* to the extent that he was able to achieve immortality.[46] His abode was later turned into a temple, and this area has continued to be a major center of Daoist worship. During the Tang Dynasty, many Buddhist temples were also built on the mountain, reinforcing the religious dimension of this mountain range.

Religious sites on beautiful mountains were popular destinations for travel excursions, and Mount Luofu was no exception. Artists and scholars composed many paintings and odes in celebration of this mountain (made up of 432 peaks and over 980 waterfalls). Xie Lansheng provided an account of the mountain in his travel diary *Changxingxingzi you Luofu riji* (常惺惺子遊羅浮日記), and executed many paintings on this theme, including a hanging scroll *Waterfall in Mount Cha*, dated 1821 (Fig. 20), dedicated to his friend Li Yingzhong (the same friend who had penned the inscription on Xie's *Lychee Grove* painting). The inscription talks about his wish, and that of his friend, to retire and run a fish farm on the mountain. Nanhai was famous for its fishponds, and Xie's reference to this local feature acts as a connection between the two Nanhai men. In this eremitic manifestation, Mount Luofu thus becomes a landscape of hopes and friendship between two old friends.

Waterfall in Mount Cha makes pictorial reference to the Ming artist Wen Zhengming and his famous *Pine Forest and Waterfall* (Fig. 21). Both paintings have a cluster of pine trees in the foreground, with a zigzagging river behind that leads the eye up the composition to a figure, clad in red, gazing at the waterfall. One of the main physical differences is that the peak of Mount Cha is soft and rounded, whereas Wen Zhengming's mountain is a tall, cascading form, suggesting that Xie altered his Wen-idealized landscape to include the physical properties of Mount Cha. Xie also added figures at the top of the landscape, undercutting the tense loneliness of Wen's solitary figure. Overall, there is less of the disjunctive tension of Wen's *Pine Forest and Waterfall*, but there are enough similar motifs in Xie's painting to see a direct debt to Wen Zhengming and the Wu school of painting.

Wen Zhengming's famous painting was dedicated to his close friend Wang Chong (王寵, 1494–1533), a well-known contemporary calligrapher. He had spent several years painting this picture for Wang after a short, disheartening spell at court. The painting is filled with pictorial disjunctions, and today's scholars have interpreted this ambitious painting in relation to Wen Zhengming's biography and his disillusion with court life that led to his early retirement. The theme of reclusion in Wen's painting can be read as a pictorial symbol for independence but also for the empathetic relationship between the artist and his close friend.[47] It is a fitting landscape painting that could be reinterpreted and presented as a gift to a friend who dreams of retirement. Li Yingzhou, the recipient of Xie's painting, was also a literatus, patronized by wealthy clients to compose poetry and write calligraphy. By referring to a famous Ming painting of friendship and dreams of retirement that may have proven difficult to fulfill, Xie added art historical references into his painting of Mount Cha, imbuing the painting with a similar aspiration for independence, even as

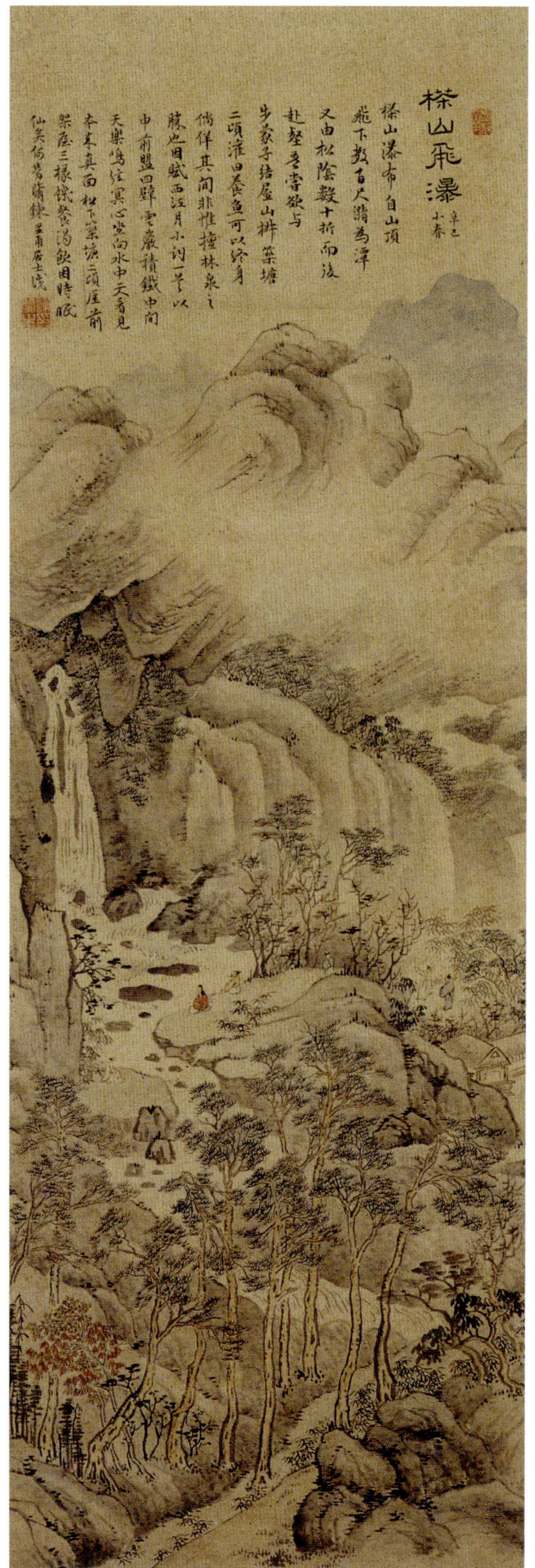

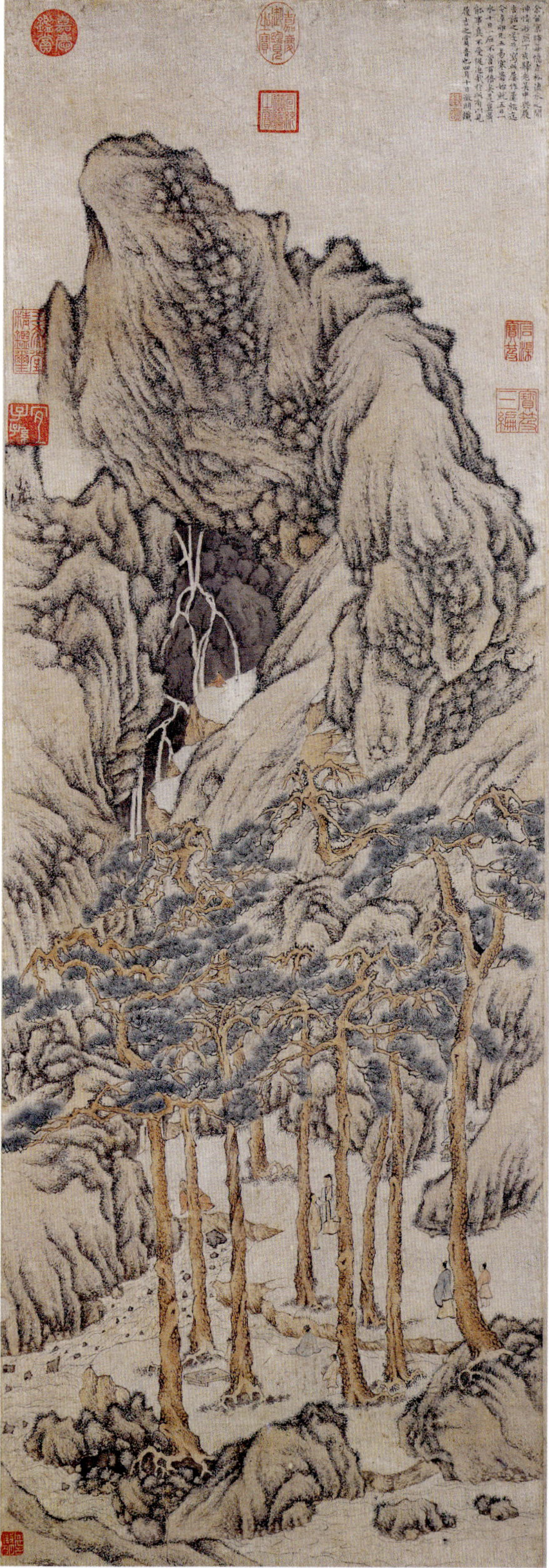

Figure 20 *(left)*   Xie Lansheng, *Waterfall in Mount Cha*. Hanging scroll, 1821, ink and color on silk, 116 × 43.5 cm. Guangdong Museum.

Figure 21 *(right)*   Wen Zhengming, *Pine Forest and Waterfall*. Hanging scroll, 1527–31, ink and color on paper, 108.1 × 37.8 cm. National Palace Museum, Taipei.

he created a landscape with literary references that would be accessible to a small group of friends.

Xie Lansheng's attempt to form a Guangdong literati tradition was cut short by historical events. After his death, Xie's friends and followers, such as Huang Peifang, did continue to paint in the literati style of the Wu school, mixed in with the more individualistic style of Shitao; however, because of the Opium War and the beginnings of rebellions, more urgent questions about the role of the literati pushed aside Xie's agenda to place Guangdong within a larger art canonical narrative. The abolishment of the Canton system in 1842 also meant that the former *hong* patrons were less active, with many dispersing their collections as fortunes fell. Later, a new generation of Guangdong art collectors emerged that benefited from the tumultuous events of the late nineteenth century, some moving to other major commercial cities like Shanghai and, in the early twentieth century, to Hong Kong and Macau.[48] For a while, Guangdong, in the early nineteenth century, capitalized on an opportune moment to form a Cantonese literati art that briefly fitted into a larger canon.

Guangdong's Open Circuit

The world of the wealthy merchants provides the backdrop to *Shenlouzhi* (蜃樓志 An account of mirages), an anonymous popular erotic novella

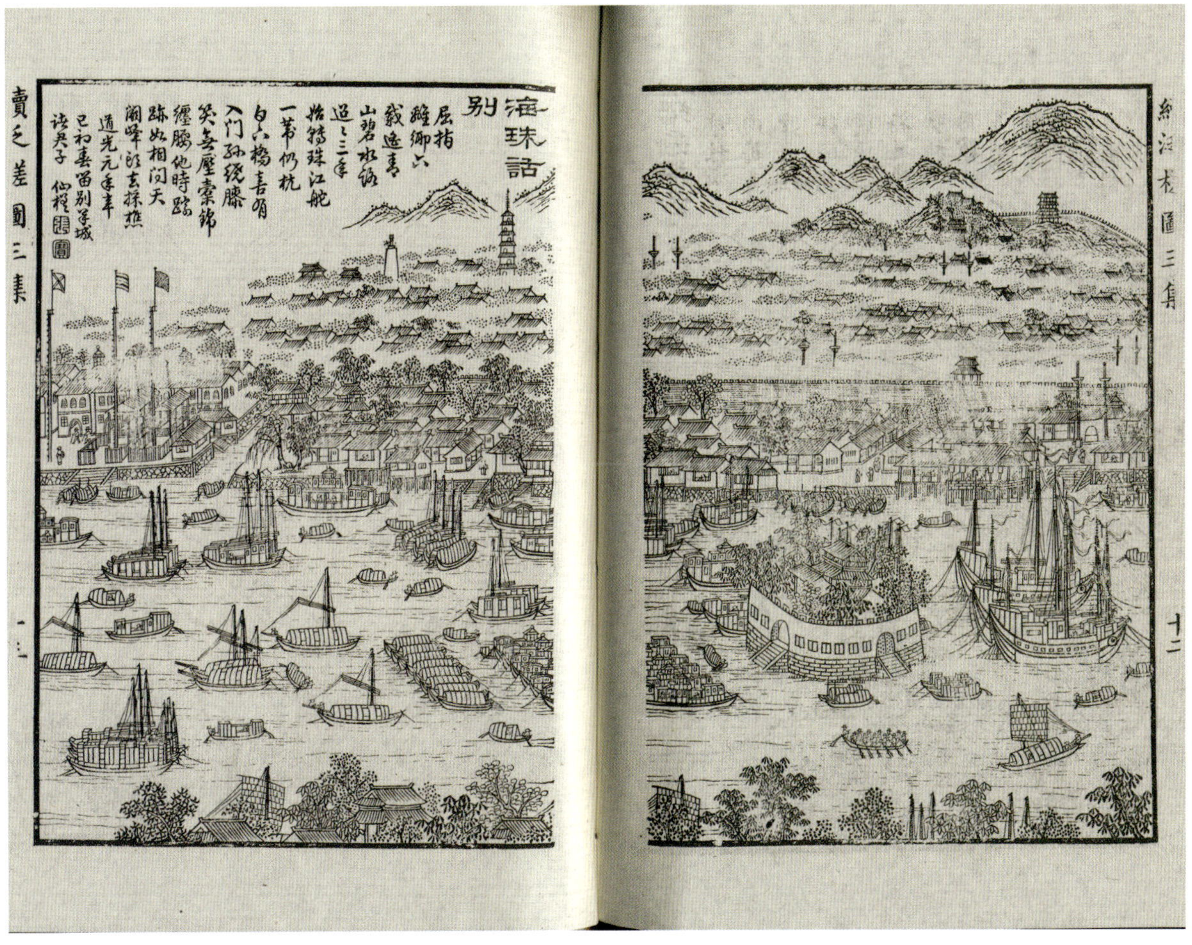

Figure 22   Zhang Bao, *Guangzhou*. From *Images of A Floating Raft*, vol. 3, 1833. Reprinted by Beijing guji chubanshe, 1988.

published in 1804. The main characters, father and son, are from an established maritime trade family, who fall foul of the scheming plots of the newly arrived and corrupt maritime customs official. Thinly disguised as being set in the Ming Dynasty, the novel offers insights into the lives of maritime traders in the late eighteenth century and suggests that the writer was very familiar with the comings and goings of the city. The novel also refers to an actual late-century person: the salt merchant Wen Zhongweng (溫仲翁, dates unknown) from Shaoxing, who in the novel was seeking to marry his daughter to a local official. As seen in Pan's family connections, this was a common practice among migrant merchants seeking to form strong connections with the local elite.[49] The novel celebrates the city as a place of intrigue but also a place where its local sons were adventurous, loyal, and quick-witted, their background as traders honing their ability to escape from constant danger.

Shenlouzhi is also, as with many late eighteenth-century novels, a story of objects. The writer's description of an encounter with a foreign gentleman leads to a lengthy description of an egg-shaped foreign watch, its face divided into twelve branches, encased in glass, edged with jade, and on a gold strap. This type of descriptive indulgence foregrounds the exoticism that appealed to readers. Excessive foreignness, however, was dangerous and a symptom of decadence and greed, as seen in one scene of a merchant's home confiscated by the state. In this scene, a *yamen* clerk enumerates, with satirical hyperbole, sundry household items, including 24 self-chiming "sing-song" clocks (Western-style automata clocks made in Guangzhou), 182 foreign watches, 24 screens made of Western glass, 418 foreign carpets, 16 beds with Western-glass decorative inserts, and 120 pairs of Western lamps. In such domestic quarters, these were the imagined exotic bricolage of everyday living among the wealthy traders. Underscoring the description of foreign objects was always a suspicion

about excess—whether in monetary or in cultural terms—that too much was too dangerous.

As an example of a diverse audience that typifies an open circuit, the novel shows how the worlds of export trade, the local merchant community, and scholar-officials interacted or intersected with one another. It also portrays the exotic world of foreign objects that were consumed by local merchants as well as the foreign community. Those who were interested in purchasing some of these goods only had to go behind the factories on New China Street although most of the buyers were foreign traders and sailors. Pictures and paintings were available for those who could not afford the actual objects. If today's volume of extant export pictures in collections around the world can be used as a crude measurement of the market, it would be fair to say that export art painting was a massive industry. Diaries and other forms of texts also provide useful information on the volume and value of these works. The head of the Dutch East India Company, Andreas Everard van Braam Houckgeest (1739–1801), acquired 38 volumes of Chinese artworks with over 1,800 images, including maps, landscapes, flora and fauna, albums of manufacturing, manners, and customs.[50] A visitor to the workshop of Lamqua, an artist freqented by Chinese and Western clients, cited the cost of having his portrait done as £8, if in Chinese style, or £10 in British style.[51] An advertisement in the 1835 *Canton Register* notes that the cost of a portrait by Lamqua was £15. Based on the exchange rate of opium from sterling to taels, an approximate calculation of £15 sterling is 0.15 tael. A comparison with the cost of Chinese ink painting collected in Pan Zhengwei's collection can provide a rough gauge of what the art market was like. The most expensive painting in Pan's collection cost 500 taels, but the average price was in the region of 35 taels. Based on the price of rice at two taels per *shi*, (the average in 1843), the price of Lamqua's portraits was very reasonable.

The low cost of an export art picture meant that it was accessible to anyone, but advertisements and writings about such paintings in the Western press also expanded their circulation. An example of this is seen in the *Canton Press* that advertised "Panoramas of Canton... As the city of Canton is one of the largest in point of size, for beauty of situation unsurpassed, the very first of Chinese cities with respect to wealth, we may take this picture of it as conveying to us an accurate idea of the towns of the celestial empire."[52] This is one of many articles that touted the accuracy of the images on offer, enticing its armchair audience.

In contrast, writings on the Chinese consumption of such objects are rare, but available fiction or anecdotal accounts are revealing. When Shen Fu arrived in Guangzhou, he visited the Ocean Banner Monastery and the flower gardens and market at Huadi, which were also popular spots for the foreign community.[53] He also went to a requisite part of any visitor's itinerary—the Western cannons and foreign factories at the edge of the New City by the river—and claimed that they looked exactly the same as seen in paintings. Again, accuracy was one of the key measures determining the value of representations of foreign things. Shen Fu's succinct comment also reveals how Chinese visitors were aware of one of the most popular subjects in export art, the scene of the thirteen factories. By the 1780s, the image of the factories—a sort of abridged panorama—had already emerged as an independent subject, principally by being copied from oil paintings to decorate porcelain punch bowls for an export market. It subsequently proliferated in gouaches on silk, on wallpapers and fans, to name but a few.[54]

Another Chinese visitor was the scholar Zhang Bao (張寶, b.1763), who composed a pictorial travelogue comprising 103 illustrations, published incrementally over fifteen years.[55] His journey began in Nanjing, via Beijing, then south to Guangzhou before he headed back north, collecting inscriptions and writings along the way. This collection of travel writing also reads as a who's who of the early nineteenth century, and testifies to the strength of transregional social networks in the mid-Qing period. Zhang spent some time in the Guangdong and Guangxi region meeting many of the local elites including Ye Menglong, Xie Lansheng and Ruan Yuan who had left their words in Zhang's volume. Many of his illustrations of Guangdong and Guangxi followed established travelogues of mountains and famous sites and, as such, he inscribes the southern region as part of a larger national narrative of scenic mountains. As with Shen Fu, he was also captivated by the western factories, and he includes a scene of Guangzhou City with the recognizable flags of the foreign factories, at the edge of the page, waving in the background (Fig. 22), further testifying to how the factories became a landscape symbol of this port city. In Zhang's woodblock image, the foreignness of the factories is heightened by the imagery of Chinese boats, pine trees, and distant pagodas. It presents a picture that would not be too out of place in an export art market, with the exception of the inscription that dominates the scene. According to the preface to chapter four of the book written by the scholar Zhu Yingfang (朱應坊, dates unknown), the book should not be read as a biography but as a tool from which one could learn things about different regions.[56] The unfamiliar and exotic sight of the factories is filtered through the idea of knowledge and mediated by the calligrapher's brush that dominates the scene. The factories are juxtaposed against a landscape of mountains and words that accentuate the contrast of "China" with the "West" and speak to the city's reputation as a trading port.

Depictions of Street Life

To pursue this investigation of intercultural contrasts and flows, I narrow my research scope to images of social types. Among the eclectic range of objects that were available in Hog Lane and Old and New China Streets were painted albums that provided a portable visual narrative of life in Guangzhou. One of the key materials used in artworks from these workshops was imported gouache pigment. As an opaque watercolor paint, gouache was not easily absorbed into paper, remaining on the surface and thus creating relatively flawless flat, bright color areas (although the color could also be easily chipped over time). Its overall effect was an attractive palette of bright hues that enlivened the subject with its decorative appeal. In some ways, the effect of the gouache watercolor was similar to that of bright enamel painting, which was another popular craft in the region. Gouache was a more direct method of painting, requiring very little manipulation of color tones, with qualities that made it easy for commercial artists to use. Its simplicity accounts for part of its popularity: Export artisans could make these works with very little training, simply by coloring in certain areas. The use of this relatively exotic medium also signifies another type of cultural exchange, which added to gouache's appeal.

An example of how popular these images were can be seen in an English illustrated book, *Costumes of China*, compiled by George Henry Mason, a professional soldier who stayed in Guangdong in or around 1790. Mason's work was also later combined in *Views of 18th Century China, Costumes, Histories, and Customs* with works by William Alexander (1767–1816), a British artist who traveled to Beijing with the Earl of Macartney to discuss trading agreements between 1793 and 1794.[57] *Costumes* was published in 1800, shortly after the Macartney Mission and was part of what Stacey Sloboda has shown to be part of "a major shift in British visual images of China away from the overtly fantastic styles in favour of the documentary picturesque. This emphasis on legible authenticity occurred in tandem with increasingly imperialistic British attitudes and activities in and

about China."[58] It is possible to consider this album as an example of that shift to the "documentary picturesque."

The images in the book are attributed to the local Cantonese export artist Pu Qua[59] and formed one of the most widely published and most influential images of China in England.[60] The album includes watercolor images of a butcher (Fig. 23), a vegetable seller (Fig. 24), a barrel maker (Fig. 25), a metal worker (Fig. 26), and a feather dusters hawker (Fig. 27). An incomplete Pu Qua album at the Victoria and Albert Museum (V&A) also includes templates of the earlier artists' images in simple outline on thin paper used for making tracing copies (Fig. 28). Chinese characters written in the corners of the tracing copies, supposedly identifying the depicted subject, but more often the labels are wrong. The inaccuracy of the words suggests that they were later additions, and given the many erroneous labeling, it is possible that the tracing copies were made after the original, with words randomly added and later used for other additions intended for a non-Chinese reading audience. At the very least, the words stood in as a label written in Chinese that may "authenticate" the image as being made by a Chinese artist and observer. The Peabody Essex Museum also has several leaves, some of which are the same as the V&A Museum's, testifying to the practice of using the templates for copying. Overall, the album portrays different types of people making things such as shoes and barrels, or selling things such as vegetables and meat. At times, the items sold appear exaggerated in size, or offer a dizzying array of goods, and all cultivated an "urban festivity" of consumer culture.

In each, the figures are set against an empty background, the subject floating in the center of the page. The persuasiveness of the images as records of "truth" comes from the isolation of the figures removes them from the lived experience of the subject by denying any sort of extended narrative usually provided by

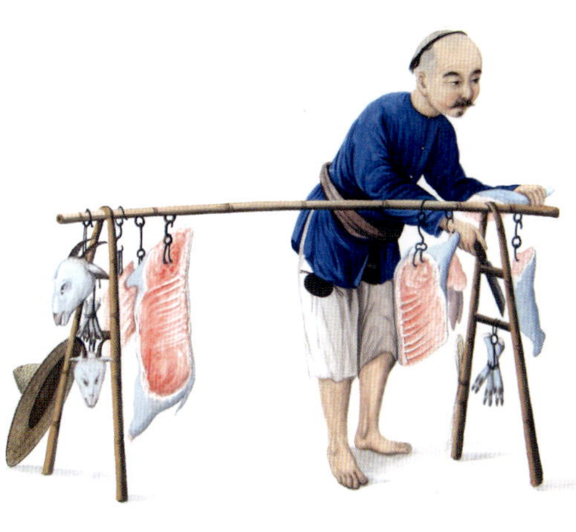

Figure 23 Pu Qua Workshop, *Butcher*. From a set of 100 sheets, dated ca. 1790, watercolor on paper, 34.1 × 41.5 cm. Victoria and Albert Museum.

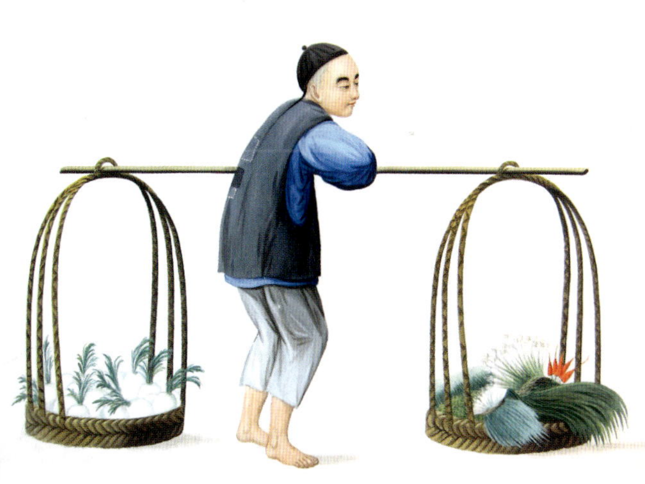

Figure 24 Pu Qua, *Vegetable Seller*. From a set of 100 sheets, dated ca. 1790, watercolor on paper, 34.1 × 41.5 cm. Victoria and Albert Museum.

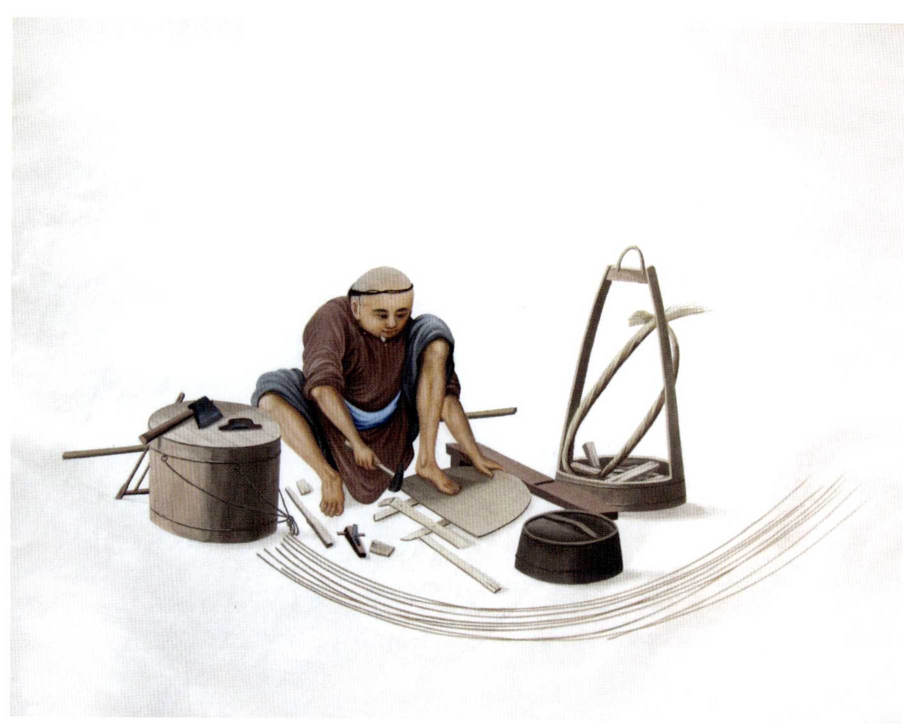

Figure 25   Pu Qua, *Barrel Maker*. Dated From a set of 100 sheets, dated ca. 1790, watercolor on paper, 34.1 × 41.5 cm. Victoria and Albert Museum.

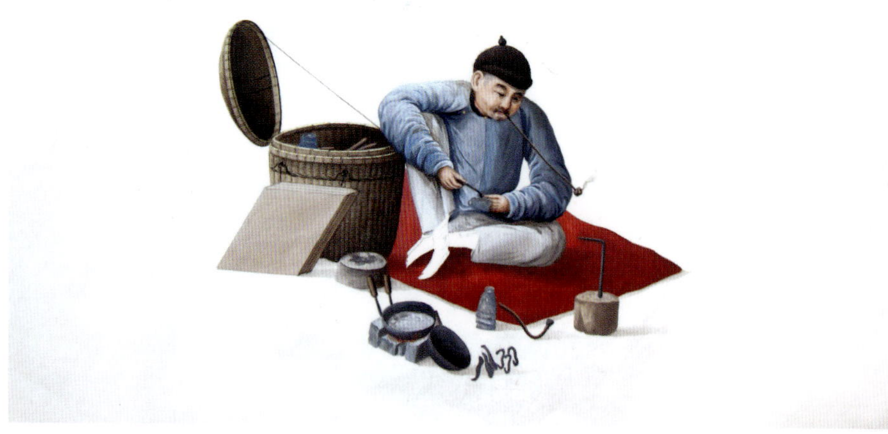

Figure 26   Pu Qua, *Metal Worker*. From a set of 100 sheets, dated ca. 1790, watercolor on paper, 34.1 × 41.5 cm. Victoria and Albert Museum.

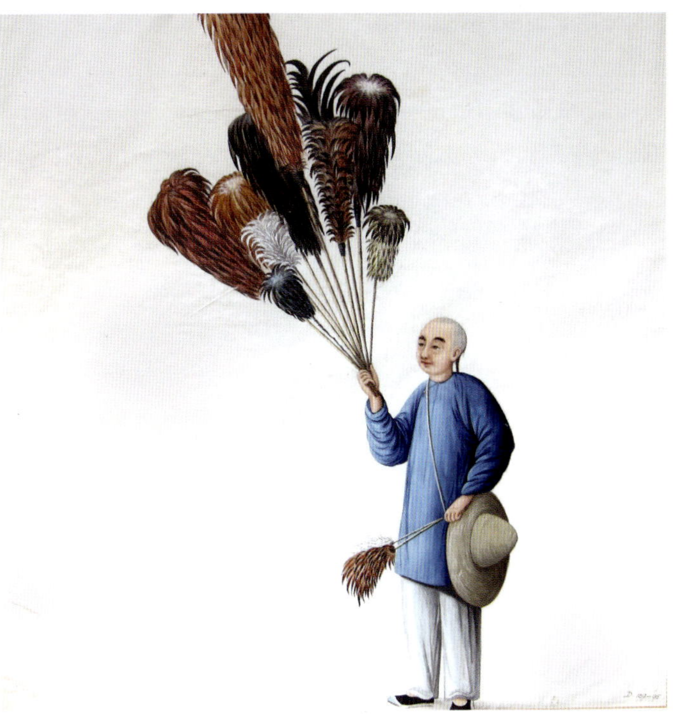

Figure 27   Pu Qua, *Feather Dusters Hawker*. From a set of 100 sheets, dated ca. 1790, watercolor on paper, 34.1 × 41.5 cm. Victoria and Albert Museum.

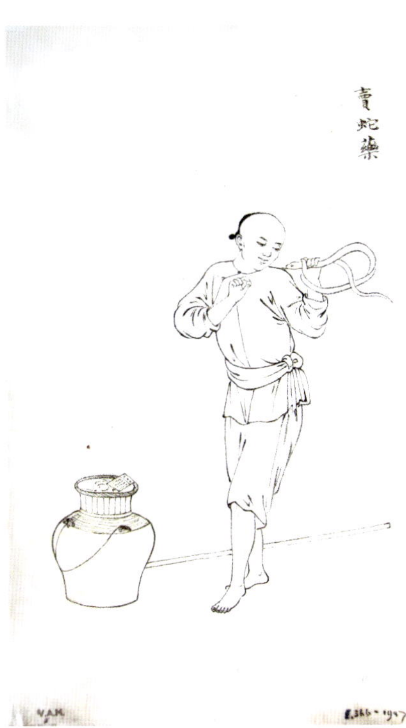

Figure 28   Pu Qua, *Street Entertainer with a Snake Tracing*. ca. 1790, paper, 34.1 × 41.5 cm. Victoria and Albert Museum.

a background. The central placement also creates a sort of invisible frame that distances the subject from the viewer and creates a physical distance that also implies an abstract distance of social and cultural differences. Broadly, these simple formal strategies contributed to a sometimes affectionate, sometimes crude stereotyping that distilled China into manageable parts.

As a form of ethnographic souvenir, these albums were compelling ways of translating China. They were cheap, mass-produced works made in workshops with clear divisions of labor: Some artisans might be responsible for coloring and others for the addition of different motifs. Systems of copying using grids meant that the copied image could become the desired size, and smaller and larger versions of the same image could be made. These types of artwork encouraged a certain amount of standardization, but that did not lessen their persuasiveness as a form of documentation. The documentary nature of the albums is also affirmed by the use of labels and thematic titles, such as "Trades of China" and "Costumes of China." As Poole argues in her work on photographs of Andean natives (which is equally applicable in Chinese export art albums of social types), by arranging labels, the images can be "classified, hierarchized, and serialized to portray the corps de metiers through which contemporary sociological discourse defined social structures."[61] In other

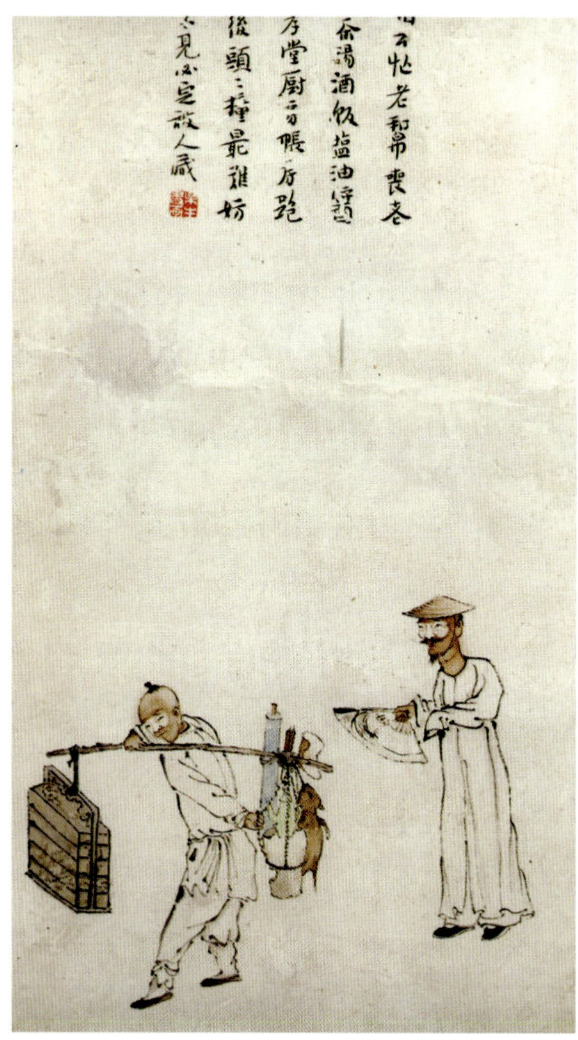

Figure 29 Ju Chao, *Operatic Comic Actor*. One from a set of 4 hanging scrolls, ca. 1840s, ink and color on paper. Reproduced by permission of the Art Museum of the Chinese University of Hong Kong from the collection of the Art Museum.

words, what made these images valuable was less their individuality and more the serial nature of albums as narrative, which made the unfamiliar familiar by giving it reason and logic.

If Western audiences valued export art (or *yang* objects, as they were known to their Chinese counterparts) because they depicted the unfamiliar, the pictorialization of the object also depended on a degree of "iconographic redundancy."[62] For viewers to understand the unfamiliar, the artist needed a familiar image as the starting point. For example, the most prevalent type of production series incorporated the most popular export commodities, such as ceramics, tea, and silk. Moreover, the representation style used some familiar elements of shadows and shading and imported gouache paint borrowed from Western conventions of painting. I would argue that the use of foreign materials and style was, in part, to make the depicted works accessible to a Western audience who found Chinese brush and ink too alien an art form. The appeal of this hybrid form was that it allowed viewers to engage with the foreign by seeing something familiar, whether in medium, iconography, or style. By extension, this type of iconographic redundancy operated as a marker of "authenticity" by seeing the same subject repeated time and again.

Reading these images from the perspective of the Western viewer limits the possibility of considering the multiple dimensions of these types of artwork. It is necessary to expand the scope of enquiry by considering the domestic market for images of social types alongside that of the export artworks. The producers of images of street life and characters were artists who were primarily based in the older part of the city where the academies, teahouses, theaters, and some government offices were based. Although foreign traders were not allowed inside this part of Guangzhou, what becomes evident in

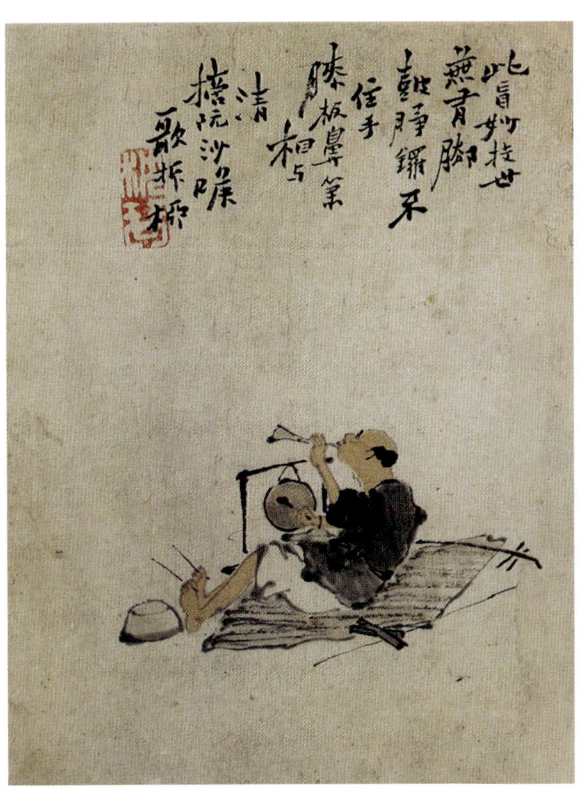

Figure 30 Su Liupeng, *Tan San* from *Album of Street Characters*. Album of four double leaves, ca. 1843, ink and color on paper, 24.5 × 18.5 cm. Guangzhou Art Gallery, Guangzhou Art Museum. After Kao Mayching, ed., *The Art of Su Liupeng and Su Renshan*, Hong Kong and Guangzhou: Art Gallery, The Chinese University of Hong Kong and Guangzhou Art Gallery, 1990, 35.

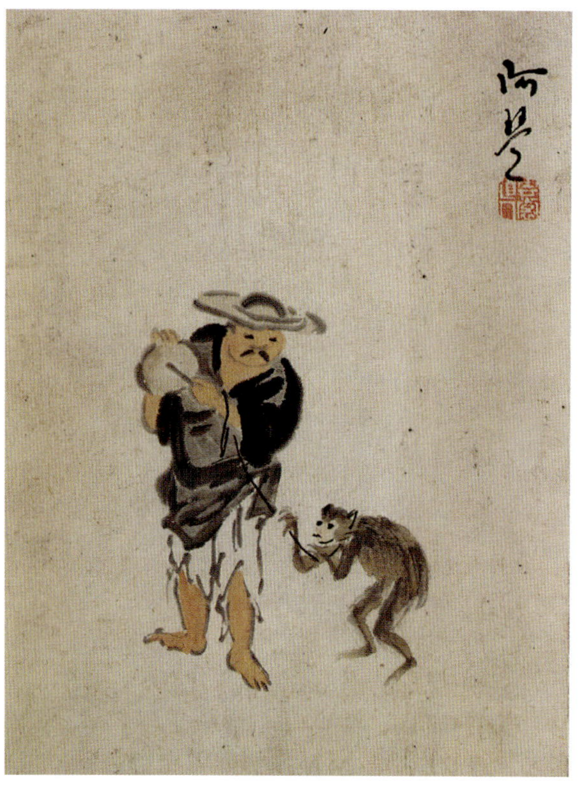

Figure 31   Su Liupeng, *Monkey Trainer* from *Album of Street Characters*. Album of four double leaves, ca. 1843, ink and color on paper, 24.5 × 18.5 cm. Guangzhou Art Gallery, Guangzhou Art Museum. After Kao Mayching, ed., *The Art of Su Liupeng and Su Renshan*, Hong Kong and Guangzhou: Art Gallery, The Chinese University of Hong Kong and Guangzhou Art Gallery, 1990, 35.

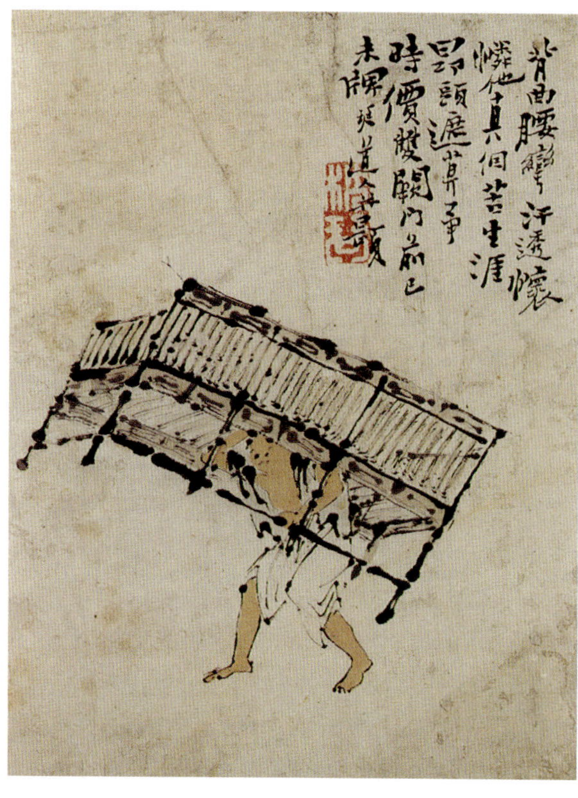

Figure 32   Su Liupeng, *Bamboo Bed Peddler* from *Album of Street Characters*. Album of four double leaves, ca. 1843, ink and color on paper, 24.5 × 18.5 cm. Guangzhou Art Gallery, Guangzhou Art Museum. After Kao Mayching, ed., *The Art of Su Liupeng and Su Renshan*, Hong Kong and Guangzhou: Art Gallery, The Chinese University of Hong Kong and Guangzhou Art Gallery, 1990, 35.

this comparative exercise is that there was a market for similar images of the daily life of Guangzhou and that there were some shared modes of depiction that suggest contacts between the two worlds.

The depiction of theater troupes was rare in Chinese art, thus making exceptional a set of four album leaves of operatic actors, dated 1849, by Ju Chao (Fig. 29).[63] Ju Chao's album of actors is an unusual venture: An inscription on each leaf refers to an opera tune. The actors in Ju Chao's album are largely comic actors, recognizable by the distinctive white patch of makeup around the nose and eyes. Comic actors are unusual characters within a play: They often improvise, enter scenes by making references to current or local events, and speak in colloquialisms. This type of intervention meant that, even with the most familiar plays, there was always a sense of the present, and, because theater troupes came from different regions, it was an opportunity to bring in regional elements, adding a sense of the local to a diverse city.

It is also within this hustle and bustle that we see one of the more successful town-based artists, Su Liupeng (蘇六朋, act. ca. mid-nineteenth century), who had a reputation for his sharp observations of city life. Su, an artist from Shunde outside Guangzhou City, moved into the city, where there were more opportunities to find patrons, and, while he never sat for the civil examinations, he worked hard to ensure that his sons had the chance to become officials. As his reputation increased, he began working for Guangzhou elite merchants and scholars, painting at their gatherings. His studio was ideally located in Shiting Alley, in the center of the Old City. Despite his relative fame (and typical of an artist of his rank), we have no more information about his artistic life.

Many of his hanging scroll paintings were executed with a high degree of spontaneous cursive style, reminiscent of the eighteenth-century Yangzhou eccentric artist Huang Shen (黃慎, 1687–1772), originally from Fujian. Su Liupeng's style highlights the immediacy of a city scene as an experiential encounter, quickly observed and depicted to playfully capture contemporary life on the streets. Representative within this genre is an album of itinerant occupational types who worked on the streets of Guangzhou. In his *Album of Street Characters* (ca.1843), with the extant four of the original sixteen leaves, he captured the range of outsiders and insiders who congregated in Guangzhou seeking jobs. Su depicts the characters floating on an empty background, bearing compositional similarity to Ju Lian's actors. One leaf is of a famous local street performer, the blind musician Tan San (譚三, dates unknown) (Fig. 30). According to the *Nanhai Gazetteer*, Tan San supposedly came across a generous Daoist priest while begging outside a temple. Tan used the money the priest gave him to buy musical instruments, which he played with his feet, hands, mouth, and toes, and became a local celebrity hired at times to perform for elite gatherings.[64] On another leaf, Su executed an image of a *Monkey Trainer* (Fig. 31), a street performer from the north. *Bamboo Bed Peddler* (Fig. 32) depicts a traveling hawker, a trader associated with southern Guangzhou, carrying his bed on his back. These leaves suggest that Su Liupeng was in part looking at the migrant workers who contributed to Guangzhou's urban landscape. Su's interest in depicting street

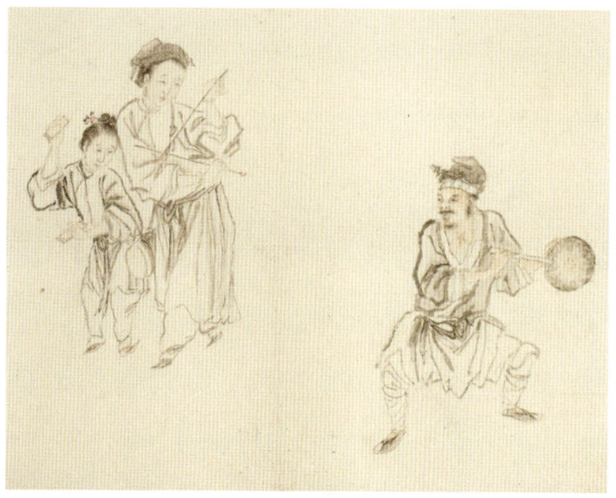

Figure 33   Huang Shen, *Street Beggars* from *Album of Figures*. Detail. Album of twelve leaves, 1730, ink and color on paper, 43.8 × 33.7 cm, University of California, Berkeley Art Museum and Pacific Film Archive. Purchase made possible through a gift from an anonymous donor. Photographed for the UC Berkeley Art Museum by: Benjamin Blackwell.

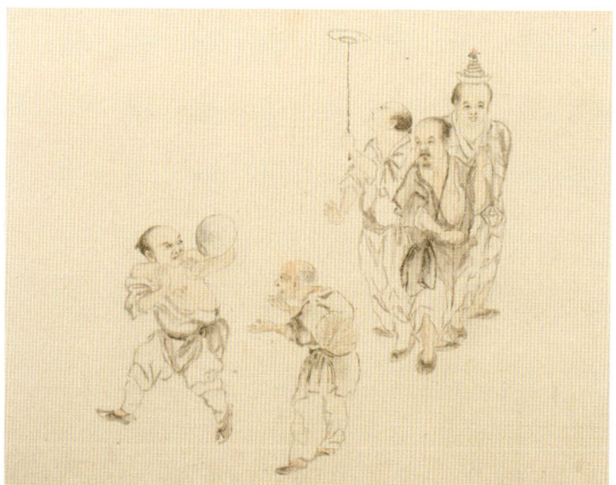

Figure 34   Huang Shen, *Street Entertainers* from *Album of Figures*. Detail. Album of twelve leaves, 1730, ink and color on paper, 43.8 × 33.7 cm, University of California, Berkeley Art Museum and Pacific Film Archive. Purchase made possible through a gift from an anonymous donor. Photographed for the UC Berkeley Art Museum by: Benjamin Blackwell.

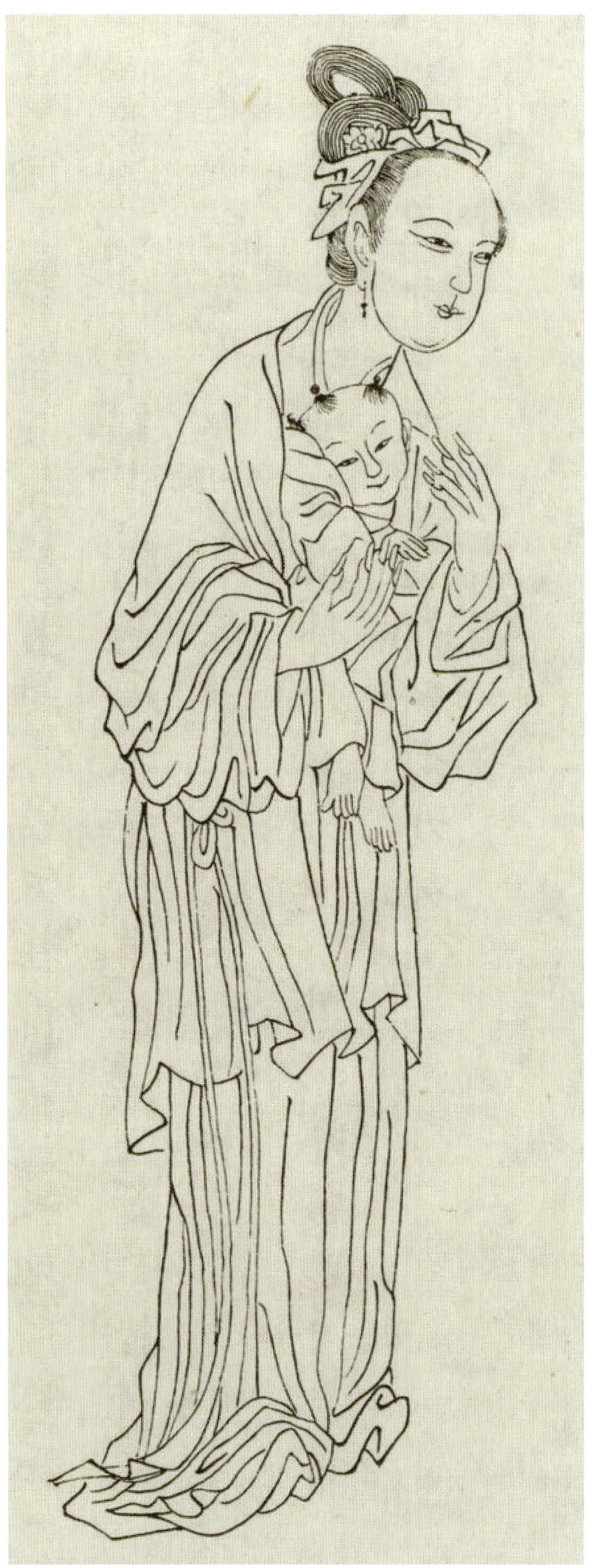

Figure 35 Shangguan Zhou, *Portrait of the Son of Duke Hua Yun of Eastern Qiu, Desheng* from *Wanxiaotang huazhuan*. Reprint edition, 1984 Beijing, 26a.

types parallels interests in the export painting, and it is possible that Su's album (being later in date) was influenced by the export painting.

However, the social types made by Su Liupeng and Ju Lian also belong to a longer history of the representations of social customs and life, loosely referred to as *fengsu* (風俗 wind-like customs) that became popular in the Song Dynasty and continued into the Ming with artists from the Zhe school.[65] Figural vernacular paintings were particularly prevalent in Zhejiang and Fujian Provinces, where the Southern Song tradition continued to be strong into the eighteenth century, with artists like Huang Shen (the Fujian artist who influenced Su Liupeng). An excellent example by Huang is his album of *Beggars and Street Entertainers*, which includes more portrait-like images of street performers and vendors. This undated album shows snake charmers, traveling musicians, and other itinerant types. Huang paints his characters with glee and liveliness. In the twelve leaves, there are old women, young children, laborers, and charming street performers who interact with one another, and Huang portrays each one tenderly (Figs. 33 and 34). Their faces are stamped with personality and spirit, and their bodies reflect the daily toll of work and the passing of years. Painted with quick strokes and light washes, these characters embody an unusual vigor and charm. They offer an intimate view of the urban space as a lived experience that draws viewers into the painting and onto the streets.

The immediacy of Huang's *fengsu* painting befits his reputation as an eccentric artist. While Huang and his style of painting are associated with Yangzhou, his training began in Fujian under the tutelage of Shangguan Zhou, an artist known for his portraits of historical characters, many of whom are depicted striking a theatrical pose. Among his artworks is a 1743 woodblock printed book of *Wanxiaotang huazhuan* 晚笑堂畫傳 (Painting record of Wanxiao hall), which portrays highly individualized historical figures (Fig. 35). Shangguan was also active in Guangzhou, where there was a high concentration of Fujian sojourners and migrant merchants, including the *hong* families discussed earlier. Therefore, we can consider that Su Liupeng's album of street types may be a combination of this *fengsu* trend from Fujian and the export art ethnographic approach to social types.

Pu Qua's album also has earlier Chinese precedent, which further complicates our understanding of how these types of images moved around in the open circuit. An earlier, and more unusual, source can be traced to *Taiping huanle tu* 太平歡樂圖 (Album of happiness in an age of peace), attributed to artist Fang Xun (方薰, 1736–99), and presented to the Qianlong Emperor on his fifth Southern Inspection Tour in 1779 by the Zhejiang official Jin Deyu (金德輿, 1750–1800).[66] Fang Xun was the painter in residence at Jin Deyu's family home in Hangzhou. He was a versatile painter who could paint literary themes and vernacular scenes. Jin came from an elite Hangzhou family, and while he never gained a high official rank, he counted among his friends some of the leading Hangzhou-based scholars and merchants.[67] The gifting of genre paintings by a scholar elite to the emperor recalls the long-established tradition of promoting greater social and political responsibility.[68] In 1689, the Kangxi Emperor (康熙帝, r. 1661–1722) was presented with the painting *Tilling and Weaving*, a Song Dynasty theme associated with the official Lou Shou (樓璹, 1090–1162) and promoting the ideals of a good official and his duty towards the people. Kangxi commissioned a set of paintings and prints on an updated version of the theme, showcasing some of the latest developments in technology such as new types of looms and different types of irrigation methods, as well as endorsing a moral vision of gender roles in which men tilled and women weaved. The popularity of the set led to numerous

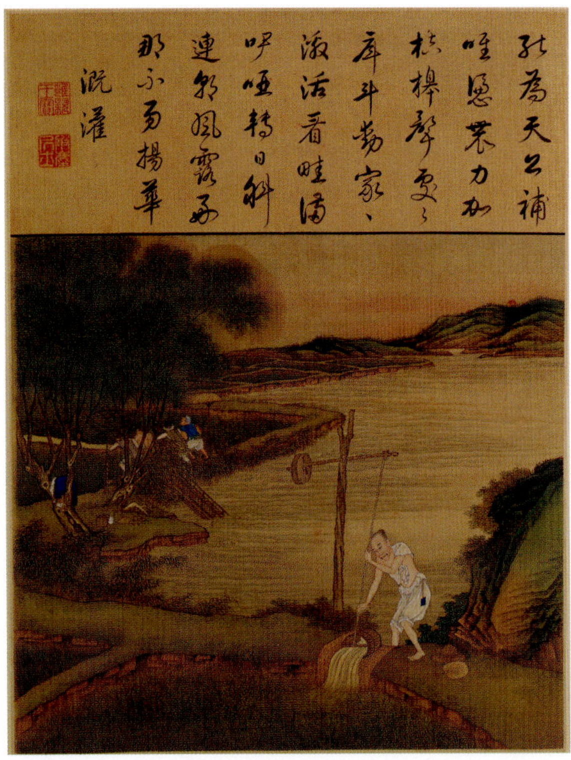

Figure 36   Anon, *Gengzhi tu with Prince Yinzhen*. Album leaf, colors on silk, 30 × 27 cm. Palace Museum, Beijing.

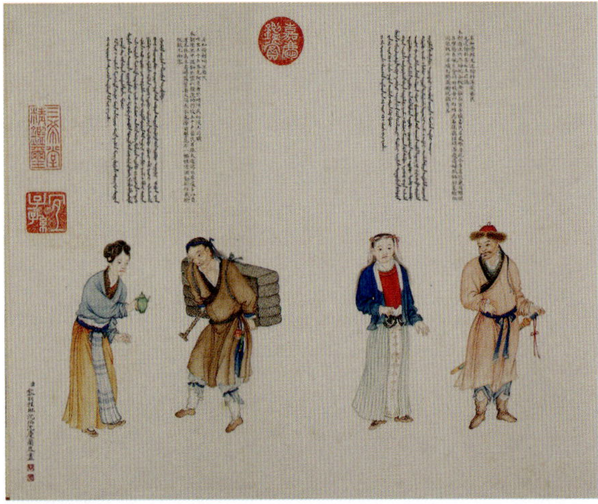

Figure 37   Ding Guanpeng et al., *Huang Qing zhigong tu*. Handscroll from a set of four, 1751–75, ink and color on paper. Palace Museum, Beijing.

versions made after it, including one in which Prince Yinzhen, the future Yongzheng Emperor (雍正帝, r. 1678–1735), presented himself and his wife as farmers and weavers as he made his bid for the throne (Fig. 36).[69] The success of the gift to Kangxi would have been well known to Jin Deyu, and he may have presented his album in the hope of career advancement.

The striking difference between Jin's gift and the Qing versions of *Gengzhi tu* 耕織圖 can be seen in the narrative structure that affects the pictorial modes used. The latter sees the protagonists set in a story told through a seasonal framework that tracks the cyclic time of farming and weaving. The former, with its empty background, presents a timeless image. As such, Jin's gift may bear more affinity with another imperial project and one closer to its own time of a set of handscrolls of ethnographic types that refers to another kind of imperialist project undertaken under the Manchu rulers. In 1761, the Qianlong Emperor commissioned the making of *Huang Qing zhigong tu* 皇清職貢圖 (Qing imperial illustrations of tributaries) (Fig. 37) and *Qiannan Miao man tu* 黔南苗蠻圖 (Illustrations of the Miao southern barbarians).[70] In both these projects, the images were considered accurate depictions that reflected a broader interest in *kaozheng* scholarship (考證 empirical studies) that elevated geography as a key discipline and visual records as empirical data. This intellectual path, followed by scholars like Ruan Yuan, supported the use of ethnographic representation in projects on different sites and places. Zhang Bao's travelogue would also fit into this type of scholarship, in which the efficacy of his travelogue as a "tool" depended on his knowledge and experience of different sites. As Emma Teng shows in her work on Chinese colonial representation of Taiwan, by the second half of the eighteenth century, the role of eyewitnesses acquired a special importance in Chinese accounts of the frontiers.[71] The empirical nature of these projects acted as an imperialist record of the Qing's campaign to conquer marginal lands and, via documentation, reduce foreignness into manageable (or conquerable) parts, which inevitably included the inhabitants of the land.

It is possible to consider Fang Xun and Jin Deyu's album as a regional approach to geography that was also aligned with these Qing court projects, especially given that Jin Deyu and his coterie of friends were ardent pursuers of epigraphy and *kaozheng* scholarship. There are a number of similarities: Gone are the narrative background scenes of happy villages or the presentation of street types in groups. Instead, we have images of the various trades presented as singular subjects that one could find in Zhejiang. By concentrating on trades, the city's mercantile reputation was emphasized, but this ran the risk of treading on morally ambiguous grounds (as seen in *Shenlouzhi*). To avoid this, the album narrated the idealized timelessness of work, which was presented as observed records, made possible through the proper duties of the official class.[72] The efficacy of this type of cataloguing of social types brings to mind the ambitions of the later export artists cataloguing China for a foreign audience.

The Fang Xun version is now lost, but Jin had copies made for himself and as gifts for others. Extant versions indicate that Fang Xun's student Dong Qi (董棨, 1772–1844) was commissioned to make at least two copies in 1828 and 1831. In 1888, a lithographic print version was made based on Dong's 1831 album. Given how proud Jin was of his gift to the emperor (and speculations that the gift was an attempt at career advancement), it is possible that many more copies were made of the album that have not survived. An examination of Dong's copy shows individual portraits of different street vendors and performers, accompanied with a text describing the various trades. The inscriptions trumpeted the importance of local products and the skills of local

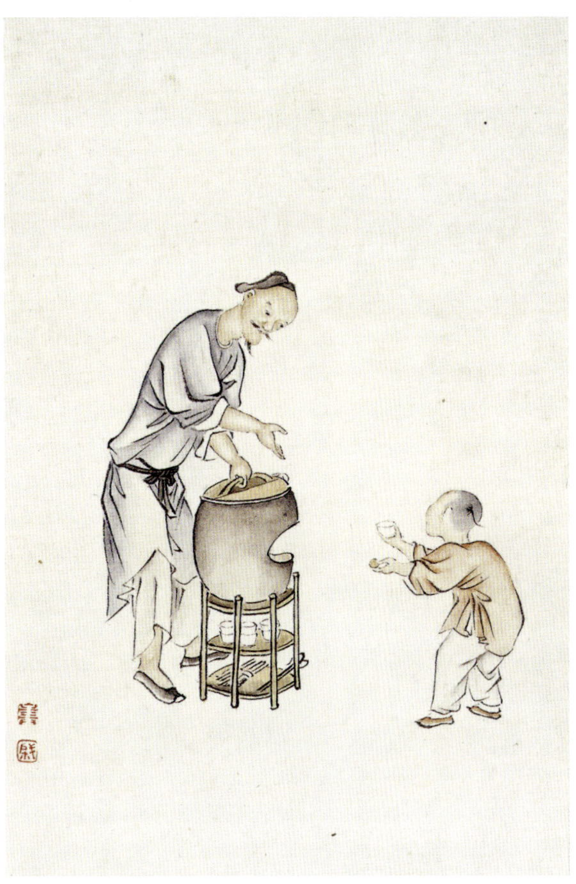

Figure 38 Lithograph after Dong Qi, *Congee Seller* from *Taiping huanle tu,* pictures by Dong Qi, text edited by Xu Zhihao. Shanghai: Xuelin chubanshe, 2003, 18.

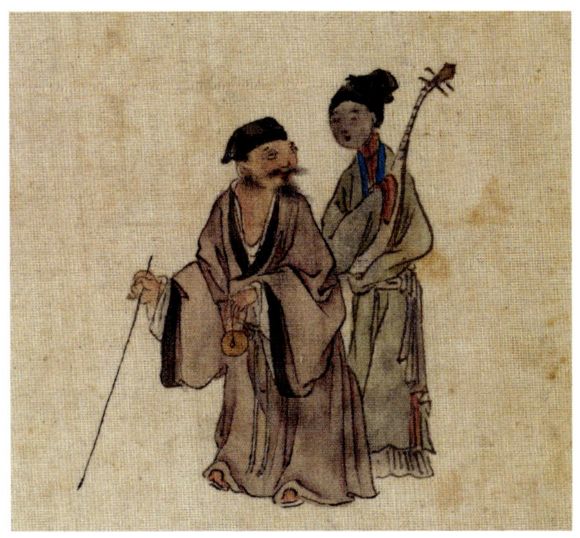

Figure 39 Zhou Kun, *Street Entertainers* from *Album of Paintings of Life in a Village Town.* Palace Museum, Beijing.

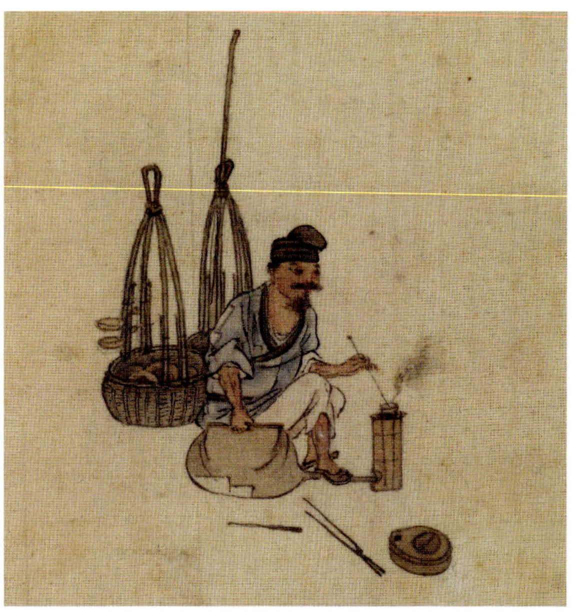

Figure 40 Zhou Kun, *Metal Worker* from *Album of Paintings of Life in a Village Town.* Palace Museum, Beijing.

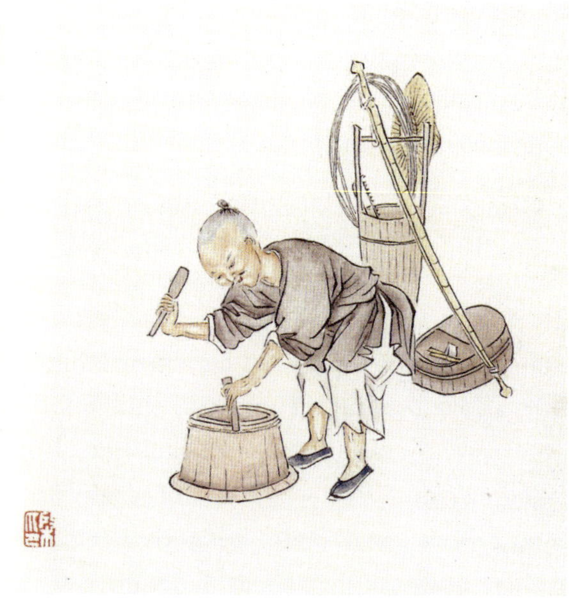

Figure 41 Reprint of lithograph after Dong Qi, *Barrel Maker* from *Taiping huanle tu,* pictures by Dong Qi, text edited by Xu Zhihao. Shanghai: Xuelin chubanshe, 2003, 108.

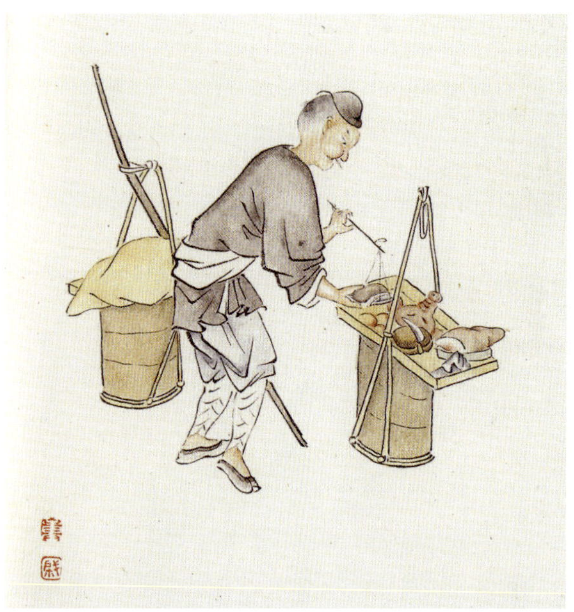

Figure 42 Reprint of lithograph after Dong Qi, *Butcher* from *Taiping huanle tu,* pictures by Dong Qi, text edited by Xu Zhihao. Shanghai: Xuelin chubanshe, 2003, 72.

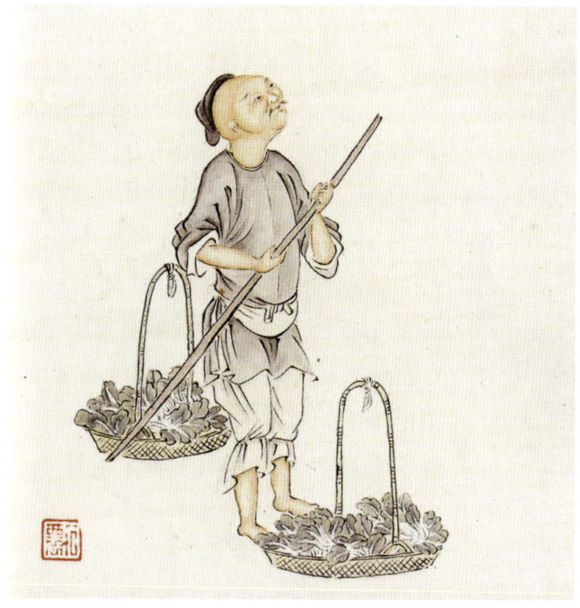

Figure 43 Reprint of lithograph after Dong Qi, *Vegetable Seller* from *Taiping huanle tu,* pictures by Dong Qi, text edited by Xu Zhihao, Shanghai: Xuelin chubanshe, 2003, 38.

vendors and used seasonal and textual references to give a literary anchor to Zhejiang life. For example, corresponding to the image of the bamboo shoot seller, the text speaks of the various types of bamboo shoots that were available in spring in Zhejiang. In the painting of the congee seller, the inscription refers to the Song Dynasty book *Ancient Matters from the Wulin Garden*, written by the scholar Zhou Mi (周密, 1232–98), about urban life in the late twelfth century, when varieties of congee were available, such as the seven-treasure congee, the five-flavor congee, etc. On the streets of Zhejiang, you can still get sweet congee that appeals to everyone (Fig. 38).

Another comparative album is an undated work by Jiangsu artist Zhou Kun (周昆, act. eighteenth century) entitled *Album of Paintings of Life in a Village Town*. Zhou, a relatively unknown court artist, made this small album of street vendors that includes street performers (Fig. 39), a fan seller, a mirror cleaner, a shoe mender, and a metal object mender (Fig. 40). It is possible that this was a court variation of the Fang Xun album. A comparison of these two court-related works with Pu Qua's album suggest that the latter may have used one of the former (or a variation) as the base. For example, the image of a man mending metal objects by Pu Qua (Fig. 25) bears some similarities to Zhou Kun's version. A variation of Pu Qua's barrel maker (Fig. 24) can also be seen in Dong Qi's album (Fig. 41), as can the butcher (Fig. 42) and the vegetable seller (Fig. 43). In general, the Pu Qua album version seems to be more elaborate and at times emphasizes the products, whereas the Dong Qi version often includes children, adding an element of community and wonder to the street. Nonetheless, the similarities, particularly the selection of types, strongly suggest that in the eighteenth century, albums of social types were being circulated both within and outside of the court, that they traveled across regions, and it may even be possible that the

Fang Xun version had a direct impact on Pu Qua's. This speculative argument is strengthened when we recognize that Fang Xun had another, more influential, patron, Ruan Yuan. Before becoming the Governor-General of Guangdong and Guangxi in 1817, Ruan Yuan was the Governor of Zhejiang in 1799–1805 and again in 1807–12. It is feasible that an album presented to the emperor, and loosely linked to one of the key figures in Guangdong, would have appealed to Cantonese audiences.

The historical connections between export art and *fengsu* painting offer only one perspective in looking at the open circuit in Guangzhou. First, genre painting continued to thrive in areas outside of direct imperial interest, particularly in Zhejiang and Fujian, developing into a regional art form that readily found appeal to a Guangdong audience. Second, there was a growing interest in urban identity that saw the local appropriation of an imperialist discourse supported by travel writings and empirical studies. Part of this appropriation was the greater acceptance of pictorial documentation. Lastly, there was a large workforce that could produce this type of art quickly and cheaply. These elements of production, exchange, and consumption formed a particular vision of Guangdong's diversity and hybridity that came to represent the urban cosmopolitanism of a port city.

◆◆◆

Shen Fu captured the diversity of a city that reaped the rewards of being a sole maritime trading port in China. As a visitor and an opportunistic entrepreneur, Shen experienced the heady delights of the new and unusual. He was not alone; many travelers also visited Guangzhou, and some stayed, becoming part of the in-migrant communities. In the art world, the flux of people and visitors had a large impact on the two dominant art circuits. In the closed circuit, the rich merchants, many of whom were from Fujian, interacted with visiting Jiangnan officials and local scholars. The establishment of Xuehaitang was an important part of the elite cultural scene, acting as a foundation of *kaozheng* scholarship in Guangdong and publishing numerous projects, some of which received national attention. In this elite world of scholars, a local Cantonese art world was also emerging, collectors and artists working towards forming a Cantonese art lineage that also fit into a national narrative. Paintings made within this closed circuit belonged to a highly codified system that was also accessible to those with enough social connections to partake in the viewing of art or the making of occasional paintings that celebrated outings to literary sites. For the merchant scholars, many of whom were from outside the city, their involvement in cultural projects helped to cement ties and relationships with local scholars and gain cultural cachet as being part of the arbiters of elite taste in the city. In contrast, in the open circuit, where local elite would also readily participate, images of the city were being formed that emphasized a hybrid Guangdong cosmopolitanism that used the street as the focus of urban activities. In parallel with travel stories and personal diaries, these images purported to be eyewitness accounts of the city. The artists would use a number of different strategies to present their accounts as being truthful while also drawing on earlier pictorial schemes. However, as Deborah Poole succinctly writes, "The meanings of the images do not come from fidelity to an original, but from the system of accumulation, classification and exchange through which they circulate as image-objects divorced from the substance they once portrayed."[73] Not only was there no singular Cantonese identity, but Guangzhou's identity as a thriving urban city was formed by the many intersections of local, regional, and international perceptions that crossed social and cultural boundaries.

Chapter Two

Su Renshan: Art in the Delta Hinterlands

According to *Lingnan hua zhenglue* (嶺南畫徵略 Summary of paintings from Lingnan) and its later supplement, there were almost 600 Guangdong artists in the Ming and Qing periods, of which more than half came from Shunde, Nanhai, Panyu, and areas outside Guangzhou. However, the majority of these artists were active primarily in the city.[1] For example, Su Liupeng was from Shunde but moved to the city, where he eventually opened his workshop. This concentration of artists in the city is also seen in other types of cultural production, including the writing, compiling, and publishing of poems and prose, which shifted to Guangzhou in the early nineteenth century. As such, information regarding artists who worked outside the city's art circles is generally scarce, and little is known other than a name and perhaps a surviving painting or two. The dearth of texts, a source considered the bedrock of the discipline, has complicated the recovery of early nineteenth-century Guangdong art.

One artist for whom there is a larger corpus of information is Su Renshan, although much of the transmitted texts are from his own hands. Su, an educated man from a relatively well-placed family in Shunde, was unusual in that he was primarily based in areas outside Guangzhou, including Cangwu, on the provincial edges of Guangdong and Guangxi. His occasional visits to Guangzhou were often short, and it is therefore not surprising that, unlike the artists discussed in the previous chapter, Su did not participate in the social networks that defined the closed circuit, nor was he a seasoned professional artist with his own workshop.

Su began painting as a side pursuit for an educated son with the promise of a career in government, ended his life as an itinerant artist, and according to his later clansman and scholar, Su Ruohu (蘇若瑚, 1856–1917), he was placed, by his father, in the local magistrate prison. Little is known about his friends and patrons, but, given the extant body of works bearing inscriptions, it would appear that he painted perhaps in exchange for board during his travels. From his early paintings days of landscapes following the styles of Yuan artist Wang Meng (王蒙, ca. 1308–85) and the Ming painter Wen Zhengming, his paintings quickly became tantalizingly odd to the extent that they do not conform to any type of *literary* art produced in the Delta hinterlands or in Guangzhou City. But they do speak to a vernacular tradition belonging to the former, with a literary bent of the latter, and offer another perspective, however individualized, of Cantonese art.

What accounts for Su Renshan's pictorial oddity is his disruptiveness achieved using different pictorial strategies: in group portraits, he directs all his figures' lines of visions in different directions that upsets the unity of the group, he juxtaposes vertical inscriptions with horizontal ones that shifts a viewer's reading experiences, and uses extreme graphic compositions for landscapes (such as zigzag structures) that allow no sense of depth or penetration. His pictorial unexpectedness gives an edge to his dense inscriptions that can be at times an angry tirade and at times an unconventional rereading of history. The words take on a peculiar presence that interacts with the images by sometimes overwhelming them by sheer contrast of scale, sometimes by taking on an imagistic quality in its arrangement of words, so much so, that it can be seen as adding a pictorialized timbre to his words. In any other period, this self-imposed marginality might be seen as no more than the eccentric behavior of an artist who indulged in the strange (*qi* 奇), a phenomenon associated with the late seventeenth-century artist Shitao. The lack of detailed information on other artists in the Delta region could also easily lead to an argument that isolates him from history as an oddball. However, to do so will undermine the potential of looking at a different type of agency: What was the appeal of a local vernacular for an artist such as Su Renshan who liked to explore the strange and the extraordinary? What are the different types of values being pursued by Su, and what made these values pertinent to a discussion on early nineteenth-century painting? To answer the first of these questions, I will outline the different social context of the Delta hinterlands and draw on Su Renshan's biography to see how he became an artist and how he fashioned an identity linked to his vernacular roots. Above all, there are three traits that form the crux of his experimental style and which I describe as a type of "literary vernacular." What is of interest is how these three traits constructed a style of painting that bridged familiar elements found within and outside the city with an end result that appears exceptional. In unraveling the complexities of this artist, the aim is to see how an outsider-artist worked to construct a regional identity that made him, at the same time, an insider.

The Delta Hinterlands

As seen in the previous chapter, Xuehaitang quickly became entrenched in Guangdong elite circles, forming a complex network of scholars, officials, and merchant patrons. Steven Miles and David Faure have shown, and to whose scholarship I am heavily indebted, the academy played a pivotal role in supporting evidential research and cultural production that included the appropriation of local culture. This appropriation of local symbols coincided with the large-scale reclamation of territory in the Sands area at the tip of the Delta and where city-based merchant families competed with the clan families in the larger Guangdong region.[2] Much of the older parts of the area outside the city, especially along the West River, were dominated economically, socially, and culturally by established Cantonese lineages that could trace their ancestry to the Ming Dynasty.

The lineage networks and ancestral trusts were powerful sociopolitical tools that garnered political recognition and authority, and maintained economic strongholds by claiming land and property.[3] Claiming common descent did not provide immediate territorial rights; ancestral properties were tied to specific ancestors, and as descent lines grew, some members became more marginal while more belonged to several descent lines, creating interlineage relations that diffused land rights. The complexities of all this meant that documentations (such as contracts and genealogies) and other cultural markers played increasingly important roles in legitimizing ancestral land and kinships. This was a powerful combination of both legal and everyday rituals that recognized and maintained the clout of lineage relations that could be sustained over time. To this day, certain aspects of these lineages are still active. As David Faure succinctly explains:

Donations to the lineage and the maintenance of lineage trusts are commonly in evidence among genealogical biographies. The penal code also gave ancestral property some protection by demanding the agreement of all descendants to its sale, failing which the seller might be charged with larceny... The rules of inheritance provided for the allotment of equity, so that the establishment of the focus of ancestral sacrifice, be it at a grave or in an ancestral hall, and continued ritual observance, would in themselves provide the opportunities for the definition of a sense of corporate membership. A contractual element is therefore inherent in agreement over ancestral history. The power of the lineage community and its ability to keep alive its markers and the power of the written word in providing a sense of historical continuity, involved lineages in a constant process of creation and recreation, all the while keeping intact the sense that the process followed from "tradition."[4]

In the late Ming and Qing, the development of landed estates and common land, expansions of market towns, and the extension of the state at local levels led to the proliferation of lineage institutions. According to Faure, by the eighteenth century in southeast China, lineages were everywhere.[5]

One repercussion of the successful economy of the Delta region was the rising value of land resources. Among the geographical features of the Delta region were the alluvia fields that were formed by the huge deposits of silt brought down by rivers and deposited in estuaries where the water velocity slowed. A plot of alluvial soil would gradually develop but still be under water. Only after a few years and much toil did the land became suitable for rice cultivation or mulberry embankments with fishponds. In order to claim the land, the persons concerned had to apply to the government for territorial rights, which in turn meant that they were liable for tax.[6] Because of the large capital and organizational skills needed, the landed elite and lineage estates dominated territorial claims.[7] It was extremely difficult for outsiders to penetrate this market, even as internal competition

between the old established lineages and the more recently established kinship networks intensified.[8] For example, the frontier edge of the Delta region, which included Xiangshan, was one of the hotly contested new territories. Academies, charitable institutions, and trade guilds based in Guangzhou City also attempted to reclaim land in this area, thus diversifying territorial claims in this region, particularly in the mid-nineteenth century when large-scale reclamation reached new heights. The most successful, however, were the powerful Delta-based clans, the Luo (羅) and the Long (龍) lineage groups from Shunde who claimed more land than any other institutions. Moreover, Long Tinghuai (龍廷槐, 1749–1827), a member of the Long lineage, used his official power to reduce the tax on new lands.[9]

The Delta lineage power base was largely concentrated in the West River basin area that included Foshan, Daliang, and parts of Shunde and Nanhai. This area was also connected to Cangwu at the borders of Guangdong and Guangxi, adding to a network of market towns linked by waterways, which dominated the distribution and circulation of prime market products such as salt and rice. While variations and competition between different townships were prominent within this region, they can collectively be considered a sub-regional area within Guangdong and provide a useful comparison with Guangzhou City. First, this area formed the largest cluster of literary institutions outside the city and boasted the highest number of examination degree holders. Local contributions for private academies were quite common, such as Rulin Academy, set up by Jiujiang elites from Nanhai to form a competitive institute, which focused on Song Learning that followed the Neo-Confucian traditions of Cheng Yi (程頤, 1033–1107) and Zhu Xi (朱熹, 1130–1200), differing from the evidential learning promoted by Xuehaitang.[10] This academy was part of an elite-managed network that was very active in local projects, such as dike management (an essential part of the well-being of towns that depended on water), as well as providing education for their local sons.

Another important facet of life in the Delta region was, and still is, its many festivals and rituals. From the beginning to the end of the year, homes, villages, and towns were engaged in activities connected to both commonly widespread festivals such as the New Year, to more regional rituals such as the lantern celebrations on the fifteenth day of the first month.[11] The range of large temples and smaller shrines was staggering. The 1805 Longshan local history lists 132 Gods of Earth and Grains in twenty-three villages.[12] Street parades of deities, opera performances, burning of offerings, and flying of banners are common sights that added to the visual culture of the place. Often, different towns and village clusters might follow the same festival, but many had unique elements that distinguished the relationship of the deity and their supplicants. Outsider officials often recorded the extravagance of some of these rituals and scorned what they saw as superstitious beliefs.[13] What is more evident is how these rituals and festivals, as key events that endorsed the social hierarchy within clans, helped to keep outsiders at the periphery of their worlds.

Against this, it is possible to see why the elite art circuit in the city, and literary production in general, can be seen as a form of competition vis-à-vis the Delta hinterlands. Literary arts provided cultural cachet to a city-based highly mobile group of individuals who were set apart from those belonging to established lineages. They claimed a local identity by drawing on the products, produces, and landscape of Guangdong, following practices in other regions, in particular the Jiangnan area. In contrast, for members of the Delta clan families, the strong ties of lineage and ancestral rights anchored their claims and authority in the region. Unfortunately, from an art historian's perspective, the visual culture of the

Delta hinterlands was largely ephemeral, and little has survived to document the various types of visual materials used in these festivals. Again, this makes a study of Su Renshan, however atypical he may have been as an artist, an important contribution to understanding a broader picture of Guangdong art.

A Biography of Su Renshan

Su Renshan belonged to a well-respected family in Xingtan, a small market town in Shunde prefecture. Shunde was part of the rich West River basin area. An 1853 local gazetteer describes the region as "an area crisscrossed by waterways easily accessible by boat. Rivers flow everywhere and roads go in every direction. The condition is particularly favorable to agriculture. There are mulberry forests and fishponds for the production of silk. Both men and women live by their labor."[14] The combination of silkworm rearing and fish farming was an effective use of land: Ponds were scooped out between dikes so that mulberry grew on the dikes and fish were raised in the ponds. It was an extremely successful means of commercial use, and much of the land in Shunde was devoted to producing cash crops.

The combination of silkworm rearing and fish farming generated a comfortable income for those with land rights and access within the community. According to the Su Clan genealogy, the family was relatively accomplished. The father, Su Yinshou (蘇引壽, 1788–1862), worked as a tax collector in Nanhai, a neighboring prefecture.[15] Locally, Su Yinshou was recognized as something of a philanthropist and was known for his poetry and calligraphy. He was wealthy enough to have had two concubines, and Renshan was the eldest of six boys and four girls. Su Yinshou's second son was a doctor; his third was, like Renshan, an artist; the fourth was involved in local village politics and management; and the youngest two were in trade.[16]

Drawing from the three autobiographical inscriptions, all written between 1841 and 1842, it is possible to structure a timeline for Su's life until he was twenty-nine *sui*.[17] The narrative style of these inscriptions follows the structure of a *nianpu*, which was an unusual format to use for an inscription on a painting (highlighting Su's pursuit of the extraordinary in text as well as in painting). On a painting now lost, but whose inscription has been recorded by Jian Youwen, entitled *Landscape Painting after Wen Zhengming*, Su writes:

> From my earliest years, I have been addicted to painting. As I grew up, I learned to admire the elegant style of this master [Wen Zhengming] and for many years I too lived by my brush. In the first year of my life, I feared cats and dogs, and I often had convulsions. At two, my mother rocked me on her lap and my father had my hair cut. This is when I learned about praise and dishonor. At the time, I was not able to speak. How could I have known about painting? At three, when others offered me food, I did not eat without my mother's permission. At four, my father taught me the *Sanzi jing*. I learned words but not yet how to paint. At five and six, I developed an addiction for writing, and I practiced on any blank wall or door that I came across. At seven and eight, I could paint landscape and its elements and my inscriptions expressed very well the theme of the pictures. At nine, I went to school, and a master taught me the Classics. Every day I had to write out what I was learning several times and had little time to paint. At ten and eleven, I painted occasionally in my spare time. At twelve, my paintings were well known in the village. At thirteen, my reputation had spread to scholars. At fourteen, I visited Guangzhou. At fifteen, I was addicted to copying old paintings and the *li* script of the Han Dynasty. At sixteen, I prepared myself for the examinations. At seventeen, I became addicted to poetry and rhyme-prose, and at eighteen, to Neo-Confucianism. At nineteen, I failed in the examination; at twenty, I immersed myself in statecraft discourses. At twenty-one, I continued my studies in dynastic rites and rituals, and at twenty-two, I went to take the examinations and again failed. At twenty-three, I gave up examinations once and for all, so I tried the arts and when I painted, my love for it returned. At twenty-four, I traveled to Cangwu. At twenty-five, I went to visit the Guilin caves. At twenty-seven, I prepared for marriage. At twenty-eight, I began to regret the many errors I have made in my words and deeds. I therefore record all of this. On the 12th day of the 10th month in the winter of the year *xinchou*, the 21st year in the reign of Daoguang, painted in Guangzhou city.[18]

His inscriptions reveal a sickly, awkward, but precocious child who began painting at a young age and was able to paint landscapes and compose adequate inscriptions by the time he was seven. Su recalls his early days as an eager child whose love of learning meant that he would write on any available surface. By the time he was thirteen or fourteen, he had traveled at least once to Guangzhou to receive a painting commission.[19] Extant works testify to his early achievements as well as to his father's proud role as an inscriptional companion to Su's painting. The earliest extant painting is a large landscape hanging scroll executed in 1827, at the age of fourteen *sui* (Fig. 44). It is a dense, well-crafted painting, exacting in its execution and composition, with stylistic echoes of the Ming artist Wen Zhengming.

A surprising number of Su's early works have survived, many of which are large-scale landscapes in ink and washes. However, it is possible to see that, even at this early stage, he was interested in compositional and structural dynamics rather than the brushwork qualities of individual motifs, by which I mean he was interested in the way lines, form, and space work together to dematerialize as well as materialize the motif. This is seen in his *Landscape in the Detailed Manner* (Fig. 45), painted when Su was fifteen *sui* and after his first trip to the city. According to the inscription, he executed this 1828 painting at the request of his father. The architectonic mountains in fine hemp brushwork evoke the works of earlier artists Wang Meng and Wen Zhengming, who, by the nineteenth century, epitomized conventional landscape traditions. However, Su's painstakingly detailed and unchanging brushwork, executed

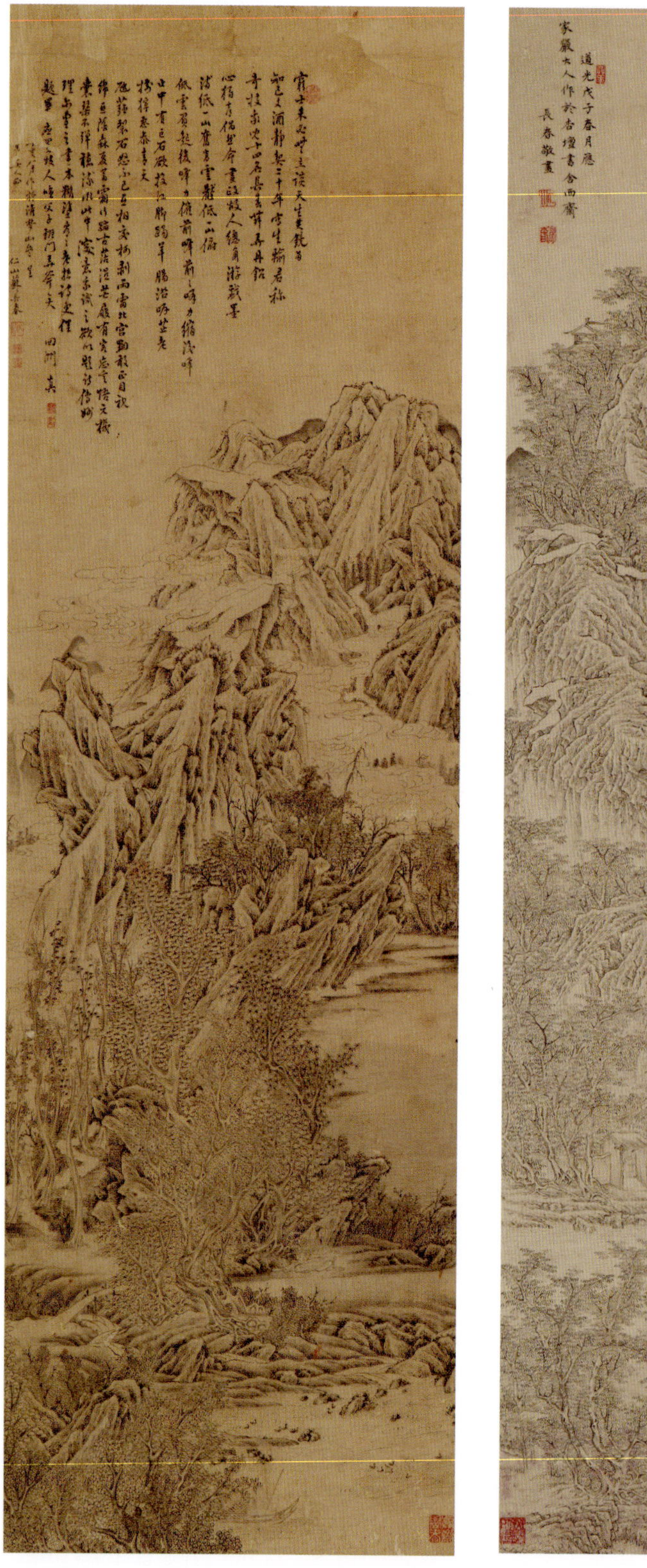

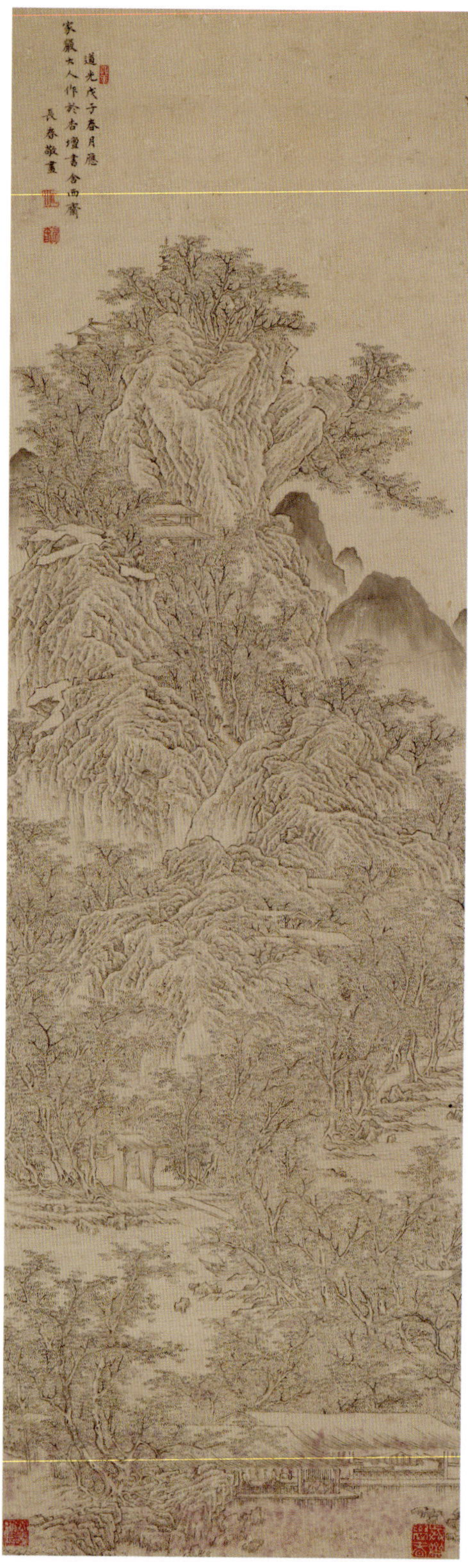

Figure 44 *(left)* Su Renshan, *Landscape.* Hanging scroll, dated 1827, ink on paper, 145 × 48.3 cm. Reproduced by permission of the Art Museum of the Chinese University of Hong Kong from the collection of the Art Museum.

Figure 45 *(right)* Su Renshan, *Landscape in the Detailed Manner.* Hanging scroll, dated 1828, ink on paper, 119 × 35.5 cm. Reproduced by permission of the Art Museum of the Chinese University of Hong Kong from the collection of the Art Museum.

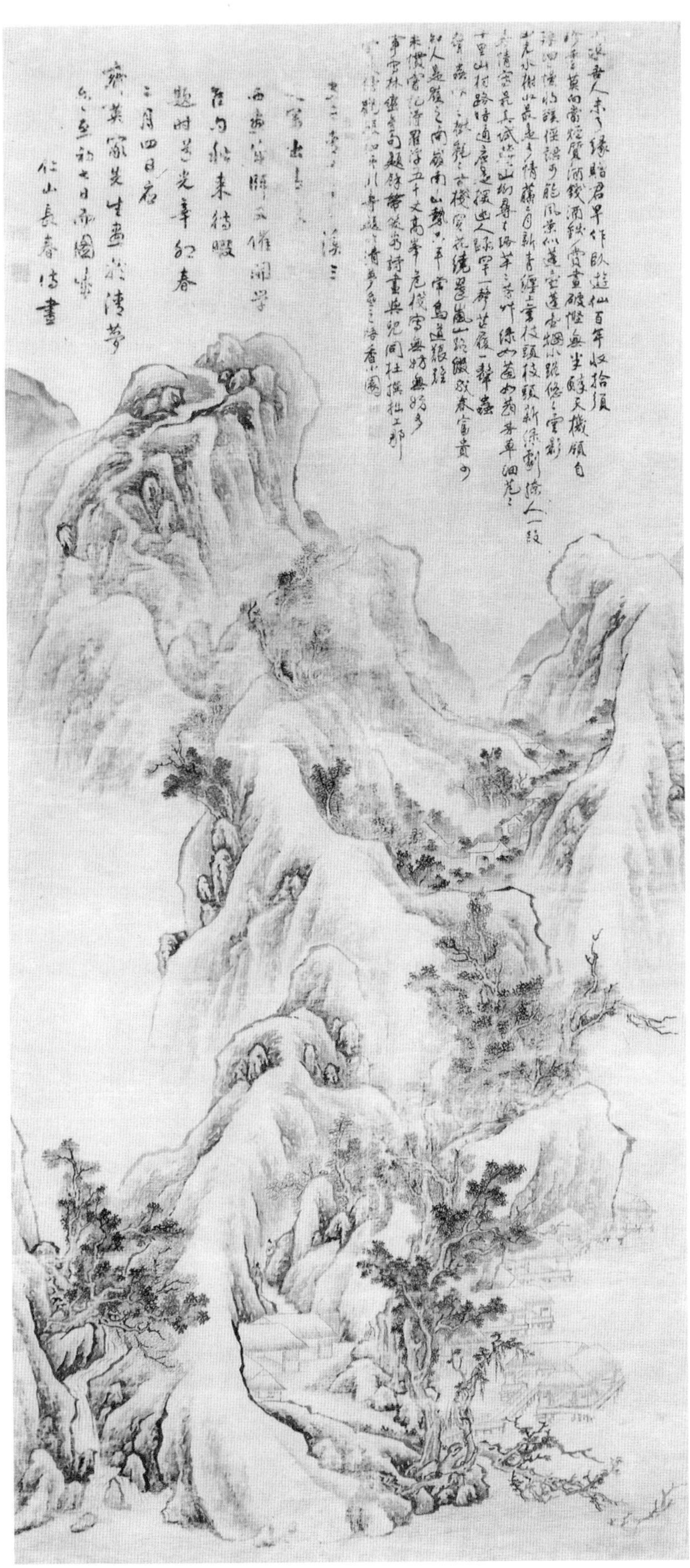

Figure 46   Su Renshan, *Landscape in Color*. Hanging scroll, dated 1831, ink and color on silk, 234 × 107.5 cm. Guangzhou Art Gallery, Guangzhou Museum. After Kao Mayching, ed., *The Art of Su Liupeng and Su Renshan*, Hong Kong and Guangzhou: Art Gallery, The Chinese University of Hong Kong and Guangzhou Art Gallery, 1990, 179.

without differentiating space and depth, flattens the image and turns it almost into a claustrophobic surface of brushwork, lightened only by the washes of distant mountains. It is a painting that takes the idea of "detailed manner" to extreme and turns it into a display of young talent.

At this time, his father would showcase Su's abilities to friends by getting his son to make paintings for them. *Landscape in Color* (Fig. 46), a large hanging scroll dated to 1831, when Su Renshan was eighteen *sui,* is a painting he made for a certain Qi Yingjia (齊英家, dates unknown). It is a very confident painting, and Su captures the parted section of a mountain with houses cradled within the valley and by the water. He uses a relatively dry, center-tipped brush employed with very little variation, in a dense repetition of forms that again recalls earlier landscape painting traditions. Su, however, has added a touch of whimsy in the lower left corner where a tree bent double, as if bowing its branches to graze the ripples of a stream, invites the eye into the painting. It took three days to finish and is an accomplished large artwork intended for display. Su painted the work in spring, when he was back at home during his studies, but as he writes in his inscription, "After the painting was completed, my teacher urged me to return to my studies. I have to wait until autumn to add the elegant poems." In fact, he never had a chance to inscribe the poems, for his father had already added his own. Su Yinshou's flattering inscription shows how proud he was of his son's achievement and begins with the following words:

> Our predestined relationship with landscape has not yet run its course. We bestow this painting so that the gentleman can soon be like an immortal wandering through the landscape. This precious painting should be treasured for one hundred years. Do not pawn it for wine money to sit in front of a fire.[20]

Su Yinshou continues the inscription with long flowery verse that hints at his obsequious nature that

later commentators speak of.[21] Although it is difficult to ascertain the accuracy of these later commentaries, the juxtaposition of this inscription that follows on from Su's declared interest of penning his own inscription suggests that perhaps father and son did not always see eye to eye.

Su's talent and love for painting might have emerged early, but he had to put them aside when he left home at the age of sixteen to attend an academy designed to train students to pass the civil examinations. Su saw this time of training as a suffocating experience, as he was forced to give up his spontaneous behavior to become a disciplined young adult studying for his examinations. When he was nineteen, he took his exams, failed, and re-sat them at twenty-two, and then failed once more.[22] In between his examinations, he returned home and was confined to studying. However, he may have, between his studies, also completed some painting commissions. Kao Mayching cites an inscription from a painting dated to year *bingshen* (1836), autumn, seventh month, night of the fourteenth, inscribed by Su Renshan during a trip to Foshan.[23] According to the *Foshan Gazetteer,* Su was, at one point, an artist in residence at the home of Liang Jiutu (梁九圖, act. ca. nineteenth century), but no dates are given as to when.[24] Liang was a Shunde native whose family had moved to Foshan. If Su was partially working, however briefly for Liang in 1836, he did continue to try for his exams, which would have also been in the same year. However, after the failure of this second round of exams, he was resolved not to sit for a third time (despite appearing to be studying), suggesting he had not shared his decision with his family and, more importantly, with his father.

The turning point in Su Renshan's life was in 1841, when he was twenty-nine *sui.* This was the year that he was scheduled to retake his exams but instead chose to escape to Guilin. It was an emotionally wrought time for many in the city, as the Opium War was waging, and tension was high in the city. It may be that he chose to escape from the events in the city, or simply that he did not want to take the exams again. According to a transcription by Jian Youwen of another inscription from a painting now lost, which is also dated to 1841, Su makes clear how little he thought of examinations, but it also shows someone who was not satisfied with his life. He writes:

> The shadow of the mountain is like a scar, so pale there is almost no trace. When I was four I studied the Classics at home. When I was sixteen, I left home to continue my studies. When I was twenty-one, I completed my studies in literature, arts and Confucian studies, and returned. There, confined beneath the bamboo roof, enclosed by the bamboo fence, I recited the officially approved texts for two or three years. I sat for the exams twice and failed. In my despondency, my thoughts turned to travel. I went to Guilin and wandered through its cliffs and caves. I saw the fragrant imposing trees known as cassia, the clear shallow waters of the river known as Li.[25] The hills are soaring yet luxuriant; the cliffs are mysterious yet unsoiled; the caves are intricate yet penetrable; they are deep and thick, yet twist and turn; they are high and protruding yet they form images [*xiang*]; deep in parts, flat at others, you can go forth or return. In admiration and joy, I uttered, "Within here, there must be a man who understands the beauty of landscapes, who has been nurtured into a great man with an admirable countenance." A long time passed, and I did not encounter such a person. I retreated into my thoughts, musing, "The grace of heaven and earth does not lodge only in a man but also be shared in women.[26] Among them, there must be one who is virtuous and good." But I have failed to encounter any of them. I cannot but help grieve in silence.[27]

Travel is a familiar motif in literati biographical writings, the journeys functioning as metaphors of inner quests for truths, and Su Renshan's treatment of Guilin is no exception. In this period, in order to reach Guilin, one had to travel by boat across rough rapids and thoroughfares plagued with bandits. Nonetheless, it was an area that was becoming increasingly popular among the Guangzhou lettered elite. Poems and diaries structured as guides became popular among scholars. It was portrayed as beautiful but also full of dangers from treacherous robbers to terrifying miasma. Su speaks of trips alone to this wild place and thus presents himself not only as a willful individual but also as a privileged scholar. Guilin became his refuge, and the spiritual overtones of wanderlust were associated with grottoes, long used in literature and paintings as magical Daoist realms that offered escape. As we shall see, Guilin was an important anchor in his life, and his work would increasingly respond to the structural qualities of the caves. The potential of the caves as inspiration for his painting was already formed when he observed their structures as being "images." We often see this imagistic grotto form in his treatment of inverted triangular forms (like stalactite icicles) fall as misshapen parts of the mountain.

The period 1841–42 also marks his departure from home, and, for the next five years, Su led a more itinerant life, possibly relying on friends and family, perhaps offering his literary skills and painting talents, as he traveled to Guangzhou City and once again to his former retreat, Cangwu, on the borders of Guangdong and Guangxi. Cangwu was also a place that had close ties with many West River Basin lineages, including members from Jiujiang, whose strong fish pond and mulberry embankment economy extended into the western regions of Guangxi and as far as Vietnam.[28] Cangwu was therefore very much part of the West River Basin geography, and it is not surprising that Su Renshan would spend time in this area. From this point onwards, Su moves more confidently away from the detailed landscape paintings from his early days. These later paintings, which best testify to Su's own pictorial ambitions, are discussed in greater detail in this chapter and those following. For now, Su's self-imposed exile was a turning point in his artistic development.

Given this dramatic change to Su's life, it is worth looking a little closer at possible reasons that prompted his move. Civil examination failures were relatively common, but in Su's instance, his failure greatly affected his family life and his relationship with his father. As the eldest son, he was burdened with the role of maintaining the family line and representing the family's prestige and standing within the village. Su, however, failed to live up to his early promise and to his father's expectations, which might have affected both his and his mother's positions within a household with two concubines and nine younger siblings.

Su Renshan also married relatively late at the age of twenty-seven (between his second and third exam attempts), and his marriage may also have hampered his ability to establish a strong familial position as an elder son who was expected to carry on the lineage. According to the Su family genealogy, Su's wife did not "cross the threshold" (*buluojia* 不落家), implying that she followed the delayed-marriage transfer custom that was popular in Shunde and other areas of the Lingnan region.[29] This was a ritual observed by families of a certain social and economic standing and particularly popular with Delta hinterland families. In this practice, a newly married woman would return to her natal home after the wedding ceremony, visiting her husband on special occasions or on arranged days. The new wife only formally moved into her husband's home after she bore a child or after an extended time (usually around three years). In Su's case, there were no children (which we know because the eldest son of

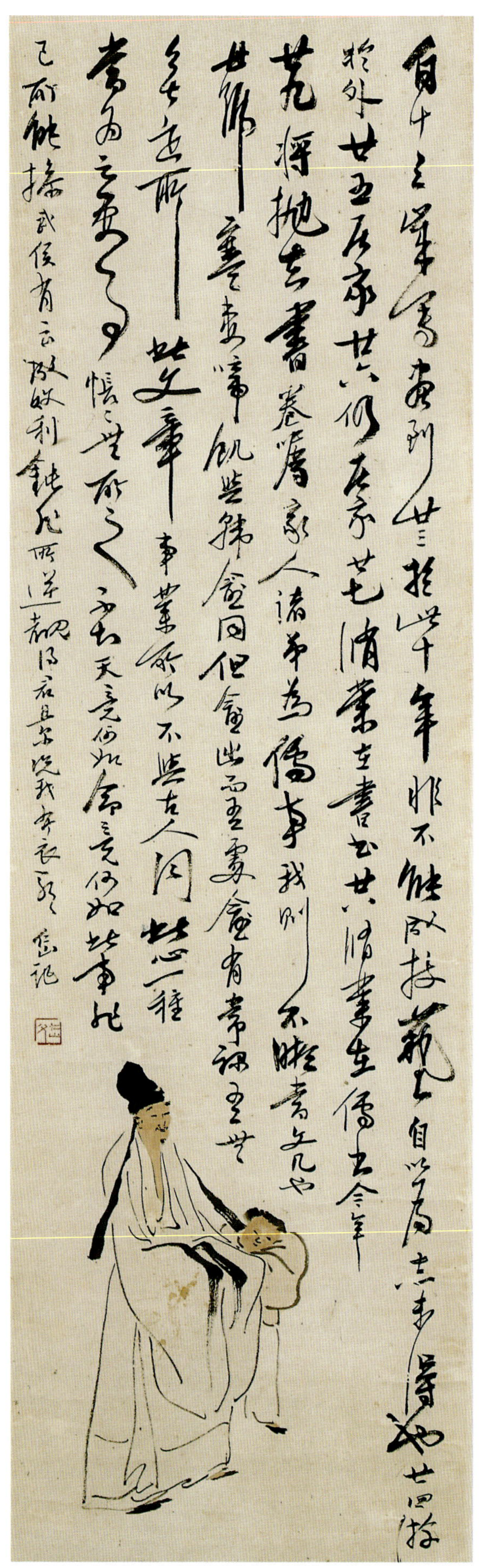

Figure 47   Su Renshan, *Self Portrait*. Hanging scroll, 1842, ink and light color on paper, 120.5 × 34.5 cm. Guangzhou Art Gallery. After Kao Mayching, ed., *The Art of Su Liupeng and Su Renshan*, Hong Kong and Guangzhou: Art Gallery, The Chinese University of Hong Kong and Guangzhou Art Gallery, 1990, 185.

his first brother was, perhaps posthumously, adopted as his in order to continue the family line). There are very few references to his wife, and it has been speculated that their marriage was not a happy one.[30] His 1841 *Remembering the Mountains* inscription, written two years after his marriage, hints at his disappointment of never encountering a woman who had the "grace of heaven and earth." At the very least, they could not have spent much time together, because one or two years after the wedding, Su decided to leave home while his wife was still living in her natal home. In the last of his autobiographical inscriptions, dated 1842, written on a small self-portrait showing a tall, gangly man (Fig. 47), the bitterness of his life's direction seeps through his writing:

> I painted from the age of thirteen until twenty-three. Within these ten years, it was not that I could not master the technique, but I had not found my true vocation. At twenty-four, I traveled outside [my home]. At twenty-five, I stayed at home; at age twenty-six, I was still at home, at twenty-seven, I applied myself to painting and calligraphy and, at twenty-eight, the Confucian classics. This year, at age twenty-nine, I have thrown out my books, instructed my family and all my younger brothers to continue their Confucian studies, for I have no time to do so myself. My mother cries from the cold, my wife cries from hunger, [I am] like Han Yu [韓愈, 768–824]. But Han Yu had a government position, and I am in retirement; Han Yu received an official salary while I do not even have a steady abode. This literary career, one where my heart differs from the ancients', is an important pursuit, but it is not for me. I am disappointed and at a loss. I know neither what Heaven's will is, nor what the fate of my path is. These are matters over which I have no control. Zhuge Liang once said, "Success and failure, advantages or shortcoming cannot be foreseen." If a gentleman can understand the value of these words, then why cannot a common person, such as me, do the same? Recorded by Renshan.[31]

The reference to Han Yu is a standard trope for poverty, but Su Renshan's reference here is also drawn from a well-known song-poem that circulated in Guangdong. It was written by Guangdong's most famous philosopher and poet, Chen Xianzhang (陳獻章, 1428–1500), who had long been incorporated as a local cult figure within a state-sponsored temple in the Delta region.[32] Chen Xianzhang was a teacher as well as a philosopher and poet, and, during his career as a teacher, to admonish students who indulged in too much women, wine, and leisure, he composed a series of vernacular song-poems. In Chen's admonishment of laziness, he penned the following lines:

> Han Yu burnt the oil block, and Sun used the reflected light of the snow (to read at night).
> Who has heard the name left behind by the idler?
> The idlers know who they are.
> Let me grace them with some well-intentioned words:
> When officials are lazy, the scribes will abuse,
> When generals are lazy, the soldiers do not care.
> When the mother is cold, the children will cry with cold, when the husband is lazy, the wife sobs in hunger.[33]

By referencing lines from this well-known poem chanted by young men training to pass the examinations in Guangzhou, Su suggests that, while he might be deemed lazy by some (most likely by his father, who appears in Su's inscription as a strong disciplinarian), at heart, he was like Han Yu. He worked hard, but the official path was not for him. By identifying with the elder former politician and famed hermit-poet, Su was justifying his position while also alluding to financial difficulties of one who no longer wanted to have an official career or one related to government service (such as his father's role as a tax inspector). The inscription suggests that Su's father had forced him to take the dramatic action of leaving home, possibly because he refused to sit the exams again. His father may have severed his subsidy for Su's living, forcing him to seek work elsewhere.

Tracing his movement from inscriptions, it appears that Su painted for survival, perhaps to seek lodgings at temples or at the requests of friends and patrons in return for hospitality. While little is known of his living, there is an increased number of paintings of figures, in particular mythical and religious beings, often with an inscription but seldom any dedications, suggesting that he may not have had intimate patronage support, such as being an artist in residence. This shift from his earlier landscapes to subjects such as immortals suggests that he was adapting to a regional market where religious rituals and festivals were an important part of daily life. He appears to have spent most of his time in Guangxi, but in the winter of 1845, at the age of thirty-two, we find him in Guangzhou City again.

By the fifth month of 1848 at the latest, he was once again in Guangxi. In an inscription on a hanging scroll painting entitled *Figures* (Fig. 103), which will be discussed in greater detail in Chapter Five, there is a rare piece of evidence on his interactions with his siblings, beginning first with a visit from his sister.[34] The inscription is first and foremost a salutation to his sister, who had made the difficult journey to see him and had discussed with him some of the calligraphy and rubbings that he owned. He compliments her connoisseurship skills, bowing to her greater understanding. However, the inscription ends with a comment that leaves a sour aftertaste, "My third brother copied my Wisdom Sutra. My second brother presented it to my father for critique. My father declared: 'I fear the original is not as good.'" Evidently, his father no longer held Su Renshan in the esteem that he once had. His third brother, also an artist, had replaced him as

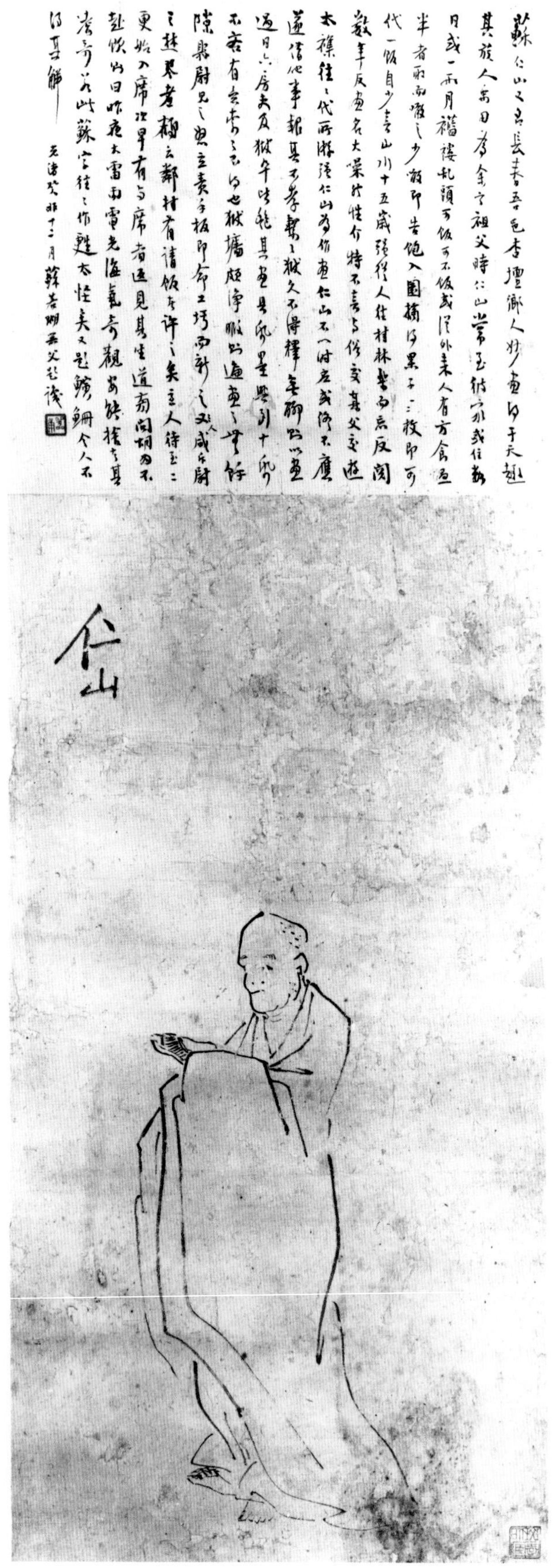

Figure 48 Su Renshan, *Bodhidharma*. Hanging scroll, undated, ink on paper, 94 × 33 cm. Reproduced by permission of the Art Museum of the Chinese University of Hong Kong from the collection of the Art Museum.

the object of his father's affection and respect as a painter.

Eventually, Su returned home, but his return must have been fraught with problems, for shortly afterwards, his father placed him in the *yamen* for filial impiety. Numerous apocryphal anecdotes later emerged speculating on the reasons for this dramatic event in 1849, but there is no concrete evidence accounting for his imprisonment.[35] It has been suggested that his writings attacking educational institutions may have been too provocative, and the family placed him in jail. Another possibility may be that Su refused to take his wife back (away from her natal home) and to start a family, hence incurring accusations of filial impiety. In the earliest inscription about Su Renshan, inscribed on the mount of his painting *Bodhidharma* (Fig. 48), Su Ruohu spoke of Renshan's personality and his later imprisonment:

> Su Renshan, also named Changchun, was from my native Xingtan, His skilled paintings are executed with an innate sense of joy. One of his clansmen told me that during his grandfather's time, Renshan often went to his family home and stayed for a few days or months on end. His clothes and hair were often messy, and he would eat or not eat at times. Sometimes when he had returned from outside, he would eat from the bowls of others, then declare himself to be full. He would go into the gardens and pick one or two fruits from the branches as a replacement for his meal. From his youth, he enjoyed painting landscapes. When he was fifteen *sui*, he traveled to Guilin, and was so happy he forgot to return home. Over the years, his fame as an artist grew, but his nature was such that he did not like to mix with the vulgar.
>
> [Su's] father had an indiscriminately selected assortment of friends and on their behalf constantly solicited paintings from Renshan.
>
> Renshan either did not complete the paintings on time or did not paint them at all. Eventually his father found an excuse to place him in jail for filial impiety, and [Su] was not released for a long time. Despondent, he painted to pass the days. The *yamen* officer and the jailer all admired his paintings. They provided him with paper and ink. When he felt inspired, he would be so generous as to paint ten paintings. But he would refuse those who intentionally wanted them. The prison walls were somewhat clean, and during his leisure times, Su would paint all over them, leaving no crack uncovered. When the provincial official saw the walls, he was angry and immediately brought him forth for punishment. He ordered him to re-plaster the walls like new. People scolded the official for "burning the *qin* and cooking the crane," in destroying such talent.[36]

Su Ruohu used standard tropes to describe Su Renshan's individualistic talent: The wild hair and messy clothing are evocative of the untrammeled hermit, and while wild, he was never vulgar (thus above the ordinary). More surprising was Ruohu's suggestion that it was Renshan's father who had dubious relations that affected the relationship between father and son. Given the importance of clan lineage and familial ideals of respect, Ruohu's slight against the father suggests that the paternal friction was substantial. But the inscription also reveals the extent of the authority of clan lineage, which was so overriding that it permitted a father to throw his son into jail for filial impiety.

Su Renshan's confinement did not hamper his will to paint, and he resorted to his childhood practice of painting on all available surfaces, even when the more vulgar official at the *yamen* jail failed to recognize his talent and had all the walls cleaned. Su's extant works of art on paper from this period also testify to this continual practice of painting, including some hastily drawn but powerful landscapes, in which mountains and rivers were changed into mere lines and geometry. His last painting dates to 1850, when he was still incarcerated. It may be that Su Renshan died while in prison, but at the very least, his painting career ceased.

The Literary Vernacular in Painting

The tragic ending of Su Renshan's artistic life often overshadows his achievements in painting. If we were to read his paintings from a biographical perspective, the unusual direction of his formal development in painting can be seen as a consequence of his difficulty in coming to terms with his status as an elder son in a Delta-based clan who was expected to achieve career success. However, by shedding light on the larger social historical readings of art practices in and outside the city, it is possible to see how Su absorbs the various forms in the region. By refusing to abide to the conventions demanded of an elder son or of a scholar, Su also placed himself outside the expectations of certain types of paintings. Instead, he made artworks that at first glance appear impossible to categorize and which reveal an interesting mix of literary references and vernacular customs. The results have been described as intellectualized folk paintings (e.g. paintings of gods with literary references), but they can equally be seen as vernacularized literary painting (e.g. paintings of literary gatherings of gods).

By using "literary vernacular" to explicate the transgressive nature of Su's art, I am aware that I have thrown two uneasy terms together. As scholars have shown, the literary versus the vernacular is a common false dichotomy that can be used to privilege one over the other despite the two often being combined in practice. An example of this combination, taken from the previous chapter, sees how regional symbols, such as the kapok tree, were elevated into an iconographic program that correlated with a canonical narrative of literati tastes. If the literary and the vernacular are often paired, how is this useful in a discussion about Su Renshan's transgressiveness? My argument rests on two aspects. The first is how Su Renshan chose different strategies and motifs that were outside the normative approach set by the cultural elite in the city. And second, he would opt for juxtapositions as opposed to absorption of elements (kapok as pine) to form anomalous details or relationships that can, at times, threaten the aesthetics of ink painting. My argument is that Su's paintings challenge existing structures through a constant tussle between seemingly contradictory aspects that makes his paintings visually confrontational.

Before examining the implications of Su's transgressive paintings, a brief summation of what is meant by literary vernacularism is needed. Literary is used here to refer to paintings that draw on the training of artists who adhere to the literati canon of texts such as histories, the Classics, and poetry. Literary paintings are embedded within a historical canon that privileges calligraphic brushwork, artistic lineage, and themes that circulated within an elite visual economy. The vernacular is more difficult to pinpoint. More recently, James Cahill recovers what he terms vernacular painting by largely examining paintings that are often marginalized in the Chinese art canon.[37] He looks at a variety of works including paintings by professional artists and workshops, and paintings for domestic use (for display in homes). Overall, Cahill's interpretation of vernacular encompasses art outside the literati as defined as a male literary world related to the civil examination. He also relates vernacular art to the academic style which uses the *gongbi* (工筆 detailed) method of fine lines and color to differentiate it from literati painting. Taking this combination of medium, style and format (where they can be some variations, for example using paper instead of silk) as the cornerstone of defining vernacular, Cahill examines one of the more common subjects that fit in this category as his primary focus: women. The depiction of women in Chinese art tends towards a style that uses detailed brushwork and a colorful palette and thematically touches on issues of desire and intimacy. Cahill repositions their importance in the visual sphere of Ming and Qing China.

I veer from Cahill's broad inclusion of representations of all beauties under the rubric of "vernacular." I also take a different path from Cahill's "literati" versus the "academy" criteria that is often used in critical connoisseurship discourse. Part of the reason behind my departure is that I am looking at a particular time and space, thus moving away from the broader, and arguably more ambitious, scope offered by Cahill. I also use the term literary rather than "literati" (even though I am referring to the canonical foundation of learning and social structures of literati culture) to include female painters and viewers, as well as artists who were trained in the literati tradition and aped literati conventions even though they never held official positions. In other words, I am considering the literary as social and intellectual practices inherent in a closed circuit, which, as seen earlier, was an effective mediator of social exclusion and pretension but which was also opened to those, such as Su Renshan, who subscribed to some, but not all values of that circuit.

My use of vernacular also differs from Cahill's by locating it within a *geographical* social matrix that places vernacular as an aspect of local, but where an urbanized local acts as its counterpart. It is a matrix that works in the Guangdong context, where cultural competition between the city and the West River basin area led to different types of expressions of Cantonese identity, each claiming some sort of local affiliation. It is also a comparison that will allow for more nuanced readings of paintings. For example, Xie Lansheng's paintings of lychees conforms to a local identity strongly tied to poetic allusions with national implications that typified an urban local identity, and as such represent a local literary aesthetic. A painting by the town artist Su Liupeng of village musicians, at first glance, suggests a genial scene of rural pleasure. However, on closer inspection of Su Liupeng's

inscription and in looking at his production of similar paintings, his country musicians are revealed to be a form of social commentary about the perils of urban living and its many temptations, rather than as definitions of a rural life. Su Liupeng's painting is part of a body of satirical works about mercantile greed and is, like Xie's lychees, more indicative of city life of the urban local.

I do, however, follow Cahill in looking at the literary novels and popular literature. This textual mode requires knowledge and literacy from its readers and writers but may be written in a vernacular voice or touch on qualities outside canonical learning, such as intimacy, desire, dreams, and fantasies. Undoubtedly, the rise of literary vernacularism in Ming and Qing paintings is heavily indebted to the growing popularity of literary novels, which provided an alternative space for scholars to write and read ideas and learning outside of canonical texts. This point is elaborated in the final chapter, when I examine Su's depiction of women and his use of the printed page. My use of vernacular also follows regional linguistic properties outside normative structures of official language. As a mode of communication connected to the spoken, rather than to the written, it is often seen as direct and intimate and associated with customs and rituals that are site specific. In the case of Su Renshan, I consider Su's brushwork, which challenges the calligraphic and textured ink brush mode as a direct form of engagement that is akin to linguistic plays that challenge official language.

To clarify my reasoning, I have isolated elements in Su Renshan's oeuvre to elucidate my reading of his literary vernacular that can be categorized as follows: an alternative Cantonese lineage, graphic trace and *kaozheng* scholarship, and depictions of local gods and immortals. These three elements are not mutually exclusive, nor are they the only defining characteristics of works by Su Renshan. However,

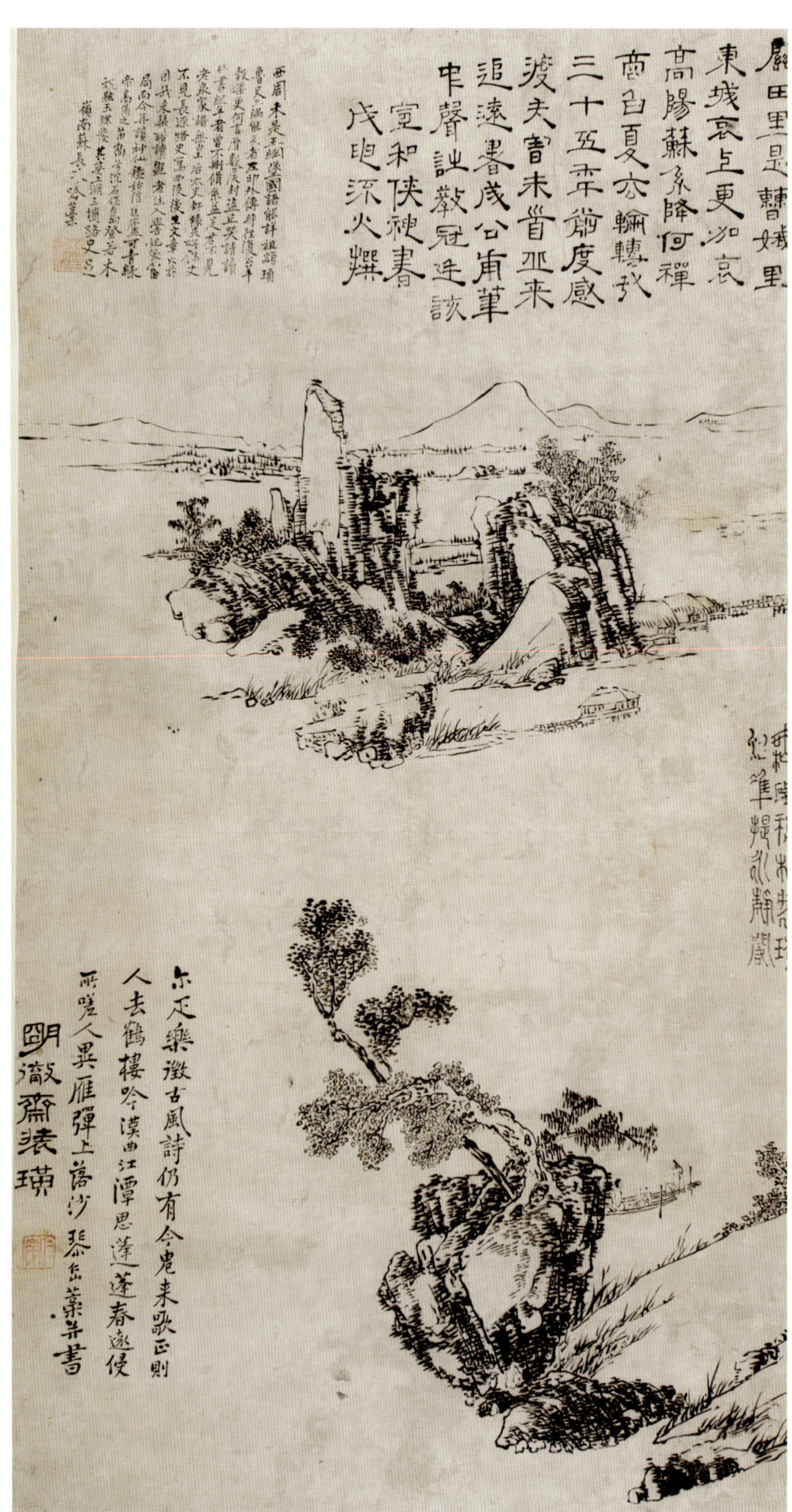

Figure 49 Su Renshan, *The Unobstructed Chan Forest Adorned with Jade.* Hanging scroll, dated 1848, ink on paper. University of Alberta Museums, MacTaggart Art Collection.

they do, collectively, reveal the most fundamental traits that speak of Su's ambitions, his approach to painting, and his affiliations with his home region in Shunde and the larger Delta hinterlands.

An Alternative Cantonese Lineage

At one level, literary vernacularism captures the bridging of the local with the non-local, such as the use of Cantonese within elite literary strategies. Su Renshan's plays with the Cantonese language follow this convention and can be seen in his sobriquets that were used to assert a multitude of identities, including literary ambitions and lineage connections. Su, primarily, only used this convention in his naming and rarely used Cantonese in his inscriptions. This makes sense given that Su, first and foremost, considered himself a scholar, and his dense literary inscriptions with numerous literary references showcase his learning. The use of Cantonese for naming, however, speaks to a formation of identity. As shown by the anthropologist Rubie Watson, naming in patrilineal societies in Hong Kong (which is applicable to areas such as Shunde) was particularly important, because it is used to classify people into kin groups, to deflect inauspicious providence, or present a public identity at different stages of one's life.[38] Su Renshan, unusually, had over sixty alternate names over a period of approximately twenty-four years. Within this large number of sobriquets are several fashioned using Cantonese homophones. Su sometimes wrote the character for his last name Su (蘇) as 甦, Renshan (仁山) as 釚潺, Jingfu (靜甫) as 靖虎, and Changchun (長春) as 祥椿.[39] Moreover, he played with names through puns and allusions. For example, he used the characters zhurong (祝融), a fire god whose descendants were from the area Su, as his last name.[40] Furthermore, fire, as one of the five elements, was designated a symbol of the south, which again ties Su to his Guangdong self. The staggering number

of alternative identities raises the question of what this excessiveness may mean.[41] At the very least, it can be seen as a willful display of individuality, but it also reflects his own internal conflicts as a son, husband, scholar, and artist.

Among his many name plays is the historical figure of Su Shi (蘇軾, 1037–1101), who, as with Han Yu (referred to in his 1842 autobiographical inscription), was exiled to the south. Su Shi was a potent symbol for Su Renshan: He styled himself as *Gaoyang miaoyi* (高陽苗裔 Descendent of Emperor Gaoyang), which alludes to the mythological emperor Zhuanxu (顓頊), grandson of Huangdi (黃帝), whose fief was at Gaoyang. The Song scholar Su Xun (蘇洵, 1009–66), and father of Su Shi, traced the origins of all Su families to Gaoyang. By this logic, Renshan and Su Shi, sharing the same last name, are bonded by descent. The importance of this fabricated lineage may have also been a response to his wandering years as he searched for a sense of belonging. In a landscape painting entitled *Unobstructed Chan Forest Adorned with Jade* (Fig. 49), dated to the seventh month of 1848, Su obliquely writes, "Thirty-five years ago I entered into a life of emotions [i.e. I was born], yet after crossing so many ferries, I am still not able to go back to the home (that I am deeply oriented to). To trace my roots I follow the Duke's brush, and the sound of the middle way and education of poetry perpetuates (my effort to connect with the past) as it should be."[42] This inscription was written while he was possibly in Guangxi. It shows how Su conflated his exile with his need to find his roots, in this instance in texts rather than in family.

The inscription continues with a description of his lineage:

> [Dating to] the final years of the Western Zhou, when the kingdoms fell into ruin, the *Discourses of the State*[43] were able to [provide] details about my ancestor Zhuanxu [顓頊, ca. 2513–2436 BCE, the legendary ruler and grandson of the Yellow Emperor]. The *Chronicle of the State*

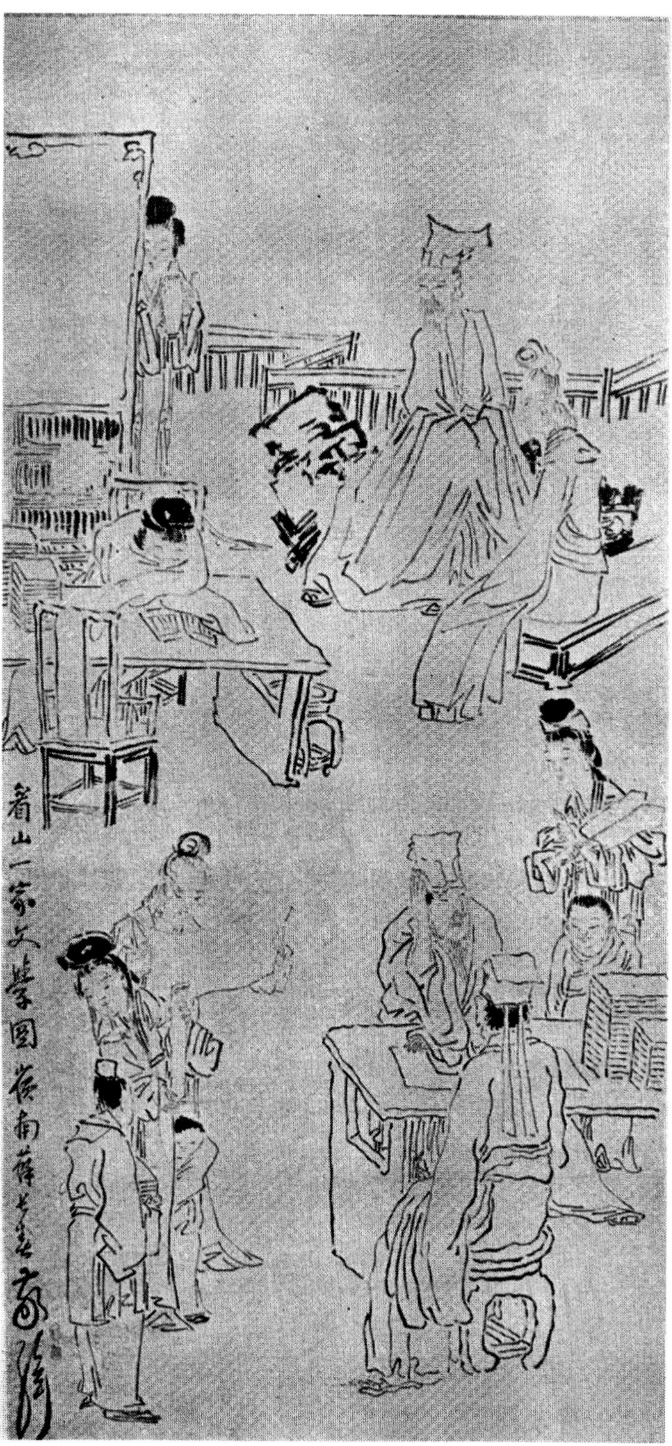

Figure 50   Su Renshan, *Portrait of Su Shi's Family.* Hanging scroll, ink on paper,
dimensions unknown. Whereabouts unknown. After Li Chu-tsing, "Su Renshan
(1814–1849), The Rediscovery and Reappraisal of a Tragic Cantonese Genius,"
Oriental Art, vol. IV, Winter 1970, 355

of Lu[44] also offers sufficient clues to reconstruct his history. Yet in *Mr. Zuo's Tradition*,[45] information about this ancient was inconsistent—not to mention (inconsistencies in) the *Commentaries of Gongyang and Guliang*.[46] Robber Confucius[47] cried over the miscalculation of the calendar and the lords' usurpation of kingly power, but his own accounts were another form of hegemony that suppressed my family's noble past. Please read the *Bamboo Annals*,[48] since in this unexpurgated book one will find sufficient information. So you see, in the Su family genealogy compiled by Su Xun [蘇洵, 1009–06] there isn't an empress dowager, and it lacks all record of the Grand Scribe [Sima Qian] and the Yellow Emperor. Don't you see, though, that in contrast, sources deemed unorthodox such as Changyuan's *Grand History*[49] recorded the ancient kingdom of Xiling,[50] and later [his] students' essays returned to fire sparks. I with my *qin* manual read of the (ancient state of) Zou,[51] and pay attention to the concubine of the Emperor Ku's[52] laughter at the authorities, and now I again read the *Mirror of the Immortals*,[53] and begin to believe what they clearly record— that I am the offspring of the Gaoyang Emperor [Zhuanxu]. A stone sinking into the ocean became an island with "Accord Trees" reaching into the heavens;[54] the God of Fire blessed the jade tablets with the prized imperial genealogy.[55] For me, to trace the source of my family history through the *Three Tombs*[56] and the *Grand History* is enough.

[Signed] Chanted and drafted by Su Changchun of Lingnan[57]

Su explicitly states his ancestral ties to the Gaoyang Emperor and moreover accuses Confucius for failing to recognize the importance of Gaoyang. By neglecting the works by Gaoyang, who was known for his contributions to astronomy and a unified calendar, Su suggests that "Robber Confucius" therefore miscalculated the calendar, causing later generations of scholars to follow his erroneous path.[58] This inscription is one of many that attacked Confucius and his mistakes, and Su's mode of attack via ancient text verification belongs to the traditions of *kaozheng* scholarship, which we saw in the previous chapter was the intellectual discourse promoted at Xuehaitang. More

is said about the impact of *kaozheng* scholarship on Su's work in the following sections. What is of interest about this inscription is how Su uses a genealogy that looks at ancestors of ancient times rather than looking at his immediate clan families, which was the standard practice of genealogies, to seek his sense of home. This painting, made during his exile, offers a look at how Delta regional practices and *kaozheng* scholarship were co-opted by Su Renshan to define a personal history.

Another example of this lineage construction can be seen in Su Renshan's *Portrait of Su Shi's Family* (Fig. 50). In this hanging scroll, Su Renshan depicts ten siblings—six brothers and four sisters—in a garden, engaged in the literary arts. This is a scene of familial congeniality with no clear hierarchy among the group; an older brother and sister sit companionably next to one another in the top right, while another sister is collapsed asleep on a desk, her face hidden within her arms. And it is precisely this self-absorption in the same space that exudes an unusual intimacy. This family scene recalls the famous eighteenth-century novel *Dream of the Red Chamber*, in which the garden was the center of familial bonding. Scholars of the novel have examined the garden as a space where family relationships were portrayed outside the patrilineal structure that separated the achievements of sons and daughters.[59] Su Renshan takes on a similar ambition in his portrait by emphasizing the informality and immediacy of family ties that disrupts a gendered reading of familial hierarchy. But there is more in this painting than a depiction of family life. Although the painting claims to be a portrait of Su Shi's family, Su Shi did not have that many siblings nor sired that many children. However, it does recall Su Renshan's family: Su had five brothers and four sisters, which echoes this family painting, and it is more likely that this is a painting of Su Renshan's siblings. If it is indeed a portrait of such, it is a most unusual subject, not least because it overturns the more traditional form of cultural inheritance (in which artists claim a singular alignment with former historians, writers, etc.) and a hierarchical family structure to create a personal image of his family.

The Graphic Trace and *Kaozheng* Scholarship

Su Renshan's paintings are distinctive for their graphic quality achieved with dry brushwork or with the use of the center tip of an ink-laden brush. These two brushwork styles suggest debts to other mediums and in particular the printed book and the epigraphy scripts. In both, the empty surface becomes as important as the quality of the inked line, and the effect is one that emphasizes a particular type of flat ground plane that creates a geometric illusion. Some scholars have interpreted the flatness of surface and the unwavering brush line as a reflection of Su's debt to painting manuals, which may have been his primary teacher. The insinuation is that an artist like Su, based in Guangdong, did not have access to good ink brush artworks and was dependent on secondary sources. However, this type of rationalizing reflects some of the pitfalls of our current understanding of nineteenth-century painting. Contrary to this bias, as outlined in the previous chapter, Guangdong was a place with large collections of paintings and artworks, and attracted artists and patrons from different parts of the country. In the case of Su Renshan, although we have very little knowledge of what he might have seen and learned from, we do know that, from the age of fourteen, he was an accomplished artist, and extant works show a man who began his artistic career painting large-scale landscape paintings with *jiehua* architecture. His later works show a more focused pursuit of the linear that upends the more familiar paths of artists who worked to erase any trace of a debt to print by using washes or through displays of brushwork. In contrast, the graphic

quality in Su Renshan's paintings was enhanced rather than subdued, particularly in his later works, suggesting that Su's print-like quality paintings were no accidents of limitations.

A comparison of his landscapes reveals how Su Renshan was pushing his painting craft from an early age. As seen in *Landscape in the Detailed Manner* (Fig. 45), discussed above, Su showcased his precocious skills with a careful rendering of a landscape using washes and short, textured brushwork that built up the layers of lush mountains in the Wu school tradition. By 1834, he had pared down the basics of landscape structure to a simple central axis as seen in his *Reading under the Tree* (Fig. 51), where a small figure sits under a bare tree whose branches stretch out to curve into a path that snakes up to the ridges of a central mountain. The lower half of the painting is surprisingly bare and goes against conventions in which the bottom of the landscape tends to be heavier, anchoring the mountain. Here, the tree and the path, which are placed in the center of the painting, are flanked by almost blank spaces. This is a very confident construction and one that Su returns to time again. What it achieves is a strong central axis that holds his landscapes together and allows him to then play with different types of distortions. By 1843, and as seen in *Liezi in a Landscape* (Fig. 5 and Fig. 52 [detail]), Su distorts this S-curve by placing an inverted triangular form of a hanging mountain face at the top, instead of a peak, that leads downwards to small pockets of space at the bottom of the composition. Again, he has flipped the traditional landscape that roots the mountain as hardy structures, but unlike the 1834 landscape, Su has created a claustrophobic surface of lines that dislodge his viewers' sense of travel through space, by making his mountain impossible to ascend. The use of abstracted forms to create strange, impenetrable landscape becomes an increasingly evident characteristic of his painting.

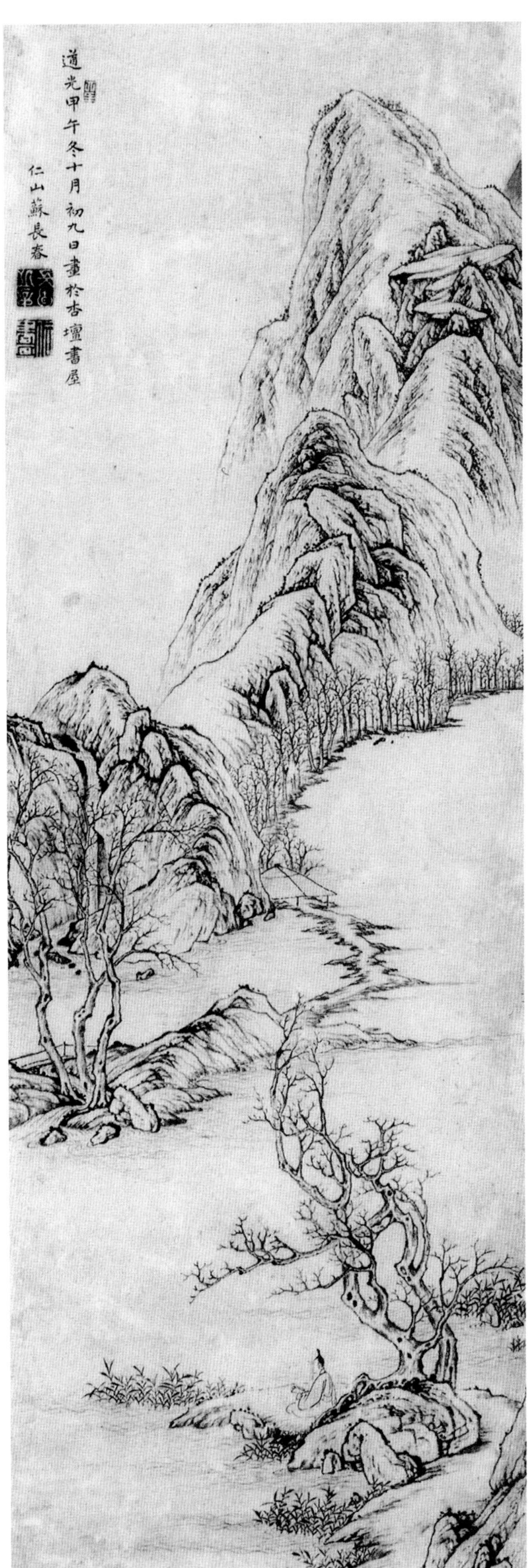

Figure 51 Su Renshan, *Reading under the Tree.* Hanging scroll, dated 1834, ink on paper, 96 × 33 cm. Guangzhou Art Gallery, Guangzhou Art Museum. After Kao Mayching, ed., *The Art of Su Liupeng and Su Renshan,* Hong Kong and Guangzhou: Art Gallery, The Chinese University of Hong Kong and Guangzhou Art Gallery, 1990, 183.

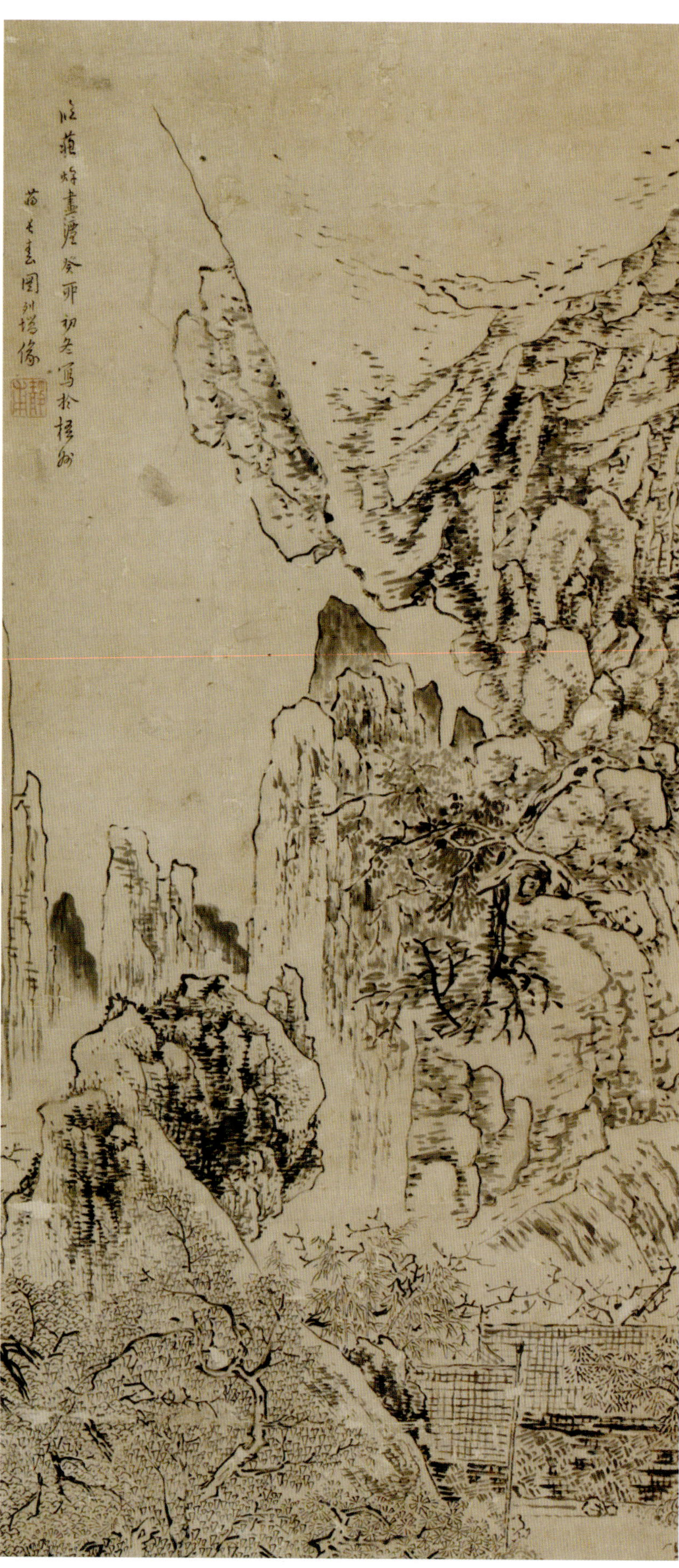

Figure 52   Su Renshan, *Liezi in a Landscape*. Detail. Hanging scroll, dated 1843, ink on paper, 192 × 46.5 cm. Reproduced by permission of the Art Museum of the Chinese University of Hong Kong from the collection of the Art Museum.

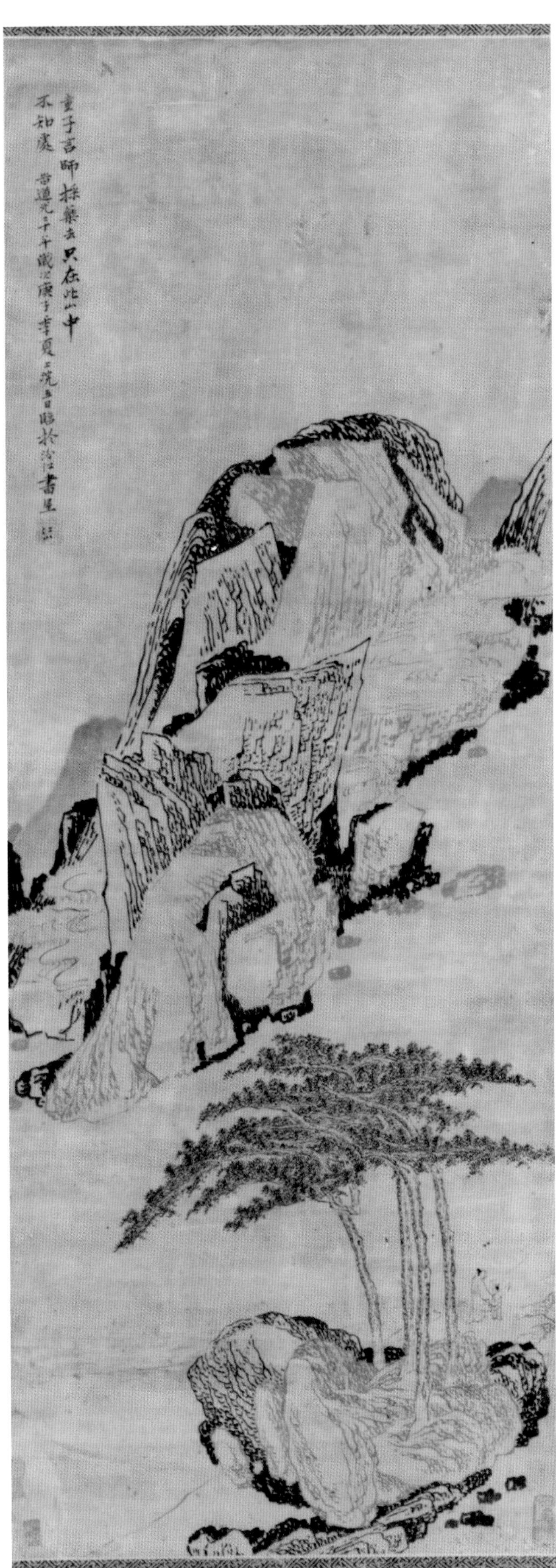

Figure 53 Su Renshan, *Landscape on a Poem by Jia Dao.* Hanging scroll, dated 1840, ink on paper, 109 × 40 cm. Kyoto National Museum.

Placing these three landscapes in chronological order, we can see how Su has moved from the standard mountain landscapes to more complex forms, and that part of this move was shaped by his pictorial experiments to pare down a painting to basic motifs, using voids and contrasts to break up conventional compositions. Moreover, his brushwork does not define the representational quality of the motifs so much as give his motifs compositional balance. For example, his rocks are executed with his familiar short horizontal strokes, which do not emphasize the materiality of the object by giving it shape and density. Rather, the strokes add visual weight to the rocks to balance the rest of the composition and to prevent the landscape from collapsing.

The pursuit of different compositional plays is seen in other, more short-lived, experiments, including the use of ink as a form of color and pattern making. In his 1840 hanging scroll, *Landscape on a Poem by Jia Dao* (Fig. 53), he uses ink as color, filling in blocks of areas with dense and wet concentrations of lines or with lighter gray wash tones and outlining the white of the paper. In effect, Su created patternized blocks that played off dark against light and big against small.[60] This block arrangement recalls images from painting manuals, and it is tempting to regard it as a derivative form and as a continuation of his early training that might have relied on such tools. Again, this undermines Su's more ambitious approach to image. What Su tries to achieve through the flatness of the image with its tilted ground plane, the repetition of forms, the consistent brushwork, and the balance of voids and lines, are ways that emphasize the pictorial *means* of the painting rather than the subject matter of a landscape.

Perhaps his most overt experiments occur when he abandons landscape logic to create forms. In his *Travelers in the Mountains* (Fig. 54), Su uses the empty areas under the tree arches and to the sides of the zigzag forms as the dominate structure of this

more experimental image where negative shapes rather than ink washes give the landscape form. This shape is his most geometric form of the S-curve, and we see it time and again in his paintings, including *Landscape with Houses* (Fig. 55) and *Landscape with Torrent* (Fig. 56), a crisscrossed waterfall flanked with imposing, sharp mountains above, which appear without any color, shading, or washes—only lines.

If Su's transgressive approach to compositions saw him overturning expectations, he embraced more fully the aesthetic qualities and the intellectual properties of ancient scripts. Writings such as the clerical script exploited the relationship between negative and positive spaces, and this can be seen in many of Su's paintings. An example is an undated small painting entitled *Two Revered Gardens of Xianjie An* (賢劫庵 Buddhist Hut of the Present Kalpa of Virtue) *and Zhuangyan Si* (壯嚴寺 Temple of the Past Kalpa of Virtue), sometimes entitled *Two Temples* (Fig. 57). The latter may refer to what is now called the Temple of Six Banyan Trees (六榕寺 Liurong Si) but was formerly known as Bao Zhuangyan Si (寶壯嚴寺 Temple of the Precious Past Kalpa of Virtue). This was a famous temple in Guangzhou with a history that dates from at least 537, when the temple's stupa was built. Many famous figures are associated with the site, including the Tang poet Wang Bo (王勃, ca. 649–76), Huineng (惠能, 638–713), and Su Shi. It was Su Shi, who, after being invited by the temple monks to write something and seeing the six banyan trees outside the complex, composed a poem and inscribed the characters *Liu Rong*, which now gives the temple its present name. It is possible that Su's small painting is a portrait of this historical site in Guangzhou: Its history with Su Shi and, as we shall see, Huineng would have appealed to Su Renshan. I have not been able to trace Xianjie An, although it could be a reference to another building within the temple complex or to the other pagodas in nearby temples that depicted the thousand Buddhas of the

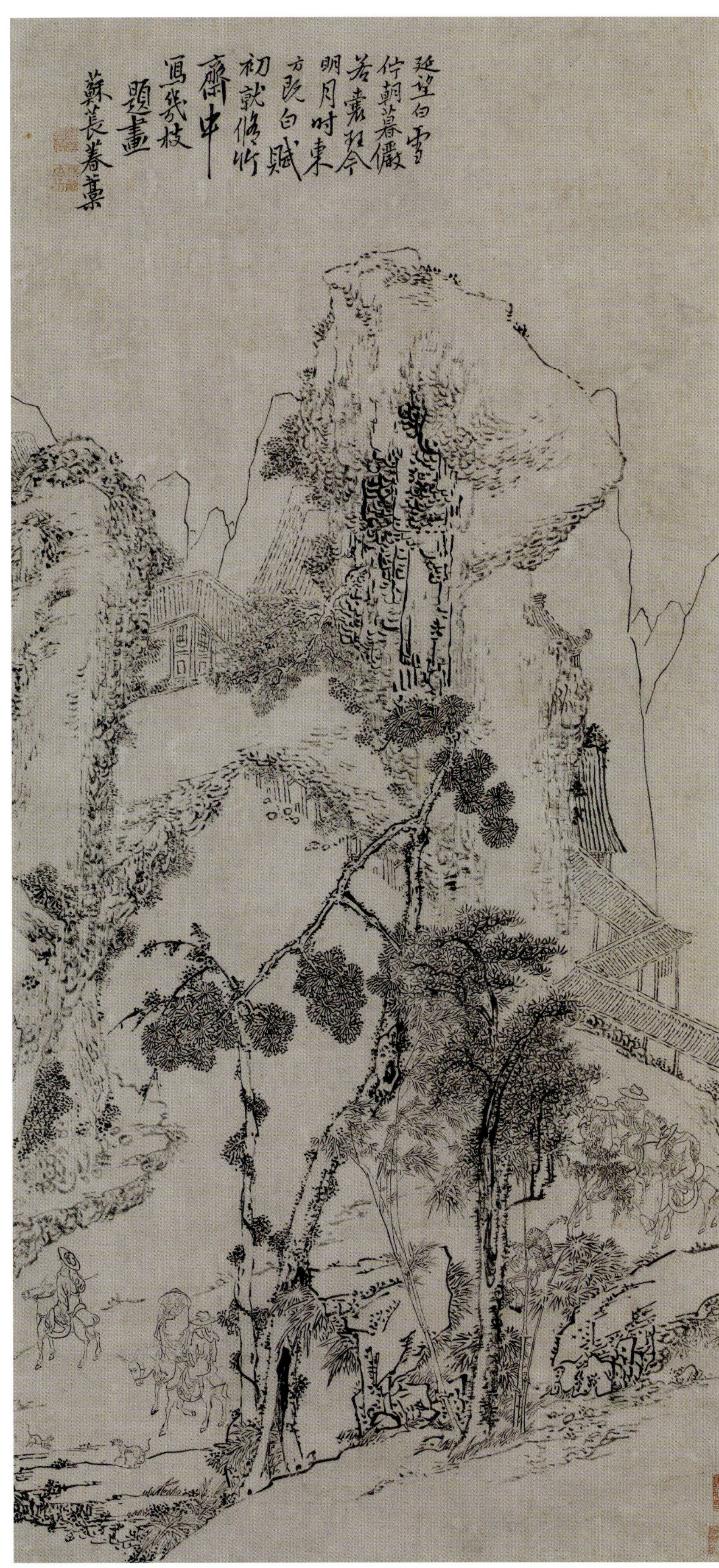

Figure 54 Su Renshan, *Travelers in the Mountains*. Hanging scroll, undated, ink on paper, 125 × 60 cm. Hong Kong Museum of Art Collection.

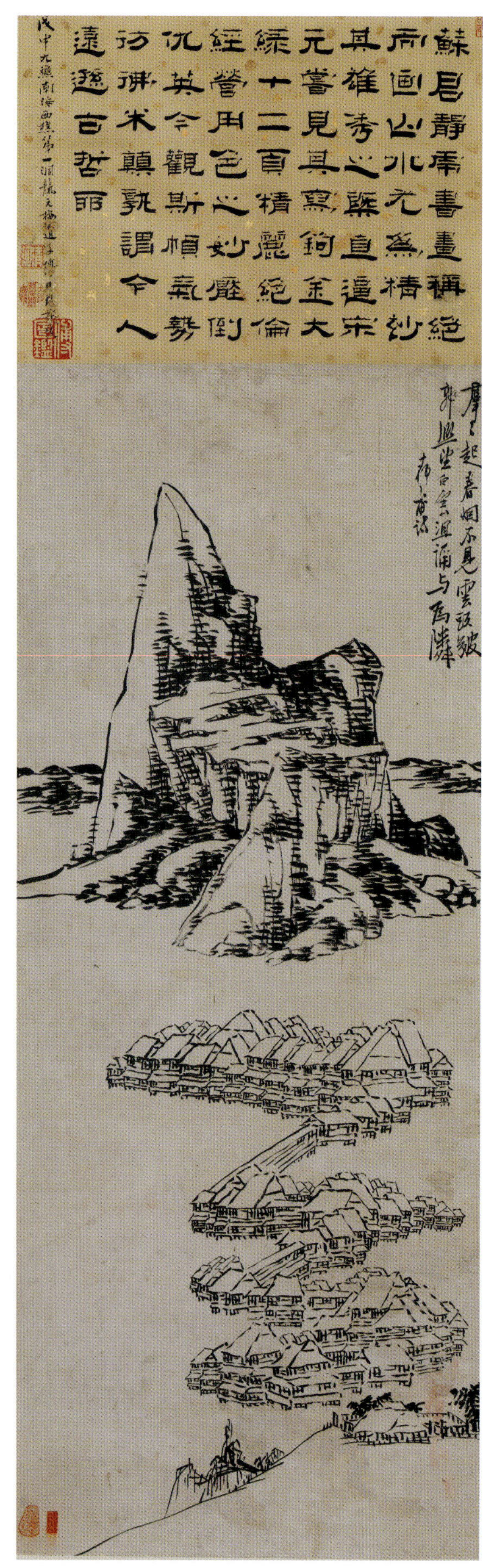

Figure 55 Su Renshan, _Landscape with Houses_. Hanging scroll, undated, ink on paper, 117.5 × 47.5 cm. Hong Kong Museum of Art Collection.

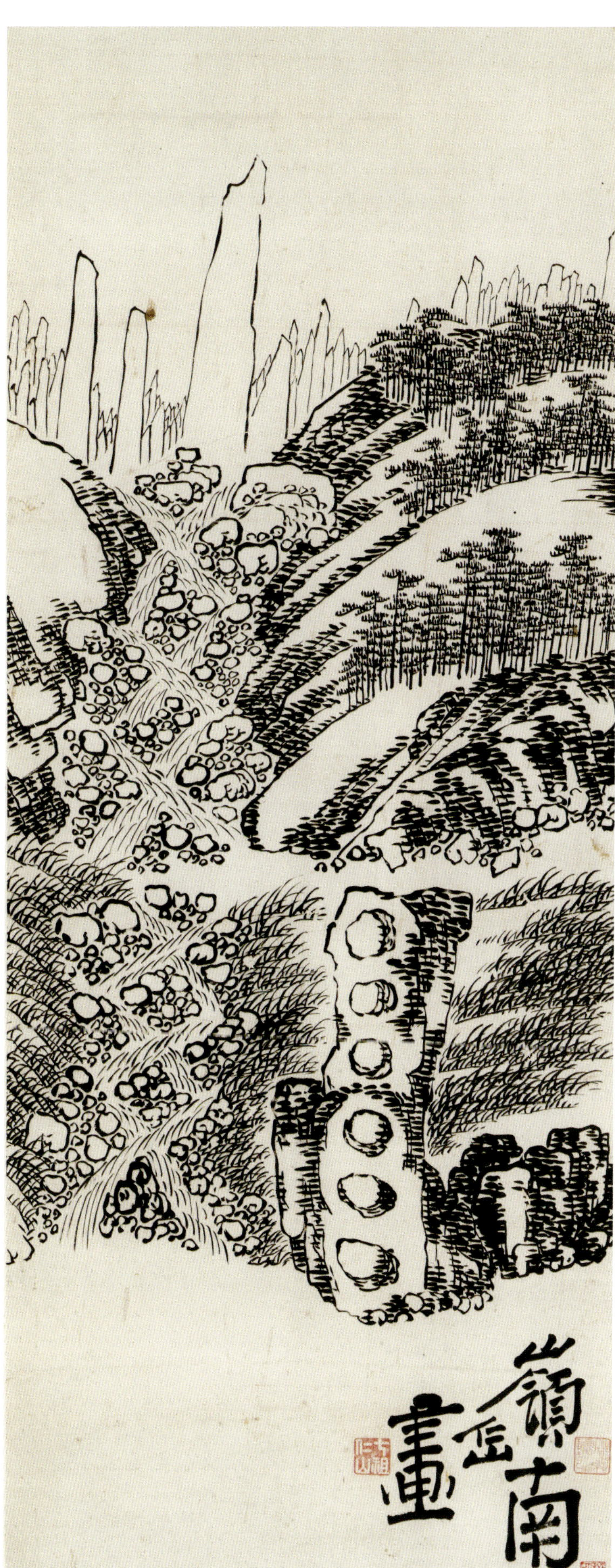

Figure 56 Su Renshan, *Landscape with Torrent*.
Hanging scroll, undated, ink on paper, 112 × 48 cm.
Reproduced by permission of the Art Museum of the
Chinese University of Hong Kong from the collection of
the Art Museum.

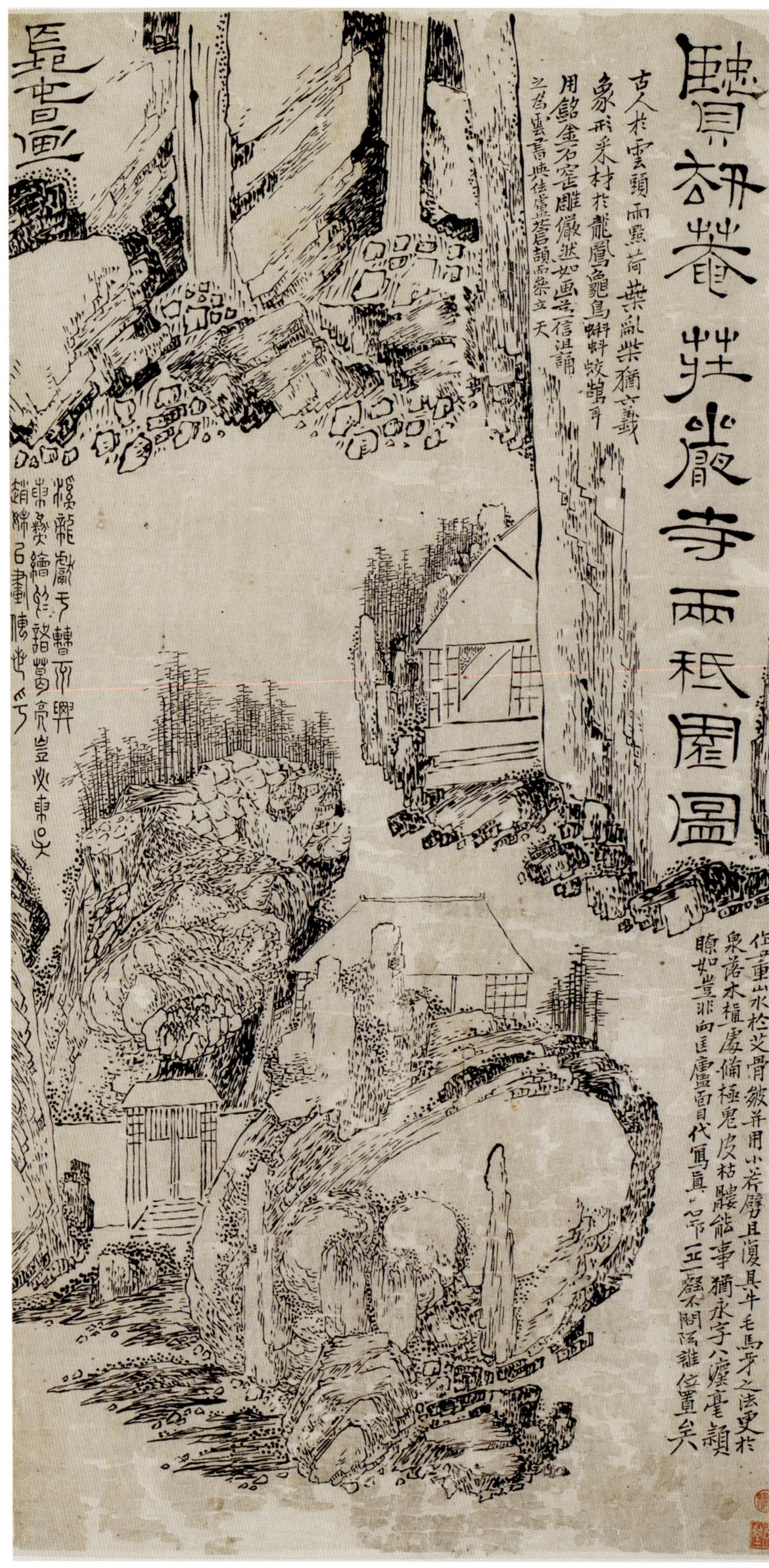

Figure 57 Su Renshan, *Two Revered Gardens of Xianjie An and Zhuangyan Si*. Hanging scroll, undated, ink on paper, 74 × 39 cm. Kyoto National Museum.

Present Virtue (Xianjie Pagoda) such as that found in Zhuangyan Si and Guangxiao Si, also in the Yuexiu area of Guangzhou. In either case, *Two Temples* can be seen as paying homage to famous temple sites.

The painting is an exploration of forms that are at once organic and geometric. Two waterfalls in the top left corner cascade onto a quilt of square-shaped boulders. On the right is a long cliff face on which is written the title of the painting in seal script. Hidden behind is an empty temple room. Below to the left are more buildings snuggled within a landscape of round mountain rocks and mini vertical peaks. An inscription flanks the right-hand side, connecting the first temple to the second, and another hovers above that, connecting the second complex to the waterfall. It is a composition that is highly aware of the frame, the landscape and the inscriptions all bordering the edges of the paper. One of the curious things about this painting is how the blocks of inscriptions direct the eye across the painting surface to the extent that the cascading linearity of the words echo the water-fall, the trees, and the rocks. The result is that we follow the movements of words that direct us across the landscape.

The inscriptions, written in a variety of scripts, are arranged in three blocks, Su's name (長春 Changchun) in the top left corner. Each of the three inscriptions refers to calligraphy and the different types of scripts and brush strokes and in particular to *cunfa* (the textured brushwork). The names of the various strokes are given imagistic properties such as "cow hair," "horse tooth," "raindrops," and "cloud's head." It is an extracted passage from painting manuals, but the imagistic description turns this list of stroke types into a landscape world of "skin of ghosts," "skeletal trees," and "lily leaves." The title of the painting is also inscribed on the cliff face and plays a double role of being an image of words on a cliff as well as words of a title.

In her work on *tibishi* (題壁詩), poems written on walls, the scholar Judith Zeitlin talks about the "writing in place" as a form of publishing, since it was a way of displaying and disseminating one's writing.[61] However, unlike a book, these are things one leaves behind to mark memories of a place, thus giving it a spatial and temporal dimension. As material objects, the walls weather and thus erode and deface the words, so that the recovery of *tibishi*, and also words carved in walls, preserves the original words but also the ghostly presence of what the original words would have once looked like. This theme of recovery and loss are evident in the ways that engraved or written texts on walls and steles have been explored in late imperial China. Novels often evoke emotions of loss through the materiality (or the lack) of fading words. Writers spoke of the "death of steles" and romanticized the written ruins scattered in forests and mountains. Wu Hung has also argued that these types of word traces perpetuate a cycle of birth and rebirth, as new steles based on old rubbings were made, or as scholars sought to make rubbings, they work towards destroying the surface of the original.[62] An example of this is seen with Ruan Yuan, who had new steles made of old rubbings of texts from Mount Hua in his collection and which he believed was the closest to the original. These steles were then placed in his school and extolled as new versions that best capture the earliest version of the original.

I want to extend this argument in my analysis of Su's painting. If we accept this painting as not only a landscape of words but also, in the *kaozheng* vein, as a landscape of a historical site, Su's evocation of an epigraphic trace suggests not only a recovery but a loss, or more accurately, an absence. A striking feature of this landscape is the lack of people. The empty windows and doorways of the two temples are tucked within a landscape of brushstrokes. The *cun* stroke piles up around the buildings, hiding it from outsiders. The temples are made up of simple lines of blocks of white surface, and while this emptiness captures the temples' meditative state, their retreat into a landscape of epigraphic presence also brings into play that double-sided materiality of words in place of a history of what has been lost as well as what is present.

Su's interest in early writings and his general interest in the engraved qualities of the brushstrokes relate to the revival of epigraphy in the eighteenth century. One of the major proponents of epigraphy was Weng Fanggang, who served briefly as an education commissioner in Guangzhou in the 1760s. Weng's impact on the elite scholarly scene was immense: Many of the eighteenth-century art collectors sought Weng for connoisseurship advice, including Wu Rongguang, as seen in the previous chapter. Members of the Pan *hong* merchant family also make claim of some relationship (as friends or disciples) with this senior politician. Shortly after his arrival in Guangdong, Weng compiled *Yuedong jinshi lu* 粵東金石錄 (Record of writings on stone and metal in east Guangdong), which was a compilation of ancient inscribed texts found in the region. Weng found many different surviving epigraphic inscriptions on old ancient sites, but there was one that eluded him: the famous stone at Yaozhou, the former site of an imperial palace from the Southern Han (917–71), where the Song scholar, calligrapher, and connoisseur Mi Fu (米芾, 1051–1107) once visited and was so impressed by the rocks that he inscribed a poem dedicated to the site. Unfortunately, Weng failed to find the site, but in 1826, Wu Lanxiu (吳蘭修, 1789–1839), a sub-director of schools in Panyu County in 1821–22 and a long-term sojourner in Guangzhou, discovered Mi's stone engraving. The engraving was badly damaged, but the discovery quickly became a key cultural symbol of Guangdong and this former imperial site.

Weng's interest in epigraphy went hand in hand with the rising influence of evidential scholarship in the eighteenth century. For these *kaozheng* scholars, early inscriptional accounts carved on stone and metal were invaluable authentic documents that provided greater insights into history. One could argue that, for these scholars, the materiality and age of the epigraphy object were deemed as important as, if not more important than, its authorship.[63] It is partly this ability to consider famous sites primarily through a pedagogical lens that *kaozheng* scholars were able to mitigate the problems that arose from looking at objects and sites that had a problematic past. This was particularly useful when *kaozheng* scholars explained artifacts that had complicated histories, such as works that are of or made references to the Southern Han (917–71), a time when Guangdong claimed political autonomy from the rest of the country as an independent kingdom.

By claiming an interest in Southern Han, scholars at Xuehaitang, and Guangdong in general, found themselves in an interesting position of reclaiming a history of an outsider kingdom that declared independence from the north. However, by emphasizing their intellectual interest, scholars were able to co-opt and reframe the unruly elements and mute the period's rebellious character (for example, emphasizing Mi Fu's inscription on a former Southern Han palace). Moreover, by emphasizing the historical and cultural richness of the period, they managed to tread, with relative ease, the fine line between insider and outsider, by claiming their status as authority to an important part of Guangdong's local history.

There are numerous sites and artifacts that reference the Southern Han, including Yuexiu Hill where Xuehaitang is based, and the popular Lychee Cove, visited by numerous Guangdong scholars. Another important site was the Guangxiao Temple. This temple can be traced to the Nanyue Kingdom

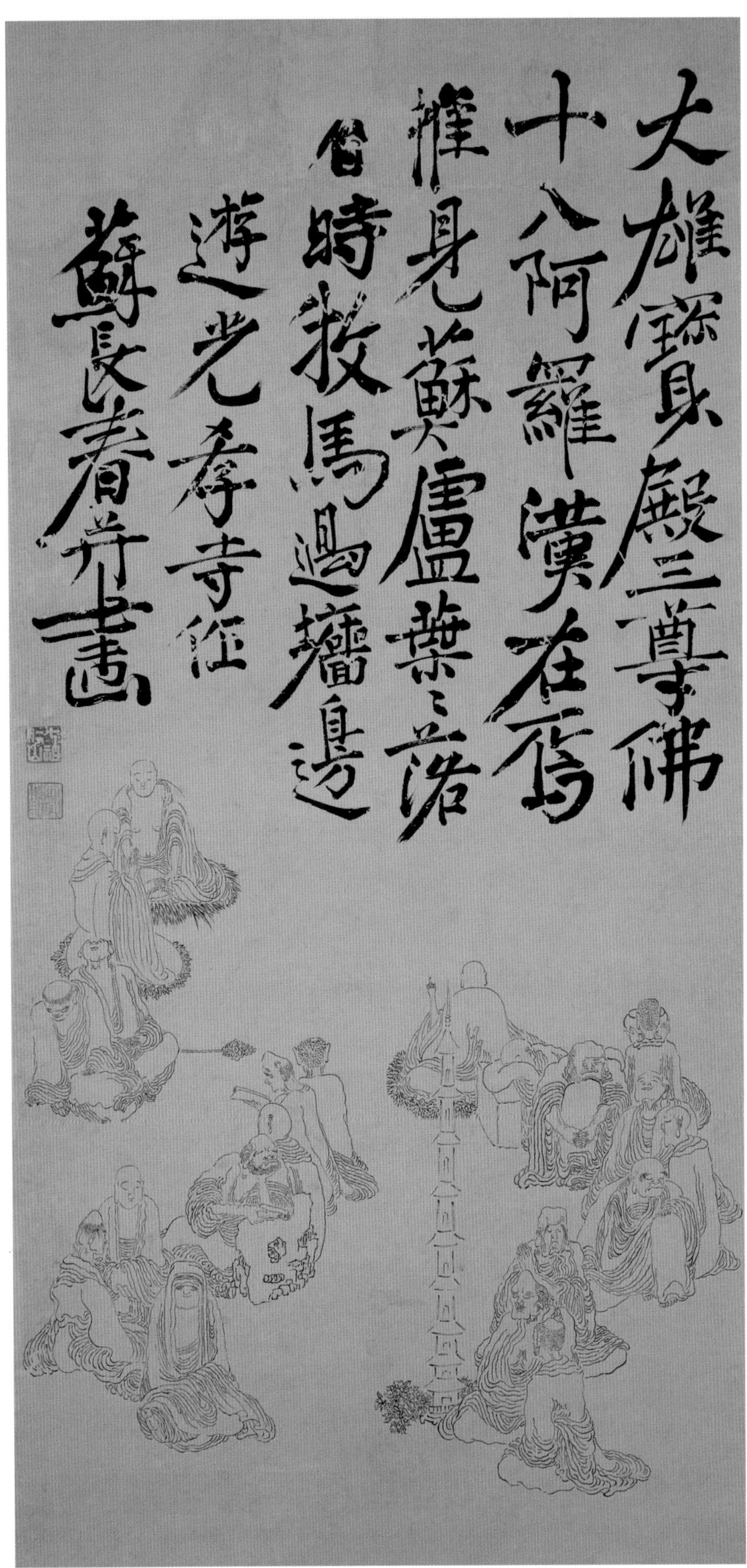

Figure 58 Su Renshan, *Guangxiao Temple Luohans*. Hanging scroll, undated, ink on paper, 124 × 59.3 cm. Guangdong Museum.

during the Western Han (206 BCE–24 CE). It is also important as the training place for Huineng, a poor peasant boy from Guangdong who became the sixth patriarch of *Chan* Buddhism. During the Southern Han period, two iron pagodas were cast with images inscribed with texts and Buddhist figures. The writings on the iron pagodas were carefully scrutinized by many Xuehaitang scholars and were an important part of Southern Han study in the early nineteenth century.

Su Renshan followed the *kaozheng* interest in Southern Han artifacts and sites. In one painting, Su depicts a scene of eighteen *luohans* (Buddhist sages) based on his visit to Guangxiao Chan Buddhist Temple (Fig. 58). Su references this pagoda in his painting of the *luohans* who are seated in groups around the motif. The most striking feature of this painting is the extreme graphic contours of the figures. The robes are delineated in blunt regular lines that recall the engraved features of the pagoda itself. It is as if the figures have emerged as carved figures from the pagoda and now sit among each other. They are, however, enlivened by the every-dayness of their characteristics and behavior. Some appear to be reading, others are slouched in contemplation, and yet more in conversations. The intimacy of the *luohans* makes them appear as if this was no more than a gathering of men, and as a result, their usual beast-like qualities such as the gnarly faces and impossible physiques are seen as being gentler, more human. That they do maintain their otherworldly presence is evident in the treatment of lines and also in the ambivalent ground on which they sit. The ground plane is tilted up high and in turn intensifies a compression of space between the flat surface of an image and the real lived, creating an in-between area that suggests an impossible world, and one where immortals can live.

Gods and Immortals

The genre of immortals and gods was a popular art form that would be hung on auspicious days or appropriate seasons. As a subject, it is the most obvious vernacular trait in Su Renshan's paintings. However, as we have seen, Su's approach to this subject differed from the general staple images, which are often colorful and appeal to a broader audience, and often anonymous. There are some by known artists such as the large finger painting by Su Liupeng of *Magu Presenting a Birthday Gift* (Fig. 59). The composition of a single figure engaged with the viewer (in this case with the offering of an immortal peach), pleasant light colors, short inscription that do not intrude the pictorial subject, and an overall theme of auspiciousness that is readily understood make this an ideal image for display.

I will probe deeper into how Su approached this subject of gods and immortals. At the most basic level, Su offered images that played with brush trace. He sometimes depicted them using dry brushwork that makes his portraits appear almost graphic, as seen earlier in his *Bodhidharma* (Fig. 49). At the other end of the spectrum is the more spontaneous inky trace of *xieyi* brushwork, as seen in his *Portrait of Li Tieguai* (Fig. 60), housed at the Metropolitan Museum of Art. In both these simple portraits, Su exaggerates the unusual qualities of his brushwork and compositions: *Bodhidharma* looks like a printed page, while the foreshortened gourd, executed with few strokes, in *Li Tieguai* echoes the pose of the seated *luohan* and adds a flutter of pictorial bravura.

His more ambitious works often involved groups of immortals and gods that allowed him to play with their interactions with one another. An example of this is his large, undated hanging scroll entitled *Immortals of the City of Five Rams* (Fig. 61). The painting refers to the legendary founders of Guangzhou, a popular subject that remains true today. According to local

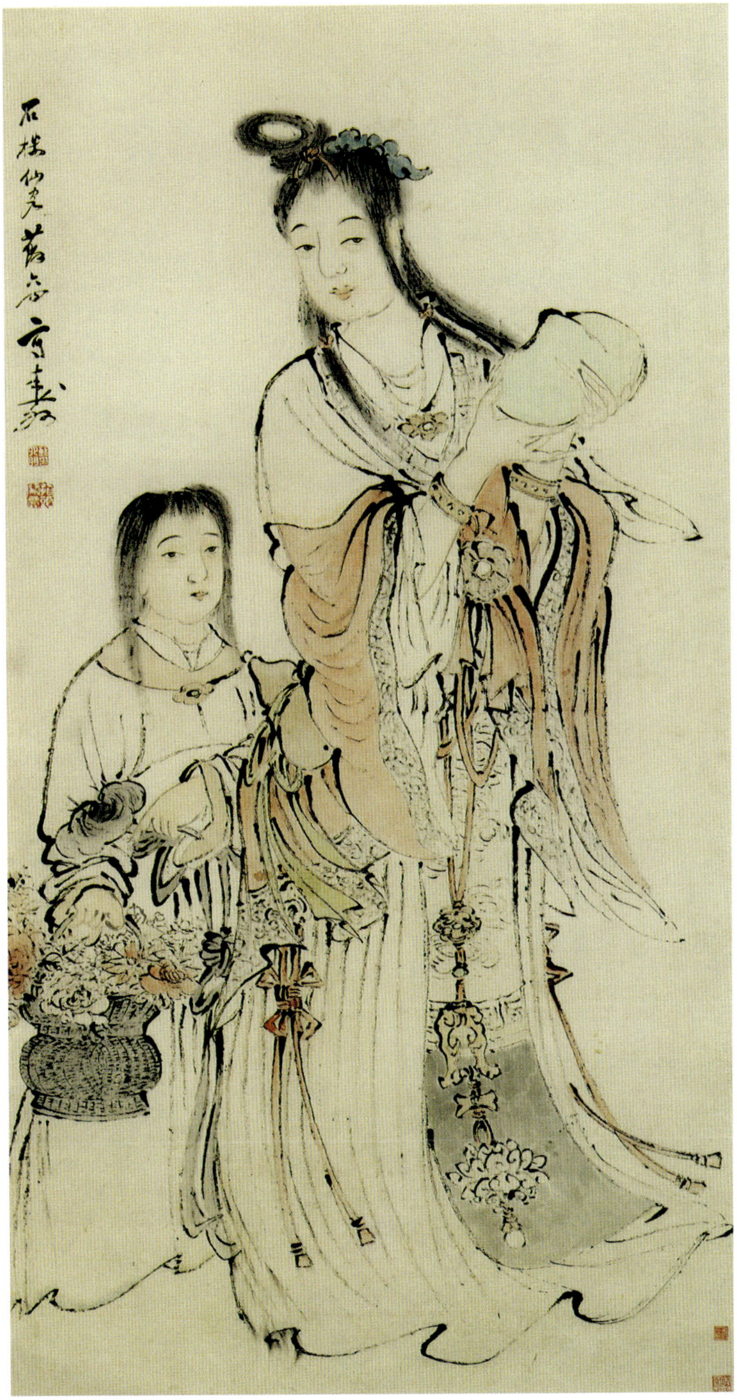

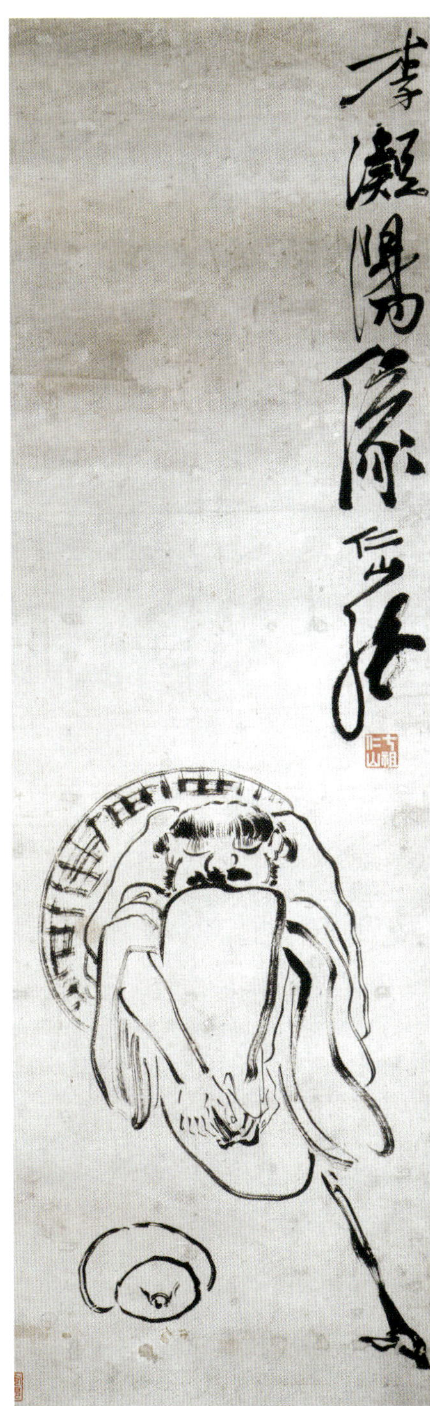

Figure 59 *(left)*   Su Liupeng, *Finger Painting of Magu Presenting a Birthday Gift*. Hanging scroll, undated, color on paper, 169 × 91 cm. Reproduced by permission of the Art Museum of the Chinese University of Hong Kong from the collection of the Art Museum.

Figure 60 *(right)*   Su Renshan, *Portrait of Li Tieguai*. Hanging scroll, undated, ink on paper, 115.6 × 40 cm. Metropolitan Museum of Art. Gift of Robert Hatfield Ellsworth, in memory of La Ferne Hatfield Ellsworth, 1986. Image © The Metropolitan Museum of Art.

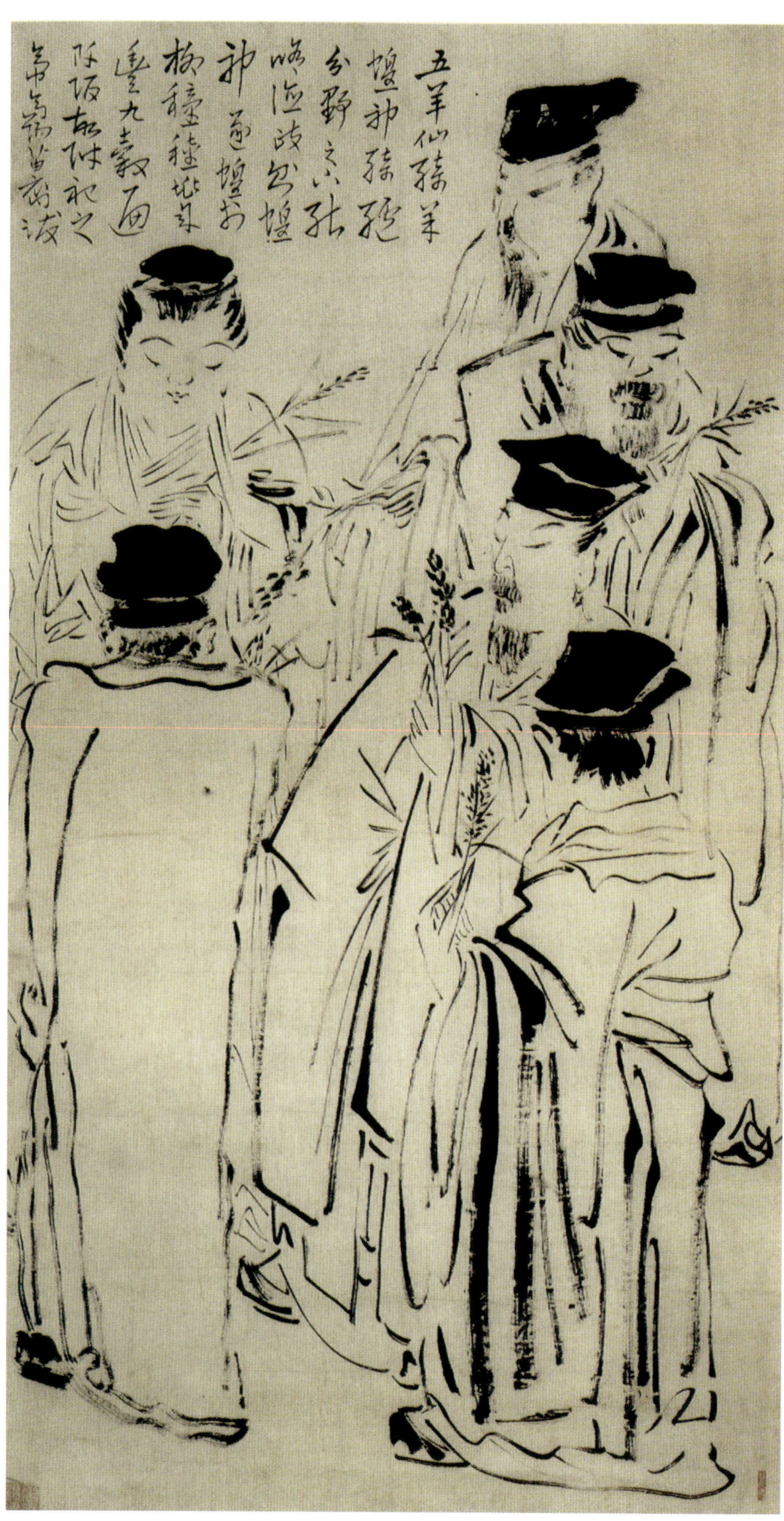

Figure 61 Su Renshan, *Immortals of the City of Five Rams*. Hanging scroll, undated, ink on paper, 136 × 72.5 cm. Guangzhou Art Gallery, Guangzhou Art Museum. After Lee Chi-kwong, *Su Renshan*. Guangzhou: Lingnan meishu chubanshe, 2011, 110.

mythology, five immortals riding on rams came and presented the people of Yue with a stalk of grain each and declared that thereafter their lands would never suffer from famine. This well-known legend also gave Guangzhou its other appellation, Yangcheng (羊城 City of Five Rams). Popular versions of this image depict these five gods in iconic poses to create a sacred presence. Su thwarts conventional iconic symmetry by depicting his immortals herded together as if in conversation with one another, even as they are all looking in different directions. The painting also veers from convention by including a figure of a woman, shown here carrying a stalk of grain. According to Su's inscription, he also included the Locust God (a male immortal), suggesting that one of his Five Immortals is female (since the legend does not identify the immortals, it is possible to reinterpret the myth with one of them as a female). Su might have interpreted this immortal as *Hegu furen* (禾穀夫人 Lady of Grains), a popular deity widely worshipped in Xiangshan, an area south of Shunde and part of the Delta.[64] This was one of the hotly contested regions for unclaimed land between the Delta clan families and the merchant guilds in Guangzhou City. Eventually, the land was gained by the Long and the Luo clans, who were established families based in Shunde. The inclusion of an immortal linked to Xiangshan traditions demonstrates how local myths were incorporated into better-known legends, and Su's identification with the Delta clan families.

Su's painting of the five immortals is intriguing not only because of his iconographic manipulation but also because of his painting style. Outlined in thick, dark lines, the voids appear solid, turning the figures into blocks that recall the traditions of steles and stone monuments. The figures fill the surface, leaving very little blank space around them but never appearing as a claustrophobic group. Su Renshan was a master of using voids, and here, the voids are contained within the immortals' bodies. The result is

a sense of spatial breathing within the subject, while at the same dematerializing their physicality into empty blocks. There is no sense of compression or airlessness despite the closeness of these figures to one another. On the contrary, there is a wonderful sense of spaciousness, the figures facing in or out in different directions, unified by their physical awareness of one another. They appear as if friends talking to each other, their mythical aura dimmed.

The theme of a community of gods is seen in another painting: *High King Avalokitesvara* (Fig. 62), which may accompany *Guangxiao Temple Luohan*. Here, Su depicts an impossible world where immortal ladies draped in ribbons and robes are grouped together among beasts and animals. A child-bearing Guanyin is seated in a cave-like structure held up on the heads of ogre-like creatures dressed in skirts of leaves. In the front is another bodhisattva seated on a lion, a peacock and a mythical *qilin* nearby. This painting refers to the magical chant of the High King Avalokitesvara Sutra, which is based on a story from the Five Dynasties (907–60), when a man imprisoned and waiting for his death was told by a monk in a dream to chant 100 sutras. The monk taught him the chant, and he managed to finish his recitations before he was taken to the executioner's block. When the sword came down on his neck, it broke in two and he was saved. The sutra chants the names of the bodhisattvas, and this painting can be seen as manifestation of the chant. At the same time, if we consider this painting within Chinese art history, the theme of the gathering of beautiful women echoes the familiar genre of palace women. In Su's reconstructions of impossible places, he has created plausible scenes (by referring to palace women), and it is at this juncture of real and unreal, possible and impossible, that Su captures the magic associated with religion.

The utopian world of immortals and gods takes on another dimension when landscapes become

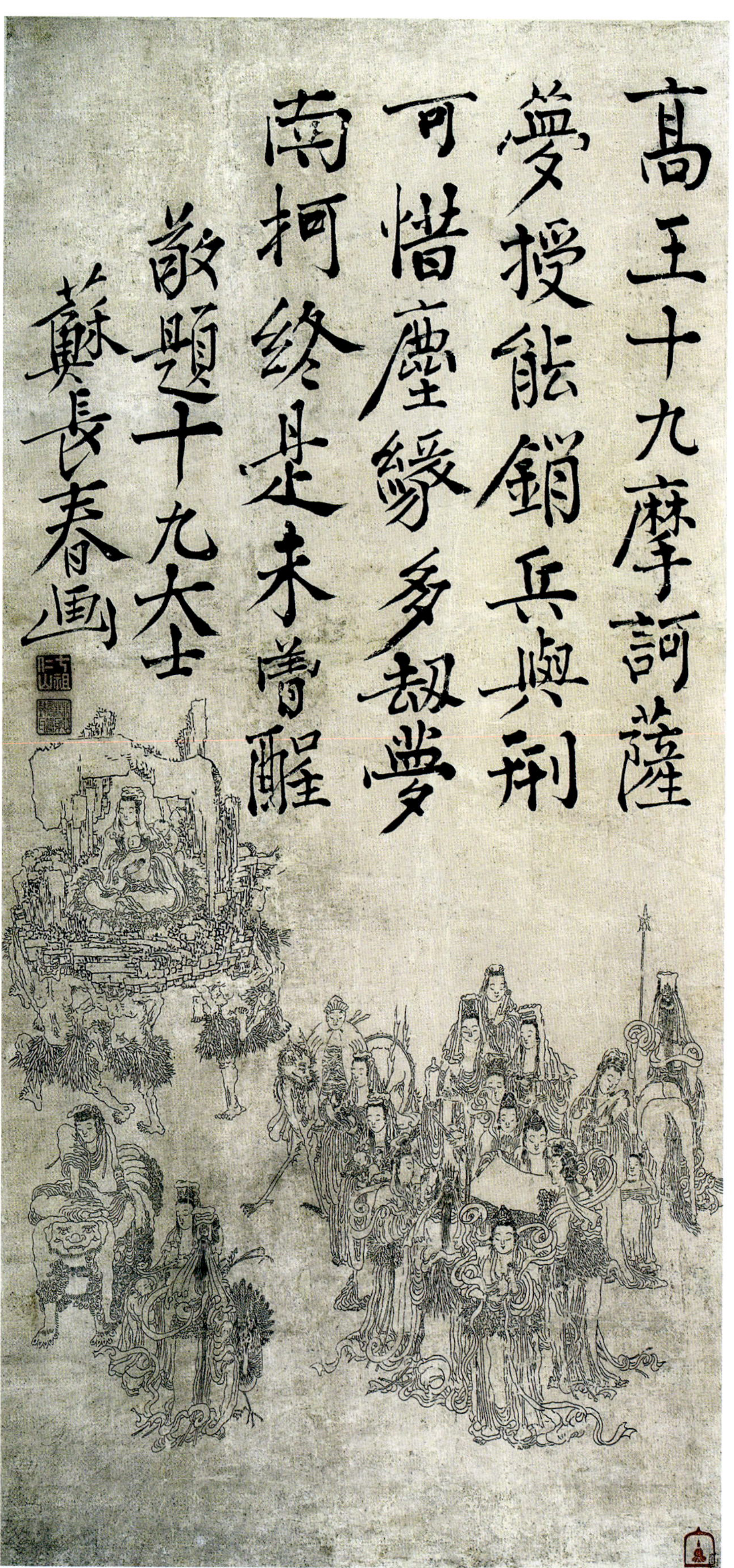

Figure 62 Su Renshan, *High King Avalokitesvara*. Hanging scroll, undated, ink on paper, 124 × 59.3 cm. Guangdong Museum.

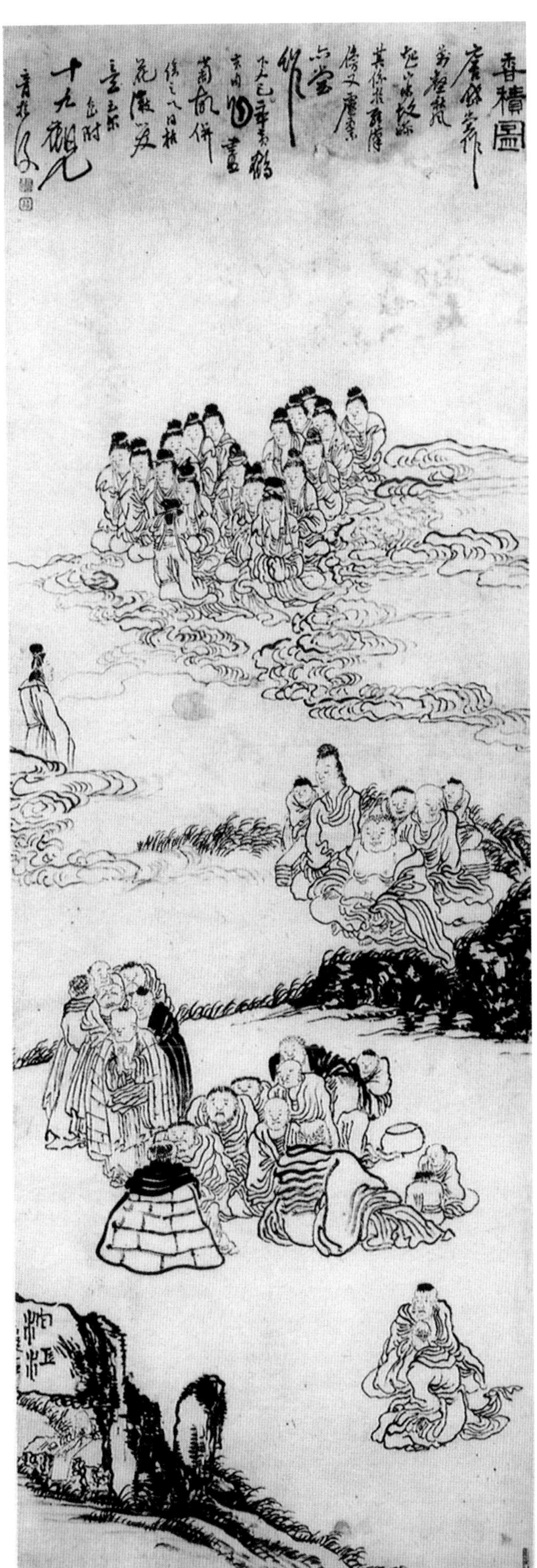

Figure 63 Su Renshan, *Xiangji tu*. Hanging scroll, undated, ink on paper, 166 × 58.3 cm. Guangzhou Art Gallery, Guangzhou Art Museum. After Kao Mayching, ed., *The Art of Su Liupeng and Su Renshan*, Hong Kong and Guangzhou: Art Gallery, The Chinese University of Hong Kong and Guangzhou Art Gallery, 1990, 282.

forms of religious manifestation, as seen in his large hanging scroll painting *Xiangji tu* (Fig. 63). *Xiangji* (香績) is a reference to the food of the Daoist immortals (the fragrant incense) and to a Buddhist place, where immortals gathered to breathe in the fragrant air. The painting is separated into three sections: At the top, there are nineteen *guanyins* (bodhisattvas of compassion) descending on a cloud, in the middle is a cluster of seated *luohans*, and at the bottom is an artist-monk tucked in a cave. The inscription at the top reads:

> *Xiangji tu.* Tangdai [唐岱, 1673–after 1751] once executed a landscape painting entitled *Wanhe qiufeng qi* (Ten Thousand Ravines as the Autumn Wind Rises);[65] therefore, I added him next to the *luohans*. Lu Yuansu [盧元素, act. eighteenth century] once composed the line "the servant left riding on the yellow crane,"[66] and composed a picture of a chrysanthemum, which I added to this painting. The intent is to evoke that of "the plucked flower and the gentle smile." Renshan added the nineteen Guanyin bodhisattvas to the back.[67]

At first glance, this painting defies rational explanation. Tangdai and Lu Yuansu were never worshipped as immortals in their lifetimes or thereafter.[68] Tangdai was a Manchu official who was also a White Bannerman and an artist known for teaching the Qianlong Emperor. Lu Yuansu was a poetess who studied with the famous eighteenth-century scholar Yuan Mei, but her military family was part of the Yellow Banner. This is a curious pairing; neither of these two eighteenth-century personalities shared any common ground other than being members of bannermen families and having no connections with Guangdong.[69] However, given the large presence of bannermen in Guangdong, some of whom were artists and poets, it may be possible to consider this painting was made for someone who had connections with Qing Bannermen.[70] Another possible local element of this painting is the reference to incense. Guangdong was known for its high-quality incense,

particularly in Dongguan, where the primary market was based and which also had easy access to present-day Aberdeen in Hong Kong. In the pre-colonial period, Aberdeen was a major site for incense tree farming and gave the name to this region as "Fragrant Harbor."[71] Returning to the inscription, if the two cited lines are combined, they form a new reading of descending on the crane cloud across the ten thousand ravines, as the autumn wind blows. It marks the journey of reaching the mythical land where immortals rested to consume the fragrance of incense. However, the unusual wit of the painting does not end here. While Tangdai is depicted as the scholar next to the *luohans* in the center of the painting, there are no obvious images of Lu Yuansu, cranes, or chrysanthemums even though Su claimed that he had included them in the painting. But a careful reading of this painting reveals Su's ingenuity. Cleverly, Su executed the shape of the cloud on which the *guanyins* descend in the silhouette form of a crane flying downwards, a reference to Lu's poetic line but also a reference to Lu's sobriquet, Cloud Crane, making this an unusual sobriquet portrait, a sub-genre of portraiture that became popular in the mid-Ming period in the Suzhou region, and perhaps the first of a female scholar.

The obscurity of this scene appears to have been deliberate, as suggested in the second-to-last line, "the plucked flower and gentle smile," which is a reference to the sermon at Vulture Peak where Shakyamuni Buddha held a flower in his hand, twirling it slowly in silence. Nobody knew what this gesture meant, except for the disciple Mahakashyapa, who smiled in response, marking the transmission of the Dharma and the beginning of *Chan* Buddhism. Like the sermon, this painting is a visual conundrum: Only by seeing beyond the explicit could one reach enlightenment. This reading takes on added resonance if we read the artist-monk in the cave as a self-portrait. Su Renshan signed this painting as "Descendent of the Sixth Patriarch of *Chan*." The sixth patriarch of *Chan* Buddhism was the monk Huineng. In the lower left corner, where signatures are usually placed, the picture of an artist-monk in the cave acts as the pictorial version of Su's seal or signature (Fig. 64).[72] Huineng was Cantonese, and it is easy to see why the *Chan* master was attractive to Su. It highlights the importance of descent to Su Renshan, even as he claimed several lineages, and the importance of religion. But it also highlights something personal–a type of pictorial wit. It is a wonderful conceit—the portrait as signature—and as with the sobriquet of Lu Yuansu, it is a playful experiment of names, words, and images.

♦♦♦

To conclude, Su's precocious ability can be seen in his early large-scale landscape paintings that are in the stylistic vein of Wu school artists. However, shortly before leaving home, he developed a style of painting that exploited his early training, which may have relied on painting manuals, but moving into a more experimental mode that reveals his transgressive personality. The large corpus of extant works of gods and immortals, and generic landscapes suggests that he may have made paintings to support himself when he was away from home. The subject matter reflects a regional taste for religious motifs in an area where local practices of rituals and rites were important. Nonetheless, in some of these works, Su also demonstrated his literary learning, and pushes his images of gods and immortals beyond the usual repertoire of auspicious images.

In his more mature works, there are three distinctive traits pinpointing what can be characterized as his style. These characteristics trace his lineage, his debt to *kaozheng* studies and its related interest in the engraved script, and reflect local practices and interests, particularly of gods and immortals. Individually, each trait has earlier precedence but when combined and juxtaposed, they instill in his paintings an unexpectedness that allows him to carve a distinctive niche in the vibrant art world of early nineteenth-century Guangdong. For more than anything, although many of his themes tie him to a vernacular tradition distinct from the cosmopolitan world of the city, his debt to *kaozheng* studies pulls him closer to the intellectual world associated with the likes of Xuehaitang—a place which few Delta-based sons had ties to. His biography also supports this reading of Su as a divided man. His autobiographical inscriptions show him to be someone who went against social mores, perhaps as a reaction against his father and his duties as the eldest son, and he has reconstructed an alternative lineage that aligns him with misunderstood

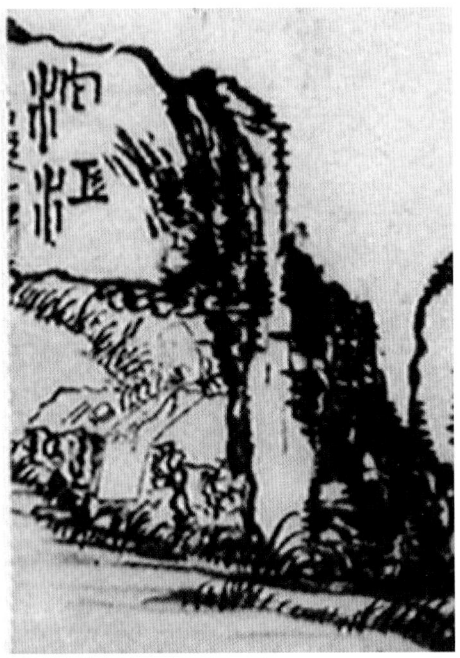

Figure 64   Su Renshan, *Xiangji tu.* Detail. Hanging scroll, undated, ink on paper, 166 × 58.3 cm. Guangzhou Art Gallery, Guangzhou Art Museum. After Kao Mayching, ed., *The Art of Su Liupeng and Su Renshan,* Hong Kong and Guangzhou: Art Gallery, The Chinese University of Hong Kong and Guangzhou Art Gallery, 1990, 282.

scholars such as Su Shi, who was exiled to the south, or legendary figures such as Gaoyang, whose intellectual prowess has been sidelined by Confucius. His argument rests on unearthing and rereading texts, and this approach, similar to *kaozheng* practices, may have been fueled by a desire to show off his learning despite, or because of, failing his exams. Whatever the reasons, by casting himself as an outsider, Su gained a greater pictorial repository and scope to experiment and to define himself as a different type of insider, a Cantonese scholar who looked at the religious practices and habits of his immediate world—the Delta hinterlands. Su Renshan's religious paintings move away from the popular and auspicious, but they are also never wholly secularized. The paintings both revere religion and demonstrate historical learning, and in conflating these two practices, he creates works that straddle both the literary and the vernacular world.

Chapter Three

Art and War in Guangzhou

A second important narrative of early nineteenth-century Guangdong is the Opium War. The war cost lives, it brought in opportunist robbers and brotherhood societies into the Delta hinterlands and parts of the city, interrupted economic stability, fuelled xenophobic frustrations, and roused volatile mobs. Not least, the 1843 Treaty of the Bogue (a more detailed supplement to the Treaty of Nanjing of 1842) also meant the de facto acceptance of the opium drug. In postwar Guangdong, as in no other place, we see elite merchants and scholars join forces with the local populace in resisting both the opening of the city and the treaty terms. Between 1847 and 1849, tension was particularly high, and the issue of opening the city was once again contested. It was only with the daring tactics of Governor-General Ye Mingchen (葉名琛, 1807–59) that, in 1849, Guangdong was able to bluff its way out of another confrontation with the British. Throughout 1840–50, these incredible forces placed state authority in the region in jeopardy and at the same time cemented connections between social groups outside the normative structures of class and kinship.

Historians have continued to discuss the importance of the Opium War in China's history and the merits of using it as a marker of Chinese modernity. They have examined its global repercussions in relation to trade, international relations, and Chinese political networks between the center regions and the peripheral cities.[1] Overall, there is general agreement that the Opium War and the ensuing rebellions collectively changed China's political and social landscape. My own interest rests on this large body of scholarship that allows me to consider the impact of the war at the local level for art and artists. From an art history perspective, the Opium War presents an interesting question: How did artists respond to the events? If the local communities were defying the treaty terms and its implementations, was that defiant energy evident in painting?

To answer these questions, I shift my focus from Su Renshan to consider a broader spectrum of artworks. Three key historical contexts provide the foundation of my arguments: the opium trade and addiction, the 1841 Sanyuanli Incident, and the failure of the diplomatic strategies that also saw, by 1850, increased hostility pitted against the waning power of the central government in Guangdong. I am aware that each of these areas has received in-depth and book-length discussions that endanger my account as being overly general. However, it is necessary to provide a sufficient context that can speak to the growing defiance seen in paintings at this time. Where possible, I will direct my examination of these three areas to consider the socio-political roles of images.

In contrast to the surfeit of texts on the war and its consequences, discussions on paintings or images that are direct expressions of war are for the most part absent. The dearth of information is symptomatic of the larger issue of why it is harder to talk about the war in images rather than in words. Unlike in Europe where certain images of war and violence motivated morality with grand transcendental narratives, in China, where such a tradition is absent, there is no system of valuing the merits of this type of work. Moreover, as social positions (and social positioning) play an important role in understanding Chinese ink paintings with its codified system of exchange and viewing practices, the relational dimension between artists and their viewers extends to the suitability of a depicted subject (such as representations of fighting). Therefore, it was doubly hard to make any pictorial attempts of such a subject when there are no conventions to readily depict or assess the work, or social events and circumstances that make such a work meaningful. Another factor is the trauma of violent events is such that it is impossible to speak directly of emotional experiences. This gap between experience, memory and expression is more often revealed obliquely and draws on narrative motifs that are repeated time and again to create references and meanings for collective sharing and individual testimonies. Drawing on trauma studies and the social aspects of painting practices, I examine art at this historical juncture. Given the pictorial conventions of ink paintings, how did artists find possible ways of exploring their frustration, anger or defiance? Looking beyond the idea of trauma is a more urgent question of how were expressions of defiance possible without overturning completely the values of the state that endorses elite painting ideals and the social status of scholarly artists? This question is directed more to the elite members of Guangdong who have been cultivating a regional identity that exploited the grand narrative of the scholarly gentleman, what sort of pictorial or stylistic means were available to them to voice protest without alienating them from the very cultural and social system that forms their social identity. At the same time, if the shared trauma of witnessing violence at home formed a collective identity within Guangzhou, how did this sharing change the social dimension of Guangdong's art

world? Looking first at the relationships between themes of violence and social positioning, I show how artists referenced old stories and historical tales to depict the ambiguities between reality (of event) and imagination (of experiences). Second, I further my examination by looking at a subgenre: the theme of beasts and ghosts where the suspended world of the extraordinary provided a spatial dimension that allowed themes of defiance to manifest. This analysis has two aims: to provide a preliminary discussion on Guangdong art in the context of war and to extend the sociopolitical parameters that will better situate Su Renshan's paintings from 1840 to 1850, discussed in the following chapters. There is also a third, more shadowy aim. I am proposing that these pictorial explorations of defiance would pave the way for the development of certain types of modern Chinese art. It is no coincidence that Guangdong artists were among the first to challenge the function of elite ink painting by producing alternative themes of political empowerment in the late nineteenth century.

Opium

Opium had long been used in China, but it was not until the eighteenth century that it came to be recognized as a widespread social ill.[2] The Yongzheng Emperor issued the first edict prohibiting opium smoking in 1729. Until then, the amount of imported opium did not exceed two hundred chests and was usually brought from India by junks as return cargo. In 1757, India's monopoly on the opium trade passed to the British East India Company, and the trade continued to flourish even after the company's demise. The Chinese authorities attempted to forbid importation in 1796 by imposing severe penalties, but the contraband trade proliferated.

From the eighteenth century onwards, opium came to be known under many different guises and aliases. It was known as *a-furong* 阿芙蓉, *yapian* (雅

片 elegant pieces), *yangyan* (洋煙 foreign smoke), *duanchang* (斷腸 ruptured intestines), *yingsu* (鶯粟 seeds of spring flowers), *yingsu* (罌粟 seeds of pitcher bowl [shaped flowers]), *wuxiang* (烏香 dark fragrance), and others, reflecting something of its many identities that changed over time.[3] For some, it was a recreational drug commonly used in brothels.[4] For others it was an effective painkiller: In its unadulterated state, it is about ten percent morphine.[5] The Guangdong artist Li Jian, the figurehead of a Cantonese literati painting tradition discussed in Chapter One, was known to have smoked the drug to alleviate his pain from an unspecified illness, especially after 1790, when his health deteriorated.[6] His friend, the scholar-official Zhang Weiping, noted that Li depended on opium to rouse his spirit so he could paint, and, in turn, relied on the sale of his paintings to purchase his dose.[7] In his 1794 *Album of Paintings and Calligraphy* (Guangdong Provincial Museum), Li wrote, "Lingering over an opportune cup of wine can also be harmful; [my] fondness of the joys of the *yinghua* 鶯花 is already too reckless."[8] Although *yinghua* can also mean spring flowers or spring scenery, it doubles here as an abbreviation for *yingsu hua* 鶯粟花, another term for opium flower. This album was made at a time when he was recovering from a bout of sickness; there is another leaf in the same set that describes his inability to walk after taking his medicine, making his reference to *yinghua* all the more telling.[9]

Pictorially, the album makes no direct reference to opium flowers or the habit, and Zhang Weiping's observations of Li Jian's drug dependency hint at a measure of the social acceptance of opium. By the 1840s, Zhang's tolerant position radically changed as he became one of Guangdong's leading opponents of the drug. The negative impact of opium smoking began its spread outside elite circles, especially after soldiers were found to be unfit for service because of their addiction. This led to debates on whether or not to legalize the drug, which intensified when it was independently confirmed that opium was used by senior members of the imperial household and by soldiers who fought and lost to the Yao rebels in Lianzhou (northwest Guangdong). The staggering data shaped a problem that was exacerbated by the increased import and smuggling of the drug despite attempts to limit its importation, production, and consumption. The number of chests of opium balls entering the country grew from 4,000 in 1820 to 18,000 in 1828, and then to 40,000 in 1839. The smuggling trade meant that the actual number of opium balls entering China was significantly higher.[10] It was a lucrative trade: In 1845, a chest of opium was worth anywhere between US$700 and $800, and 40,000 chests of opium could make $28–32 million.[11] To pay for foreign opium, China increased its output of silver, the international currency. Increased supply lowered the value of silver. Domestic taxes were paid in silver, so taxes were increased, leading to widespread consternation. Concerns about the declining imperial coffers, which had never fully recovered from the numerous suppressions of frontier rebellions in the late eighteenth and early nineteenth centuries, also affected the debates about legalization, blurring moral responsibilities with fiscal anxieties.

Opium was domestically cultivated in southwest China, but it was the imported, processed variety that was desired by users, partly due to a consumer trend for foreign goods and partly due to its illicitness. The cosmopolitan reputations of Guangzhou, and later Shanghai, also reinforced the pleasurable dangers of opium smoking.[12] And while it was largely considered to be part of an urban experience, it was a practice that spread to rural areas and increased in all sections of society. Opium's reputation for its pick-me-up allure meant that it became associated with the doldrums and failures of life and was presented as a drug used by the unsuccessful scholar, the harassed shop owner, or the discontented farmer, who were too weak to overcome their desire for escape. This image of the weak addict was a compelling one that provided moral fuel to arguments against the drug.

Lin Zexu's (林則徐, 1785–1850) strict approach to curbing the opiate marked the beginnings of the escalation of violence on the streets of Guangzhou City (Fig. 65). In 1838–39, tension was particularly fraught: Chinese smugglers were publicly executed in the factory square, a hot-headed Scottish merchant shot fire-arrows at the customs house, and rioters gathered outside the British factory, throwing stones and using battering rams to destroy the gates.[13] Efforts to stem the use of opium extended beyond the factories: Dai Xi (戴熙, 1801–60), a Jiangnan scholar-official who was appointed Education Commissioner to Guangdong in 1838, at the height of the opium debate, was a stern opponent.[14] In 1839, he, along with local officials and scholars, including his friend Zhang Weiping, worked in a non-official bureau based at Dafo Temple, set up by Lin Zexu. The group helped the state receive deliveries of surrendered opium and smoking equipment, and maintained surveillance within the community of degree holders who constituted a large group of opium smokers. Dai wrote a compelling piece entitled "Lamenting the Feebly Sick," in which he connects opium smoking with war:

> Simmer the flower to make a paste, a paste that is poisonous. Place it into a clay bowl and inhale using a bamboo pipe, filling your entrails and bowels until your essence is all used. Its corruption will slowly carve its way inside; your muscles will gradually be wasted. Flesh is used to soothe its use. Why bother to use your flesh or muscle? The joys of the skull and skeleton—what do the people know? You feel drunk, yet you are not, you dream, yet it's no dream. Slowly you wait for death but unknowingly you luxuriate in happiness. You thirst, but this love is the hardest to sever. You can endure hunger, but this path is the hardest from which to depart. Last night, I heard that my southern neighbors were dead, and my northern neighbors are gathering arms. Today, you'll eat your fill—tomorrow, you'll quit.[15]

An 1854 album attributed to Su Liupeng also depicts the dire consequences of addiction. The three leaves depict the addict's demise and begin with a man smoking opium on his bed while his wife sits sobbing (Fig. 66). The second leaf depicts a wife who, according to the inscription, was "like a female general," her raised hand holding onto a cleaver, about to destroy the accouterments of his habits "into bamboo shards" (Fig. 67). The final image of an opium addict is a powerful painting of a body in pain, an unusual subject matter in pre-twentieth-century Chinese art (Fig. 68). This weary creature, with disarrayed hair and a prematurely aged body, is made all the more pitiful by the sad eyes of a man too aware of the whispers and gossip that follow his steps. The fate of Su's opium addict is dramatized by his treatment of the lush landscape: The gnarled figure of the addict, whose twisted body looks like a worn old tree stump, made even more so when contrasted with the background setting of tall young pine trees, a typical symbol of the moral righteousness of the upright scholar. While Su Liupeng may have looked at export art for precedents,[16] his use of traditional motifs, and in particular the contrasts of tall young pines with a decrepit body of an opium abuser, touches on the greater social concerns of addiction: the downfall of young, educated men and the future generation of officials and scholars.

Sanyuanli Incident and Local Militias

Frederic Wakeman's pioneering study on Guangdong during this period shows how social disorder, characterized by anti-foreignism and regional consciousness, was supported by organizations led by lettered elites and lineage clans. In particular, Wakeman's research centers on the crucial 1841 Sanyuanli Incident, which marked a major turning point in popular revolt.[17] On the morning of May 25, 1841, the British warship *Nemesis* successfully captured

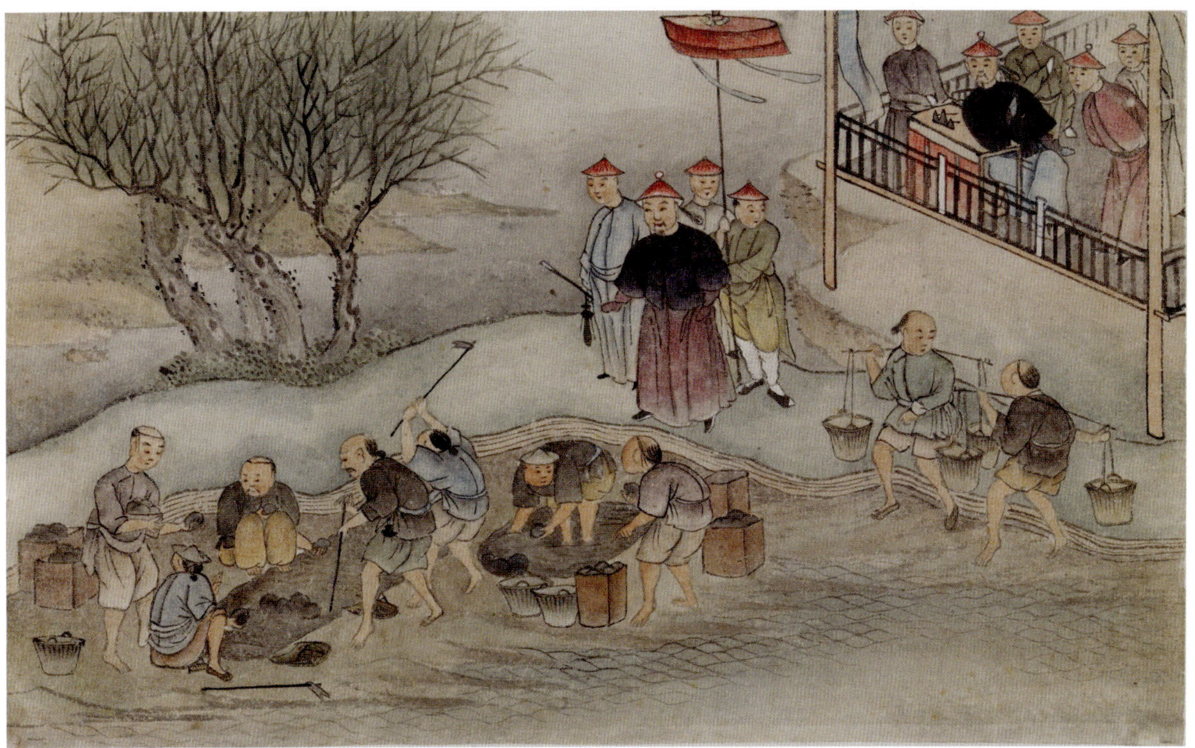

Figure 65 *(top)*   Anonymous, *The Destruction of Opium by Commissioner Lin.* Ca. 1840, watercolor on paper, 147 × 25 cm. Hong Kong Museum of Art Collection.

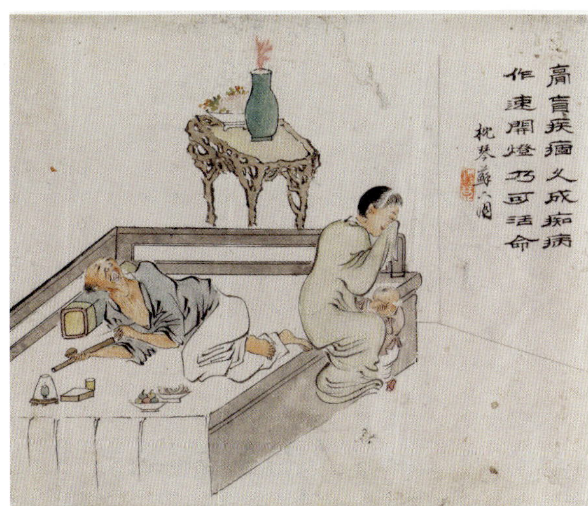

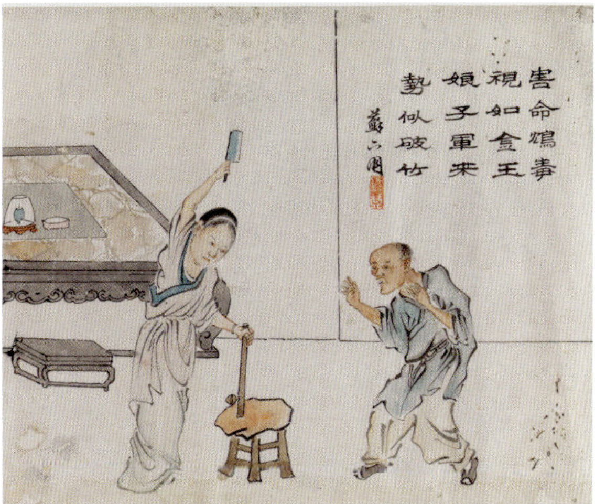

Figure 66 *(bottom left)*   Su Liupeng, Leaf a, *Giving up the Addiction to Opium.* Album of three leaves, 1854, ink and color on paper, 28.3 × 35 cm. Hong Kong Museum of Art Collection.

Figure 67 *(bottom right)*   Su Liupeng, Leaf b, *Giving up the Addiction to Opium.* Album of three leaves, 1854, ink and color on paper, 28.3 × 35 cm. Hong Kong Museum of Art Collection.

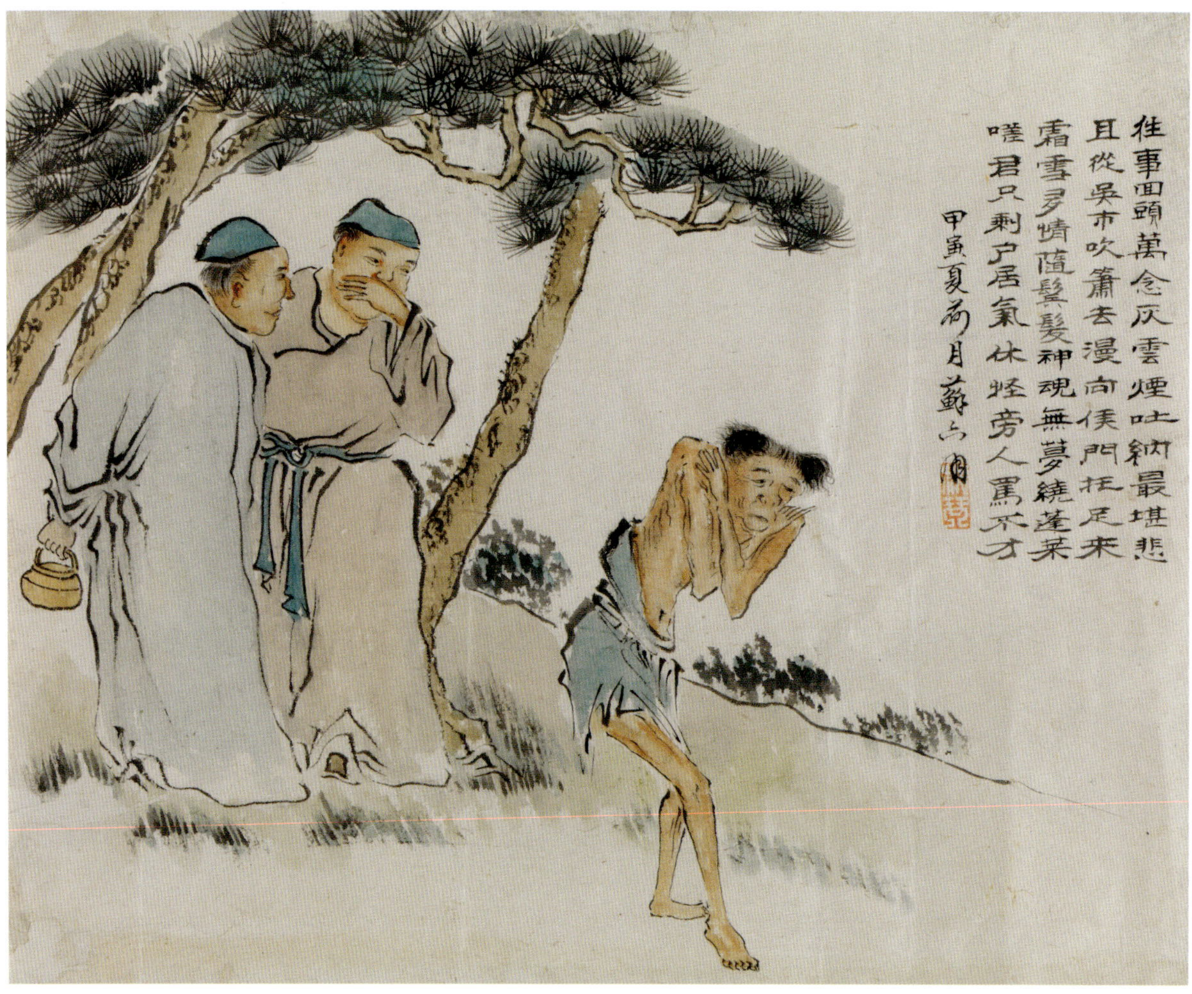

Figure 68   Su Liupeng, Leaf c, *Giving up the Addiction to Opium*. Album of three leaves, 1854, ink and color on paper, 28.3 × 35 cm. Hong Kong Museum of Art Collection.

Guangzhou City, taking over five forts just outside the north gate. The city prefect paid an indemnity of £6 million for the British forces to withdraw on May 31. During negotiations, the British soldiers tramped around Foshan and Sanyuanli, north of the city. This illegal wandering led to accusations by Chinese local communities of plunder and rape. Thirteen scholars from the neighboring areas of Nanhai gathered to discuss ways of organizing a militia to drive out the British. Three men were chosen as leaders, took a blood oath, and went around the countryside to rouse men into battle. One hundred three villagers flocked to the call, and more continued to join the volunteers. Many of these men came from the surrounding towns of Guangzhou City, and Nanhai, Panyu, Xiangshan, and Xian'an counties. The British called for help from the Governor-General of Guangdong and Guangxi, who ardently pleaded with the militia to disperse, as a peace agreement was already in place. Eventually, those in charge slipped away and the volunteers returned home.[18]

Wakeman considered the Sanyuanli Incident to be "an ideological watershed because it marked the beginning of anti-official agitation and fervent anti-foreignism."[19] Philip Kuhn also observed that the "tide of local militarization that swept the Canton area during the Opium War was not generated by officialdom but was a challenge to which officialdom had to respond."[20] Such was the event that stories circulated widely and were even published in Japan. The rise of the people was, and still is, celebrated by Chinese Marxist historians, who have hailed the occasion as the first sign of Chinese nationalism. At the time, this popular victory fired imaginations, and reports of the incident exaggerated the scale and consequences of the event. The symbolic significance of the episode was celebrated with patriotic enthusiasm from scholar-officials as well as the populace. Zhang Weiping penned a poem celebrating the heroism of those who fought at Sanyuanli, which begins:

> They roared like thunder before Sanyuanli
> A thousand, ten thousand, assembled at once,
> Righteousness behind rage and rage behind the braves,
> While the villagers' force broke the enemy's ranks
> Fields and villages—all must be manned.
> None waited for the drum's snare to awaken his zeal.
> Wives were of one mind with their heroic men,
> Mattocks and hoes turned to weapons at hand.
> Around the hamlets, far and near, flashed the
> Banners of every color and hue;
> One brigade, then a hundred, over the hills beyond,
> While the barbarians looked on and suddenly paled.[21]

The Sanyuanli Incident was only one of many resistance campaigns. A citywide autonomous organization was created in 1840 to guard against the forced entry of the British into the Old City. This organization, directed by a number of the elite and headed by Wu Bingjian (伍秉鑒 or Howqua, 1769–1843), received cash donations to create a militia, each shop and family donating the equivalent of a month's rent. The money was then collected by the pawnshops; if there were no pawnshop in the street, the money was donated to "a rich and honest shop." As Wakeman points out, this new administrative and fiscal system was created in parallel to but independent of the official system.

Growing xenophobia galvanized anger towards officials, especially against the Manchu Governors-General and those who supported them. Memories of the Sanyuanli Incident continued to irk, and on September 16, 1841, when Governor-General She Baochun (佘葆純, dates unknown), the same official who had offered the ransom money for the release of the city and dispersed the militia group at Sanyuanli, went to administer the prefectural examinations, he was met with an uproar. The students accused him of being a traitor and threw inkstones at him. More magistrates were needed to appease the unruly crowd, but they were told to "wear their honorary peacock feathers at the front instead of the back of their hat."[22] The students refused to sit the examinations until She Baochun resigned; he had no choice but to cede to their demands.

The success of the 1841 Sanyuanli Incident exemplified the local elite's abilities to call on existing grassroots structures. Centered at academies and funded by local merchants, the supervision of militia groups fueled the moral authority of local leaders both in the city and the provincial towns. In Shunde, 1842, a stele was carved and erected denouncing the British and the increased presence of bandits in the area. The stele reads:

> Opium from across the sea has poisoned our China to the extreme! Because of this foreign Opium, the buds of the rebellious barbarians have seeped through! Because of these rebellious barbarians, the treachery of traitors[23] has also become secretive! Because of the traitors, the bloodied sacrificial vessels of the mountain robbers have been nourished and ablazed! Within these calamities, we cannot forget our summons. Disasters are formed by the gradual

building up of things; are they really the results from one day one night? The august virtue of the imperial court has been spread wide and far, for two hundred years, the people have been happy and at peace.

In the year 1841, the injudicious British barbarians, against regulations, attacked Shunde. They are crafty and militant. At one time, the traitors within our lands failed to recognize the loyalty that comes from sharing the same enemies, they went against and helped the rebels' plot, and the bandits who were once hidden in brushes returned by jumping over beams, climbed walls, and hid in bushes . . .

We live in our village by the banks of the sea. The boats and ships come forth, they disembark and cross planks laid across the sand, connecting to the distant seas. We often receive imperial decrees to increase our vigilance in our resistance. Every scholar, every person is united in our hearts against our enemies; together we joined forces to raise money, a total sum of public funds exceeding four hundred *taels* and more. Now, our work to protect [our homes] can be relied upon.[24]

The stele speaks of mountain robbers (土賊), and their sacrificial vessels refer to the marginal forces of secret societies and brotherhoods that skirt the Delta sands borders. There is a long history of these groups active in southeast China, including Fujian, Guangdong, and Guangxi. Indeed, it was in this area that named societies, such as *Tiandihui* (天地會 Heaven and Earth Society)[25] and *Xiaodaohui* (小刀會 Small Knives Society),[26] began to proliferate in the eighteenth century, as a growing population and increased trade brought in young male workers to the area. Although many secret societies were associated with the revival of the Ming, most were formed based on cultural practices in traditional communities and attracted marginalized young men in the region, such as laborers and the working poor, who were outside the established social networks and lineage groups. These men (there were some women in these groups, but they formed a very small subset) set up a different type of brotherhood that aped other

forms of founding rituals to include origin myths and customs, including the use of sacrificial vessels and blood initiations.[27] As David Ownby has shown in his research on secret societies, blood oaths were important to cement brotherhoods, for they "signified more than fictive kinship at both popular and elite level. On the one hand, blood oaths carried connotations of solemn purpose in dangerous circumstances, and they are frequently associated with rebellion. On the other hand, blood oaths also carried the taint of barbarian license, or dark, dangerous heterodoxy."[28] The Shunde stele was about defending against such bandits and testifies to the potential dangerousness of these brotherhoods.

The stele's inscription ends with a long list of donors, a broad cross-section of trades people and scholars, testifying to the abilities of the local community to band together and call on resources outside the central government. Again, there is precedent for this type of local activism that included protection but was also in response to local feuds. In the past, Qing officials treated these feuds with leniency, often looking the other way, because they considered the situation a mechanism for a "balanced violence" that drained the resources of local rivals and enabled the population to be more easily governed.[29] However, in the 1840s, as a result of the escalation of fighting and general discontent, militia groups and local activism became part of an ongoing process of looking for alternative means of authority as government influence on local politics waned.

The Failure of Diplomacy

The Sanyuanli Incident was China's only success during the first Opium War, and that was achieved through local militia groups rather than through imperial guards. In 1842, China agreed to a peace treaty, fueling the sense of betrayal of the local communities and inciting xenophobic responses. The

Treaty of Nanjing included the abolition of the *hong* monopoly, a substantial indemnity, and the opening of the five ports that allowed foreign traders to set up a colonized enclave governed by laws from their home country. Local activism in and outside the city dominated the political affairs, as rumors and gossip of poor war strategies implemented by the Manchu officials fueled disillusion and placed the blame on the Qing throne.[30] Unofficial militias in rural areas attacked foreigners who dared to venture into the countryside, town dwellers mounted virulent proclamations, and mob gatherings became commonplace. The elite in Guangzhou held an assembly and set some rules for its defense against the British: Militia were to be hired, and households and shops had to protect themselves from fires and equip themselves with stones and other materials to counterattack any barbarian attempts to infiltrate the city.

Qiying was faced with a truculent Guangdong, a suspicious Beijing, and an impatient Great Britain. He had to keep the foreign plenipotentiaries happy and away from a Guangdong that rippled with anti-foreign sentiment and quickly erupted into violence.[31] Caught within all this, Qiying's approach focused largely on relationships with his foreign counterparts and on assuring the emperor of the

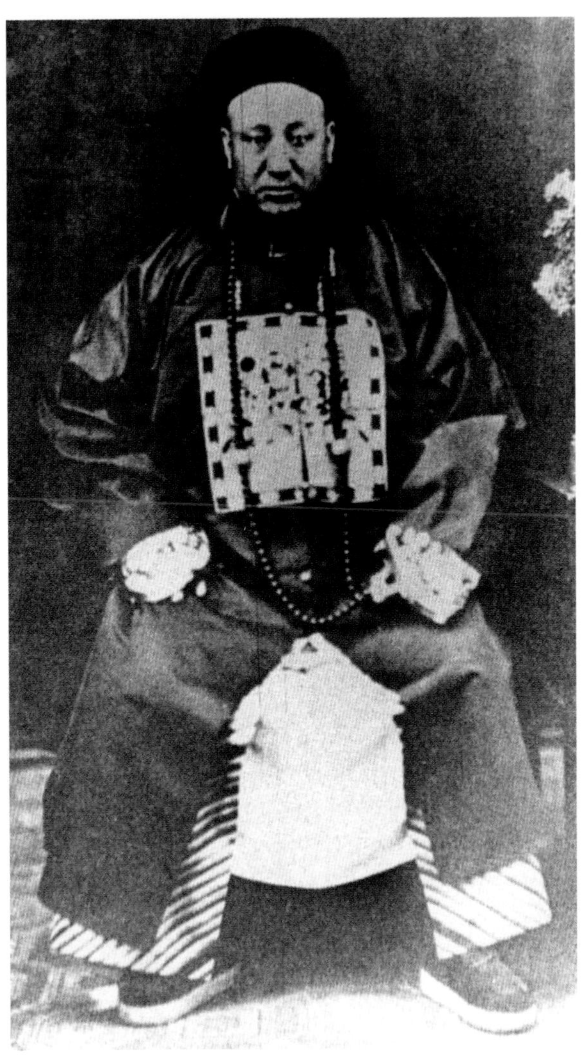

Figure 69 Jule Itier daguerreotype of Pan Shicheng, whereabouts unknown.

negotiation process. He did depend on a small team within the local community for support, including Pan Shicheng (潘仕成, 1804–73) (Fig. 69), a salt merchant who was related to the *hong* merchant and art collector Pan Zhengwei. The family's connections with the local and foreign communities placed him in a strong position to act as an advisor and help facilitate negotiations. Pan, like his cousin, was a collector of the arts, but was better known for his impressive library, which included translations of many Western medical books, geographies, and technology that reflected his interest in science and knowledge.

Large segments of the local scholars and officials, however, were distrustful of the new powers, especially with the removal of Lin Zexu from office. James Polachek has detailed the complex factions in the capital with networks that had led to shifts of power to Manchu politicians. Polachek has also shown how Lin continued to influence the local Guangdong community that sided with the Fujian official's arguments, particularly against Lin's first replacement, Qishan (who was later replaced by Qiying). The arguments against Qishan were for ceding too much, too quickly to the British and foreign powers. The provision for the permanent presence of foreigners in the city was strongly opposed by the Cantonese, and, as pointed out by Wakeman, the locals and officials were mutually alienated.

The relationships between the Manchu officials, their foreign counterparts, and the imperial courts were also precarious. Qiying's modus operandi was using an "appeasement policy"[32] with a twofold strategy: to impose acts of conviviality as a means of converting hostile impulses, and to maintain intimate relationships with envoys, whereby he could achieve a sort of personal ascendancy and therefore influence the course of their China policies. Qiying even transcribed the word "intimate" in Chinese: 因地密特 (yin-di-mi-te) to be used in his correspondence when addressing foreign dignitaries.[33] Another example of

his cultivation of friendship, which aped the practices of *hong* merchants, was to foster friendships through gifts, and in particular exchanging portrait gifts, with his foreign counterparts. This was a dangerous move, in part because portraits held different social capital: The importance of physiognomy meant that there were strict guidelines related to formal portraits, especially in their ritual use. Underscoring these guidelines is the relationship of realism between image and sitter. In certain situations, a portrait could be used to stand in place of the physical person and as such was a potent social tool (such as affirming familial hierarchy). If this is extended to the world of diplomatic exchanges, where the gifting of a portrait was always also a presentation of oneself, the potential ownership of the recipient of a part of the emperor or his representative was therefore a transgressive act. To counter charges of excessive gifts, Qiying places the blame on his foreign counterparts and reported to the emperor, in his memorials, that he did so only to make them think of him as a friend so that better terms could be achieved. This double dealing had dangerous consequences, not least because, from the perspective of the supporters of Lin and other Guangdong communities, Qiying was overly friendly and ceded too much to the West.[34]

It is clear that Qiying underestimated the resilience in Guangdong. In March 1847, tension brewed once more. During an outing near Foshan, six English hikers were stoned. When Qiying failed to punish the culprits, General d'Aguilar led a vicious attack on the Bogue Forts and threatened to enter the city forcibly. In response, the local elite gathered resources, forming protective militias to resist the British. This private police enterprise again demonstrated how quickly local leaders could mobilize mercenaries when needed. Qiying had to comply with an agreement that the British could enter the city after two years, during which time he would calm the xenophobes. However, in December, another six

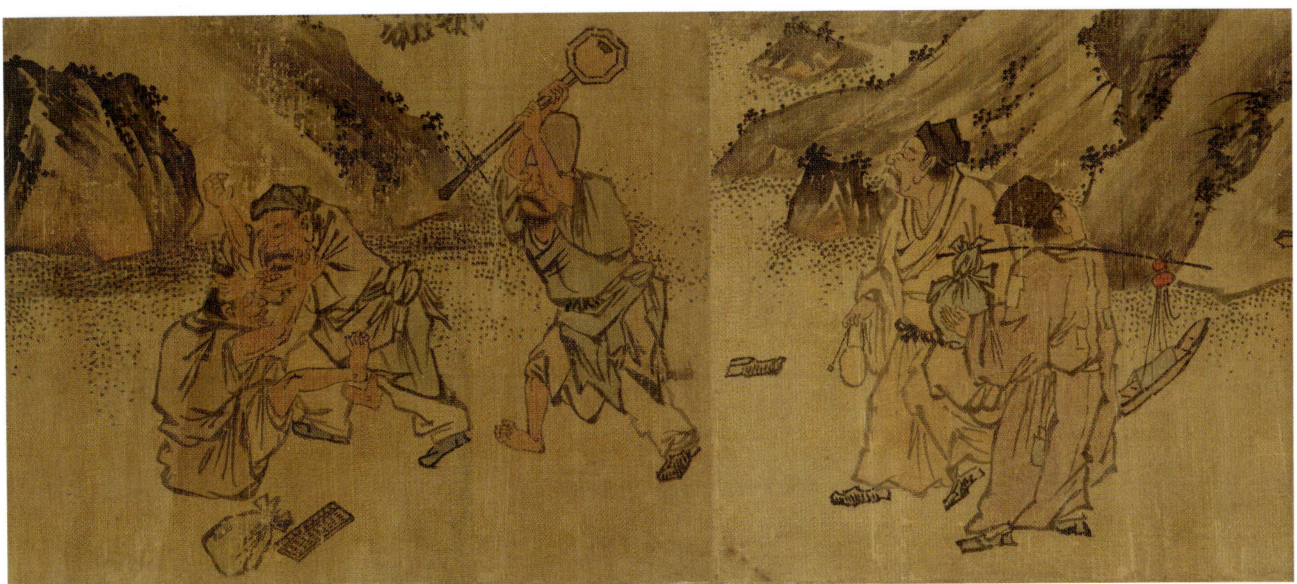

Figure 70   Wu Wei, *Strolling Village Entertainers*. Detail. Handscroll, ca. 1500, ink and color on silk. British Museum.

adventurous English hikers were killed, mutilated by swords during their jaunt though the suburbs. Fearing another Bogue disaster, Qiying beheaded four men, and fifteen others were arrested and tried. Again, this led to huge rifts between the local populace and the government as protests erupted. Placards denounced officials as traitors, crying: "Our cannibal mandarins have hitherto been the accomplices of the English robbers in all acts that the latter have committed against order and justice. For five years to come our nation will mourn the humiliation it has been forced to undergo."[35] This time, the emperor agreed that Qiying did not act in the interest of the people and sent a replacement. The failure of Qiying's reconciliation diplomacy was all the more poignant when, in the second Opium War, his memorial to the emperor, justifying his portrait gifts as necessary tokens to ameliorate the "pathetic barbarians," was uncovered and translated by the British. The embarrassment this caused led to his ritual suicide by strangulation.

Pictorial Responses to Violence

As a cultural expression of power and moral values, violence is generally absent in Chinese visual art. This is, in part, because militarism was largely insignificant to the male literati class, the cultural arbiters of arts.[36] In other arenas, images of violence were often "controlled" by restricting access to the images and displaced into the popular art realms of religious tales and fiction. For example, at court, paintings of sanctioned violence such as war scenes and military campaigns were commissioned as records celebrating the success of emperors and did not circulate outside the court. In the religious sphere, violence was displaced in the realm of Buddhist Hells or folklore and generalized as malevolent forces that needed protective talismans. In addition, illustrated images of fighting and violence celebrated the heroism of the knight-errant or showed the immoral adventures of bandits and robbers. As fiction, these images did not impinge on the values upheld by the socially

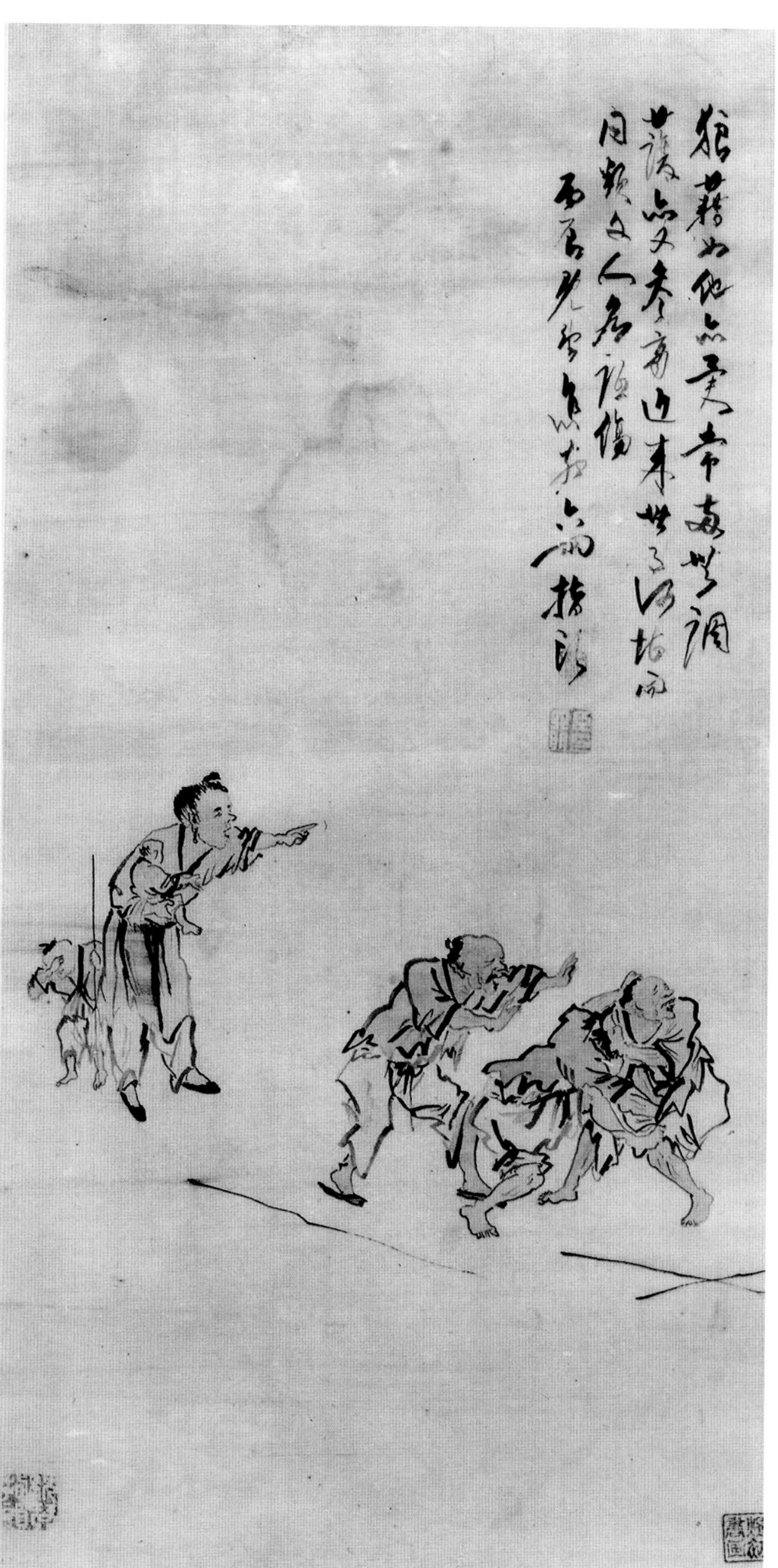

Figure 71 Su Liupeng, *Blind Men in a Fight*. Hanging scroll, dated 1856, ink and color on silk, 70 × 36 cm. Guangzhou Art Gallery, Guangzhou Art Museum. After Kao Mayching, ed., *The Art of Su Liupeng and Su Renshan*, Hong Kong and Guangzhou: Art Gallery, The Chinese University of Hong Kong and Guangzhou Art Gallery, 1990, 97.

differentiated world of the close iconic circuit that privileged a moral intellectual system that is extended to and reflected in the quality of the ink brush-trace. As printed works, such images operated outside the moral and social codes of ink painting.

The relative absence of violence in images does not imply that it was absent in the day-to-day world. Indeed, as Craig Clunas notes in his study on Ming art, in the elite world of literati ink painting, the consciousness of violence was repressed in the pictorial form, and the role of violence in the elite imagination was inversely proportional to reality.[37] There are some exceptions, such as a handscroll painting by the Ming artist Wu Wei (吳偉, 1459–1509) of a musicians' brawl in his *Strolling Village Entertainers* (Fig. 70). Clunas suggests that Wu Wei's background as a member of a military family (as opposed to a literary background where such a theme may be considered inappropriate) accounts for this exceptional representation. If this was the case in mid-Ming China, the historical context of similar paintings in mid-nineteenth century Guangdong suggests a different type of reading. The image of brawling villages as a form of social commentary takes on greater resonance under the brush of Su Liupeng. Su Liupeng, who often used blind men to speak of urban life and the corruption of merchants, depicted them in a fight, while a mother and her children stand in the distance and another man attempts to step in. The inscription on this 1856 hanging scroll painting, *Blind Men in a Fight* (Fig. 71), is revealing.

> They were different from the hoi polloi, but the two, without benevolent protection, became like Orion and Lucifer (opposing forces). What have you heard about the recent affairs of the world? Literary men of the same type slander and hurt each other. On the 16th of the lunar month, 1856, Shenshu depicted this with his fingers.

His inscription refers to literary men, but Su has depicted ordinary men who were blind.[38] The juxtaposition of different social classes within the painting alerts the viewer that this is no ordinary fight. Painted at a time when violence ravaged the country with rebellions and war, Su Liupeng's painting therefore has an added historical urgency. To follow Clunas's argument that social identities of the artist may determine the suitability of this type of subject matter, Su Liupeng was not a literatus (he did not take the civil examinations) and therefore could paint such a theme. To add to the argument, Su used the performative style of finger painting that further removed him from the values of a certain ink brush mode associated with the paragon literatus. Finger painting was popular in Guangdong by the region's association with the famous seventeenth-century finger painter and Han bannerman artist Gao Qipei (高奇佩, 1660–1734). First, Guangdong has a large concentration of bannermen military in the city that included members known for their paintings. Also, and more relevantly, in 1771, Gao's grandson, Gao Bing published *Zhitou huashuo* (On finger painting) in Guangdong and may have contributed to the circulation of Gao Qipei's paintings in the region.[39] It is no coincidence that, at this time, there was a flourish of finger painting by Guangdong artists that continued into the nineteenth century by artists such as Su Liupeng.[40] In his examination of Gao Qipei, Jonathan Hay points out how "the intensified physicality of finger painting resonated with the importance of martial values among the bannermen."[41] Given how the seventeenth-century painter was revered in Guangdong, it is possible that Su Liupeng chose to depict his fighting scene using his fingers to reference the martial quality associated with this mode of depiction.

If we are to follow this line of reasoning—that the depiction of violence was only possible for those who were either socially removed or used a style that positioned them outside the critical discourse of literary arts—the moral dimension of violence comes under scrutiny. Violence is related to anger and the cultivation of moral feelings, which are complex ideas pursued, since the very beginning, by Chinese philosophers who have tried to distinguish the various shades of anger, the acts that led to its expression, and its consequences. For example, the difference between *nu* (怒) and *fen* (忿), both translated as anger, is a difference of time, the latter being an emotional response that is sudden and short. Anger is also associated with other cognitive forms including resentment, disgrace, courage, and ethics. It is these associations that can render anger as either appropriate or inappropriate. Very broadly, according to the Song philosopher Zhu Xi (朱熹, 1130–1200), acts of violence are triggered by anger, which operates on two levels: violence pertaining to the physical body, and that directed by morality.[42] Moral anger is an emotional response to harm and injustice directed at others; this emotion is best expressed with a certain amount of detachment. Raw responsive anger, leading to a force exerted on a body, such as fisticuffs, was deemed unsuitable behavior for a gentleman. As such, the depiction of angry village brawls would position the artist as someone who did not uphold these values. However, it is much more complicated. As we have seen, the depiction of urban genre scenes was part of a growing interest in regional identity and urban cosmopolitanism, and street scenes of fighting fall into this category. It would have been difficult to verify whether Su Liupeng was using fight scenes to speak of social behaviors on the street, or whether he was making a reference to the social situation of postwar Guangdong, if it were not for his inscription. The inscription speaks of brothers from the same socially elite group fighting one another, thereby putting the issue of moral anger into precarious territory. In short, Su Liupeng is co-opting the theme of street fights to speak of, if not directly depict, behaviors that are outside the social norms. If we consider this painting alongside his album of

the opium addict, it reveals yet another image of an anxiety towards the fate of young scholarly men.

The lack of pictorial precedence of images of violence and anger makes a small body of works from Guangdong made between 1842 and 1850 all the more remarkable. A question that has to be asked, even if only speculatively, is: Why was it possible in mid-nineteenth century Guangdong to develop different type of images related to violence? What was different about the Opium War from earlier experiences, some arguably more catastrophic? One answer, touched on earlier, is that the Opium War only truly affected the southeastern regions, thereby increasing the growing animosity towards the state and outsiders in general. By considering the Opium War as a regional event, it may be possible to see how a collective form of trauma was formed as many who saw themselves as being abandoned or marginalized by a government who rallied with the foreign invaders. As such, this sense of being marginalized fueled their own particularly brand of heroism and loyalty. It is possible to see this period as an intensification of a regional identity that resisted the state in postwar Guangdong.

In looking at postwar representations, Cathy Caruth's groundbreaking writing on the psychoanalytic theory of trauma shows it is not the experience itself that produces the traumatic effect but rather the remembrance of it.[43] There is a period of latency when forgetting is characteristic between an event and the experience of trauma, and many art forms that are expressions of this type of trauma are often formed after the event. As a reflective process, trauma manifests itself in different types of narratives and representations that link the past to the present, but the gap between the experience and the memory of it is often manifested in stories that are incomplete, fragmented, or displaced but which nonetheless are understood, explained, and made coherent through sharing. Representations, through text and image, are forms of empathic witness that support the narration of the trauma to come and are part of the healing process of postwar experience. These aspects—fragmented narrative, delayed response, and the healing process—allow the affective dimensions of experience to find means of representation. More specific to this chapter, I will be looking at narratives formed after the war, which were centered on the possibility of defiance and martyrdom that, at the very least, hint at political action (even if none is taken), spurred by strong emotions, including anger. These narratives, told and retold, formed a sense of community, and in this instance of a Guangdong loyalty after the trauma of war.

Rania Huntington's work on writings on the Taiping Rebellion also provides a useful case study.[44] Looking at memory and the *biji* and *zhiguai* genre, Huntington considers how memories about the rebellion are recalled in genres in which it is not the primary subject. By looking outside the historical rationalization of this traumatic event, Huntington considers these more complex memories as a scar that "has the twin purposes of closing a wound and marking its presence, so the literary records of an age of chaos, recalled from an era of stability, have the same two functions. The stories both narrate disorder and ultimately attempt to restore order."[45] Huntington also shows how memories as a narrative device were effective means that not only recollected things past but also could be used to speak while in the midst of chaos. Looking at themes such as destiny, martyrdom, and haunting, Huntington investigates how memory worked at both the individual and collective levels by considering perspectives from the writer and the reader. The writings discussed fall within the gap between traditional and modern systems of history and imagination, and its own fragmentary nature also makes these types of text, however unwieldy, a type of raw voice

to be recovered. Following this argument, paintings, like the *biji* and the *zhiguai* genre, do not attempt to historicize the events or depict the objects of their fears. Instead, they too, from their vantage points, offer insights into the symptoms, the scars, of having experienced war and violence.

Paintings of Defiance

The difficulty of using paintings to respond to the growing tension in the city is most evident in ink painting that circulated within the elite scholarly world. The lack of a vocabulary—of motifs and style—that can equip them for the task, and the long-held belief that anger and violence were not responses that befitted a gentleman, made any possibility of a desire to use painting as an affective vehicle difficult if not impossible. Nonetheless, given the active role that scholars had in organizing militia groups and banning opium among their community members, it is not surprising that there were attempts, some not wholly successful, to develop means to overcome the limitations of the pictorial craft.

For Guangdong's educated elite, the threat of Western ships at their coastline was a daily reminder of their defeat and possible further loss of territory. Huang Peifang painted a pair of album leaves in the winter of 1848, but which was later viewed and inscribed on, including at a literary gathering to appreciate chrysanthemums in the tenth month of 1849. In 1848, Qiying had left Guangdong and was replaced by Xu Guangjin (徐廣縉, 1797–1869), who with Ye Mingchen were ardent anti-foreign officials. Instead of ceding to British demands of opening Guangdong at the agreed date of April 1849, Xu and Ye supported local militia rallies against the British from entering Guangdong. The juxtaposition of an elegant gathering to admire chrysanthemums and the sober reflections of the current situation has a longstanding tradition in Chinese texts. Inscriptions

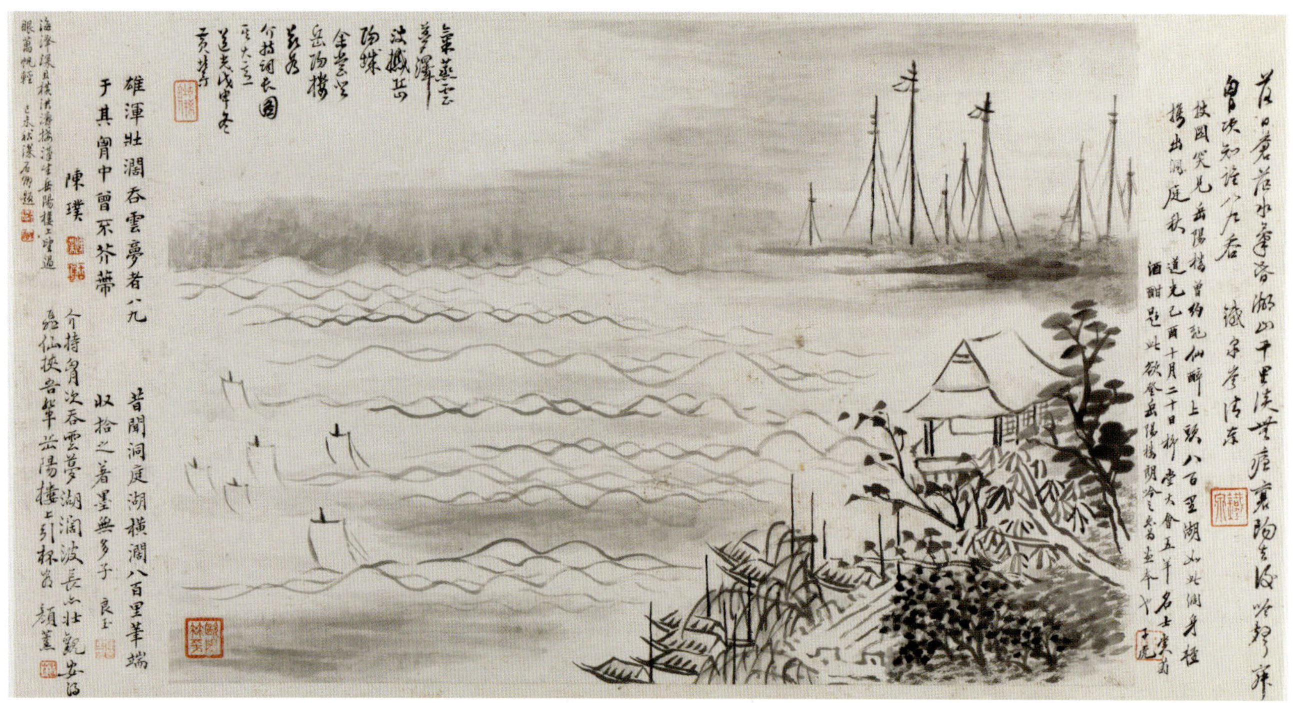

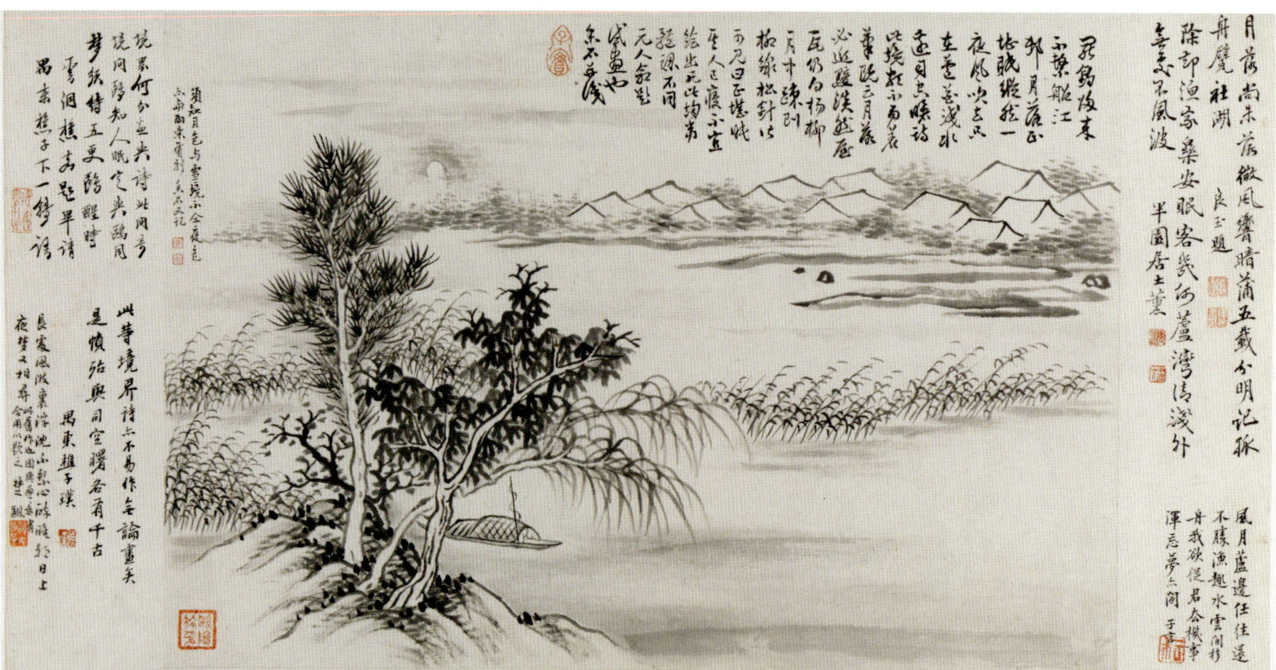

Figure 72 *(top)*   Huang Peifang, *Yuefang Tower*. Leaf one of a pair collected in an album of 6 leaves, earliest date on the pair of leaves is 1849, ink on paper, 30.5 × 58 cm. Hong Kong Museum of Art Collection.

Figure 73 *(bottom)*   Huang Peifang, *Yuefang Tower*. Leaf two of a pair collected in an album of 6 leaves, earliest date on the pair of leaves is 1849, ink on paper, 30.5 × 58 cm. Hong Kong Museum of Art Collection.

written in response surround the images and offer glimpses into the conversations shared among these men at the gathering. Huang's inscription recall poetic lines by Meng Haoran (孟浩然, 689–740), of misty vapors rising from the Yun and Meng Marshes, and waves crashing the city walls of Yueyang.[46] Meng's valiant image refers to Yueyang's history as a military base for boats during the Three Kingdoms. Meng's poem is often explained as reflecting his ambivalence about serving at court, and this appealed to later poets who had similar misgivings. His followers include Du Fu (杜甫, 712–70), who penned the poem "Ascending Yueyang Tower," but now refers to Lake Dongting from which Yueyang Tower overlooked. Here, Du Fu's ambivalence is also underscored by a melancholic reflection of the An Lushan Rebellion (ca. 703–57), and the chaos and lost opportunities thereafter. These poetic allusions were later appropriated by Song loyalists and, as seen here, continued in nineteenth-century Guangdong.[47]

As a pictorial device, the strategy of using history as a mirror for contemporary events, a type of double telling, was also a conventional approach of expressing the pain and anxiety of political chaos. This strategy communicates by the connotative (rather than descriptive), and seamlessly interweaves concepts of "history," "memory," and "imagination." Huang's pair

of album leaves offer two different scenes. One leaf depicts a lone skiff drifting at night (Fig. 72), and the other is of a sea view seen from Yueyang Tower (Fig. 73). The lone skiff on the lake, under the moon, is set apart from the city of rooftops, emphasizing the individual response, and one aligned to Du Fu and his line from "Ascending Yueyang Tower": "Old and sick, I have one solitary boat. War horses are riding north of the mountain pass, I lean on the rails as tears flow."[48]

In contrast to the sad stillness of the lone boat, a stormy sea with a group of Chinese boats, emphasizing the collective experience, is depicted on the accompanying leaf. The choppy waves enhance the sense of danger as they submerge the sails of the boats. A layer of ink-wash covers the scene and captures what one scholar at the gathering describes as "the heaviness of heart," but Huang was keen to make sure that readers understood his painting and explained that the wet ink did not depict mist or fog but was to capture *qi* (氣 energy). This is a painting of defiance, or, as Zhang Weiping, the elderly scholar who penned "Sanyuanli Ode" and who partook in the Chrysanthemum-viewing party, wrote: "In the past one heard the waves at Lake Dongting [where Du Fu composes his famous poem]. Today, we see the *qi* from Lake Dongting. This painting may be only a few

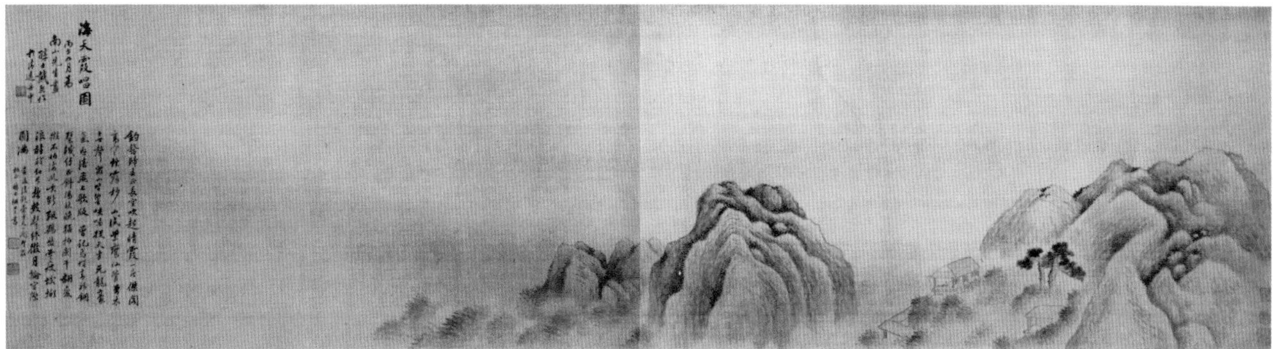

Figure 74 Dai Xi, *Singing in the Red Haze of an Ocean Sky*. Handscroll, 1846, ink and color on silk, 36.5 × 137.7 cm. Guangzhou Art Gallery, Guangzhou Art Museum. After Kao Mayching, ed., *Paintings of the Ming and Qing Dynasties from the Guangzhou Art Gallery*, c294–295.

feet tall, but its strength measures a thousand *li*." The difficulty of recognizing this transcendental power of energy in pictorial form required the depiction of the object of their defiance, here represented by the distinctive masts of European ships looming menacingly at the edge of the painting in the upper right corner. The illustration of the Western sails in a Chinese ink painting is an unexpected anomaly and breaks the boundaries of a time-honored visual rhetoric that seldom depicts the threat of violence.

The local scholars who gathered at Huang's home also had like-minded friends outside Guangdong. One such individual was Dai Xi, the official who penned the poem on opium addiction and who returned to Beijing after being promoted to vice-president of the Ministry of War. Nonetheless, he maintained a strong emotional bond with his friends in the south. In 1846, he painted a handscroll painting for his good friend Zhang Weiping, in which Dai reiterated the need for heroes and wise men to aid a country that was failing. In *Singing in the Red Haze of an Ocean Sky* (Fig. 74), Dai depicts a quiet landscape that opens with the scene of the upper rooms of a building nestled on top of a mountain range. The weightlessness of his brushwork is used to great effect as he depicts a mist that stretches across the expanse of the painting and ends with two upright pines painted in darker ink, the most distinct motifs among the haziness, making their presence deeply haunting. The painting refers to the friendship of the two men, the two pines (a common trope for friendships) and the tall pavilion a symbol, perhaps, of their Xuehaitang days. An expanse of mist stretches across the scroll, evoking the contemplative air of scholarly communion between two like-minded friends connected despite their geographical separation. Both the threat and the saviors are located on the borders, leaving a precarious uncertainty, captured by a landscape shrouded in mist. The mist is also, however, the

symbol of the awakening of heroes as evoked by the valiant tempo of Dai's inscription:

> They returned after fishing for turtles, the vast sky opens. In their wake, an expanse of red mist rises.
> A tall pavilion sits high on the mountain where misty smoke caresses the tips of trees.
> Light whispers of sound from the purple *luan* bird's immortal pipe; the wood is quiet, the myriad hills echo,
> [The tune sounded] like speech, a trail of words that fills the sky.
> The ferocious billows of waves, with the martial prowess of Yuanlong, leap forth from the pages of the song.
> I remembered wearing my blue-sleeved gown and black gauze silk hat, with a bronze *pipa* and iron clappers, playing as the descending sun's ray swept across the autumn evening.
> With vigor I clapped the railings of the balcony, turning my hands, changing the rhythm with clear tones.
> I was not afraid that the stormy sea and wind will disrupt my tune.
> Listening to the clapping of my clappers,
> A lone crane flies against the clouds and the *jiao*-dragons thrash against the waves.[49]

Dai Xi uses literary references to parallel contemporary events. The men who had been fishing for turtles are references from the Daoist classic *Liezi*, in which warrior-like men captured giant turtles to carry the five immortal mountains and prevent them from drifting to sea.[50] The tower where the pipes of the purple *luan* are heard refers to Xuehaitang: A path leading to the famous Yue King Terrace, near Xuehaitang, is named Huluan Way (Cries of the *luan* Path). Yuanlong, or Chen Deng (陳登, 170–208), was a famous strategist in the Eastern Han period known for outsmarting a larger force that had arrived by boats, gaining his title as the General Who Subdues Waves (伏波將軍). The *jiao*-dragon thrashing in the waves refers to mythical malevolent beings that are believed to be creatures of chaos in the south.[51] Dai Xi's use of different allusions adds drama to his heroic words backed by the iron clappers and the lute. They form a battle cry rallying the spirit of former heroes to subdue the creatures of chaos that circle the sea in the south.

The quiet landscape, in contrast to the upbeat tone of the inscription, feels disconnected, in part, because of Dai's conservative painting style, but he also exploits this "quietness" to engage his viewers in internalization and contemplation of the words. This creates a double narrative, one circling around the other, finding a meeting point in the mist—here, both a contemplative device and a red haze (as suggested in the title)—that acts as an atmospheric omen of defiance.

Painted in 1846, Dai Xi's scroll, showing the promise of returning heroes who can resist the dangers at the gate of the city, would have been welcomed by the recipient, Zhang Weiping, who was in Guangdong when he unrolled the scroll. Painted two years before Huang's album leaves, this handscroll is an earlier example of a landscape of defiance. It was also a prophetic omen: Between 1848 and 1849, the people in Guangzhou did precisely that and managed to hold off the opening of the city. Meanwhile, Dai Xi wrote, in a memorial to the emperor, an account of the British trying to force their way into the country, but his inflammatory narrative did not gain the approval of the emperor, and he was forced to retire. His commitment to his country was further tested when the rebellion army, the Taiping, grew in strength and penetrated farther north into the Jiangnan region. In 1860, the Taiping attacked Dai's home city, Hangzhou, and, in response, he committed suicide.[52]

The use of poems and narratives of the past to act as the vehicle of displaced emotions extends to the popular tales of bravery. In Su Liupeng's undated *Album of Figures*, the illustrative images capture pivotal moments in the narrative to focus on the act that transformed the everyday protagonists into cultural heroes. In each of the leaves, the backdrop of the story involves violent themes, also popular in novels at this time, of cannibalism, banditry, murder, and war, dramatizing contemporary events. The four leaves are also interconnected, creating an episodic progression of stories that depict increasingly extreme displays of loyalty. The first begins with the meeting of two arrogant men, a beggar and merchant, whose flawed characters led both to death. The second leaf, of sibling loyalty, shows two starving brothers caught by bandits but released after one offers his life in return for his brother's freedom. The third is of a filial daughter scolding a pirate for daring to capture her father; she kills herself as a demonstration of bravery and piety. Each of the first three narratives were common fodder for readers of popular illustrated novels, and all speak of violent deaths; however, the

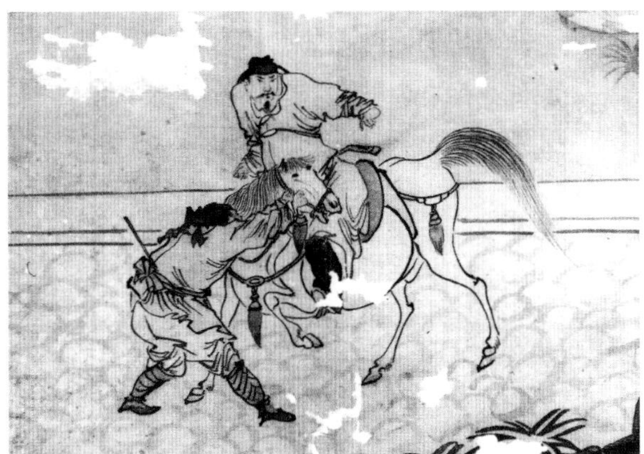

Figure 75   Su Liupeng, *Whipping the Horse to go to the Imperial Court*. One leaf from *Album of Figures* of four leaves, ink and color on silk, 30.5 × 52.3 cm. Detail. Guangzhou Art Gallery, Guangzhou Art Museum. After Kao Mayching, ed., *The Art of Su Liupeng and Su Renshan*, Hong Kong and Guangzhou: Art Gallery, The Chinese University of Hong Kong and Guangzhou Art Gallery, 1990, 73.

last leaf of the album indicates that Su Liupeng was also responding to a more current story that was circulating in Guangdong.

The last leaf (Fig. 75) refers to story of the Ming Emperor Jingtai (景泰, r. 1450–57), who wanted his son to be his successor, and not the heir apparent, the son of his brother. An unnamed Guangxi official who had killed his brother in order to achieve his official position sought to escape punishment by supporting the Ming Emperor's desire to displace the rightful heir. The Guangxi official sent a memorial suggesting that the heir apparent should be given a lesser position and that the emperor's son should be his legitimate successor. Zhong Tong (鍾同, dates unknown), an official of high moral standing, objected to the entire affair and went to court to challenge the memorial, knowing that his protest would lead to his death. Su Liupeng's inscription ends the story with "Before Tong was about to go to the imperial court, he went to prepare his horse, but the horse refused to get up. Tong scolded him saying: 'I am not afraid to die, so why are you doing this?' The horse untangled his legs, got up on all fours and together they left. When Tong died, his horse neighed several long wails and then died."

Continuing in the richly colored and detailed style, Su Liupeng celebrates the moral righteousness of Zhang Tong and, equally, the loyalty of Zhang's horse. The distressed horse is shown with a groom struggling to calm him, while the general sits precariously on his back. The entangled limbs convey the drama of the story, capturing the moment when Zhang was willing to face death and the emotional love and loyalty of a horse that feared the outcome. I believe this painting echoed an event that had prompted many literary works that were circulating in mid-nineteenth-century Guangdong.

General Chen Liansheng died in the twelfth month (January 1841), while fighting with the British. Many tributary works were composed by scholars,[53] including texts by Wang Zheng (王拯, 1815–76):

> When I went to Guangzhou, I heard the tragic stories of how General Guan Tianpei and General Chen Liansheng died. Later, Zhang Nanshan (Weiping) composed *Yima tu shice* 義馬圖詩冊 (Collected poems for the painting of the loyal horse) and recorded the woeful tale of General Chen . . . Chen had a horse that lamented his death. When the barbarians got hold of the horse, it refused to eat. The barbarians were angry with the horse and left it stranded on a barren island. A kind person brought it back. A painting was made and poems were composed to tell others of this affair.[54]

The painting and poems are now lost, but the many extant eulogies about the two generals indicate the veracity of Wang's comments. According to Wang Zheng, this story had circulated in Guangzhou, and it is likely that Su Liupeng would have known of it, not least because he was an acquaintance of the author of the collected stories of the loyal horse, *Yima tu shice*, Zhang Weiping, for whom he painted literary gatherings.[55] Su's album leaf can therefore be seen as part of a body of literary and pictorial memorials for a famous contemporary general and his horse.[56] This example shows another means by which stories were shared between groups of people: the widespread circulation of poems, narratives, and, now, paintings that eulogized the heroic action of a general. Unlike Dai Xi and Huang Peifang, who were recognized scholar official artists, Su Liupeng's social positioning may account for the different approach that referenced popular stories rather than poetic traditions and classical historical allusions. Nonetheless, Su's reference to General Chen does reveal how similar stories circulated in many literary forms and speak for collective experience. As such, it offers a glimpse of how different forms of the same story circulated, some crossing social classes and all circumventing the thorny relationship between representation of violence and the social positions of artists.

Of Beasts and Ghosts

Related to this corpus of artworks responding to the Opium War are images of beasts and ghosts from the *zhiguai* literature tradition. Throughout the 1840s, xenophobic protests came in strong waves. After rumors of the Treaty of Nanjing terms leaked to the public in 1842, a public meeting was held on December 2, during which fears of an immediate British intrusion into the city caused uproar among the elite who attended the meeting. These fears were also exacerbated by the untimely visit of British women for the first time in Guangzhou. The heated discussions did not reach any consensus, and government officials stepped in and banned public displays of placards and general meetings. The bans were short-lived. On January 14, 1846, Guangzhou's citizens again gathered to protest against entry. Placards announced that any barbarians would be killed and scorned the high officials:

> They do not reflect that the English barbarians (夷 *yi*) are born and grow up in wicked and noxious villages beyond the pale of civilization, have wolfish hearts and brutish faces, the looks of tiger and the suspicion of the fox, and that the cause of their not presuming to covet our Guangdong consists only in their not getting into the city to make enquiries respecting the true state of the country and hear the reports on affairs.[57]

The portrayal of the barbarians as having bestial physiognomy was not uncommon at this time. Wang Zhongyang (汪仲洋, *juren* 1801) described the British as having "the beak of a [hawk], the eyes of a cat, red beards and hair."[58] He continues to mock how the bandaged legs of foreigners made it impossible for them bend their knees and therefore they could not run.[59] This composite image of beast-like qualities comes from a long history of rhetoric that differentiates the "Chinese" from the "barbarian." Marc Abramson's work on cosmopolitan Tang China notes how physiognomy assisted the construction of the

non-Han as bestial, "for it asserted that animal-like features reflected a correspondingly animalistic nature and vice versa." An important physiognomy text completed shortly after the end of the Tang, *Mayi xiangfa* 麻衣相法 (The hemp-robed master's physiognomic techniques), explicitly states that people who look like animals will have a character and suffer a fate appropriate to their animal counterpart, using pigs and tigers as examples.[60] Moreover, he shows how widespread this type of association of beasts and foreigners was by looking at both popular and court circles.

Despite Confucian skepticism that criticized arguments for a relationship between outward appearances and inner nature, at times of civil unrest, such as during the An Lushan Rebellion (755–63), these bestial terms became more commonplace. As a type of discourse, images of animalistic foreigners on the frontier served as a means of dealing with ethnic differences during times of conflict. Then, as it was in mid-nineteenth century Guangdong, vehement words describing the British intruders as having "wolfish hearts and brutish faces, the looks of tigers, and the suspicion of foxes," was part of this longer tradition of portraying the foreign intruder.

The same qualities assigned as bestial can, however, be associated with imposing or heroic qualities when applied to a Han person. Therefore, the semantic mobility of words associated with terms referencing ethnic differences makes any discussions of "barbarian" a complex enterprise. For example, the poet Du Fu (who wrote of Yueyang Tower), in a poem entitled "Painted Hawk," wrote: "Body strains, its thoughts on the cunning hare, its deep eyes turn sidelong like a barbarian in despair."[61] The deep eyes is part of the making of an ethnic identity of non-Han, and in this instance the word for foreign person is *hu* (胡), a term used for foreigners from China's northwest borders. Early description of these areas often spoke of the hard life of the nomads and the terrain of their homelands. By extension, their physiognomy was adapted to their lifestyle: The deep, despairing eyes would scour the far-reaching desert and endless skies. In his analysis of Du Fu, Stephen Owen speaks of the poet's interest in the paradox of painting something lifelike on a two-dimensional surface, and the last line of this poem captures this idea with the rhetorical question: "When will it strike the common birds? Bloody feathers strewn across the weed-covered fields."[62] If Du Fu was pondering the ability to depict something lifelike, his description of the hunting hawk with its despairing eyes (愁胡) was aptly cited in an inscription on a painting of a hawk by the Ming Cantonese artist Lin Liang. Lin was a court artist known for his paintings of birds in the wilderness in their heroic might, which became metaphors for the emperor. How are we to understand a fifteenth-century use of bestial characteristics written by a ninth-century poet? Lin's citation has a double meaning of being both a reference to Du Fu's reflection on representations and to the might of a hunting hawk, whose frontier origins (胡 *hu*) as a form of barbarianism is neutered in this reframing. This cautionary example emphasizes the need to consider not only the social context of the painting but also the people involved in making and viewing the painting.

Lin Changyi (林昌彝, 1803–76), a Fujian native who is a relative of Lin Zexu, published a collection of poetry composed before and after the Opium War, primarily from Fuzhou scholars, in 1851. Given Fujian's close relationship with Guangdong, this collection is relevant to the discussion of regional responses to foreign forces. The collection is entitled *Sheyinglou shihua* (Poems and prose from the Tower of Shooting Hawks). In his preface, he explains the title of the book:

> There is a pavilion to the northeast of my study. It faces the Jicui Temple on the Back Rock Hill that is now the hiding place of a flock of hungry eagles. They have built their nests and reside in them since. Whenever I rest my eyes upon the spot, the sight of it disgusts and embitters me. My first impulse is to snatch my strong bow and shoot a deadly arrow at them. But alas! My dart will not be fatal, and I relinquish my purpose in despair! To console myself I have sketched a painting to which I have given the name "Shooting the Hawks and Chasing the Wolves." Hence I named my study the Tower of Shooting Hawks.[63]

Black Rock Hill was the location of an abandoned Buddhist Monastery, Shenguang Si, where the British consul gained residence within Fuzhou. In 1850, two Protestant missionaries sought to reside within the city. Protests broke out and demonstrators argued against any foreigners, other than the consuls, living in the city despite the terms of the treaty agreement. Violent opposition soon ensued, not least from Lin Zexu, who was back in Fujian. Eventually, the missionaries relinquished their right to stay at Shenguang Si and moved to another site on the mountain that had previously been used by the interpreters for the British. Lin's "Tower for Shooting Hawks" refers specifically to the British on Black Rock Hill and plays with the homophonic relationship between the character for "English" (英 *ying*) and the character for "Hawks" (鷹 *ying*).

Lin also painted a smaller scroll entitled *Shooting Hawks and Driving out Wolves*, adorned with many colophons and inscriptions, suggesting that his sentiments were shared by many of his friends. Among his friends was Wen Xun (溫訓, 1787–1857), a Hakka official scholar from Changle in east Guangdong and a former co-director of Xuehaitang. Wen, in response to the painting, inscribed the following poem:

> I have heard that to shoot hawks from a high wall requires exceptional skills. The sea hawks, how they twist and soar to the extreme! The white feathers from the bow lift high and are released. A rain of blood, a wind of hair and feathers scattered down across the ground. The claws and the beaks are as uncompromising as unyielding metal. From hereafter, Heaven and Earth calm

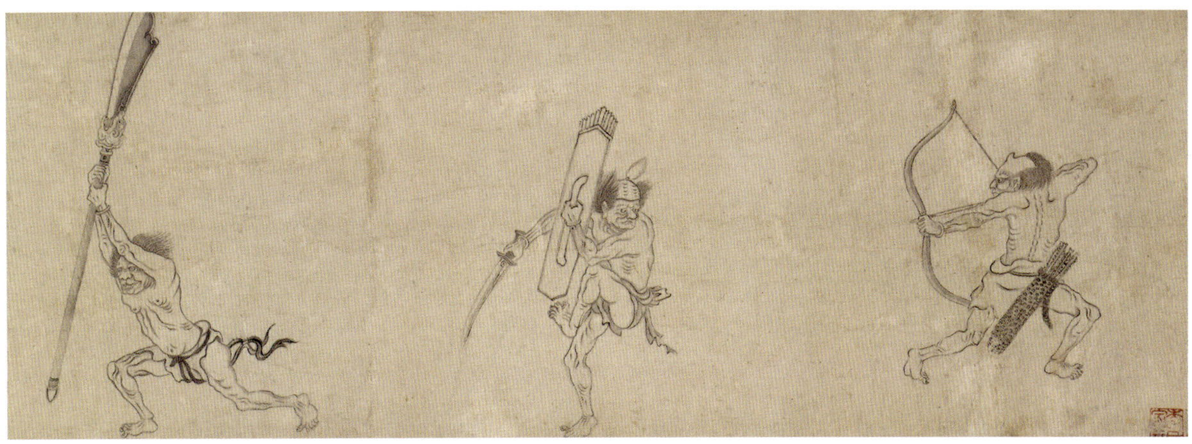

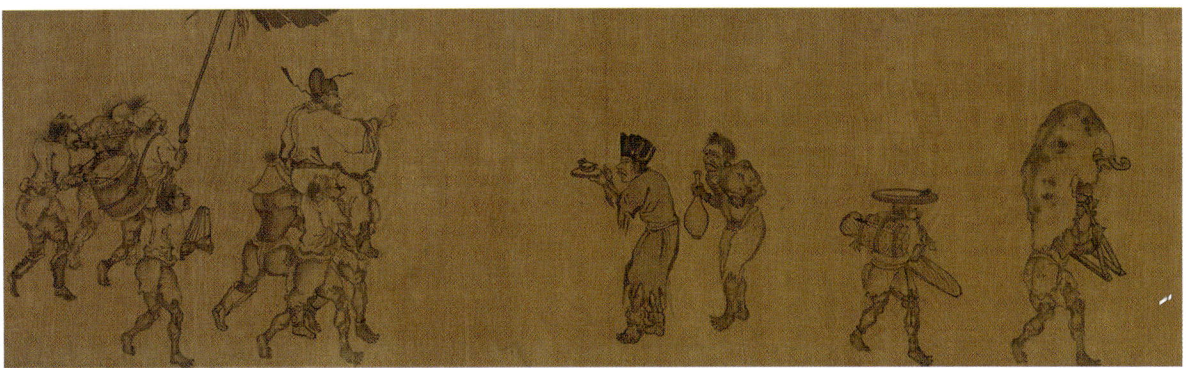

Figure 76 *(top)* Zhang Mu, *Zhong Kui Goes Hunting*. Handscroll, dated 1673, ink on paper, 28.5 × 481.5 cm. Hong Kong Museum of Art Collection.

Figure 77 *(bottom)* Yan Hui, *Night Revels of Zhong Kui* (or Lantern Night Excursion of Zhong Kui). Handscroll, ca. 1300–50, ink and light color on silk, 24.8 × 240.3 cm. Cleveland Museum of Art (1980.12).

the ominous atmosphere. Above the tower, a shadow of a bow is cast on the sea; it has subdued the barbarian hawk with its eyes of despair by drawing its bow into the evening clouds.[64]

In this ominous poem, there are two types of hawks. The "barbarian hawk with its eyes of despair" refers to Du Fu's poem, but it no longer refers to foreigners from the northwest; it does draw on the poetic conventions of bestial frontier. In contrast, the sea hawk (or arrow) is praised for its unyielding strength, and its imagery is sharpened by the description of whiteness as it pierces through the evening clouds.

The two paintings, however, survive only in textual sources. Nonetheless, the theme of hunting as political resistance echoes earlier works by the Guangdong

Ming Loyalist painter Zhang Mu (張穆, 1607–83). Zhang Mu was known for his skill at riding horses and at using swords. When the Ming fell, he and his friend, the Southern Ming martyr Zhang Jiayu (張甲玉, dates unknown) recruited soldiers in Huizhou and Chaozhou to fight back the Manchu invaders.[65] Their ambitious plan soon crumbled, Zhang Jiayu was killed, and Zhang Mu returned to his home in Dongguan and dedicated his life to painting. He became known for his painting of wild animals, and admirers spoke of the humanlike quality of his representations of birds and beasts, for which he was extolled as a superior artist. Among his large body of works are handscroll paintings of hunting scenes such as *Hunting Deer* and *Zhong Kui Goes Hunting* (Fig. 76), both in the Xubaizhai Collection.

Surprisingly, few of Zhang Mu's paintings bear inscriptions with political allusions, and his writings can be oblique in talking about the tragic events in early Qing Guangdong. However, the seventeenth century was a precarious time to be a loyalist in the southeast region, and Guangdong, as the last stronghold of Ming loyalists, suffered violent reprimands from the Manchu court, including a five-day massacre in 1650 that made many wary of further direct confrontation although ties to Taiwan and Ming resistance continued. Nonetheless, Zhang's paintings suggest that he was aware of the potential of hunting images as a *yimin* statement, even if there are no direct references. For example, in *Zhong Kui Goes Hunting*, Zhang cites the famous Song *yimin* artist Qian Xuan (錢選, 1235–1305) as an influence. Zhang's painting, however, bears greater similarities to another Song loyalist artwork by Yan Hui (顏輝, act. ca. late thirteenth century), whose *Lantern Night Excursion of Zhong Kui* (Fig. 77) was considered by its contemporary viewers as a political response to the demise of the Song under the Mongols. In both these earlier paintings, the ethnic tension between Song loyalists and Yuan Mongol rule was readily transferred into the realm of demons. It appeared to have been used in the Ming and Qing transition by Zhang Mu, and I will argue that another dimension of this theme can be seen during the time of the Opium War.

Ethnic tension in the mid-nineteenth century was exacerbated during the writing of the treaties when the British refused to have the word *yi* (夷 barbarian) used in legal documents because of its barbarian connotations. Lydia Liu has shown that this point of negotiation, centered on translation, underscored the clashing of signs of sovereignty. Despite the semantic range of *yi*, it was deemed at this time by the British negotiators and their team that *yi* meant "barbarian"

and was part of the arrogant sinocentric world of the Chinese who perceived all those beyond the Middle Kingdom as being inferior.[66] By winning the Opium War, the British had adequate grounds to ban that word in diplomatic language between the two nations, and eventually by 1858, in Article 51 in the Treaty of Tianjin, the word *yi* was forbidden.

A counterpart to the word *"yi"* was the more popular character *gui* (鬼 ghost/devil) which had a broad semantic range in Guangdong; the eighteenth-century novel *Shenlouzhi* uses the term intermittently with *yang* (ocean). Similarly, in the arts world, popular New Year images of Zhong Kui (鍾馗) (Fig. 78), the demon-queller, as a foreigner, blurred the symbol of auspicious wealth with ethnicity. The use of *gui* as a type of racial slur with political potency appeared to have gained traction only after the 1841 Sanyuanli Incident.[67] In the Chinese accounts, this event was mythologized as a great victory and spurred numerous victory-style poems and chants. Its memorialization in poems, popular chants, and stories made it a powerful symbol of both the elite and the grassroots. As Lydia Liu suggests, the popularity of *gui* and *fangui* can be seen in contrast and as a response to the diplomatic discussion of *yi* and again registers the importance of drawing on the vernacular as a form of protest.

The foreign community in Guangzhou was also well aware of the growing spread of the term *fangui*, as testified by a report in the local newspaper, the *Chinese Repository*, which explained, "*Fan* was a term given to the petty groveling island savages living in the southern ocean… when foreigners first came to the shores of China, their close fitting dress, their squeaking shoes and cocked hats, their blue eyes and red hair, their swords, their unintelligible talk, their overbearing carriage, and the roaring guns of their ships, all astonished people who exclaimed 'Kwei! Kwei!' Thus the term came to use… the term is, however, the only one in common use among the people in this region to denote foreigners, yet if the people entertaining any particular respect for us, they would soon use a better term."[68]

The regional use of the term *gui*, which was negative at this time and understood as such, pushes a familiar subject of *gui* into the unfamiliar territory of a collective form of xenophobia and fear in texts, and more tentatively in the pictorial arts. An example can be seen by a poetic response by Pan Shicheng, using a famous painting in his collection, to speak of the foreign traders, after he became disillusioned by events. This change of heart is particularly poignant,

as Pan Shicheng played a very active role during the treaty negotiations. The painting in question is *Guiqu tu* (鬼趣圖 Ghost amusement scroll, Fig. 79) by the Yangzhou eccentric artist, Luo Ping (羅聘, 1733–66). It was Pan's prized possession, and he continued the tradition of inviting famous scholars to view and inscribe the scroll. The inscriptions are as important as the painting and form a larger portion of the scroll. They offer an extensive history of the painting's transmission over the years and a list of famous scholars, including the influential Weng Fanggang.

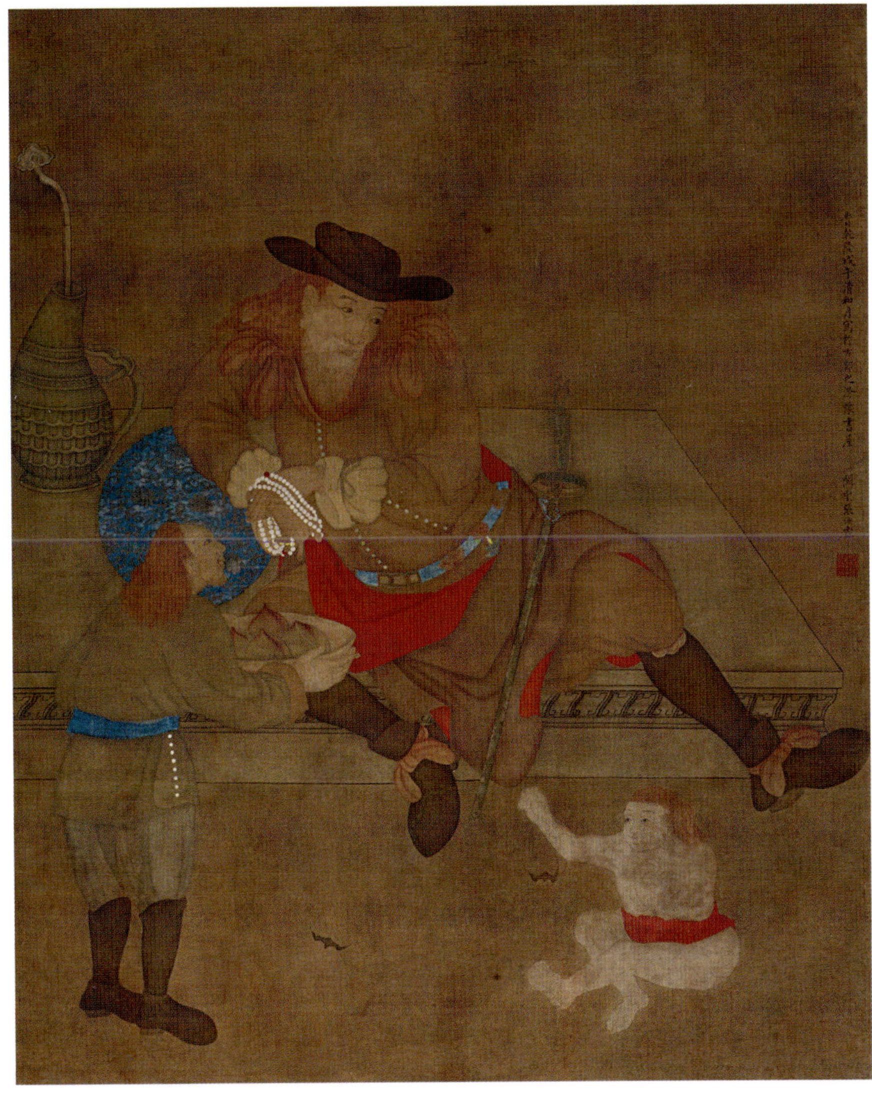

Figure 78 Anon., *New Year Painting of Zhong Kui*. Hanging scroll, 1738, ink and color on silk. Rijksmuseum, Amsterdam.

In 1851, Pan Shicheng wrote the first manuscript of the painting's colophons, *Inscriptions from the Guiqu tu,* to which he added his own preface and postscript.[69] The manuscript followed earlier examples of documents extolling the historical and aesthetic significance of the artwork, and, in his preface, Pan rejoiced in his good fortune at finding the painting. In the postscript, however, he penned a long and powerful poem entitled "Writings to Curse Ghosts." The title alludes to the Han Dynasty poet Wang Yanshou (王延壽, ca. 124–48) and his famous poem "Nightmare." Wang claimed to have collected certain demon-cursing writings and, through their incantations, he was able to expel the aura of spectral influences lingering around a person who had experienced a bad dream. Pan evoked his own incantations to dispel the demons haunting his world:

> [I have] also heard of ghost worlds at the four frontiers, where the people roam at night and hide during the day. At the extreme, they are

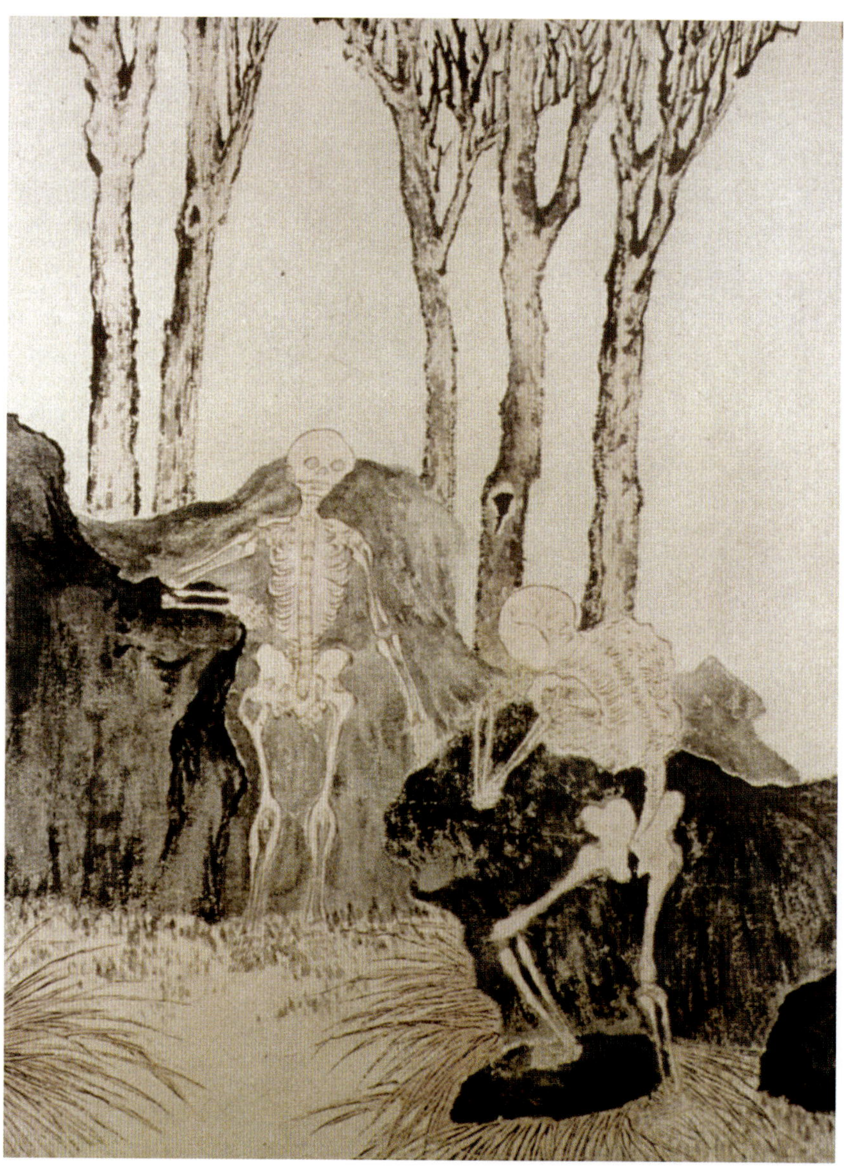

Figure 79 Luo Ping, *Guiqu tu.* Detail. Pair of handscrolls with paintings and colophons, undated, ink and color on paper, 35 × 1500 cm, 35.5 × 1000 cm. Resell Fok Family Collection.

like Ye Cha and Luo Cha in their ghostly caves. These ghosts are not ghosts, and they come from ten thousand *li* across many oceans. When the ghosts first came to set up their ghost markets, their assortment of wares dazzled our eyes and ears. With valuables on the one side and fire on the other, they went upriver and downriver. Bales of cloth were transported using carts and boats. With the changing of the winds, their steam-powered ships sailed away in haste . . .

The slanderous ghost and the flattering ghost—they rape with force; the poor ghost and the hungry ghost—their teeth gnaw [at us] on behalf of the ghost commissioner. The superiors do not believe in the principles of Heaven; those below them do not have the principles of men. Now we realize that these non-ghosts are ghosts [all the same]. We call them ghosts on account of their lies.[70]

Pan's angry poem made no attempt to hide the contempt felt for the "ghosts." This angry and bitter poem sharply veers from the image of a semi-diplomat who opened his home to the political representatives of France and the United States. Here, Pan's poem is the more powerful because of the vehement range of how he used the term ghosts to portray the foreign traders as deceivers who raped the country with their greed and cunning. He taps into a folkloric imagination using vernacular terms and images of Buddhist ghosts that raped, bit, and lied, and echoed the grassroots resistance of placards and demonstrations.

Pan's lament is also structured as a magical chant used to dispel "fright," a practice usually associated with popular Daoist rituals to dispel evil forces.

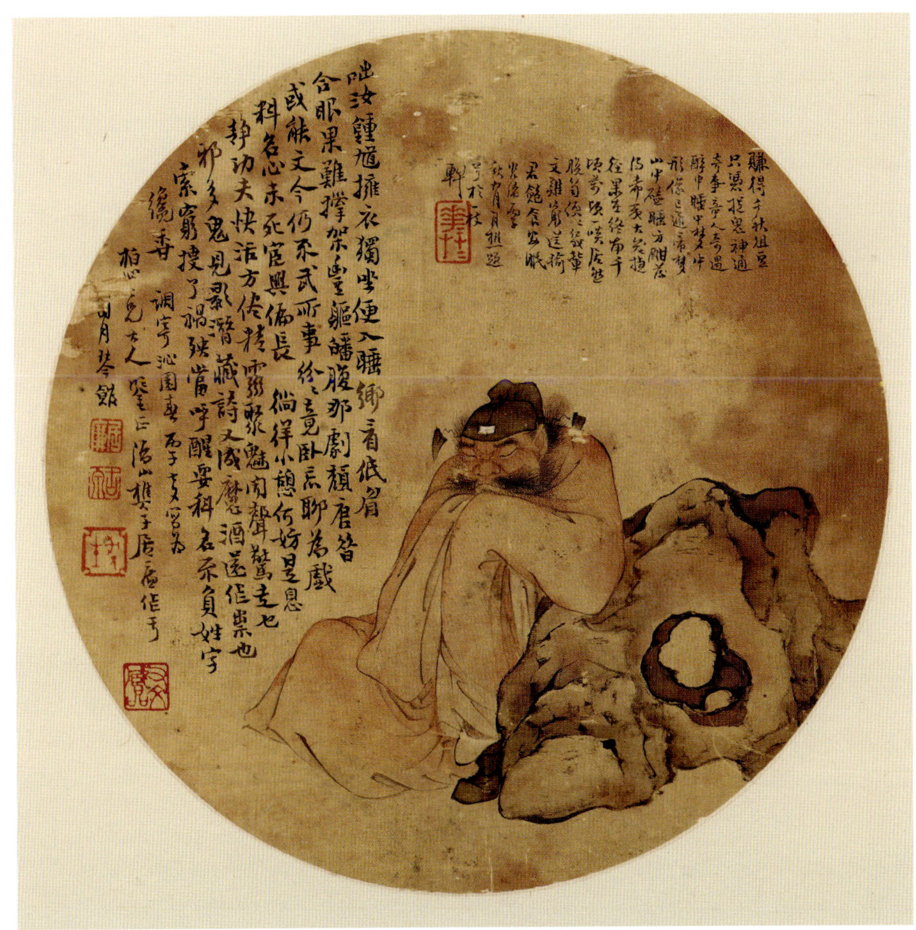

Figure 80 Ju Lian, *Sleeping Zhong Kui*. Fan or round album leave, 1876, ink and color on silk, diameter 26 cm. Reproduced by permission of the Art Museum of the Chinese University of Hong Kong from the collection of the Art Museum.

Suffering from "fright" is also a pathology that links the physical body with emotions and is a disease that is often associated with, but not limited to, children's health.[71] Pan's use of Wang Yanshou's exorcism poem links his work to a literary past and proposes a way to heal the country that has become ill by suffering from "fright." One of the early anecdotes about Zhong Kui's origins is that he was a failed martial examination student who committed suicide because he could not serve the emperor. However, the emperor, suffering from an illness that no doctors could cure, had terrible nightmares (a symptom of someone who suffered "fright").[72] One night in his dream he saw Zhong Kui appear, killing the demons in the emperor's nightmare. After quelling the demons, Zhong Kui declared that he was a loyal subject of the emperor. On waking up, the emperor honored Zhong Kui with a posthumous title. Pan must have been aware of this popular anecdote because his evocation of a magical chant to end nightmares corresponds with this reading of Zhong Kui as a protector who hunts in dreams.

Pan's poem shifts our reading of Luo Ping's handscroll, which is now seen within a political reading against the British who were once more threatening the shores in 1851, when the poem was written. This reading does not negate the other interpretations of Luo Ping's handscroll and, more importantly, it shows how a painting can take multiple social and political meanings at different points in history. In this instance, it adds a regional and folk dimension to the call for martial rebirth, a theme that we have seen in Huang Peifang's album and in Dai Xi's handscroll of a defiant *qi*. Here, the narrative integrates local practices and folk origin stories with references to a literary past and offers an example of this larger realm of collective memory-making that blurs the line between social classes.

Similarly, the line between linguistic charms and pictorial arts was also blurred, as local artists made paintings of Zhong Kui, in square format that echoes the shapes of talismans that were often pasted on doors and walls. The artist Ju Lian, a younger cousin to Ju Chao, who had depicted the images of actors, executed numerous paintings of the demon-queller after Luo Ping. He takes on Luo Ping's drunken demon-queller, a theme that was supposedly invented by Luo's teacher, Jin Nong. In the eighteenth century, the drunken demon-queller evoked earlier representation of untrammeled scholars and immortals, such as the Seven Sages of the Bamboo Grove, and was a popular figure in the arts. As such, and this can be no more than speculative, Ju Lian's decision to depict a Zhong Kui after Luo Ping (as opposed to any other artists) raises the question of whether Ju was aware of Pan Shicheng's "Writings to Curse Ghosts." One of Ju's patrons was Li Bingshou, a Jiangxi native based in Guangxi and known for his calligraphy, connoisseurship and his garden. Li was a friend of Zhang Weiping, who went to Guilin to visit him, and it is also likely that Li knew members of the Pan family given their shared interest and connections to Zhang. Given these connections, it is possible that Ju Lian would have known of Pan Shicheng's poem written in response to *Guiqu tu*, which was very famous in Guangdong, and Luo Ping's paintings of Zhong Kui.

In Ju's *Sleeping Zhong Kui*, dated 1876 (Fig. 80), Zhong Kui is now sleeping, not in drunken stupor but to re-energize in order to take up the sword and regain his earlier position as a martial official. In Ju Lian's fan painting of a sleeping demon-queller, intermingling classical Chinese with the Cantonese vernacular, Ju suggests that it was in a dream state that the malevolent specters could be expelled. He writes:

> In the past, it may be that [Zhong Kui] was capable of literary skills. Today, he still does not possess martial skills. In the end, the confusion of affairs can be forgotten in sleep. For war, to make sure that our destinies and hearts never die, the officials' provocation is lengthy. [However] with a quick nap, we can stop wavering. It is in rest

and peace that martial strength can be quickly regained. We depend on our energy to capture the ghosts, and when they hear us, they shall flee. Whatever evil, however many ghosts, we'll see their forms dissipate and vanish.[73]

The inscription tackles the problems of the martial qualities of China's official elite by referencing the iconographic properties of Zhong Kui, whose earlier transformation into a literary figure forced his military might to lay dormant. But, as with Pan's evocation of Wang's "Nightmare," Ju also uses sleep and dreams as a transformative trope that can rouse people into action and drive out ghosts. Thus, the drunken scholarly Zhong Kui theme is charged with the promise of martial rebirth. Ju Lian, like Pan Shicheng, was using the rhetorical tropes of marginalization—vernacular speech, popular myths, and eccentric art—to establish a collective identity at a time when boundaries were being threatened. By restoring Zhong Kui with martial strength to confront "ghosts," the demon-queller gains another layer of meaning as protector of the country. The new, reinvigorated Zhong Kui will become more popular in late-nineteenth-century Shanghai, brandishing his sword with the swagger of a knight-errant, as protector of the nation. For now, in mid-nineteenth-century Guangdong, he re-emerges as a symbol, a myth of a man that permitted the utterance of things that were otherwise inexpressible: the defiant hero who appealed to all classes, and, more importantly, exorcised the phantomic powers of foreign danger that lurked in dark shadows of fear.

◆◆◆

In trauma theory, memory acts as a form of narrative recovery. Often fragmented, it provides glimpses, impressions, effects, and other intangible qualities at both individual and collective levels, but these recollections also reveal much about the unspeakable nature of trauma. As such, those who witnessed such an event often use different modes of revelation, including paintings, to speak of the unspeakable. Huntington's work on Taiping *biji* concurs with such an analysis and uses the trope of scar and ghosts to talk about the various frameworks used and the effects of such works. But looking at Chinese art through the lens of trauma can also be frustrating as it rests too much on the idea of the unspeakable as a psychological condition. My own findings suggest that the unspeakable in mid-nineteenth-century Guangdong was also conditioned by the social practice of art itself and its influence on what can or should be made. While the social status of artists, as seen in Chapter One, is always relative, what does the role of art have, if any, in Guangzhou where local elites have been working towards establishing a regional scholarly identity and depended on the rhetoric and ideals of a literatus gentleman? More simply, what happens when the depiction of violence is socially conditioned and its depiction can be deemed too transgressive? I have argued that one way around this is to create intangible spaces that speak of the potential of acting, rather than the act of violence itself; in other words, to speak of what can be done, even as artists draw on themes of memory through recollections of former times. It is in this collapsed time-space where the future and the past converged in the present that themes of defiance become a powerful tool. The blurring of the present time is inevitable because, unlike dynastic transitions where there is a before-and-after that allows memories to take form, the artists discussed continued to live in an age of chaos (to borrow Huntington's useful phrase). They actively sought a "cure" to restore order by renewing an inner energy that was able to purge their land of foreign invaders. Defiance should also be seen not only as an act but also as a mechanism that allowed them to speak at a collective level with a regional dimension and as a personal response to the changes taking place. It is, however, only one possible route and as we see in the following chapters, for an artist such as Su Renshan, whose frustrations were directed at the social conditions of being an artist at this juncture in time, different approaches were also being explored. The mid-nineteenth century marks the beginning of a momentum in art that radically see the possibility of defiance, of the renewal of a martial force, and, as we shall see, of breaking with the values of scholarly ink painting that paved the way for modern Chinese ink painting.

Chapter Four

Su Renshan: Politicizing the Vernacular

If Guangzhou-based artists were beginning to respond to the political situation through pictorial depictions with an emerging theme of defiance, a second type of response could be mapped outside the immediate circles of the city based elite. Returning to Su Renshan, we see how he forms alternative responses to the war by focusing on the failures of the government to protect the people rather than the subject of foreign invaders. At the heart of Su's cathartic reasoning was the problem of violence itself, or how violence begets violence. His logic was this: The moral and pedagogical backbone of Confucian institutions reinforced canonical writings that, in his eyes, served little purpose and, arguably, endorsed a hypocrisy that has slowly damaged the country by sanctioning violence as a legitimate method of rulership.

Su formulates his arguments with investigations of older texts and historical figures (often loosely tied together) and conflates them in a manner that creates an alternative space that indirectly talks of the present. By attacking canonical histories in his inscriptions, his revised interpretations of the past pinpointed areas of dispute. Su's critiques of Confucius and Confucian learning, and in particular the civil examinations, echoes earlier eighteenth-century scholars, but they also differ for two main reasons. First, the historical circumstances provide a political urgency to Su's attacks, and secondly, Su extends his argument into the pictorial realm by overturning the representational system associated with elite practices and undercuts the social values associated with certain brushworks, motifs and compositions. Moreover, I would argue that there is a rawness of emotions in his paintings that can be described, and at times only, as violent. If notions of anger can be differentiated into two types—one that is raw and directed at the physical body and the second of a detached moral response—Su's paintings arguably straddle the two. Although Su's arguments rest on a moral anger and do not depict acts of violence, his markings and compositions have an unusual somatic quality. This is perhaps not a surprising path, and possibly an inevitable one. Given that the social positioning of the artist is a crucial element in determining whether the subject of violence is appropriate, and that Su, as seen in Chapter Two, placed himself as an insider on the outside, he was, as a contrary character, suitably placed to be transgressive. He could, and did, express anger in his painting and in a manner mediated through his interest in literary markings and revised histories. It is my contention that more than any other artist, Su demonstrates how violence in paintings is not only an act in itself, but also a performative display of destruction.

In 1842, Su was at a different stage in his life: He had left home after abandoning his pursuit of an official career. His experience of the war would have been different from that of other artists in the city and his personal life may also have shaped his responses. Certainly, his disillusion with familial expectations and social mores must be taken into account in

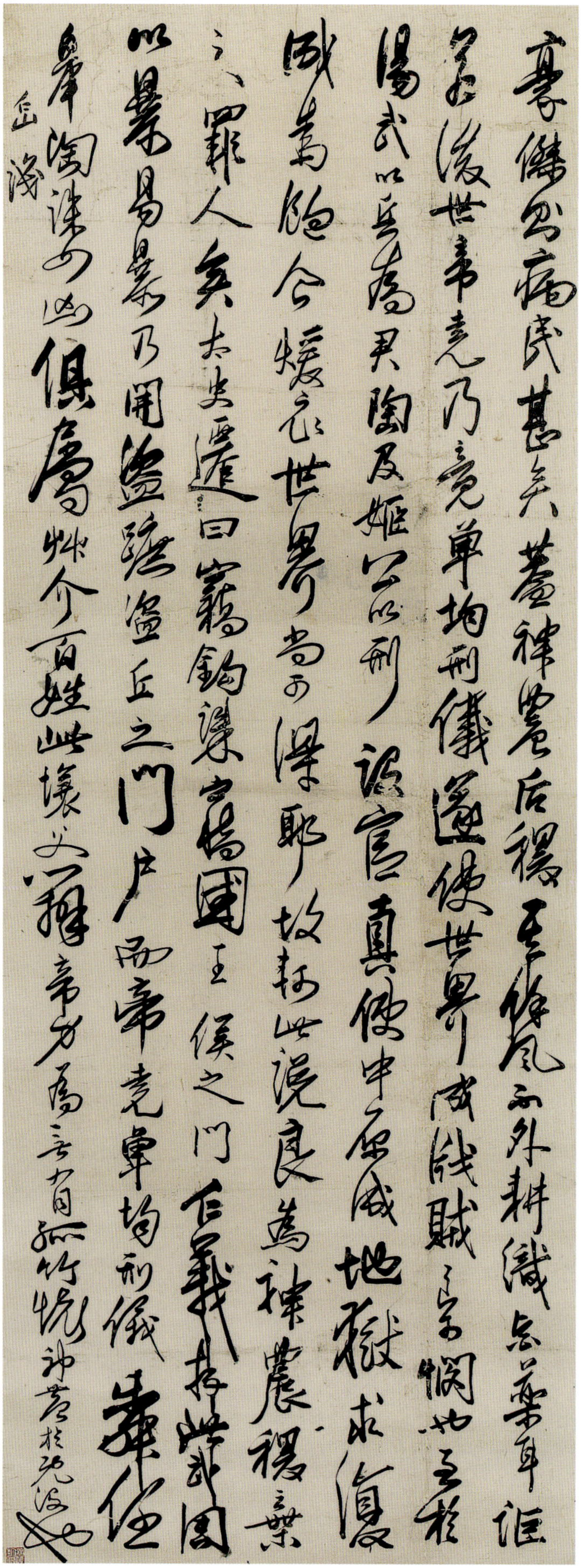

Figure 81 Su Renshan, *Calligraphy*. Hanging scroll, undated, ink on paper, 166 × 62 cm. Reproduced by permission of the Art Museum of the Chinese University of Hong Kong from the collection of the Art Museum.

his criticism of Confucian institutions and formal learning as inadequate instructors. Su frames his disillusion by directing his frustrations with the moral and intellectual backbone of Confucian learning and constructing two primary themes: the problems of heroes, and the relationship between order and chaos. I will examine this intersection of history and biography where Su's approach of the literary vernacular gains momentum as a political force. In the unfolding of this and the following chapter, Su's disruptive and doubled-edged gestures provide a parallel argument of narratives of trauma discussed so far. More poignantly, the palpable physicality of Su Renshan's brushwork and his open discontent may well have led to his undoing as he ends his painterly life in prison.

Paragons and Heroes

For Su Renshan, the traditional hero celebrated in poems, prose, and art fostered warped ideals. What if, Su asked, the paragons of the past had erred by endorsing violence and implementing their actions as law? Was this what the mythical rulers of the past had intended? In a compelling calligraphic piece (Fig. 81), Su laments how histories celebrate false paragons:

> Heroes! They are detrimental to the well-being of the people! Now, the legacies of [the cultural heroes] Shennong [神農] and Houyi [后稷] were none other than the knowledge of farming, sericulture and medicine. Who would have thought that Emperor Yao [堯] would single-handedly enforce a system of discipline and punishment that would force the world to violence? How mournful indeed! Tang [湯 of Shang] and Wu [吳 of Zhou] used weapons to gain their crowns. They provided the model for Duke Ji [姬, Duke of Zhou] who used punishment to establish official authority. They transformed the Central Plains into Hell. How can one seek to return to a world where there was enough to eat and warm clothes to wear. Therefore, Mencius said this: The good

> resided in Shennong; when Duke Ji abandoned [Shennong's way], he became a criminal.[1] Sima Qian said that he who steals a belt buckle pays with his life, but he who steals a state becomes a ruler. Humanity and righteousness reside in this.[2] Wu of Zhou used violence and begat violence. He opened the gates to Robber Zhi and Robber Qiu. Yao single-handedly enforced punishment and Shun bestowed power on Yu to kill all four evils. In all these cases, the people were treated like trifling dregs. The difference between the power of a father and the emperor is little. This is why the elderly man Rangfu [壤父] considered the emperor as having no real power, and Guzhu [孤竹] lamented the demise of Shennong.[3] Inscribed by Renshan.[4]

This calligraphy piece reframes historical accounts as a succession of sanctioned violent events that have turned the country (Central Plains) into Hell. The legendary Emperors Yao, Tang, and Wu are considered to be exemplars for all later emperors but are here criticized for their sanctioning of violence; likewise the Duke of Zhou who is generally regarded as the archetype official. Above all, Su mocks Confucius with the derogatory title of "Robber Qiu." This name comes from an encounter, recalled in *Zhuangzi*, of a robber named Zhi, an eloquent philosopher, who scolded Confucius with the following statement: "Now you cultivate the way of *wen* (文 literary) and *wu* (武 martial), monopolizing the world's debate to instruct posterity. In your flowing robes and cinched belt you lie and trick to fool the world's rulers. In your lust for eminence, there is no robber greater than you. If they call me 'Robber Zhi,' why don't they call you 'Robber Qiu'?"[5] From this Su concludes how sanctioned violence has trickled down from the emperor to a father at home. In Su Renshan's challenge to history, he vehemently announces that it was these men who turned Central Plains (China) into Hell.

By examining closely a small number of works by Su Renshan, it is possible to determine how he structured his criticisms against Confucius, and to consider them as part of a larger narrative against the hypocrisy of sanctioned violence. With close readings, I will show how Su exploited the formal modes of the illustrated book and *jinshi* (金石 stone and metal) texts and crafted arguments that extended across the social spectrum of popular reading and canonical histories.

In his hanging-scroll painting *Story of Xuanhe Times* 宣和時事圖 (Fig. 82), executed in the *baomiao* style, Su Renshan has depicted a heroic figure standing proud, looking at a donkey with its head bowed low. It is based on a story entitled "Xiafuren" (俠婦人 The knight-errant's wife), from *Jianxia zhuan* (劍俠傳), a collection of martial arts narratives compiled by Wang Shizhen (王世貞, 1526–90) that included a number of women whose bravery and learning made them worthy heroines. The male protagonist of this story, Dong Guodu (董過度), was working as an official during the Xuanhe period (1119–26), based near the northern frontier. When the Jin attacked, and the Chinese capital was forced, in 1127, to move to Hangzhou, Dong was trapped in the north, unable to return to his southern home. His landlord and friend took pity on his loneliness and arranged for a concubine to help look after his needs. This concubine, a beautiful and accomplished woman, helped Dong by purchasing donkeys to grind grain to make flour, and thus the couple was able to sustain themselves, and, over time, prospered. Despite the comforts of their new life, Dong was often melancholic and later confessed to his concubine that he missed his family. On hearing this, the concubine made arrangements with her brother, a large, burly northern man with a big thick beard, to take Dong home across the border. This was a dangerous task, as both men could be punished; but as her brother owed her a favor, he reluctantly agreed. Dong was suspicious of the two and was in tears thinking about the potential dangers of the journey, but the patient concubine comforted Dong and presented him with a quilt. She instructed Dong never to take money

from her brother, no matter how tempted he might be, and, if the brother persisted, to raise the quilt to show her brother. Puzzled, Dong left his border home, and together the two men encountered adventures on their journey, and throughout the brother tried to find ways to leave Dong. In a last effort, the brother offered a large sum of gold to Dong, hoping that he could pay off his debt to his sister. Dong raised the quilt up in the air; when the concubine's brother saw this, he laughed, and claimed his sister as being cleverer than him and agreed furthermore to bringing his sister to the south. Dong, still puzzled, did not fully understand why holding the quilt up proved to be so exceptional, until his wife, one day, realized that the concubine had sewn gold leaves inside the quilt patches, ensuring the family's financial future. On seeing this, Dong recognized how smart his concubine was and, her safe journey to the south complete, the family lived happily ever after.

The story, as suggested by its title, is about the concubine; but in Su Renshan's painting, it is about the heroism of a male *wuxia*, with windswept hair, standing proud on his bare feet. The hero's confidence is informed by the sparse clarity of this painting, which also suggests that this was made in the mid to late 1840s, when Su's style reached maturity. As with Su Liupeng's narrative paintings discussed in the previous chapter, this painting recalls depictions of *wuxia* found in illustrated versions such as the *Shuihu zhuan* (水滸傳 Outlaws of the marsh). However, unlike Su Liupeng, Su Renshan depicted his *wuxia* hero in simple ink lines against an empty white background, and, as such, it belongs to a different tradition of *wuxia* representations. We have seen in Chapter One, albeit briefly, the impact of the Fujian artist Shangguan Zhou, and Su Renshan's painting bears similarities to the elder artist's *Wanxiaotang huazhuan*, a printed illustrated book of historical characters (Fig. 83). Shangguan's work, in turn, followed that of Chen Hongshou (陳洪綬, 1599–1652), who had vitalized

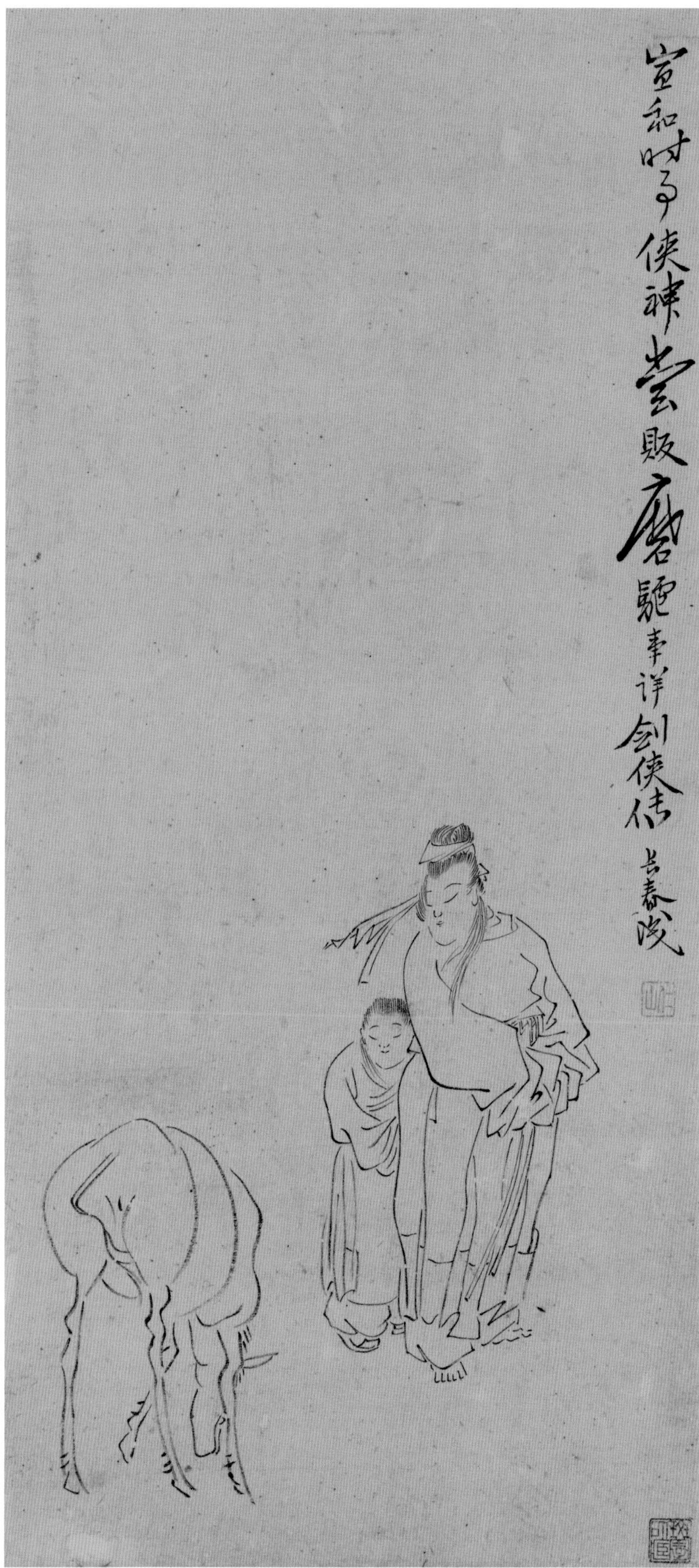

Figure 82 Su Renshan, *Story of Xuanhe Times*. Hanging scroll, undated, ink on paper, 70.5 × 32 cm. Reproduced by permission of the Art Museum of the Chinese University of Hong Kong from the collection of the Art Museum.

the market for good-quality printed illustrations with his theatrical and witty pictorial style. Chen depicted figures without scenic backdrops, using only facial expressions and postures to convey personalities and the subjectivity of the characters. Su Renshan draws from this reservoir of inspiration by using his brush to mimic the qualities of the printed line. It is a fitting style for the subject matter of a hero that has been celebrated through popular printed novels and texts.

Su's treatment with minimal lines conveys one simple aspect of what makes a *wuxia* hero: the psychophysical presence of valor. Su's hero stands tall, in a theatrical stance, his arms twisted to one side and his downward-cast eyes turned to the other. It is powerful in its simplicity and theatricality. The protagonist, however, is depicted barefooted, suggesting that this is not our conventional sword-wielding hero. Bare feet were associated with the poor, farmers, or other types of manual worker. However, it may be used here to hint at how Dong was transformed by his northern concubine from an official who was often tearful and melancholic into a heroic-type laborer. In his study of the Qing Empire in the northwest region, Peter Perdue examines how the Manchus used nature to reinterpret the so-called New Borders (Xinjiang) in order to bridge the gap between the Mongols and themselves. In particular, under Qianlong, by actively transforming grasslands into cultivated fields and thus linking the steppes as part of the interior, the Manchu rulers were able to present a categorized history that made the region appear less alien.[6] The efficacy of this project is borne out by Qing writers who recognized that the landscape of Xinjiang imbued their inhabitants with a distinctive character, some going so far as to say that Han emigrants would benefit from the harsher surroundings, their martial spirit being reinvigorated.[7] This interest in marginal frontier qualities runs parallel to the bestial Zhong Kui's recharged attraction as a vigorous fighter, seen

in the previous chapter. Su's painting of the miller hero, therefore, can be seen alongside Zhong Kui's paintings that popularized the martial qualities of heroes. However, without further evidence, it is difficult to push this speculative argument of a martial figure as a defiant character during the Opium War, even if it is tempting to read the Song/Yuan dynastic context as a historical reflection of contemporary events.

Another possible reading of this painting is to consider how the subject of Su's painting does not explicitly reveal the female focus of the story but lets the female protagonist linger in the title, casting her ghostly shadow. I would also argue that there is a second trace of a feminine presence. Dong's stance with his arms twisted arms to one side, his eyes cast downwards, and standing on bare feet echoes a popular way of depicting the compassionate bodhisattva, Guanyin, which can be traced to the Tang painter Wu Daozi (吳道子, 680–740) (Fig. 84). This type of portrait that conflates the image of an immortal with a real person can be seen in works by earlier artists such as Luo Ping's *Portrait of Jin Nong Reading a Sutra* (Zhejiang Provincial Museum) where the image of Jin and a *luohan* are fused as one. Similarly, especially given Su's Buddhist beliefs and that he has depicted numerous paintings of the bodhisattva, it is possible that the depiction of the shoeless miller forced to live in the northwest outer regions may have been conflated with a portrait of Guanyin, who is usually depicted as a woman, acting as a talisman that protected Dong on his return home to the south. To the side of the knight-errant stands a donkey, its head low, as if kowtowing. Su Renshan has chosen to illustrate the donkey as a foil to the hero. A hero needs adulation, and, here, the adoring audience is a grain-grinding donkey. Is there an element of satire here? Or is it possible to read the donkey's kowtow in recognition of Dong as Guanyin? It is likely that there are multiple readings at work here, and the theme of

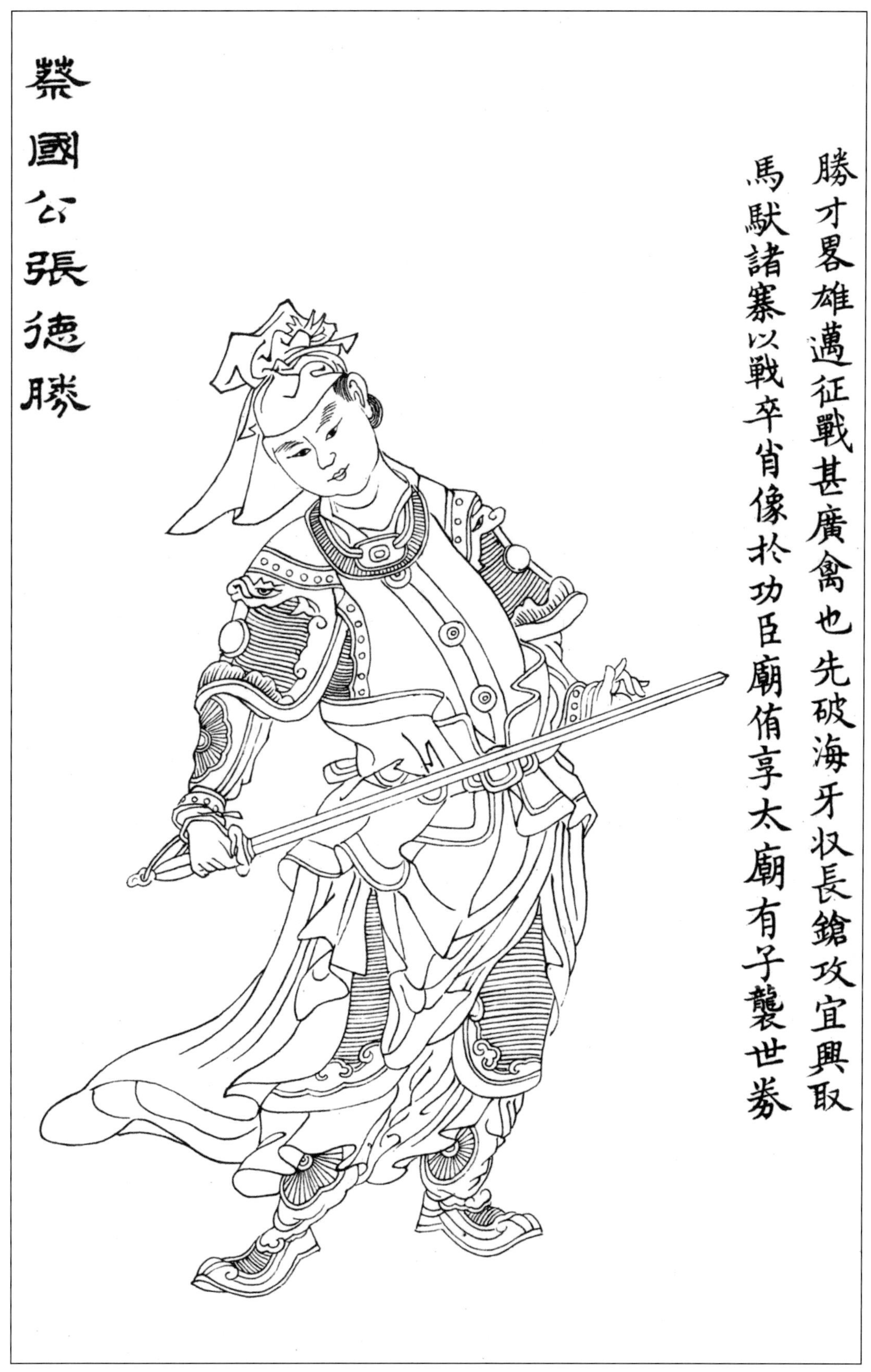

Figure 83　After *Portrait of Duke of Caiguo, Zhang Desheng* by Shangguan Zhou, *Wanxiaotang huazhuan*. Beijing, vol. 2, 32a. 1984 reprint.

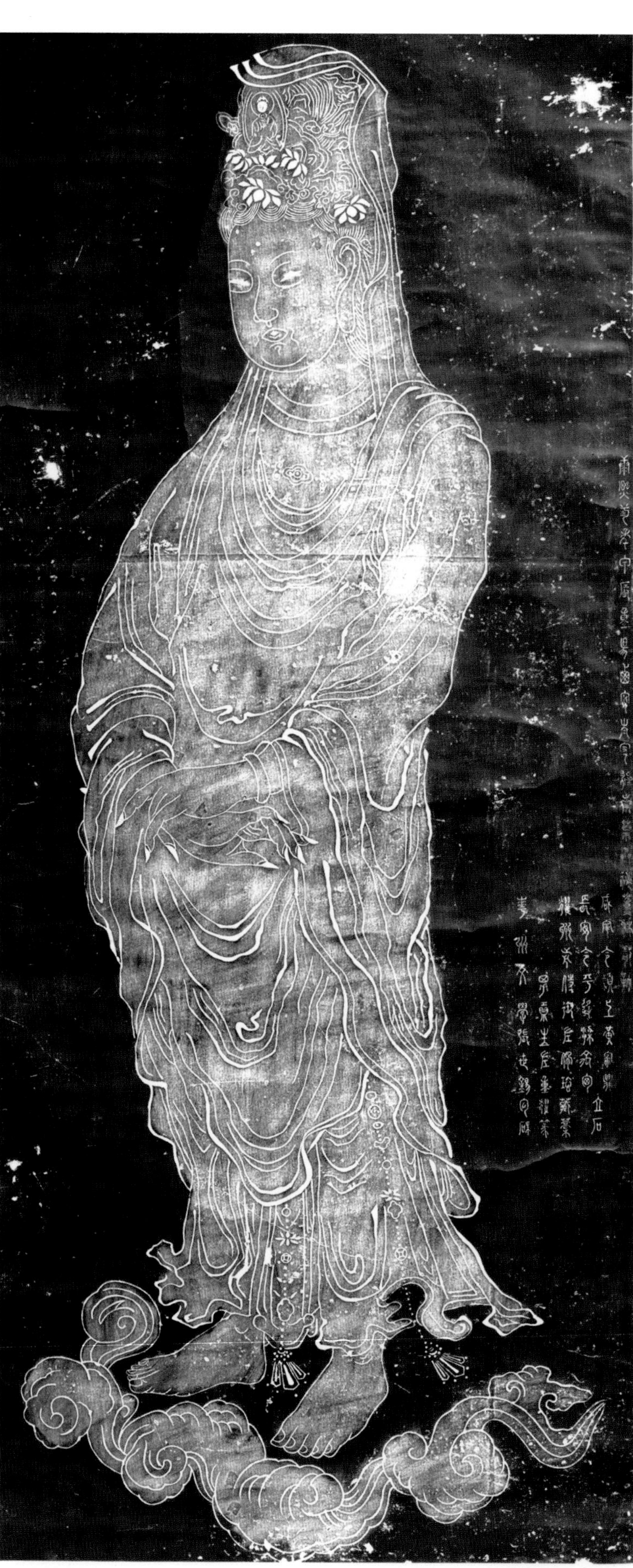

Figure 84 Portrait of Guanyin, re-engraved after an engraving traditionally said to be based on a painting attributed to Wu Daozi (ca. 689–ca. 758). Rubbing mounted as hanging scroll, undated, 173 × 79 cm. The Field Museum, #CSA38754.

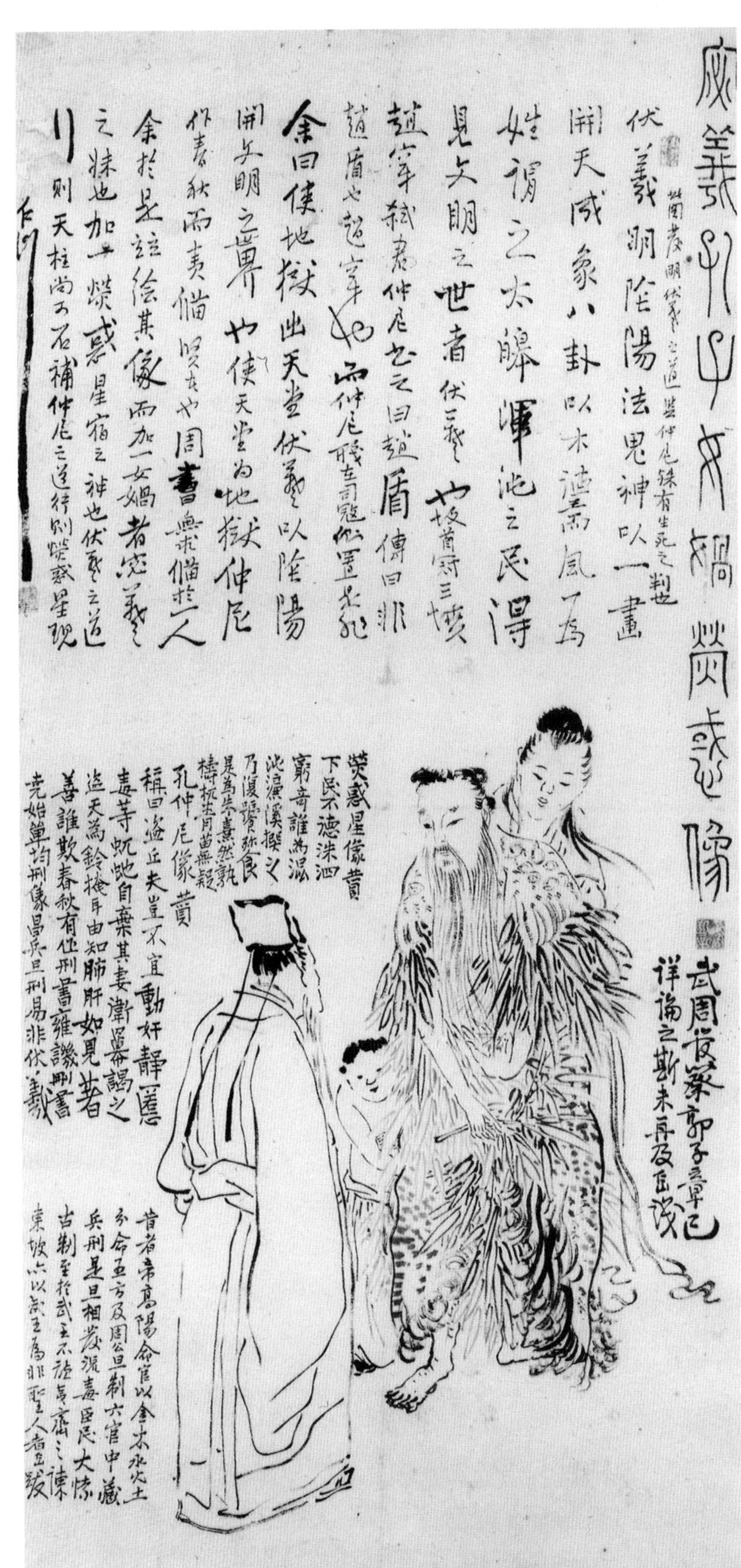

Figure 85 Su Renshan, *Portrait of Fuxi, Confucius, Nuwa and Yinghuo*. Hanging scroll, undated, ink on paper, 121 × 57.5 cm. Guangzhou Art Gallery, Guangzhou Art Museum. After Kao Mayching, ed., *The Art of Su Liupeng and Su Renshan*, Hong Kong and Guangzhou: Art Gallery, The Chinese University of Hong Kong and Guangzhou Art Gallery, 1990, 275.

gender inversions as a doubling device is examined more closely in the next chapter. What is clear is that the depiction of Dong as a *wuxia*, who can take on properties that hint at a female god and a barefoot worker, makes Su's hero more complicated.

If heroes were ambiguous figures, it was easier to define who was bad. Confucius, as seen in his calligraphy piece, was the main target of Su's tirade. Su also depicts images that problematize the figure of Confucius in history. In *Portrait of Fuxi, Confucius, Nuwa and Yinghuo* (Fig. 85), Su Renshan presents an atypical portrait of four historical and mythical gods: Fuxi, legendary god of agriculture and writing, is depicted as a robust man garbed in feathers and skins; Nuwa, the female complement to Fuxi, is his sister and stands behind Fuxi; a young, bare-chested servant boy, the baleful star Yinghuo (Mars), coyly stands behind Fuxi's right-hand side; Confucius, depicted as an old man, is shown with his back turned to the viewer, facing the trio, in his scholar's cap and robes. He is represented alone, confronting a family unit of legendary gods resisting his patriarchal authority. Su took iconographic license by representing Yinghuo as a child instead of the usual mythical man-animal, to complete a family unit of gods. Nuwa and Yinghuo hide behind the protective barrier of Fuxi, who stands with his left hand raised, as if warding off Confucius. Yinghuo (Mars) is a star that is associated with the Lingnan region,[8] and here, centrally placed, he acts as the surrogate for Su's readers, teetering on the precarious borders of Su's recreated world. His downcast eyes, youth, and fear suggest an introspective innocence caught up in the clutter of angry words:

> Portrait-image of Fuxi, Confucius, Nuwa and Yinghuo. This painting elucidates the *dao* of Fuxi, which, surely, when compared with that of Confucius is as different as life and death. Fuxi enlightens the difference between yin and yang, he regulates the ghosts and spirits, and with one stroke, he opens the skies and formed

the eight trigrams. Fuxi of the clan name Feng [風] is also known as Taihao [one of the three sovereigns of ancient China]. When the people of the primordial state of Hundun want to see the progenitor of civilization, they saw Fuxi. Zhao Chuan [趙穿] killed the ruler, but Confucius in his book claimed that it was Zhao Dun [趙盾]. But according to the biography, it was Zhao Chuan and not Zhao Dun. When Confucius was a criminal judge, he mixed up right and wrong. I say that when Fuxi used yin-yang to create civilization, he separated Hell from Heaven. When Confucius, as seen in his *Spring and Autumn Annals*, condemned a good person, he turned Heaven into Hell. The books of Zhou did not demand that one person encompass completion, hence I painted their portraits [of Fuxi and Confucius], adding those of Fuxi's sister, Nuwa, and Yinghuo, the God of Mars. When the way of Fuxi is followed, the Pillar of Heaven can still be repaired. But when the way of Confucius is followed, the Yinghuo Star appears.[9]

Su's inscription shifts from historical commentary to narrative by mixing history with myths. The coexistence of mythical and historical characters echoes the narrative style bequeathed to literary novels from traditional oral storytelling. Here, temporal incongruities are suspended by the introduction of human pathos into the narrative portrait of how families should resist the authority of Confucius, presented as a father figure, whose moral attributes can be detrimental to the shared love between siblings and family. One of the key ways that Su introduces this idea of responsibilities and family is through the theme of double readings. In the opening section, he writes about the Fuxi clan, naming Fuxi as Taihuo, who, as one of the first clans in Chinese history, had the family name of Feng (鳳), sometimes replaced with the character for wind (風). He continues this alternative word usage when he speaks of the people of Hundun (渾沌), which can also be written as 混沌, adding potential layers of meaning. The literal meaning of the characters *hundun* is "muddled chaos" and describes a primordial state before Heaven and

Earth were separated. *Hundun* (混沌) also refers to Pangu (盤古), a mythological character and one of the creators of the universe and a figure associated with the southern region of Lingnan. Therefore, Su's line of "the people of Hundun" (混沌之民) can mean both those who are from Lingnan and those who live in times of chaos.

The play of double meanings continues as Su writes of the famous historical story of Zhao Dun and Zhao Chuan recorded in the *Spring and Autumn Annals*, one of the Five Classics within the literati canon and compiled by Confucius. The well-known story of Zhao Dun and Zhao Chuan demonstrates the importance of the official scribe as history keeper and moral judge. Su's inscription refers to the story without recalling the details of the murder of Duke Ling of Jin State. He assumes his readers are familiar with the story of the duke, a bad ruler, who, despite Minister Zhao Dun's remonstrations, neglected his duty. Tired of Zhao Dun's criticisms, the duke attempted twice to have him murdered but failed. The minister left the court and sought refuge at the borders of Jin State. Meanwhile, his brother, Zhao Chuan, a more hot-headed individual, assassinated the duke. On hearing the news of the duke's death, Zhao Dun returned to the capital. Without punishing his younger brother, he gave him the task of bringing the duke's successor to Jin State. The historian and official scribe for Jin State, Dong Hu (董狐, Spring and Autumn Period), recorded that the minister was culpable because he had failed to impugn his brother. Dong Hu's accusation, which the prime minister accepted, meant that Zhao Dun would permanently be recorded in history as a murderer and be judged for his action. Confucius also recalls this story but adds his judgment praising Dong Hu for recording the truth and Zhao Dun for consenting to be judged by history. Therefore, Confucius, through his praise, exonerated Dun of his crime. Confucius's judgment exemplifies the authorial agency of commentaries to write a moral dimension into a history that becomes a new focus for later readers.

Su's inscription takes on the commentary format, a standard textual form used to respond to famous historical texts, to narrate his story, focusing on a secondary storyline—naming Zhao Chuan as the assassin—and therefore insists that Confucius made an error in his historical record. Su is thus setting up a position to offer a new commentary. In the context of this painting, and as seen in his calligraphy piece on heroes, Su suggests that Confucius's sanction of violence affected the family unit and should be resisted, because Confucius's moral argument was based on a lack of fastidious checking of facts. Su's deliberate reading or misreading is one of the many strategies that he used to intervene in historical records to reshape a version of history that supports his point of view.

Su follows his commentary with a philosophical reading, making it possible to consider his depicted figures as the humanized embodiment of Heaven and Earth, and who, when in harmony with one another, assure a state of order with everything in its proper place, allowing things to flourish. This basic principle that integrates human moral achievement and cosmic harmony is found in both Confucian and Daoist interpretations of order. In broad strokes, disharmony is caused by extreme actions that upset the centrality of this order; for example, extreme expressions of basic emotions such as joy, anger, grief, and pleasure.[10] It is important to note that anger (or any other emotion) is neither good nor bad but a potential that can be negotiated in relation to a person's "natural tendencies" (*xing* 性).[11] Every perspective (interpretation of an act) is a negotiation of emotions and natural tendencies that must be harnessed properly to achieve a proper focus and harmony. Scholars debate different interpretations of the nuance of these concepts, but they agree that, according to early philosophers, the idea of balance, from the individual to the state, was crucial.[12] However, as in this instance, when Heaven and Earth are not in harmony, extreme behaviors such as anger and violence not directed at a proper focus become both symptoms and causes of disorder.

The emotional drive behind Su Renshan's ardent objections is emphasized by the visceral presence of his words that capture both the descriptive and prescriptive idea of anger. In this *Portrait of Fuxi, Confucius, Nuwa and Yinghuo,* and throughout most of Su's later works, his mode of writing and the format of his inscriptions provide unusual structures to his painting. The title is written in seal script, an ancient style connoting historical authority.[13] The rest of the inscription is written in standard script, forming several blocks that frame his figures with an L-shape on one side and smaller square blocks of writing on the other. This odd arrangement of words requires viewers to shift their gaze abruptly across the surface in order to read the inscriptions, preventing any lingering gaze and adds to the general flatness of the image. There is, moreover, too much writing in this painting, and only a small blank space in the right lower corner. In effect, the writing threatens to drown the presence of the depicted figures and makes words the central component of the painting.

By drowning his images with words, Su creates an unusual disharmony that results from being both familiar and unfamiliar at the same time. The familiar is in the combination of words and images and evokes the tradition of calligraphic ink-trace that epitomized the identity of the educated elite who upheld moral standards and a highly prized moral aesthetic. The excessiveness that threatens the pictorial presence, however, undermines this long-held standard and borders on being iconoclastic. With such excess, he challenges the exclusive world of eloquent inscriptions and elegant writings and questions "readability" as a form of aesthetic harmony. The argument can be pushed further by aligning this excess with the anger of what is being said as imprints

of an imagistic presence that is akin to rage against Confucian hypocrisy.

Subverting the Pictorial Order

Ink brush painting has long been theorized as an embodiment of *qi* (氣 energy) that provides the depicted objects with a "life" and elevates them from mere ink traces. It is at the heart of a number of aesthetic theories, including the Six Laws by Xie He (謝赫, act. ca. fifth century). These aesthetic principles have been the subject of numerous scholarship and form the backbone of Chinese art history. My reiteration here is a reminder of the importance of these aesthetic principles as a foundation of Chinese painting. To take but one eloquent example from John Hay, who explains in his article on the hierarchical evolution of structure in Chinese art, "Some of the most basic factors in the development of landscape are found in the question of how pattern is mapped into the process (of painting), and an evolutionary key to this question is provided by the perception of hierarchy. The stratification of *t'ien* (天 Heaven), *ti* (地 Earth), and man is clearly related to the structure of an imperial/aristocratic society that evolved in China up through the +10th century."[14] Thereafter, in landscape painting, pattern is processed through an accepted order that includes qualities of brush trace, iconographic program, and genre categorizations that cohere to social hierarchy. This patterning process is shared with the viewers, who understand and admire the artist's endeavors, to convey certain common ideas of the subject or object depicted. Equally, if pictorial order is fractured, it creates a sense of estrangement that arguably can contribute to and result from a disruption, even violence.

Su Renshan has talked in his inscription of the disorder created by the misalignment of Heaven and Earth through the acts of men in his *Portrait of Fuxi, Confucius, Nuwa and Yinghuo.* How far does he push this idea of "misalignment" in the pictorial? I will argue that certain paintings within his oeuvre address this issue of pictorial disorder, and, by extension, cosmological order. One example is a large hanging-scroll painting *A Celebration of Myriad Birds* (Fig. 1) introduced at the beginning of the book. The ink painting, whose size would indicate that it was used for public display, is badly damaged, especially at the top of the painting where a title was once written. What little exists of the title are two characters: 祟圖 (*sui tu*), meaning a painting of *sui*, which can mean either an ominous force, or the calamities caused by evil ghosts and spirits. It is easy to misread this character as "崇" (*chong*, esteem), which may explain the name of the painting used today. It is tempting to think that Su took delight with his choice of characters, playing with the similarity of the words' structures. Although the incomplete title hinders a more conclusive argument, if this is a painting of ominous forces or of calamities caused by evil spirits and ghosts, it would fit in with the artworks discussed in the last chapter. But it is also arguably more potent because Su overturns, rather than continue, with established conventions. Here, Su draws on the well-established theme of *bainiao tu* (百鳥圖 One hundred birds) (Fig. 86), in the genre of bird and flowers, which, since the Song Dynasty, was used as a message of imperial peace and prosperity. In the early Ming period, the subject matter was revived, and court artists experimented with variations of the symbolic and homonymic associations of bird motifs. The revival of this type of court painting in the early Ming attracted artists from around the country, including Lin Liang, arguably the only Guangdong artist recognized in the current Chinese art history canon.[15] Many of the other Ming court artists, including Bian Wenjin (邊文進, ca. 1356–ca. 1428) and Lü Ji (呂紀, act. ca. 1477), came from the Fujian (Bian) and Zhejiang (Lu) regions, and, collectively, these men are said to have contributed the most to

a "golden age of bird and flower painting."[16] This amalgam of coastal provincial artists reflects the connections formed by the shipping trade and a shared identity of being at the peripheral to the center of cultural production in the capital and Jiangnan area, which tie together artists from these regions. In the Ming Dynasty, Zhejiang and Fujian had some of the highest concentrations of markets and people, and, as Guangdong became increasingly important as a commercial seaport, they formed a connection that is evident in the arts, and which continued, as seen in Chapter One, into the nineteenth century.

The variety of Ming Dynasty bird and flower paintings was great, but most followed the large format of hanging scrolls and played with rebuses to concoct auspicious works befitting public rooms in both private residences and the imperial court. For example, hawks (鷹 *ying*) are symbols of strength that share a homophone for hero (英 *ying*); magpies (喜鵲 *xique*) stand for happiness (喜 *xi*); and bats (蝠 *fu*) for prosperity (福 *fu*). Together with different symbols in Chinese painting, such as bamboo for virtue, or plum blossoms for talent, the many combinations of birds in landscapes provide a huge variety of symbolic paintings. The theme of *A Celebration of Myriad Birds* belongs within this genre and can be extended by adding new birds or objects to add another layer of meaning to the traditional theme. For example, a phoenix (鳳 *feng*) added to the *baoniao* genre takes on the title *Bainiao chaofeng* (百鳥朝鳳 One hundred birds paying respect to the phoenix), in which the phoenix becomes the symbol for a ruler. Similarly, the hundred birds can take on another familiar iconographic theme of "three friends" (pine, bamboo, and flowering plum that together captured the lofty character of the scholar-official), thus offering another popular court art theme.

In Su Renshan's version of the theme, the dominant array of birds is a group of double-tailed swallows. Swallows are symbols of early spring and

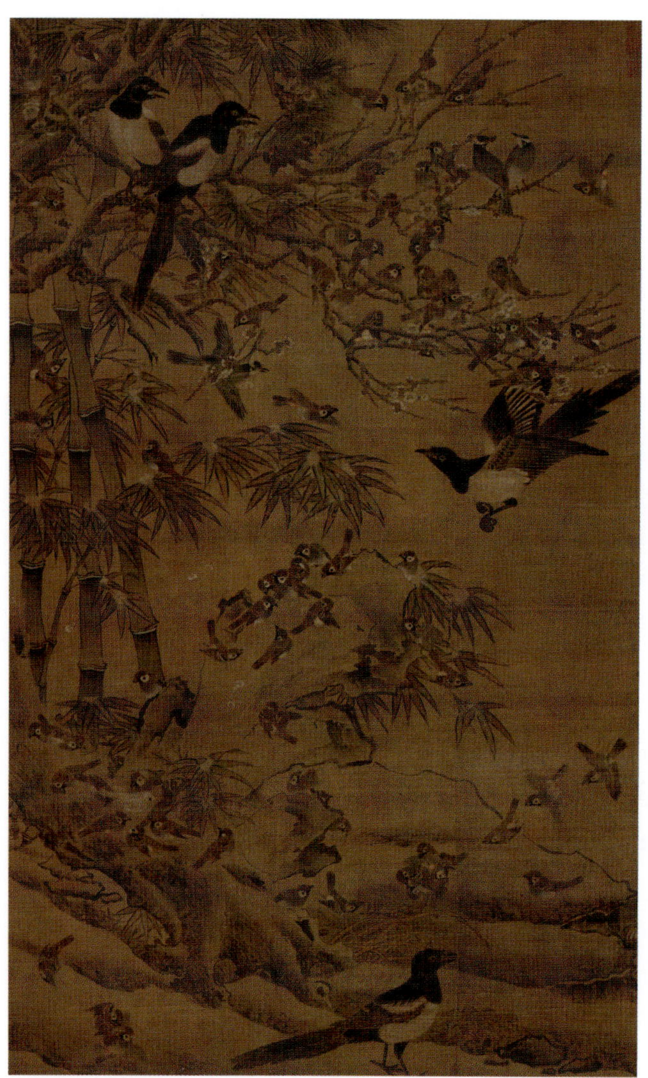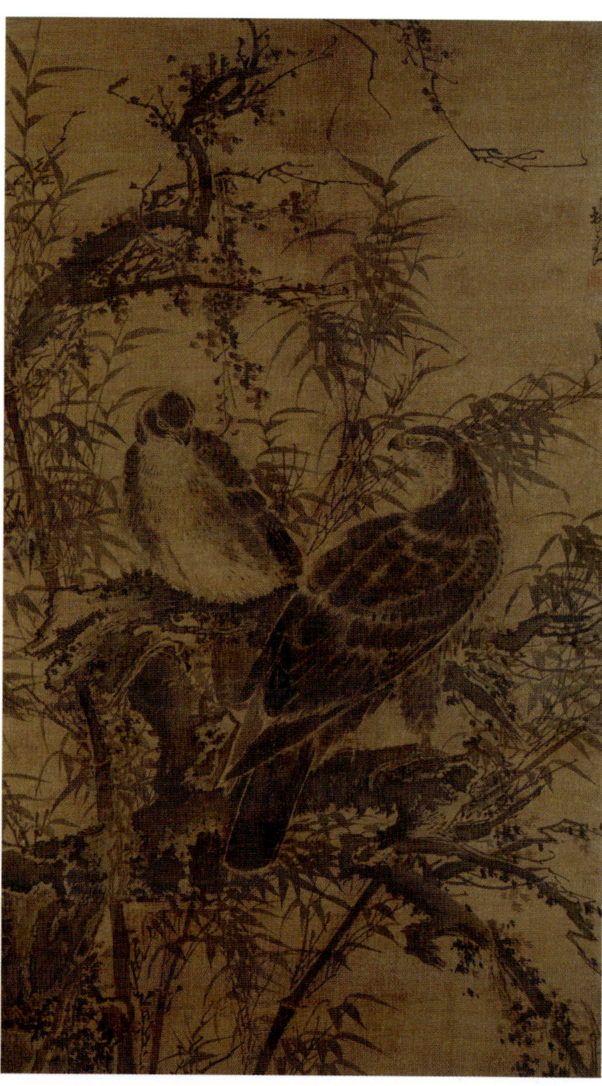

Figure 86 *(left)*   Bian Wenjin, *The Hundred Birds and Three Friends.* Hanging scroll, ca. 1413, ink and color on silk, 241.25 × 108.75 cm. Cleveland Museum of Art.

Figure 87 *(right)*   Lin Liang, *Two Hawks in a Thicket.* Hanging scroll, fifteenth century, ink and pale color on silk, 149 × 84 cm. Metropolitan Art Museum.

a fitting subject matter for an auspicious New Year's painting. They are often conceived as harbingers of happiness, returning home to the north after migrating to the south during wintertime. However, Su Renshan depicts his swallows with sharpened tails and dagger-like wings that cut into one another. The busyness of the birds and the sharp wings and tails display an aggressive chaos, bringing violence and disorder rather than peace and harmony.

At the bottom of the painting are a hawk and a crane sitting on a pine tree, a pair of Chinese francolin, a pair of bulbuls, a pair of doves, and possibly a pair of partridges, forming five pairs of birds. The distinctive group of five pairs of birds may refer to another popular sub-theme of the *bainiao* genre known as the *wulun tu* (五倫圖), referring to the Confucian Five Ideal Relationships: between ruler and subject, father and son, husband and wife, elder and younger brothers, and between friends. Sung Hou-mei's work on Ming paintings demonstrates that, while it is difficult to ascertain the genesis of this genre, it was a theme that became popular in the sixteenth century and often sees four pairs of birds with an avian symbol for the emperor.[17]

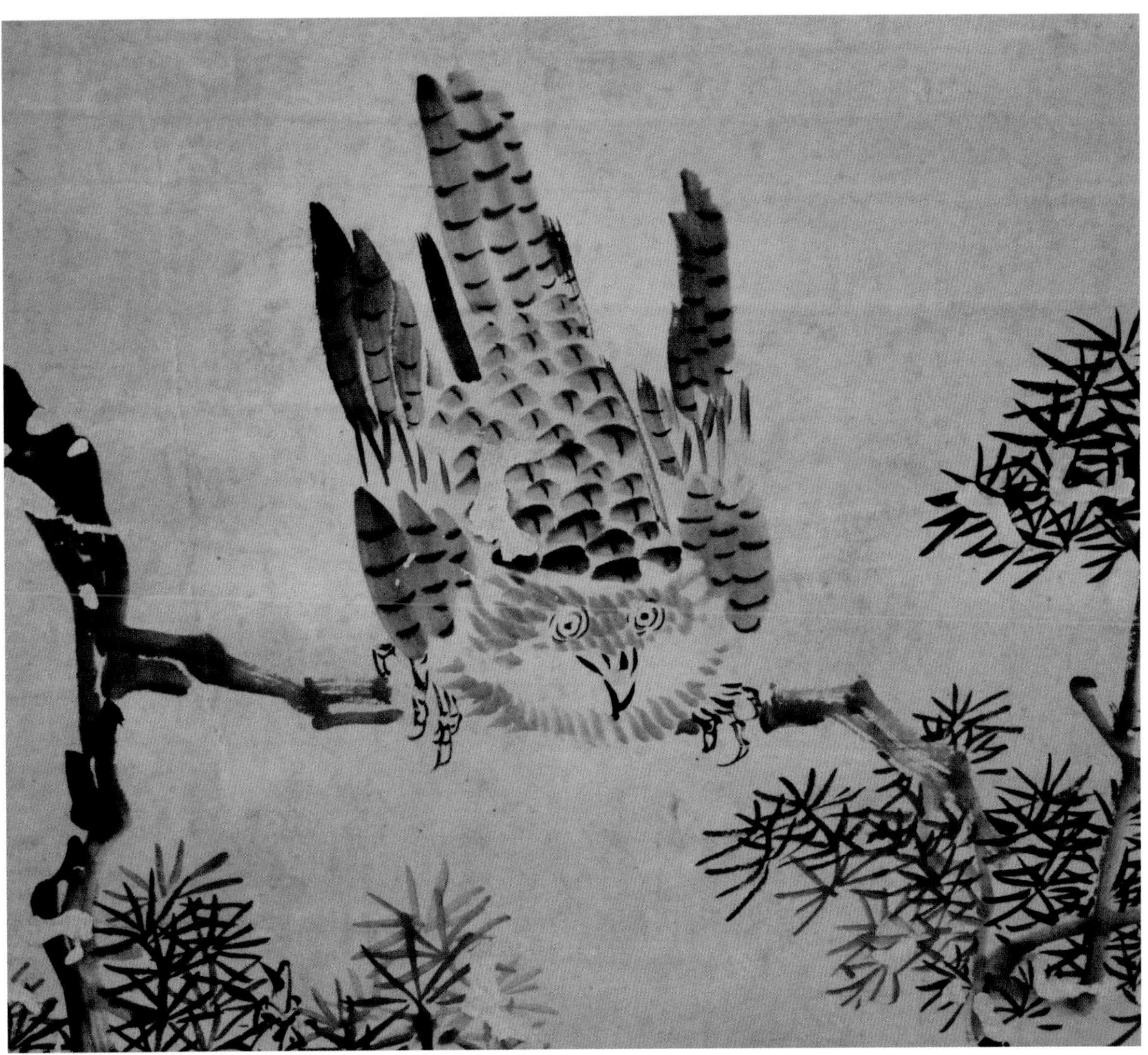

Figure 88 Su Renshan, Detail from *A Celebration of Myriad Birds*. Hanging scroll, undated, ink on paper, 243 × 123 cm. Kyoto National Museum.

In Su Renshan's pairing of the birds, these symbols of partnership are surrounded by flora, including narcissus and peonies, which bears out their auspicious status. Doves, narcissus, and tree peonies are common symbols of spring and fit in with the return of the swallows. The hawk and crane, however, are an unusual pairing although each has a long tradition in Chinese art. The Cantonese Ming court painter Lin Liang was well known for the heroic naturalism of his hawk, and his subsequent fame has made his ink hawk synonymous with early Guangdong painting (Fig. 87). In typical representations of this bird, the hawk is perched on mountain peaks and pine trees or nestled within wilderness, looking majestic, and, in Lin Liang's paintings, as representative of the emperor. Su adopted a different approach from his regional predecessor by positioning his hawk at the bottom of his scroll, reduced in size, perched on a young pine tree, and looking down at the floor (Fig. 88). Far from being majestic or imperial, Su's

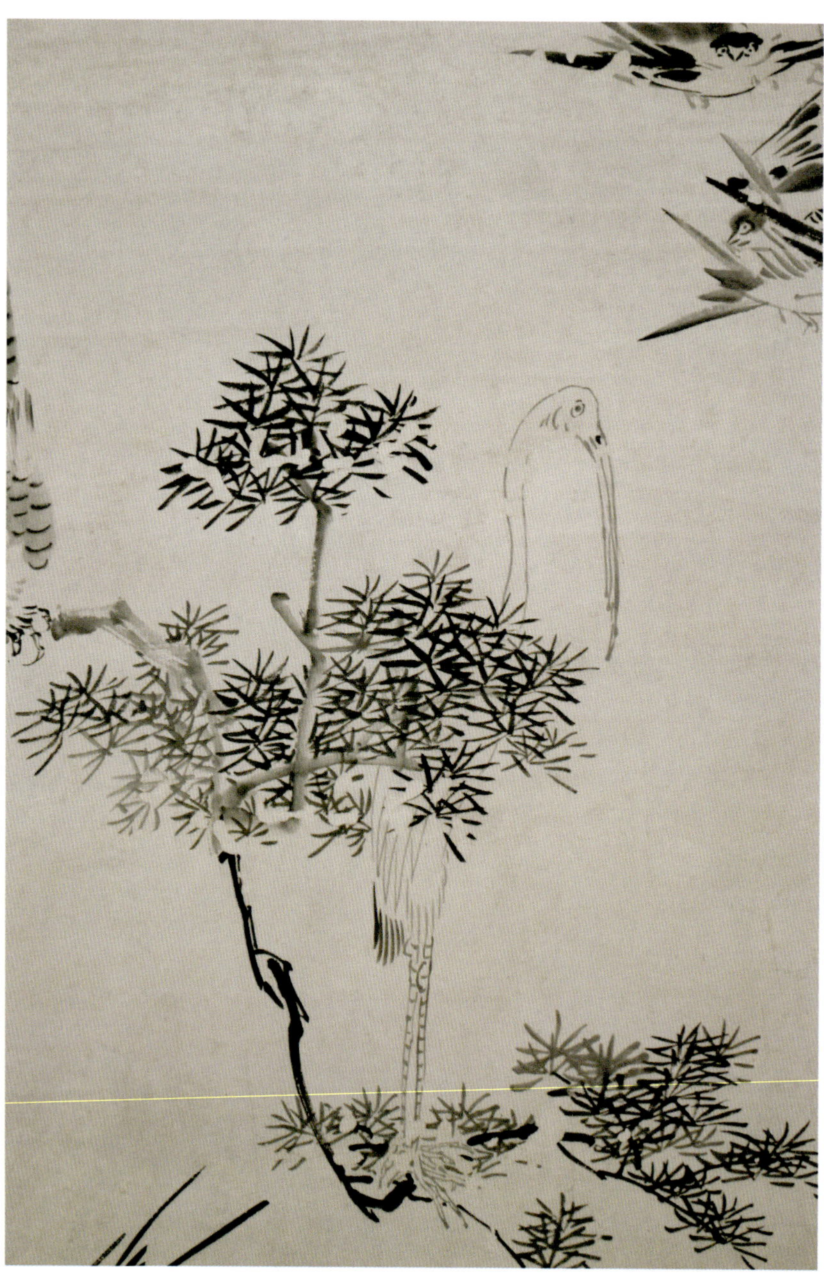

Figure 89 Su Renshan, Detail from *A Celebration of Myriad Birds*. Hanging scroll, undated, ink on paper, 243 × 123 cm. Kyoto National Museum.

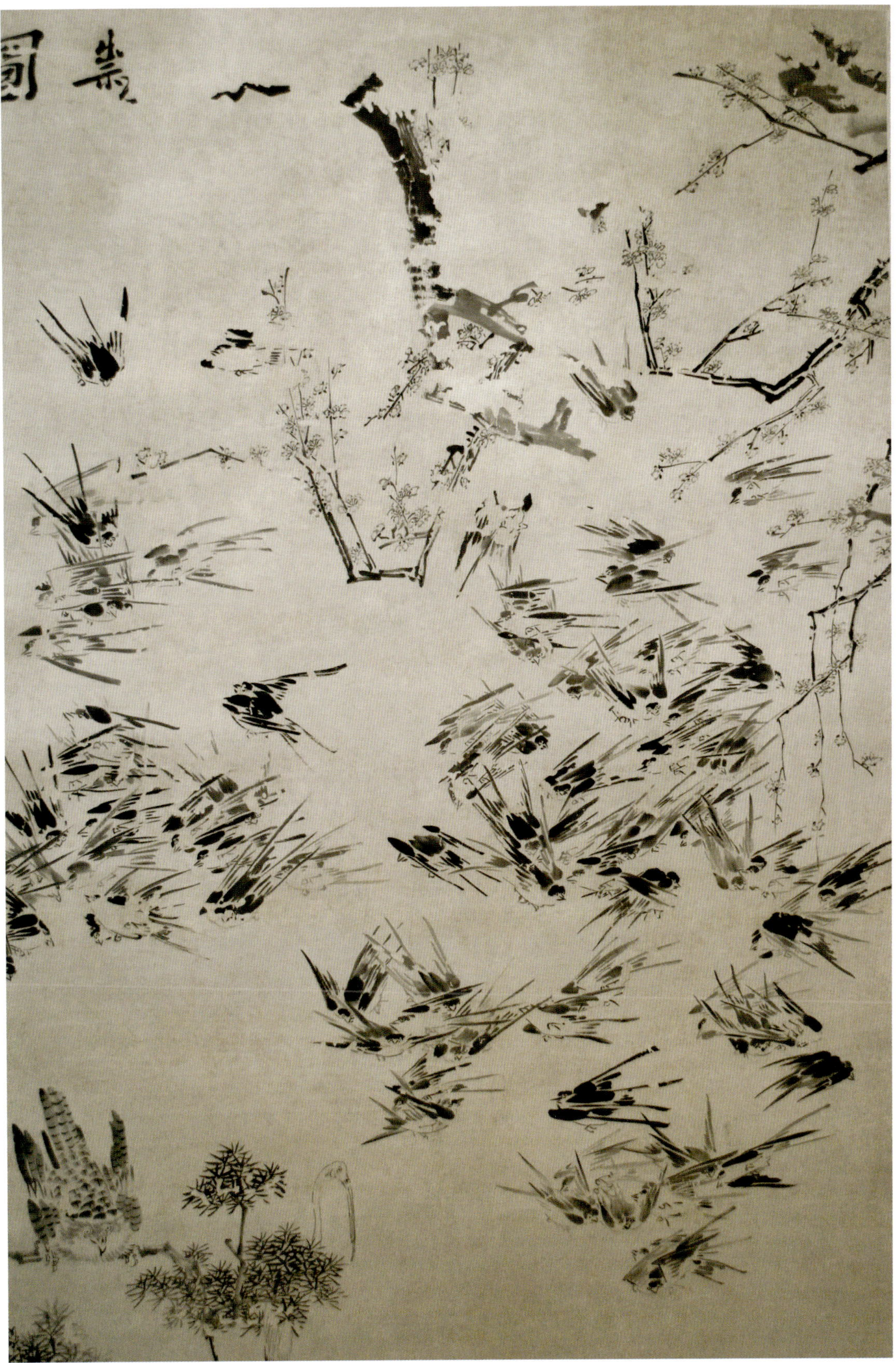

Figure 90   Su Renshan, Detail from *A Celebration of Myriad Birds*. Hanging scroll, undated, ink on paper, 243 × 123 cm. Kyoto National Museum.

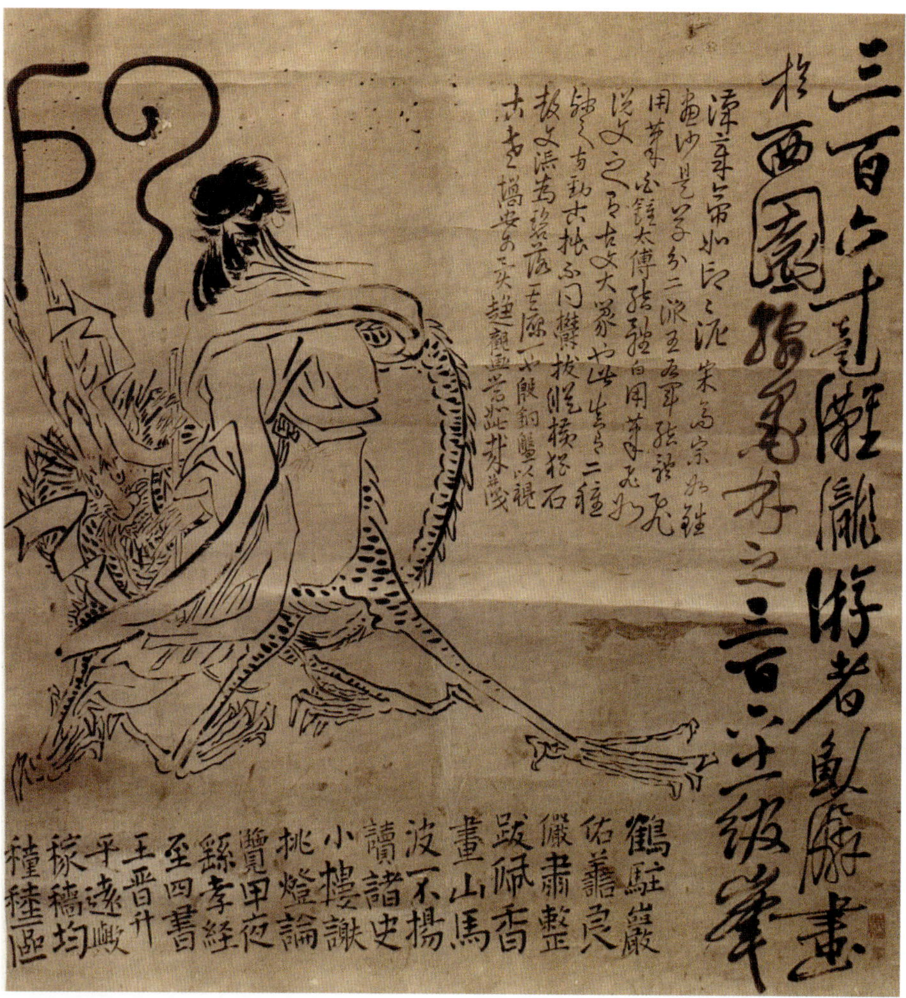

Figure 91 Su Renshan, *Riding Dragons*. Detail. Hanging scroll, undated, ink on paper, 254 × 118 cm. Reproduced by permission of the Art Museum of the Chinese University of Hong Kong from the collection of the Art Museum.

ying is depicted as small, self-absorbed, and unaware of the chaos swarming over his head.

The crane perched next to the hawk on the pine tree is also an oddity, having an unusual drooping beak (Fig. 89). Cranes are common auspicious creatures that have a large repertoire of iconographic meanings in Buddhist, Daoist, Confucian, and vernacular traditions. The cry of the crane can evoke the recruiting of loyal officials, the moment of enlightenment in Buddhism, or the auspicious sign of goodwill to come.[18] Although it may be difficult to ascertain the meaning of the crane in this painting, it is possible to suggest that Su's meek crane with a bent beak has lost its power to cry. Following this argument, if the hawk and crane suggest a pairing of official and emperor, the highest-ranked relation within the Confucian ideal *wulun*, Su Renshan has rendered the relationship useless. It is also possible to read the hawk and crane pairing as the martial and literary qualities. Pushing the rebus further, the word for swallows is *yan* (燕), the ancient word for Beijing (燕京 *Yanjing*). The chaos of the swallows (Fig. 90) may further emphasize this idea of disorder in the capital. However, there is another possibility. Returning to the unusual title, the character sui can be used in the compound "災祟" (*zaisui*) which can also refer to "災蝗" (*zaihuang*) meaning a calamity caused by locusts.[19] There are numerous historical accounts of the destructive power of the migratory plagues of locust, and in the Western Han primer text, *Ji jiu pian* (急就篇 Primer for quickly learning Chinese characters), there is the phrase "災蝗不起，五穀孰成" (if the calamity of locusts do not rise, the five grains will ripe).[20] We have seen how Su Renshan often drew on themes related to harvests (Fig. 61) and in the next chapter, the painting, *Ripening of the Five Grains* (Fig. 98) depicts an outing of women with a pair of swallows above. Is it possible that the sharp-tailed and angular-formed swallows recall the sharp and angular forms of locusts?[21] This may explain the haphazard arrangement of the flock of swallows as a swarm of insects, and if so, could it be that they represent an ominous force, or the calamity brought on by evil ghosts and spirits that have led to the cowering of the hawk and the silencing of the crane? I may have pushed my interpretation of Su's play of traditional iconography too far, but it is impossible to deny that the chaos of the swallows prevents any possible reading of the Su's *Birds* as a symbol of peace and prosperity.

In 1848, when Su was in Guangxi, he produced a pair of unusual paintings based on a famous story, *Chui xiao yin feng* (吹簫引鳳 Leading the phoenixes by playing the flute) (Fig. 91), taken from the *Biographies of Various Immortals* attributed to the Western Han scholar Liu Xiang (劉向, 80–9 BCE). The story is about Princess Longyu (弄玉), who was a young beautiful woman and a talented musician. One day, she climbed to the top of the palace platform and played her flute. Her music was enchanting, but midway through the piece that she was playing she felt another musical presence playing alongside her. That night in a dream, she met another talented musician from Mount Hua, Xiao Shi (蕭史), who claimed to have heard her play. She woke up, aware that it was a dream, but was never able to forget this young man. Her father, the emperor, sent his men to Mount Hua to look for Xiao Shi and, eventually, the

two musicians met, fell in love, and married. They became known for their musical abilities and their performances, and many young couples likewise followed their example of performing and playing music. The emperor became concerned about how this frolicking might affect society. His daughter and son-in-law, on learning this, fled the palace to Mount Hua, where they were able to play without affecting the country. Their music was such that it lured the mythical phoenixes to fly down and take them away. On their ascension, they became immortals. Su's pair of paintings, *Leading the Phoenixes by Playing the Flute* (Fig. 3) and *Riding Dragons* (Fig. 2), captures the main story, which has since become recognized as both a love story and a story about the transcendental power of music.

The striking feature of this pair of paintings is that, instead of portraying the gentility of palace scenes (which was how earlier artists depicted this story),[22] Su depicts the lovers using bold, and almost brutish, lines that undercut the sensuality of romance. The expressiveness of the lines is also buttressed by the scattered large writing that fills every surface of the painting. His calligraphy is deliberately crude, almost primitive, in the way the wet ink blots are almost too wet and the lines are almost too thick. Compositionally, the writing has a graffiti-like presence, the words crowding one another, and pushes the aesthetic limits of the colophon writing tradition. The inscriptions vary, but inevitably they refer to calligraphy, including carvings of words on walls and steles. On *Riding Dragons*, he writes about the various types of cursive and standard scripts; on *Leading the Phoenixes*, he writes of seal scripts and clerical scripts. Su also provides historical examples of each group, including Wang Xizhi's (王羲之, 303–61) *feibai* 飛白 (flying white stroke), Zhong Yao's (鍾繇, 151–230) *kaishu* 楷書 (regular script), Li Si's (李斯, act. ca. 280–208 BCE) *xiaozhuan* 小篆 (small seal script), and Xu Shen's

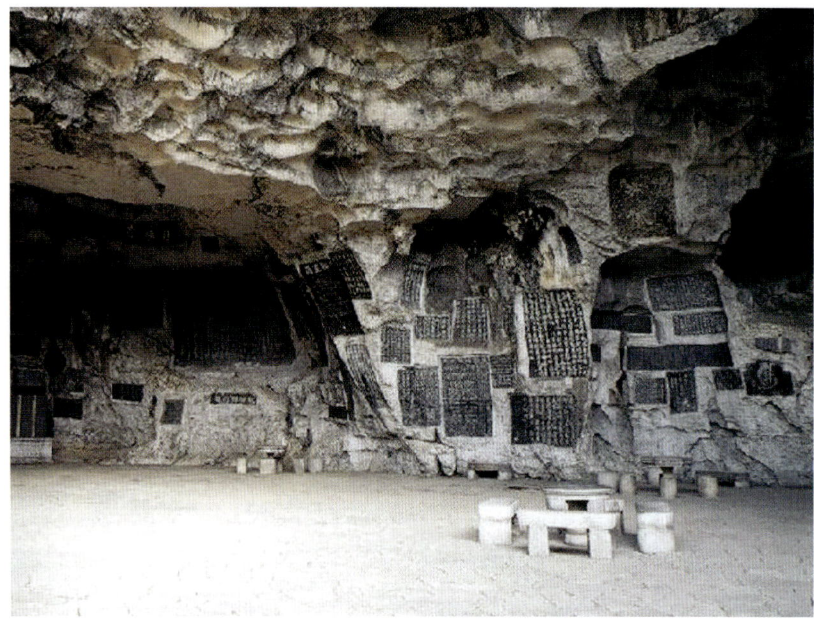

Figure 92 Photo of inscriptions on cliff.

(許慎, act. ca. 58–147) *lishu* 隸書 (early seal script) based on bronze inscriptions. According to his inscription, Su Renshan identifies himself as *Sanbai liushiyi tanlong youzhe* 三百六十一譚龍游者, literally "Visitor to the three hundred sixty-one rapids," indicating that he made the painting at the Western Garden of the Hanmolin, the Forest of Brush and Ink, otherwise the Guilin grottoes where the caves and cliff faces bear numerous inscriptions (Fig. 91). It may be that the defaced surfaces of cliff inscription (Fig. 92) were the inspiration for the paintings.

What is the relationship between this popular story and carved inscriptions? One possible reading is to understand the story as the transformation of talents that are so pure that they (the music and the musicians) can transcend the everyday and ascend to the heavens. Simlarly, good calligraphy has long been described as ascending dragons and complements the phoenixes as another type of transformation of talent. This argument can be pushed further by looking more deeply into the philosophical roots of writing. According to the *Book of Changes*, the invention of calligraphy was formed when "Fuxi (the mythical god and creator) looked up and saw the images of Heaven; he looked down and examined the patterning of Earth. He contemplated the markings of birds and beasts and the adaptations to the regions."[23] In other words, the markings of birds and beasts (which represent the traces of ink and brush), when adhering to a pictorial order or the circulation of energy, should reveal a cosmological order. This idea of patterning follows John Hay's argument about the development of Chinese aesthetics and social order. Traditionally, these ideas have been used to talk about the inner state of the artist-scholar, and paintings and calligraphies as the manifestation of their inner energy that can have transformative powers. This premise underscored the learning and training of scholar-officials whose ability to wield the brush, particularly in calligraphy, was seen as a measurement of their moral worth and ethical duty. Here, the character for letters (文 *wen*), with its loaded meaning for the educated elite, also refers to the word for pattern (紋 *wen*). When pattern and words conjoin, they form an ideal cosmological order.

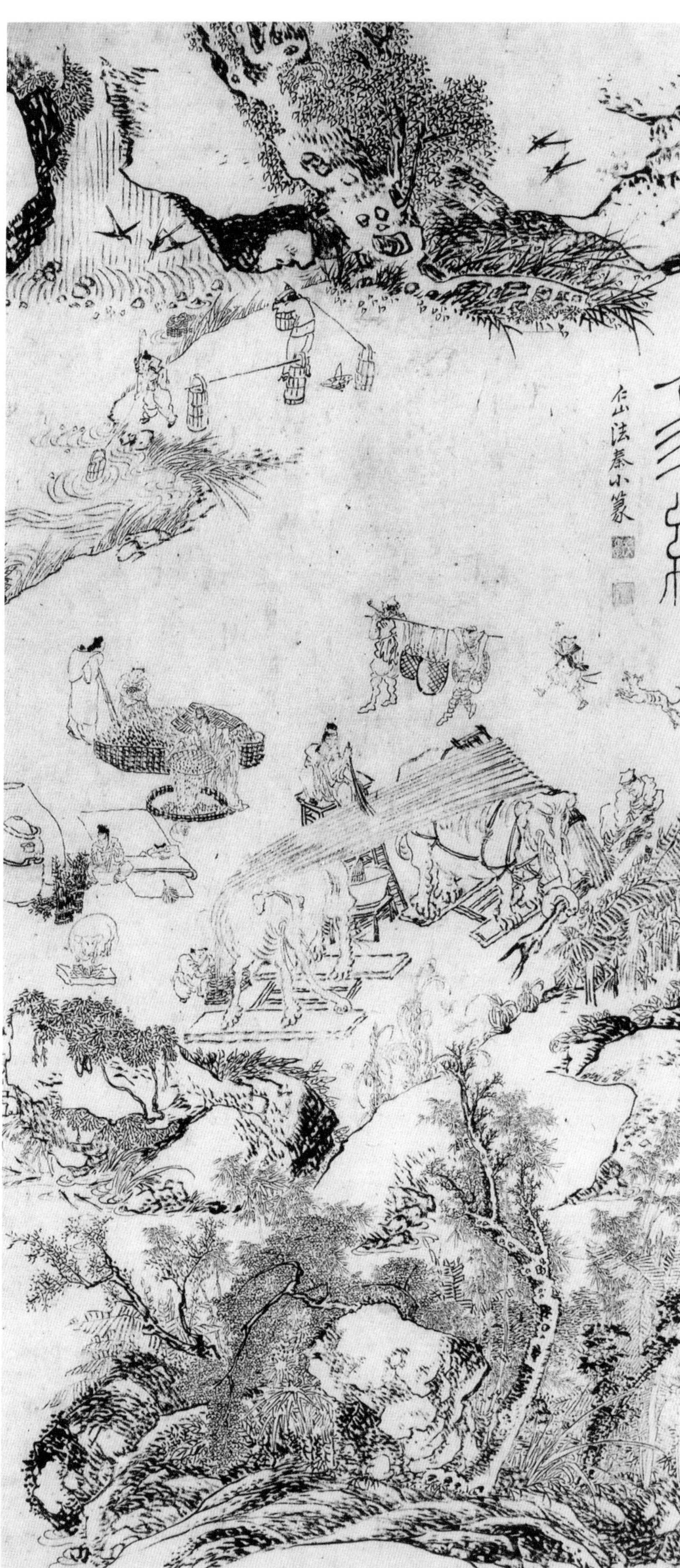

Figure 93 Su Renshan, *Xiangjing tu*. Hanging scroll, undated, ink on paper, 127 × 60 cm. Guangzhou Art Gallery, Guangzhou Art Museum. After Kao Mayching, ed., *The Art of Su Liupeng and Su Renshan*, Hong Kong and Guangzhou: Art Gallery, The Chinese University of Hong Kong and Guangzhou Art Gallery, 1990, 255.

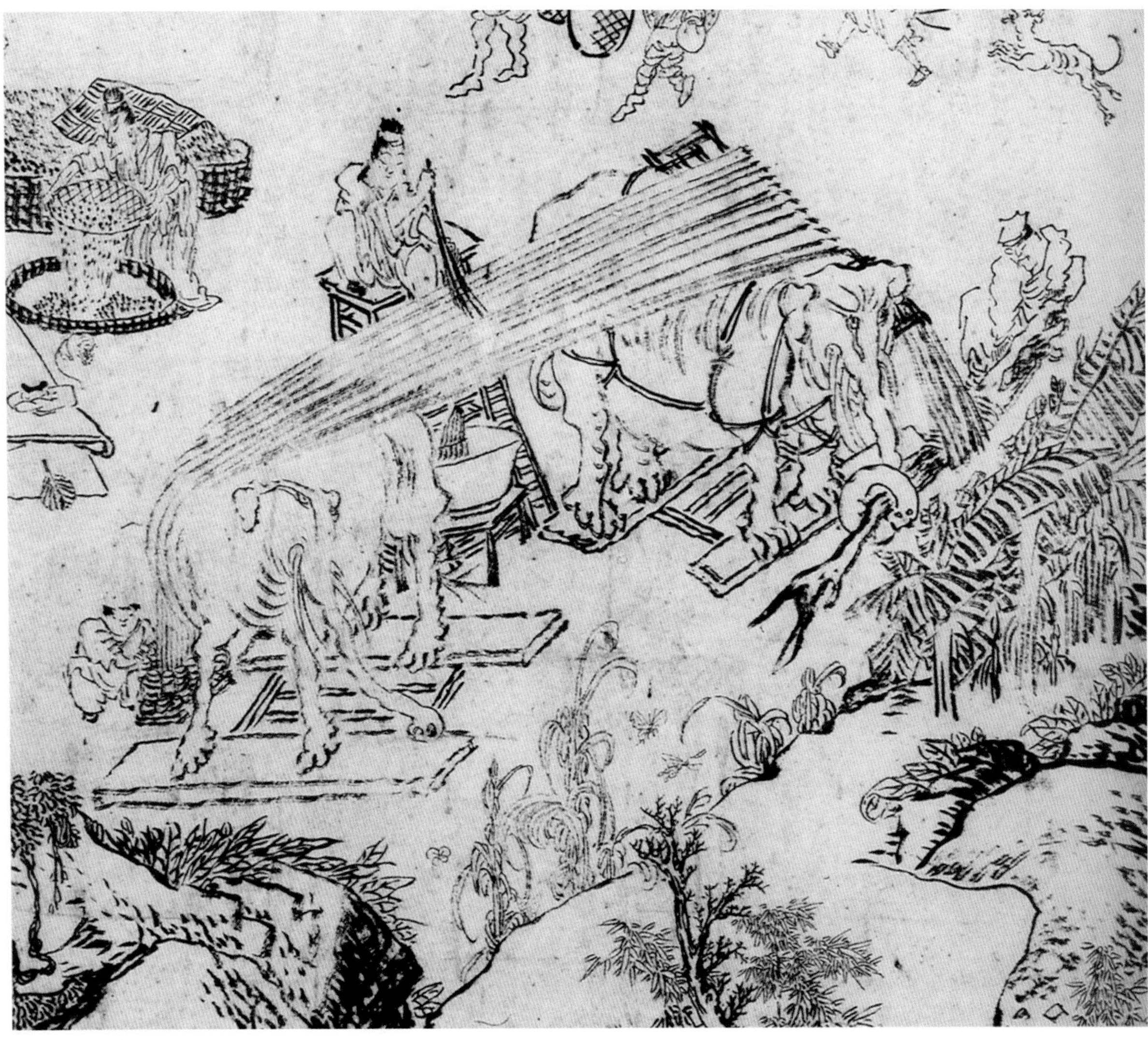

Figure 94 Su Renshan, *Xiangjing tu*. Detail. After Kao Mayching, ed., *The Art of Su Liupeng and Su Renshan*, Hong Kong and Guangzhou: Art Gallery, The Chinese University of Hong Kong and Guangzhou Art Gallery, 1990, 255.

In this pair of paintings of birds and beasts, the transformative power of love, unity, and talent evoke the imagistic properties of words. We wonder whether we are supposed to see the dragon and phoenix not as phenomenological descriptions but as the manifestations of calligraphy, the ultimate root of creativity. But as Su Renshan's chaotic markings deface the elegance of writing, we have to ask whether creativity, a cosmological manifestation, is itself in danger. If we follow this reasoning to its logical conclusion, is the disorder of the image a disorder of the world? This argument can only hold if the paintings were not accidental flurries of ink experiments but belong to a larger body of works that collectively, though not necessarily systematically, challenged the morals and values of elite *wen* communities, where painting and calligraphy acted as social and ethical barometers.

I contend that Su Renshan's paintings can be seen in this light: that his paintings present excessiveness as a deliberate attack on conventional pictorial order.

The graffiti-like inscriptions of Su's large *Leading the Phoenix by Playing the Flute* and *Riding Dragons* are perhaps the best examples of how bold and almost ugly strokes can overwhelm orthodox ideals of beauty. The graffiti quality of the image also gave him license to write random words and inscriptions that are not necessarily tied to one another, such as the exaggerated script he uses for the single word "cloud," and shaped as a continued curved line that does not fit in with the other inscriptions. This disconnected logic of words also permits, as in this instance, blurring the line between figurative and literalness of words and images. His haphazard display of words is not only about disruptions but also about failures, and in particular about the failure to recognize individual talent in this mass of people. He writes: "Painting is similar to the *qin*, who can differentiate the medium within the gathered crowding of *tong* trees and *zi* trees. The silk is like the stops on a *qin*, who has the will and knowledge to differentiate the depth and heights in order to control [the tone]." It is a telling end of an inscription that rhetorically questions the ability of viewers and listeners to understand and differentiate the good from the average. His rhetorical stance reflects his own life—his failure to pass the exams and his father's displeasure at his lack of success. While this theme of unrecognized talent is not uncommon in Chinese painting, Su's method of portraying the theme is. He disconnects the viewer from the protagonists of his portraits by portraying the couple facing one another at an angle. Instead, the viewer can only read the words that are scattered across the painted surface and is not allowed to penetrate deeper within. As a result, this impenetrable space draws our attention to the fractures, the spaces in-between the words.

If Su Renshan equated the present world with a hell where violence was sanctioned, the flipside was a utopian world where people followed the path of Shennong and Houyi. In an unusual painting,

Xiangjing tu (象經圖 Painting of the classic of the image) (Fig. 93), Su depicts a bucolic scene with a multigenerational grouping of people engaged in many activities, including cloth-making, where the loom is made up of two elephants. Leaving aside the unusual elephant loom, Su's village scene recalls some of Su Liupeng's paintings of village life and Huang Shen's album of street characters that portray the liveliness of the average person. As such, Su's painting can be considered alongside these works as images of intergenerational community of the non-elite. In the background, Su has depicted fishers sorting out their day's catch, a group of people sifting grain husks, a boy and a dog playing, and double magpies in the back, also a rebus for happiness. It is a landscape teeming with congeniality, reflecting the rich lands of Shunde, known for their unusual combination of fishing and mulberry fields. This interest in depicting different types of local production can also be seen in another Guangdong-based art world, the export art market, which produced images for a Western audience of Chinese vernacular life, including the production of tea, silk, and ceramics.[24] Su's depiction of silk production would have resonated with viewers who lived outside the city, if it was not for the unusual elephants (Fig. 94).

The title of the painting, *Xiangjing* (象經), refers to *Classics of Image Game*, a treatise on chess. The text is believed to have been written by Emperor Wu of Northern Zhou (周武帝, 543–78) in 569 but has since been lost. However, the preface to the book, written by Wang Bao (王褒, act. ca. 552–81), a notable poet, has survived. Wang notes that the game represents phenomena of heaven and earth, the principles of yin and yang, the passing of the seasons, the eight trigrams, filial relations, the order of government, and orderly conduct. The game appeared to encapsulate an idea of order, and, according to Wang, military thinking and strategy were an important part of moving the pieces across the board. Although textual evidence suggests that the game played in the sixth century differs from modern versions, some of the characters of the chess pieces remain consistent. For example, the character *xiang* can mean elephant (象) and Grand Councilor (相 *xiang*), thus playing the same role but on opposite sides. Similarly, chess strategies, as suggested by Wang Bao, are related to battle metaphors and warfare similes. But how does this tie in with weaving and textiles? It is no coincidence that the making of cloth provides several of the most fundamental metaphors of social and intellectual order in Chinese thought. The character "to govern" (*zhi* 制) is the same word as "to reel silk," "canonical texts" (*jing* 經) as "warp threads," and "philosophical discourse" (*lun* 論) as "silk yarn." These metaphors were used in a famous passage found in a text entitled *Lienü zhuan* (列女傳 Biographies of exemplary women), in which one of the main proponents, Mother Meng, instructs her son, Wenbo (Mencius), by drawing an analogy between weaving and government. In one of her famous passages, she makes an analogy between eight offices and eight parts of a loom. The relevant section reads:

> When Wenbo was minister in Lu, Jing Jiang said to him: I will inform you about what is important in governing a country; it is entirely in the warp [*jing* 經]. The selvedge [*fu* 幅, the straight border of woven cloth] is the means by which you straighten what is twisted and crooked. It must be strong; therefore, the selvedge can be considered as the General [*jiang* 將]. The painting [*hua* 畫; or the activity of creating the trigrams][25] evens what is uneven and reconciles what is not adjusted. Therefore, the pattern can be the Director [*zheng* 正] ... The one who can fill an important office, travel a long road and is upright, genuine and firm is the axle. The axle can be deemed Minister [*xiang* 相].[26]

Accordingly, the axle equals a minister, a *xiang*, but in chess, as a black piece, it corresponds to its red equivalent bearing the character for elephant. It is possible, therefore, to read Su's painting as a form of visual punning, in which the loom literally takes on

the form of an elephant, a homophone for minister in chess—one who was responsible for keeping the country running by being upright and virtuous. In his recreated contented world, the people are better off having elephants than ministers. With elephants, at least the people can (in the words of his calligraphy piece) "return to a world where there was enough to eat and warm clothes to wear."

Su's vision of this utopian rural scene has an additional political charge, because the pictorial theme of a self-sufficient rural household is related to the imperial-commissioned printed books that also supported the idyllic lifestyle of country estates and farming households and the long-established genre of tilling and weaving. The didactic properties of the tilling and weaving genre, briefly touched on in Chapter One, show how the genre became associated with the Kangxi Emperor and was continued by the Yongzheng and Qianlong Emperors as homage to their father and grandfather. By the eighteenth century, the theme of weaving and tilling was associated with the court and their rhetoric of what formed a peaceful and productive world. Moreover, as scholars have shown, in late Ming and early Qing, reforming officials wanted to imbue woman's work with a moral activity linked to a gendered identity. Although agricultural and textile production involved men and women, in representations, there was a distinctive move towards images of idealized "womanly" work.[27] It is possible to see how the Qing court appropriated this ideal where tilling and weaving were codified and segregated according to gender and hierarchy, and affirmed the natural order of gender and production under the Qing, and presented a contented world under their auspices. In contrast to the imperially endorsed image of a Confucian rural world, Su's painting shows a larger community where men and women of all ages worked and played together. We are not given any other means of assessing the reasons for this painting, but it is possible to read it as an image of a happy intergenerational place where the *xiang*, literally elephants, serve as a loom in a village that can only exist as an impossible place, a utopia.

Conclusion

At times of political changes, values are often questioned and paintings become a space where these values are explored. What is unusual here is the degree by which Su challenged the status quo and questioned the foundation of the educated gentleman's moral and social barometer. It is impossible to look at the paintings discussed in this chapter and not be struck by how different they appear to other early nineteenth century works. Their extreme differences—from iconographic programs, brushwork treatment, to overall themes and sentiments, however, make sense when we consider not only the political situation of war and violence, but also of the dynamics between those based in the city and those outside. Excess is perhaps the best description of what Su has achieved. More than any artists around him, he pushed the boundaries of pictorial conventions and it is exactly what best reflects his frustrations and anger directed at the state.

Expressions of anger are difficult to pinpoint as deliberate acts in artworks. While there is rawness in Su's paintings, his works are also carefully constructed and undercut the idea that they are spontaneous expressions of emotions. For example, he attends to the relationship between the qualities of form making and the subject matter, as seen in how he uses graphic lines when drawing on themes from illustrated novels, and exposes the heavy engraved markings of carving on hard surface when thinking about calligraphy and inscriptions. He also draws on the intellectual history of the scholarly gentleman even as he questions the philosophical and historical roots of learning. It is important to remember that Su's paintings can and should be seen as part of his biography as a son from the Delta region. As such, even as Su's experiments may appear to be a modern enterprise in appearance, they are anchored in traditional ideas of pictorial order, and it is at this juncture where his excess gains meaning.

Chapter Five

Su Renshan: In the Company of Women

Shang Wan[ren] [商畹人], Wu Ruohua [吳若華], and Zhong Wenzhen [鍾文貞] are like the legs of a *ding*-vessel, together following Yan Shirui [顏士睿] of Tongcheng. Can it not be said that these four women are the equivalent of Wang [Ao 王鏊], Tang [Shunzhi 唐順之], Gui [Youguang 歸有光], and Hu [Youxin 胡友信]? It is a pity that their extraordinary writings [奇文] have not been appreciated together. This truly draws a deep sigh of regret from writers of similarly arousing works.[1]

These are the opening lines of the inscription of Su Renshan's last dated painting, written while he was held at the *yamen* in 1850. They provide a counterpoint to his tirades against Confucius and ambivalence towards the pursuit of examinations. Here, Su considers the four literary women, who were from the Ming and Qing dynasties, as representatives of an ideal intellectual lineage, symbolized as the supporting legs of a *ding* vessel, a metaphor used to recognize distinguished talent. He suggests that their talents are comparable to the four famous Ming scholar-officials considered to be responsible for formalizing the eight-legged essay (八股文 *bagu wen*), the principle prose style for civil examinations. Given that women were not allowed to take part in the examinations, Su's comparison is provocative. Su's line "It is a pity that their extraordinary writings have not been appreciated together" recalls a line by the Jin Dynasty poet, Tao Qian (陶潛, 365–427): "extraordinary writings we appreciate with one another" (奇文共欣賞), from the poem *Moving House*, and refers to Tao Qian's fondness for *qiwen* after his retirement

from court.[2] Although there is no specific definition of what is meant by *qiwen*, it is generally accepted as referring to non-orthodox texts. By comparing the talents of four literary women with four men whose writings set a standard considered to be orthodox by the nineteenth century, Su proposes that the writings of women belonged to the sphere of extraordinary texts. If Su Renshan found the Confucian scholars (especially those who excelled in the eight-legged essay and therefore achieved government posts) at fault and responsible for the demise of the country, perhaps it was the female scholar who offered an alternative moral and intellectual barometer?

In this chapter, I conclude my analysis of Su Renshan by looking at his writings and depictions of women and, in so doing, bring together my earlier examinations. So far, I have shown the various elements of Su Renshan's painting seen against two early nineteenth-century narratives: the making of a Guangdong identity before the war, and the impact of the Opium War thereafter. I have spoken of how Su developed a literary vernacular approach to painting that differentiated from his peers, and how he used that approach to portray his frustrations against Confucian hypocrisy. These two overlapping narratives present an image of a contrary artist who has been relegated to art history's margins of oddity and madness. In this chapter, I situate his work in a framework that places him in the center and see his works as a continuation of ideas explored by his scholarly predecessors, namely, writers of literary novels. What Su shares with these writers is a common interest in the representation of women. In this final chapter, I demonstrate how Su's alternative benchmark of social, moral, and intellectual duties, explored in earlier chapters, belongs in the larger world of books.

My brief introduction of Qing novels sets the foundation for a more in-depth examination of women represented in Su's paintings, the sources of his images, and the significance of this hitherto unexplored characteristic of his paintings: the portrayal of intimate female sociality. To push my argument further, I would also suggest that one way of understanding Su's interest in the graphic line is to consider it as an extension of his interest in the literary novel and the printed page and how this may ultimately affect the way that viewers were meant to engage with Su's artworks. I am following the trajectory set by other scholars, such as Zhang Hongxing and Anne Burkass-Chasson, who have examined the impact of production advances on reading/visual engagement as responses to changes in the scroll format and the codex structure of paintings and books.[3] For example, titles, prefaces, inscriptions, and colophons on paintings act as forms of paratext that frame the painting, and artists exploit this paratext by engaging the audience in "reading" the scroll as codex, or the codex as scroll. By considering Su's interest in the graphic line as a deliberate mimicry of the printed line that directs, even if only rhetorically, his viewers to "read" his paintings, Su exerts an authorial presence that ultimately makes him as much a writer as he is a painter.

The Qing Novel

The Qing literary novel showcases the author's knowledge and moral values through strong intra-textual prose, a rich repository of motifs and characters, and literary ambitions. The dominant forms of storytelling strategies include a personal narrative voice, a profusion of commentaries, and internal voices of dreams and visions. Crucial to these developments was the shifting role of the author. Early novel writing, such as *Shuihu zhuan* 水滸傳 (Water margin), involved revisions by several writers who often used a vernacular voice inherited from oral traditions. By the late sixteenth century, the autobiographical genre was becoming increasingly fictionalized, and by the seventeenth and eighteenth centuries, novels were being written by single authors who brought personal experiences and learning to their stories.

Many of the new writers were accomplished scholars, and their novels are redolent of their scholarship. History, classics, mathematics, science, and geography blend with folk legends and mythical tales. This layering of genres resists a singular definition of the novel, but the writer is often perceived as a social critic or astute observer of society. Common patterns employed by the writer include destabilizing the normative order of canonical texts, ironic devaluation of the surface meaning of orthodox texts, and debunking cultural heroes, old virtues, and puritanical moralists. In particular, writers devised morally ambiguous plots that exploit the tension between ironic gestures and moralizing tendencies, as seen in many of the famous eighteenth- and nineteenth-century novels, including *Rulin waishi* 儒林外史 (The scholars), 1750, by Wu Jingzi (吳敬梓, 1701–54); *Honglou meng* 紅樓夢 (Dream of the red chamber), ca.1791, by Cao Xueqin (曹雪芹, act. ca. 1715–64); and *Jinghuayuan* 鏡花緣 (Flowers in the mirror), 1821–28, by Li Ruzhen (李汝珍, act. ca. 1763–1830). Again, each of these books has been thoroughly mined by scholars, but a quick summary of key points that are relevant to paintings by Su Renshan can contextualize my following analysis.

The significance of *Honglou meng* as an expressive vehicle of eighteenth-century angst and aesthetic sensibilities is undisputed. This lengthy text follows the romantic fate of a young man whose love for his ailing cousin is doomed by his obligations towards a family increasingly riddled with financial problems. It captures the mercenary careerist with a satirical bent echoed in many later novels. Similarly, the playful banter and literary amusements that celebrate the cultural, rather than the social, ideal of the literati are familiar motifs that can also be found elsewhere. The primary protagonist of this novel is Jia Baoyu (賈寶玉), who, throughout his life, refused to accept any of the traditional roles of the literati and escaped to spaces where social regulations and expectations were temporally suspended, such as in the garden where men and women, boys and girls, openly interacted. Su Renshan's painting of Su Shi's family is an example of how the garden was exploited as a space where the siblings casually interacted to create an unusual sense of intimacy. As scholars have argued, in the late eighteenth and early nineteenth centuries there was a search for authenticity in emotions that finds literary shape in women and the natural, and the development of an iconography of *qing* (情).[4] The garden became a space where these emotions were explored.

At the heart of this novel, and a theme continued by others, is the self-image of the literati. Most studies agree that there was an epistemological crisis in the eighteenth century that called for a reconceptualization of the role of the literatus.[5] This theme of the problems of forging self-images is most evident in *Rulin waishi*, considered the foremost satire of the literati world, focusing on the corruption of officialdom and the limits of literary mores. Set in the Ming period, the novel presents the unofficial history (*waishi*) of scholars and a series of interlinked stories that attack the obsessions with civil examinations and the consequent sterility of learning. One of the key storylines, and the climax of the novel, is the failure of the Taibo (泰伯) Ceremony held to honor

the ancient Confucian sage, and allows the author a plot where he scrutinizes and criticizes the limits of the very foundation of the scholarly class. This was a very popular novel and it is possible to regard Su Renshan's own thoughts on Confucian scholarly teachings as nineteenth-century echoes. What is also striking about this novel is the use of a vernacular that separated the book from the official language endorsed by the Classics. The combination of literary style and vernacular voice earmark the importance of this Qing novel.

Another novel that had an impact on Su Renshan is *Jinghuayuan*. As indicated by its title inspired by the Buddhist metaphor "flowers in the mirror, moon in the water," the novel is about the ephemeral and elusive qualities of an image, be it a literatus, an immortal, or a queen.[6] It is a topsy-turvy adventure story in which female immortals are invited to take the civil examinations usually reserved for male scholars, and both satirizes and celebrates the meaning of literati and other fictional reconstructions of identity. The author, Li Ruzhen, continued to work on this novel between 1821 and 1828. Thereafter, it was published several times, including as illustrated books that portrayed some of the main characters found in the novel. One extant illustrated version was published in Shunde in 1841, and it is possible that Su Renshan was acquainted with this book.

Jinghuayuan is a highly formalized work structured in two halves. The narrative begins by following the main protagonist, Tang Ao (唐敖), who, suffering from examination failures, decides to embark on a sea voyage with his brother-in-law, merchant Lin, and an old male servant. They travel to exotic islands where they come across various talented females who later turn out to be the incarnated fairies (Chapters 7–42). Tang Ao's daughter, who believed her father was lost, initiates a second journey and encounters more fallen fairies (Chapters 43–53). The second part of the novel marks their return and their journey to the capital to participate in a special examination designed for talented women set up by Empress Wu Zetian (武則天, ca. 625–705) (Chapter 68, Fig. 95).[7] As the literary scholar Stephen Roddy has argued, this gender-reversal story achieves "the feminization of intellectuality and its liberation from Confucian ethical and political exigencies and the corresponding effacement of men who became preoccupied with the demands of political loyalty."[8]

At the core of all three novels is the nature and value of traditional *ru* (儒 Confucian) scholarship. By following literary texts, novelists sought to emulate the philosophical teachings of the ancient sages, *rujia* (儒家). The paragon sage embodied benevolence, righteousness, and virtue, and textual and ritual competence. As scholars who had themselves received the training that forged these values that are now under scrutiny, what came increasingly to be at stake was the very core of their identity—the purpose of *ru* scholarship. These concerns, expressed in writings, use different means to question the value of *ru*, and from which are three key elements that are relevant to Su Renshan: the use of spaces where non-hierarchal relations are formed and where intimacy overturns social structures, the combination of vernacular and classical literary texts that operates as a form of social and political commentaries, and the use of mirroring or opposing structures to speak of what is and what can be.

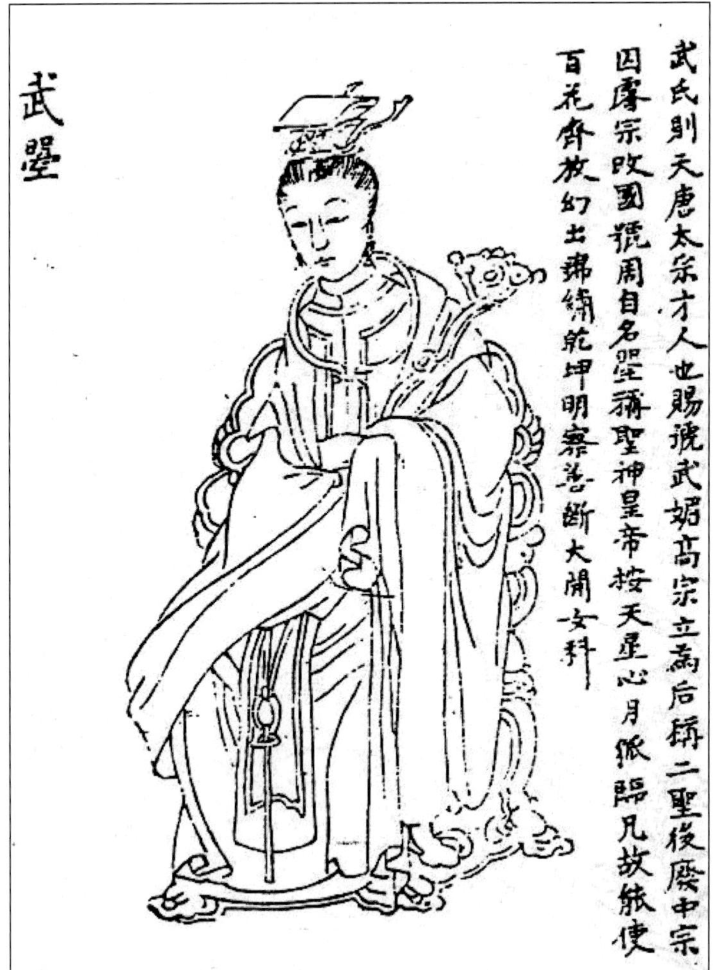

Figure 95 Image of Tang Empress from *Xiuxiang Jinghuayuan: Jieziyuan cang ban*, text by Li Ruzhen, images by Xie Yemei, 1841 preface date, Shunde, n.p.

In the Company of Women

I have borrowed the idea of "literary vernacular" in recognition of Su Renshan's indebtedness to the genre. I would suggest that he not only borrowed themes found in novels, but the manner in which he depicted them was in the position of the writer. This idea of the painter taking on the narrator's voice is evident in Su's hanging scroll painting of *Ladies Reading a Poem* (Fig. 96). This painting depicts two women, each with her own servant boy, holding an unrolled scroll on which Su's poetic inscription is written.

> A five-character and eight-line rhyme, in imitation of *Chongshan tie*
> A work produced with imperial authority with elegance by Empress Changsun [長孫皇后]:
> Ma Xuanxuan [馬玄玄], was too reckless, and Xue Susu [薛素素], was like an immortal.
> Bo Shaojun [薄少君] was truly generous, while Guo Zhenshun [郭貞順] guarded the frontiers.
> Wang Jiyuan [王激源] equaled others, and Xu Wan [徐媛] was slightly better than her teacher.
> There was Dongshan Xie [東山謝] from the Jin Dynasty, and the Song Loyalist who transformed into a pheasant-like bird from the waters.
> Nothing hinders Xu Jingfan [許景樊], and there are many dyed red paper slips belonging to Xie Tao [謝濤].
> Who knows the works of Empress Yang [楊太真], which are similar to that by Concubine Yang of the Song Dynasty?
> How many are there who play the nomad flute like Wang Qiang [王嫱]?
> Drafted and penned by Renshan.[9]

The inscription is a poetic list that celebrates the achievement of women, most of whom were famous poets dating from the Han to the Qing Dynasties, but they were also known for other skills and achievements.[10] The women in Su's re-created list do not fit with the virtuous and literary list of women found in orthodox histories but are of the marginalized types who do not conform to normative moral ethics. Xue

Susu (fl.1575–before 1652), a Ming poet based in Jiangsu, was an acclaimed horseback markswoman and considered herself a female knight-errant.[11] Xu Jingfan (1563–89) was a talented Korean poet who crafted Chinese-style poems. The Song Loyalist who was transformed into a pheasant-like bird is Lin Mo (林默, dates unknown) from Fujian, who, with her father, a coast guard officer, often went on rescue missions. There are numerous stories about Lin Mo, and of these the most popular is how, when she was young, her father and brother were out at sea when a storm suddenly arose, and they were thought to have been lost. Despite the hopelessness of the situation, Lin Mo went back out to sea alone, finding her father, and later returned with her brother's body. The traumatic event left her determined to remain unmarried and devoted to healing the sick and rescuing ships. After her death, she was believed to have turned into a mythical bird and flew into the mountains, and thereafter came to be the Mazu Goddess who rescued sailors.

Su's inscription is the central focus of the painting, and the two women holding onto the scroll are depicted absorbed in the act of reading. It is their shared experience of reading that makes this an unusual painting. The woman on the left has rolled up her sleeves, and, although exposed arms usually carry eroticized undertones, here, because of the lack of sensual treatment of the folds and the intense focus on the figures on the scroll, the rolled-up sleeves appear to emphasize a necessary practicality. The lack of sensuality or playfulness, characteristics commonly found in images of group female activities, suggests that Su's *Ladies Reading a Poem* belongs more to the tradition of male literati gatherings. Moreover, Su's female readers are actively absorbed in reading history, the cornerstone of moral scholarship. The history that is being read debunks historical canons that privilege a male center and addresses an audience that welcomes female literary company.

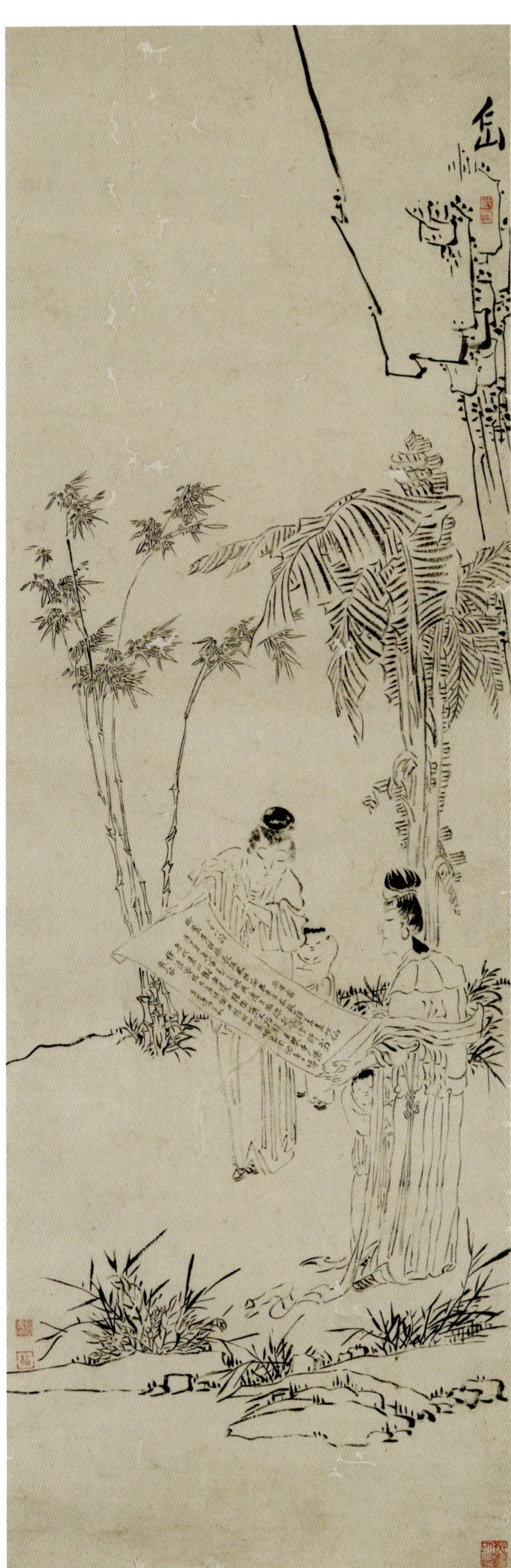

Figure 96   Su Renshan, *Ladies Reading a Poem*. Hanging scroll, undated, ink on paper, 121 × 38 cm. Reproduced by permission of the Art Museum of the Chinese University of Hong Kong from the collection of the Art Museum.

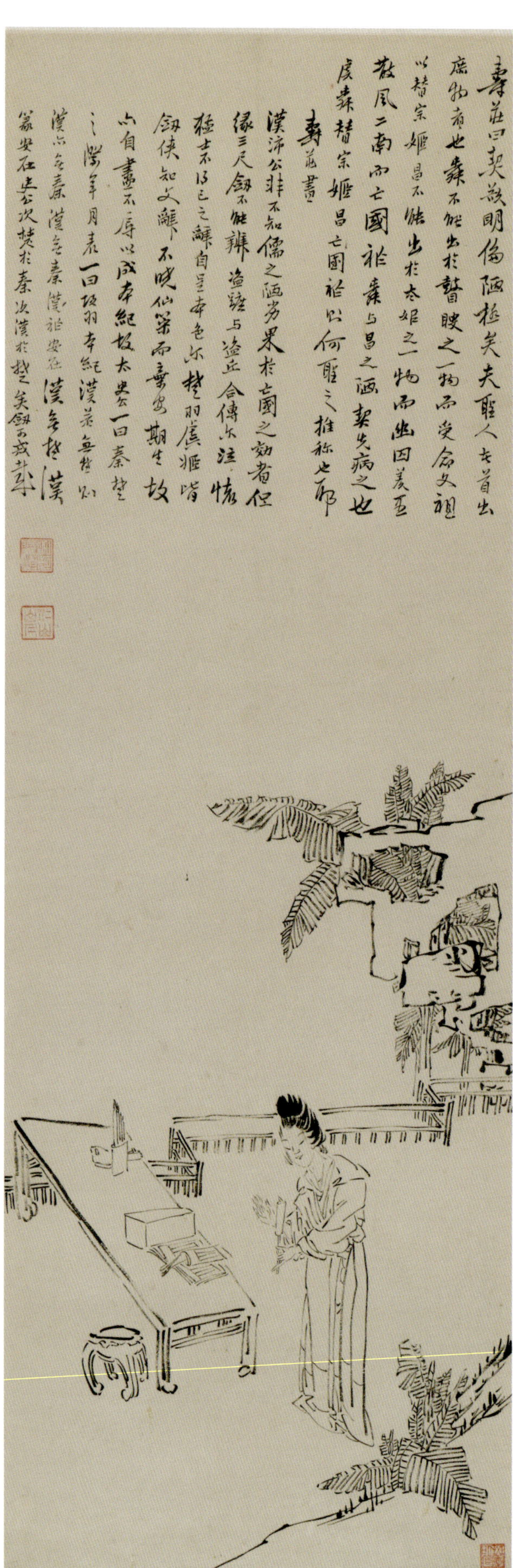

Figure 97 Su Renshan, *Lady with a Candle.* Hanging scroll, undated,
ink on paper, 120 × 41 cm. Reproduced by permission of the Art
Museum of the Chinese University of Hong Kong from the collection of the
Art Museum.

But within this world of female literary talents he has placed his words as the narrational focal point of the painting.

The theme of female readers can also be seen in another hanging scroll painting, *Lady with a Candle* (Fig. 97). In this painting, Su furthers his argument against the hypocrisy of the Confucian world through the filter of a female audience. Here, set in a garden, the female protagonist is shielding a candle as she moves toward a stone table on which are placed books, brushes, and an inkstone—the four treasures of a literati studio (the ink being implied). The theme of a solitary literary evening in the garden is not unusual. It evokes ideals of intimate reflections and yearnings. Above are two long inscriptions, the second of which is more pertinent to the present discussion:

> Shouzhuang [Su Renshan] says …
> … The Duke of Pei [劉邦] was not ignorant of the cruelty of Confucianism. In modeling himself on those who had lost their nations [i.e. his Qin and Chu predecessors] he solely depended on the three-foot sword and was unable to distinguish and thus jointly transmitted the heritages of Robber Zhi and Robber Qiu (Confucius). One laments the unwilling withdrawal of valiant men who were reduced to vaunting their natural talent.[12]
>
> [Xiang] Yu [項羽], [King] of Chu, and his concubine Lady Yu [虞姬], were both skilled sword-fighters. They were literate, but they did not understand the [writings on the] bamboo slips of the transcendent and rejected [the advice] of the immortal An Qisheng [安期生]. So they committed suicide to avoid dishonor, and in so doing completed their own annals. Thus the Grand Historian [Sima Qian, 司馬遷] gave [the story of Xiang Yu] the alternative titles of *The Monthly Annals of Qin Chu* and *The Annals of Xiang Yu*. If Han did not acknowledge Chu, it would not have been able to acknowledge Qin. If Han did not have Qin, where could the Han throne have sat? If Han had no Chu, where can the Han seal script be traced from? The Historian placed Chu after Qin, and Han after Chu. How can the sword be avoided?[13]

Duke of Pei, Liu Bang (ca. 246 BCE–195 BCE), during his quest to become ruler, he came up against Xiang Yu (項羽, or Yu of Chu), from a noble family, who had proclaimed himself the King of Chu. Liu Bang, a peasant, focused his efforts on developing agriculture (to supply food for his army) and training his men. After he had strengthened his military base, he launched a war against Xiang Yu. The war, dramatically documented in Sima Qian's *Shiji*, recalls how, when Xiang Yu was left with only a handful of retainers, he committed suicide. Despite the bloodiness with which the country was won, Liu Bang set up a model empire that would remain intact until the late nineteenth century. He introduced a centralized government, as opposed to a confederacy, vested in a single emperor, and his officials formed the imperial polity. The war between the two combatants demonstrated the death of the old heroic mode and the emergence of a new type of ruler.

The first line of Su Renshan's inscription accuses Liu Bang of harming the country because, even though he understood that *ru* scholars were crude, he adopted their "three-foot sword," a reference taken from *Shiji*, that came to symbolize a system of laws and punishments. An Qisheng (act. ca. Qin Dynasty), who later became worshipped as an immortal in Guangdong, was an official under the Qin Kingdom.[14] An Qisheng's words of warning were ignored, thus leading to the war between Xiang and Liu Bang held at Gaixia. The final stage of the war between Xiang and Liu Bang was held at Gaixia. Liu Bang ordered his army to sing songs from Xiang Yu's native home of Chu so that Xiang and his army would falsely believe that the Han army had defeated them. The morale of Xiang's troop flagged, and many left. Xiang Yu was in despair, and his beloved consort Lady Yu (act. ca. late Qin, early Han Dynasty) committed suicide. Sima Qian recalls the sad parting of Xiang and Lady Yu:

[Xiang] rose in the night and drank within the curtains of his tent. With him were the beautiful Lady Yu . . . Xiang Yu, filled with passionate sorrow, began to sing sadly, composing this song:

My Strength plucked up the hills,

My might shadowed the world;

But the times were against me,

And Dapple (his horse) runs no more.

When Dapple runs no more,

What then can I do?

Ah [Lady] Yu, My Yu.

What will your fate be?

He sang the song several times through, and Lady Yu joined her voice with his. Tears streamed down his face while all those about him wept and were unable to lift their eyes from the ground. Then he mounted his horse, and with some eight hundred brave horsemen under his banner, rode into the night, burst through the encirclement to the south, and galloped away.[15]

Sima Qian's narrative does not record Lady Yu's suicide. It was the later popularization of this scene that refocused the story of Lady Yu and her subsequent suicide using Xiang Yu's sword. It was a scene that was later immortalized in the much read Ming novel *Jinpingmei*[16] and disseminated in many different forms including popular songs, operas, and illustrated books. In this novel, and other popular versions, Lady Yu performs a sword dance before killing herself because she would rather die for the sake of loyalty than survive Xiang Yu.

Xiang Yu occupies an unusual position in Chinese history because he is often portrayed as a bad and aggressive leader whose arrogance was such that he ignored his wise advisors, yet at the same time, he is sympathetically treated. Sima Qian includes him in two different sections of his historical narrative. Xiang was included in the *Annals*, a title generally reserved for recording major events involving the emperor and his ruling bureaucracy. By including Xiang Yu in this section, Sima Qian was also recognizing Xiang Yu as a ruler, even though he never truly established a unified kingdom. This chapter is one of

Sima Qian's most widely admired and anthologized works. Xiang Yu is portrayed as possessing a noble spirit that his opponent, Liu Bang, lacked. The death of Xiang Yu, while tragic, was inevitable, with Sima Qian uncharacteristically questioning the meaning of justice and fate.[17]

In the rest of the inscription, Su Renshan takes a similar sympathetic view of Xiang Yu and likewise focuses on the emotional attachment of the lovers to evince a deeply human connection of devotion and loyalty, in contrast to the imposition of rules and laws set up by Liu Bang. As such, he combines Sima Qian's writing with popular portrayal of the lovers. The combination is not unusual, but it is rarely used to direct the pictorial theme of an image.

In the painting, Su uses a female reader (or perhaps a writer) as the filter through which this story is retold. The opened book with the corner of a page turned, and writing tools on the garden table would suggest that the lady in the painting is returning to her task of reading the story, and perhaps writing a response, bringing a candle with her to continue into the night. Ellen Widmer's recent work on the literary world of female readers and writers discusses the production and consumption of female-centered fiction.[18] By the 1800s, a strong network of female fiction readers was already in place endorsing not only works by women but also works by male writers such as Li Ruzhen and Cao Xueqin. James Cahill's work on vernacular painting also devotes substantial effort to looking at paintings made for a female audience, including paintings of women engaged in literary activities.[19] However, there is a considerable difference between genre scenes of women reading and this painting by Su Renshan. The depiction of the scene in ink on paper moves it away from the more familiar use of color that is commonly associated with female literati in their studios or similar spaces. Su's painting is also unusual because of the substantial amount of text in relation to the pictorial image. Su is not only presenting an image of a literary woman, but he is also presenting his words that blur history (by his references to certain texts and dynastic lineage) with fiction (Lady Yu's sword-dance suicide). At one level, the viewer is a companion to the literary woman reading these historical tales. At another, we are reading history as told by Su Renshan. The first inscription begins with the words, "Shouzhuang says," Shouzhuang being Su Renshan. He begins his inscription as a commentator and takes this device to showcase his own words and interpretations of a famous story. It is an interesting juxtaposition and one that makes it difficult to argue that depictions of women can determine the social or gender status of the viewer.

Another interesting aspect of Su's portrayal of the company of women is the incorporation of *kaozheng* elements. This is clearly seen in his *Ripening of the Five Grains* (Fig. 98). The inscription reads: "Ripening of the Five Grains. On Han steles, the character *shu* (熟) is written as *shu* (孰), to instruct [the people] that when the grains are not ripe, it means hunger (餓) is ripe."[20] This inscription is rooted in the definition of the character denoting hunger (餓) and may have had political implications or referred to a stele or a site that I have not been able to trace. What is more conclusive is that, by referencing Han steles and the etymology of words, Su's inscription follows the pedagogical roots of empirical studies.

In contrast to the dry clarity of the inscriptions, this painting revels in the intimacy of familial bonds. A young child smiles while clasping a toy as he clings to the *amah*, an old woman in sandals; her one leg raised appears as if she is about to take a large step forward. Behind is a small boy carrying bushels of ripe grain and looking down at a barking dog in mid-leap. A pair of magpies, a common rebus for happiness, flies above their heads and has caught the attention of the *amah*. Next to her is a younger woman, her hair tied in a topknot, indicating her married status. She

appears to be carrying a fishing rod and hat, which may reference regional agricultural practices of combining fish with rice paddies or with mulberry dikes, particularly in the West River basin area that includes Shunde, Su's home. The combination of farming provided very fertile land and generated substantial incomes for families. This is a painting of an outing of a mother with her children and her *amah*, perhaps going to or returning from the temple to wish for a bountiful harvest. The theme of harvest suggests that this may be related to *Shennong* 神農 (God of five grains), whose birthday falls on the twenty-sixth day of the fourth month.

Su has foregone all the usual pictorial conventions of color or rural background that one expects in genre paintings. Nonetheless, he has achieved a sense of intimacy by literally melding the bodies but has prevented them from becoming a jumbled ball of lines by breaking through with the strong diagonal line of a stick. This pole opens up the tight space of the group and balances the weight of the heavier dark ink above. Also, the general lack of color and empty background enhances the graphic appearance of the image coupled with the use of strong, unwavering ink that has all the appearances of lines being cut into a block of wood or into stone, like a Han stele.

The overturning of pictorial conventions is seen in an astonishingly large painting (120 cm × 247.5 cm) of a hundred women engaged in different duties in a palatial setting and recalls the premise again of *Jinghuayuan*. The painting, *One Hundred Duties* (Fig. 99), made when he was 33 *sui*, is an ambitious painting that captures something of the utopian environment of *Xiangjing tu* (Fig. 94), and the community of palace-like ladies in *High King Avalokitesvara* (Fig. 62). The horizontal scroll depicts clusters of females in different activities, such as preparing food, looking after horses, stacking books, and arranging antiques. Because it is situated on empty ground, it is difficult to ascertain the setting of this extraordinary

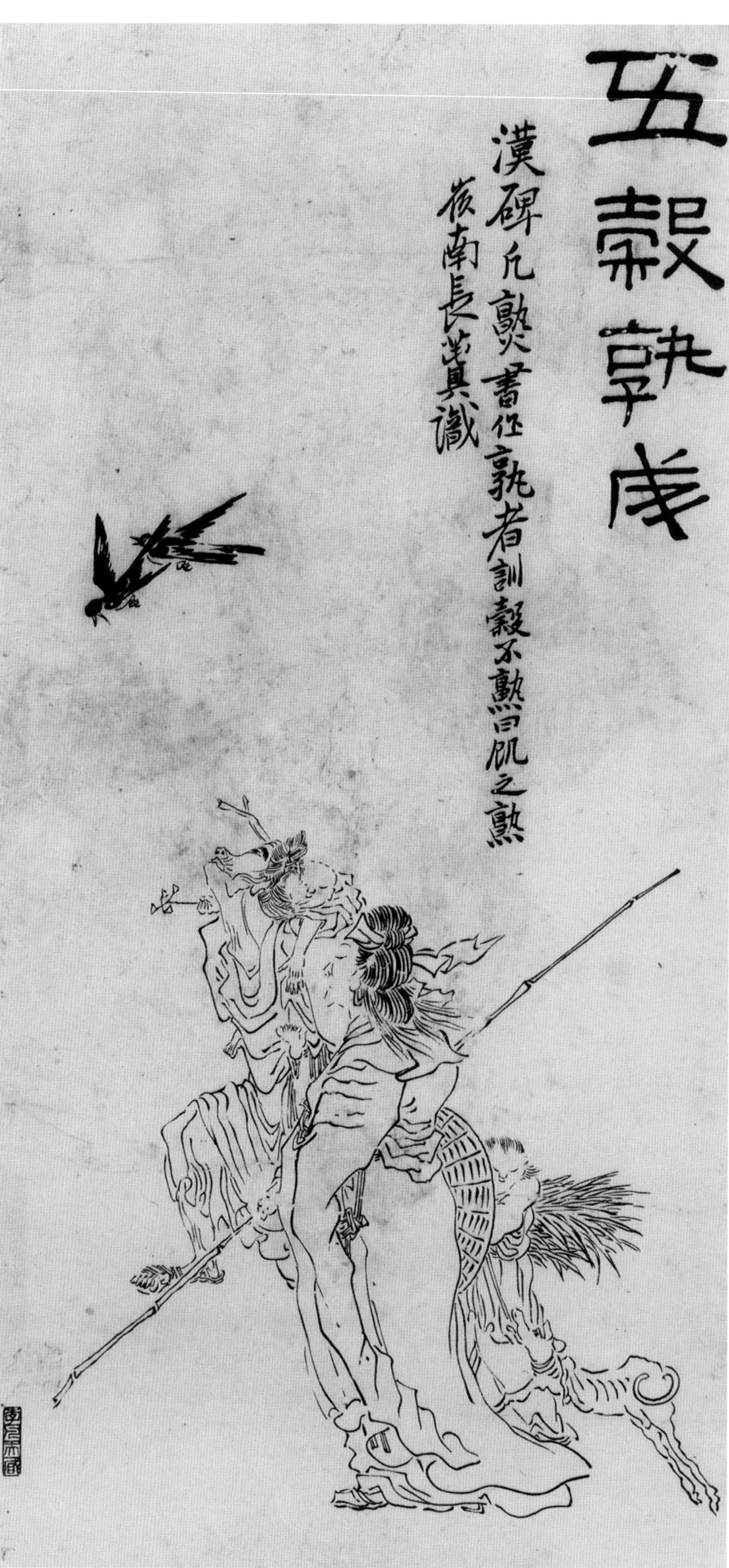

Figure 98 Su Renshan, *Ripening of the Five Grains*. Hanging scroll, undated, ink on paper, 62.5 × 29.5 cm. Guangzhou Art Gallery, Guangzhou Art Museum. After Kao Mayching, ed., *The Art of Su Liupeng and Su Renshan*, Hong Kong and Guangzhou: Art Gallery, The Chinese University of Hong Kong and Guangzhou Art Gallery, 1990, 221.

painting although there are enough visual clues to suggest that this is the world of elite women, and, possibly because of the large numbers of women, this is a scene of palace ladies. The women appear happily at leisure, looking at painting scrolls with friends, or, more frequently, doing household duties (Figs. 100 & 101). Happy smiles adorn a group of cooks who appear to be preparing for a feast. All the women at work have their sleeves rolled up and are bent over as they carry out their chores.

This is an unusual painting, because it refers to the theme of *One Hundred Beauties*, which is the more common framework for depicting large groups of women. It also echoes the familiar theme of *Spring Morning in the Han Palace*, painted by the likes of Qiu Ying (仇英, 1494–1552) in the Ming Dynasty and by Jin Tingbiao (金廷標, d.1767) in the Qing. More often such depictions carry a voyeuristic charge of erotic promise.[21] It could be that the women are preparing for a festival such as the Double Seventh Festival, and preparing for the silk making, feast, and other rituals connected as seen in paintings such as

Court Ladies Preparing Silk, attributed to Emperor Huizong (宋徽宗, 1082–1135) after Zhang Xuan (張萱, ca. 710–748). But while Su may reference these well-established themes, stylistically, his painting does not belong to either type. In Su's painting, the women vary from the young to the old; they differ in class status, with servants and the elite. The usual pictorial techniques of conveying sensuality (such as colors and patterns) are absent, and the women do not display any theatrical self-consciousness of being looked at. The ease with which these women conduct their various duties enhances the intimacy and everydayness of this domestic environment.

The painting is one of a pair; the other, depicting men, is entitled *One Hundred Sages of Xingtan* (Fig. 102). The companion painting depicts men sitting on mats, or standing clustered in small groups, engaged primarily in conversation, but some are alone in contemplation. The theme of *One Hundred Sages* is a play on Confucius and his many disciples. Xingtan (杏壇), meaning "Apricot Altar," was where

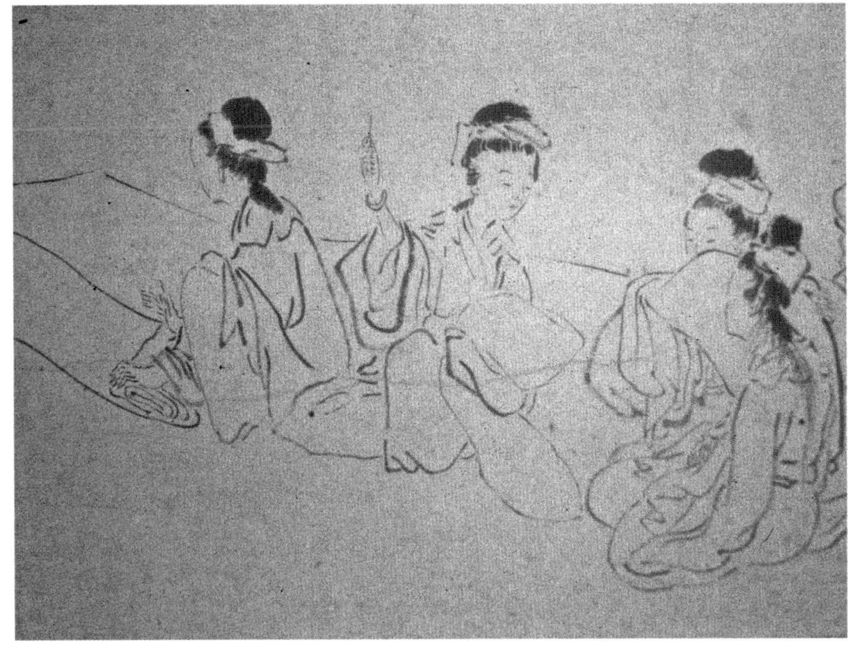

Figure 99 Su Renshan, *One Hundred Duties.* Detail. Horizontal scroll, undated, ink on paper, 120 × 247.5 cm, Guangzhou Art Gallery, Guangzhou Art Museum.

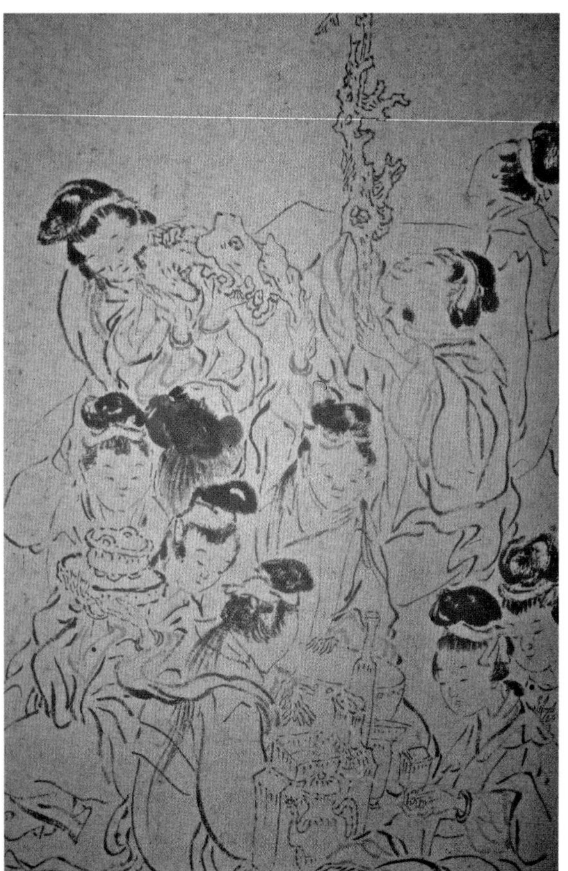

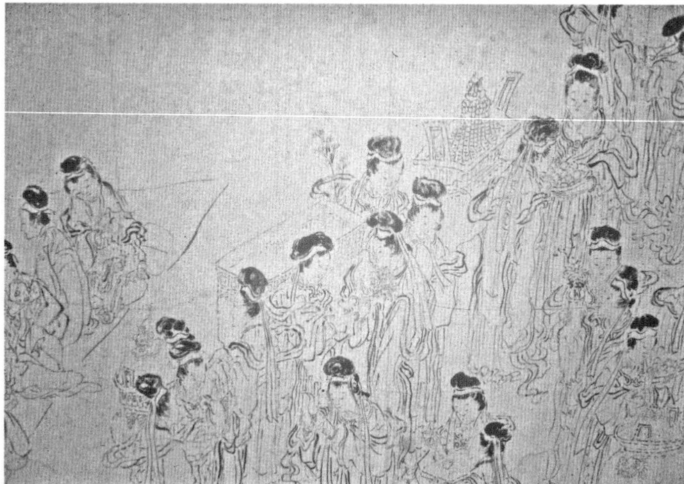

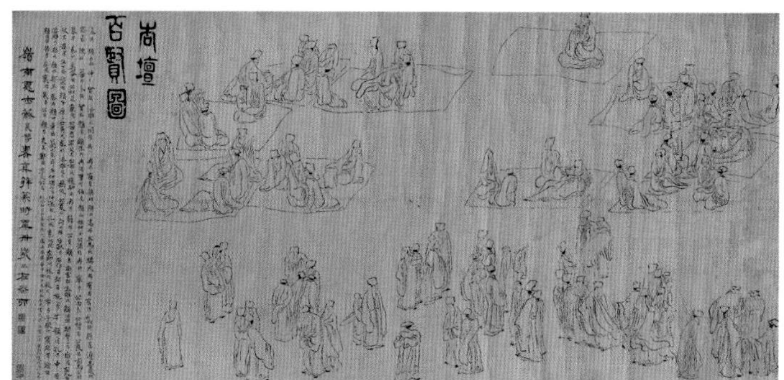

Figure 100 *(left)*   Su Renshan, *One Hundred Duties.* Detail. Horizontal scroll, undated, ink on paper, 120 × 247.5 cm, Guangzhou Art Gallery, Guangzhou Art Museum.

Figure 101 *(top right)*   Su Renshan, *One Hundred Duties.* Detail. Horizontal scroll, undated, ink on paper, 120 × 247.5 cm, Guangzhou Art Gallery, Guangzhou Art Museum.

Figure 102 *(bottom right)*   Su Renshan, *One Hundred Sages of Xingtan.* Horizontal scroll, 1843, ink on paper, 115 × 241 cm. Reproduced by permission of the Art Museum of the Chinese University of Hong Kong from the collection of the Art Museum.

Confucius presented his first lesson and is the name of Su Renshan's home village. At the top of the painting sits Confucius, with his tall cap and flowing long beard. It is a simple, almost cursory, execution of one hundred male scholars, with very little detail and variation between the figures. The absence of a background and the juxtaposition of the groups of figures on an empty background recall the simplicity of painting manuals of figures. In comparison, Su depicts a wider variety of female types and with greater individuality in their faces, dress, and postures.

It is the active world of women that Su marvels at. As a response to this new representation of a community of women at work, Su includes an inscription of one hundred female names—a genealogy of famous women that complements Confucius and his list of disciples—and gives identity, however imagined, to the individuals depicted in the painting. Once again, Su uses history, or, more precisely, his historical narration, to speak of a female utopian world.

The ability to intervene in, or invert, the familiar in Su Renshan's paintings intersects with the themes in *Jinghuayuan* and its dominant theme of the making of large female communities such as the Island of Women or a female dominant court ruled by Empress Wu. The conceit of the novel uses the theme of the mirror as a parallel conduit that extends to the structure of the novel of one hundred chapters, which can also be divided into two parts. It is likely that Su Renshan was familiar with this novel, not least because an illustrated version was printed in Shunde in 1841 (Fig. 95). This novel may also appeal to Su Renshan because the protagonists are from the Guangdong region, and their travels are based in the outskirts of the South China Sea. It has been suggested that the fantastic islands and events in the first section of the book evoke something of the exotic appeal of Lingnan in early nineteenth-century popular consciousness.[22] Furthermore, situating the novel in Lingnan also emphasizes the theme of marginality (in relation to the center), thus establishing a relation of opposites, in accord with its principal narrative strategies of contrast and mirroring.

This is taken literally in his 1848 painting *Figures* (Fig. 103), which includes an unusual description of his second sister. The relevant part of the inscription is revealing:

> In the fifth month of the summer of 1848, my second younger sister came to my humble abode to examine some rubbings. They dated from the Qin and Han Dynasties to the Song Dynasty. She approved of only a few of them. Only a rubbing of two lines by Wang Xizhi [王羲之] in his grass script from the stone inscriptions of the Yuelu Academy evoked a sign of approval. As for Yan Zhenqing's [顏真卿] Manjusri rubbing, she declared that it was not as good. I then pointed out the "flying white" script of Zhong Yao [鍾繇] and Wang Xizhi; moreover, it was the rubbing from Prince Su's *Model Calligraphies from the Imperial Archives of the Chunhua Era*. As for the rubbing by Lady Wei she said: "[The inscription to] *One Hundred Beauties*! Lady Wei? Her calligraphy is like this?" Afterwards she said, "How many female critics of poetry are there?" We examined the passage

of *Plum Blossom in Hot Summer* by the Taizong Emperor of Tang. The more she described it, the more she liked it. Later we turned to parallel prose and finished by discussing the preface of *One Hundred Beauties*. She left with one hand grasping a cloth umbrella and took off like a hawk on its first flight, all female duties of needlework abandoned.[23]

In 1848, when this painting was executed, Su Renshan was based in Guangxi. His sister had made the difficult journey from Guangdong to Guangxi, which was a route often besieged by bandits and robbers.[24] Her literary talents matched Su's as they spend the day engaged in an aesthetic and intellectual discussion of works in his collection. She was certainly as opinionated as her brother, as she easily dismisses one work after another, and she questions the absence of women as respected literary critics. She scoffs at the so-called attributed calligraphy of Lady Wei, the female teacher of Wang Xizhi, preferring the writings of the Taizong Emperor. Su's affection and admiration for his sister can be seen when he compares her with a hawk, a male symbol of virility, and notes that she no longer performs her needlework duties—abandoning the pursuit of feminine virtues. What is unusual in this inscription is that it is an example that shows how women were not merely figural ciphers but hints at a reformist possibility of truly believing that women were intellectual equals.

Su's painting shows a group of women with children. On the left, an old lady tenderly rests her firm hands on the shoulders of a young child. To the right, a young mother holds a baby in her arms. In the center is a figure dressed in formal robes. The figure is wearing a torque, a belt, and carrying a *ruyi* scepter, and follows the traditional depiction of a court emperor or high official. However, on closer inspection, the figure is depicted wearing a phoenix crown, identifying the figure as a woman. It is possible to examine the painting as a portrayal of intergenerational bonding, where the group of figures

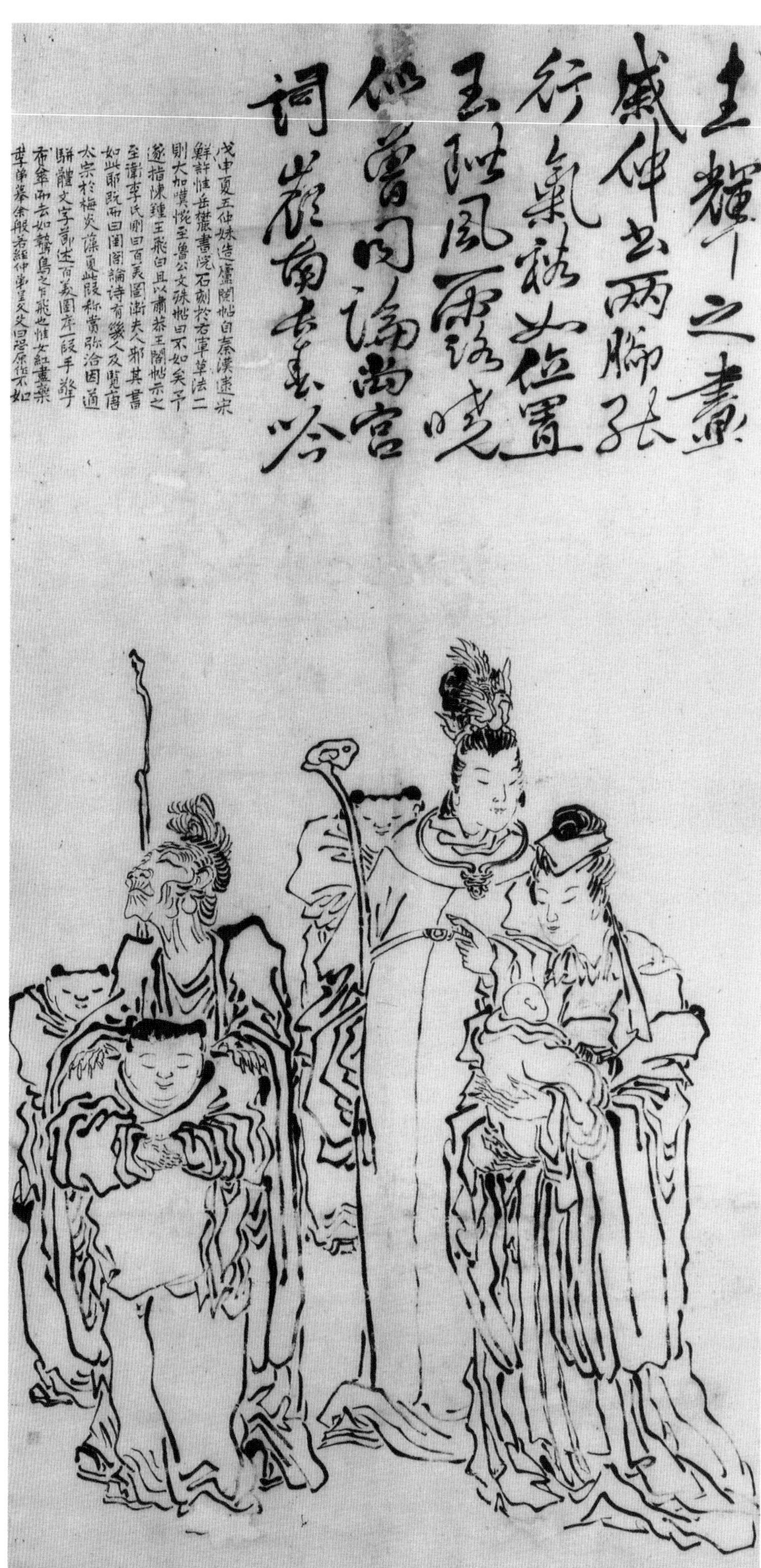

Figure 103 Su Renshan, *Figures*. Hanging scroll, 1848, ink on paper, 237 × 119 cm. Guangzhou Art Gallery, Guangzhou Art Museum. After Kao Mayching, ed., *The Art of Su Liupeng and Su Renshan*, Hong Kong and Guangzhou: Art Gallery, The Chinese University of Hong Kong and Guangzhou Art Gallery, 1990, 267.

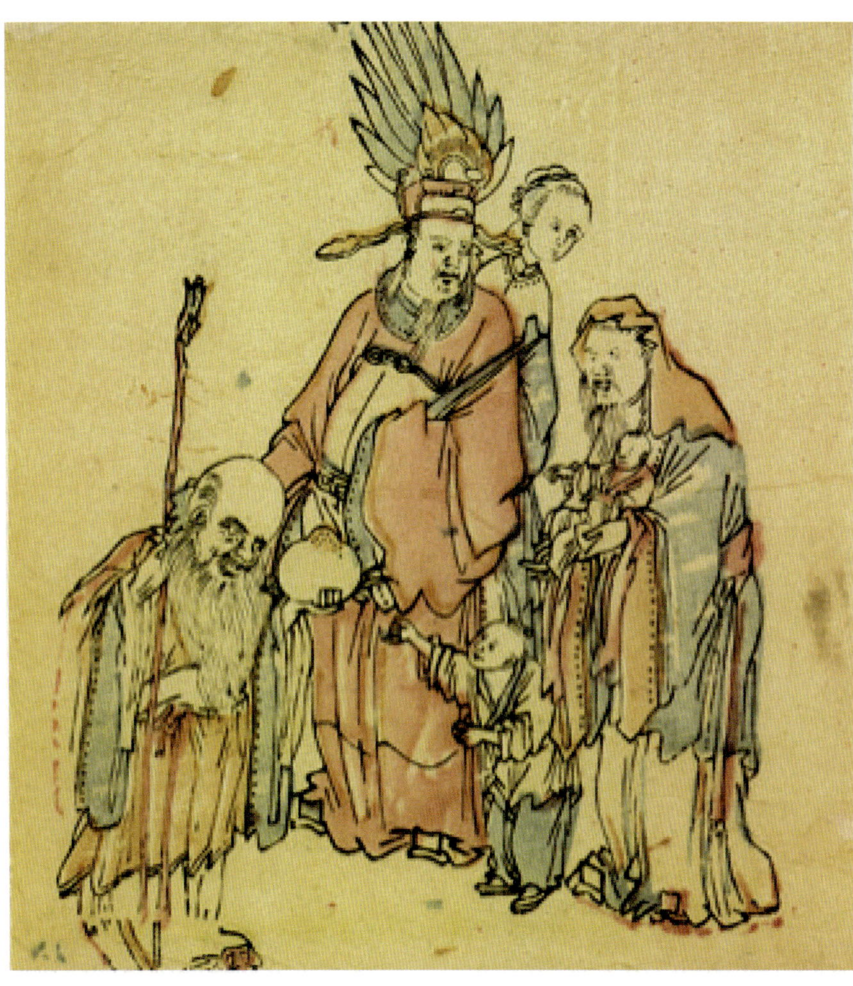

Figure 104 Anon., *Fu Lu Shou,*
print. Whereabouts unknown.

has melded into an organic mass, emphasizing their bond. Intimacy is also reflected through the depiction of touch: the old grandmother with her hands on the grandson, and the young mother clasping the newborn child.

The conceit of this painting is again a play on the theme of reversal seen in the novel *Jinghuayuan*. The three key characters—the imperial figure, the young mother, and the old woman—demonstrate a gender reversal of a more familiar auspicious iconography, the three Daoist star gods: Fu (福 wealth and happiness), Lu (祿 affluence and achievement), and Shou (壽 longevity). They are often represented as a gentleman-official (Fu, or Jupiter), an imperial official at court (Lu, or Ursa), and an elderly gentleman (Shou, or Star of the South Pole). In traditional astrology, the planet Jupiter was believed to be auspicious, generally seen in scholars' dress or holding a child. Lu is worshipped as the deity associated with imperial examinations and dressed accordingly, and Shou, as an elder gentleman, is often depicted smiling. As auspicious symbols, images of the Star Gods were very popular, especially from the Qing Dynasty onwards and were found on an array of art forms, including ceramic designs, paintings, and folk-art prints. It is possible to read Su Renshan's *Figures* as the gender reversal of the Three Star Gods, the empress as Lu, the young mother as Fu, and the elderly woman as Shou (Fig. 104). Su, with great wit, suggests that a propitious tomorrow was to be found in the alternative world of women.

The Aesthetics of Print

The relationship between painting and the literary novel is more than one based on an illustrative premise in which the image works with the text to narrate an episode, or where the artist is trying to project himself within the referenced stories. I will suggest that what Su is exploiting in his painting, and what makes him an unusual artist, is how strong his authorial presence is. By authorial presence, I am referring to the imprint of the narrator who offers both a "voice" (telling a story) and a "perspective" (opinion in the story) that directs the meaning of the painting. Moreover, I will demonstrate how paintings by Su Renshan require the audience to "read" (讀 *du*) as much as "view" (觀 *guan*) his works. My argument for different ways of looking follows the work by Craig Clunas, who distinguishes between *du* and *guan* and postulates that the viewing experience is dependent on the duration of time spent looking: With *du* the eye travels across the surface, whereas with *guan* the eye penetrates the surface.[25] Clunas further emphasizes the element of study or learning that is involved with *du* in comparison to the sensory perception of *guan*. As such, different ways of looking embody different performative acts. While terms associated with looking are often interchangeable, Clunas's premise for *du* and *guan* is a useful guide. I will argue that the flatness of Su Renshan's paintings, the density of his words, and the learning required by his audience suggest that Su assumed the roles of both writer and painter, and his audience of viewers and readers.

At some level, most Chinese paintings reveal glimpses of an "author" because of the long-standing self-reflexive relationship forged between painting and inscriptional text. The legibility of the storyline (achieved through time and space development) is largely effaced by the potent psychological effect of capturing a story-moment. An example of this can be seen in paintings by Ming artist Tang Yin (唐寅, 1470–1524), who often drew upon earlier stories to capture a narrative climax and projected himself into the story as the commentator of that captured moment.[26] With his inscriptions, Tang directed his reader to dissect the allusions and metaphors of the original texts by drawing parallels with current events, situations, or people.

The imprint of authorial presence, as argued here, pushes that strategy further by suggesting that artists anchor the "I" of the painting by directing the viewer by means of a first-person narrative voice in the inscription and using devices and motifs borrowed from the literary-novel genre. This charged "I" claims an authority and intimacy over an image that, when linked to its inscription, dramatically alters the textual source(s) through reframing and misreading. As such, the authority of the "I" also makes it harder for readers to project themselves into the work, and this maintains their status as readers of the work.[27] We have this, above, in the way that he imposes his voice into paintings such as *Ladies Reading a Poem* and again in *Lady with a Candle* and uses the composition and the relation between text and image to emphasize his authority as a writer.

If, as I am arguing, Su Renshan draws inspiration from and identifies with writers of literary novels, it sets up an interesting pictorial problem. In many ways the literary novel is a complex text to "translate" into a painting, as it involves multiple roles and passage of time (so often lengthy in pages), portrays morality that is less straightforward than that proposed in didactic works, and moves beyond the allusions more commonly associated with poetry. I have hinted at some of these problems in my mapping of Su Renshan's paintings of women. I would go further by suggesting that he was not only borrowing the craft of storytelling from literary novels and translating it into paintings by compressing plot devices and meshing well-known stories into a single frame of a hanging scroll or an album leaf, but he adopts the visual element of the printed book to emphasize a distinctive readability that, when exaggerated in size as a hanging scroll, pushes painting conventions. It is through this type of intervention in familiar stories and in the pictorial craft that he is able to create an entirely new fabula, making him a writer and painter.

The Mimicry of Print

As argued here, Su Renshan's paintings create a collaborative space using themes and strategies found in literary novels, such as gender reversals and mixing the vernacular with the literary; the paintings ultimately form a new "text." This approach, while not entirely new, set the groundwork for Su's later paintings. My close reading of paintings in this section looks at how far Su Renshan pushed the creation of a collaborative space in which the relationship between narrating and reading reconfigures the relationship between text and image. I suggest that he exploited the representational qualities of his painterly craft by appropriating the graphic quality of the printed page. He turned to the emulative process found in painting manuals, printed books, and rubbings, which initially had been part of his training following the standard model of learning in Chinese art.[28] However, in most instances when artists started with a printed medium as their source material, they would transcend the process of replication by a painterly display of brushwork that defined them as artists and erased their debt to the printed source. In contrast, Su Renshan renders print as the final product of his painting. This is no less a performance of his artistic abilities, but Su would also have been attracted to the ideals of the print as a medium that crossed class and gender boundaries.

In *Landscape with Willow*, a large hanging scroll dated to 1846 (Fig. 105), Su depicts a landscape of disjointed compositional parts. The basic structure

of this landscape is typical of Chinese landscape painting. There is a foreground of a village among banks of willow trees, and a lone fisher to the side. The middle ground sets the space for anecdotal details. Above, floating in space is a band of mountain peaks, and to its right is his inscription. However, none of these sections are connected to one another but are presented as fragmented landscapes. In contrast, an almost congenial atmosphere is evoked in his inscription:

> In the deep shade of willows, summer growing late.
> There lies a still pond of the mansion at the hamlet's edge.
> A neighbor carrying a box takes advantage of the morning cool.
> He is coming to settle the outcome of yesterday's game of chess.
> Copied at the Waterside Studio of Whales and Flying Fish in *bingwu* year in early autumn.
> Renshan wrote the character 贏 (to win) as 盈, Liuru smiled and said, "In my lifetime, I have only composed poetry or offered rhymes. Today, do you want to introduce sounds? Renshan laughed, and said, "Elder gentleman, you pretend that you do not know sound, I pretend that I do not know words." Liuru laughed loudly; Renshan also laughed loudly. This was their meeting amid mountains and forests.[29]

The inscription reveals Su Renshan's more playful side as he teases the boundaries of time and space in his imagined landscape where friends laugh and play chess together. However, Liuru, Su's friend, is Tang Yin, the famous Ming painter and poet. In this reconstructed landscape, Su goes back to the past, to converse with a kindred spirit, another literatus who failed to gain an official position but, more importantly, someone who was also highly intelligent and would use non-canonical writings, such as plays and drama, as intellectual and creative stimulants. They laughed at phonetic mistakes, the character for winning (贏) wrongly written as "盈," a homophone. The mistake created by writing

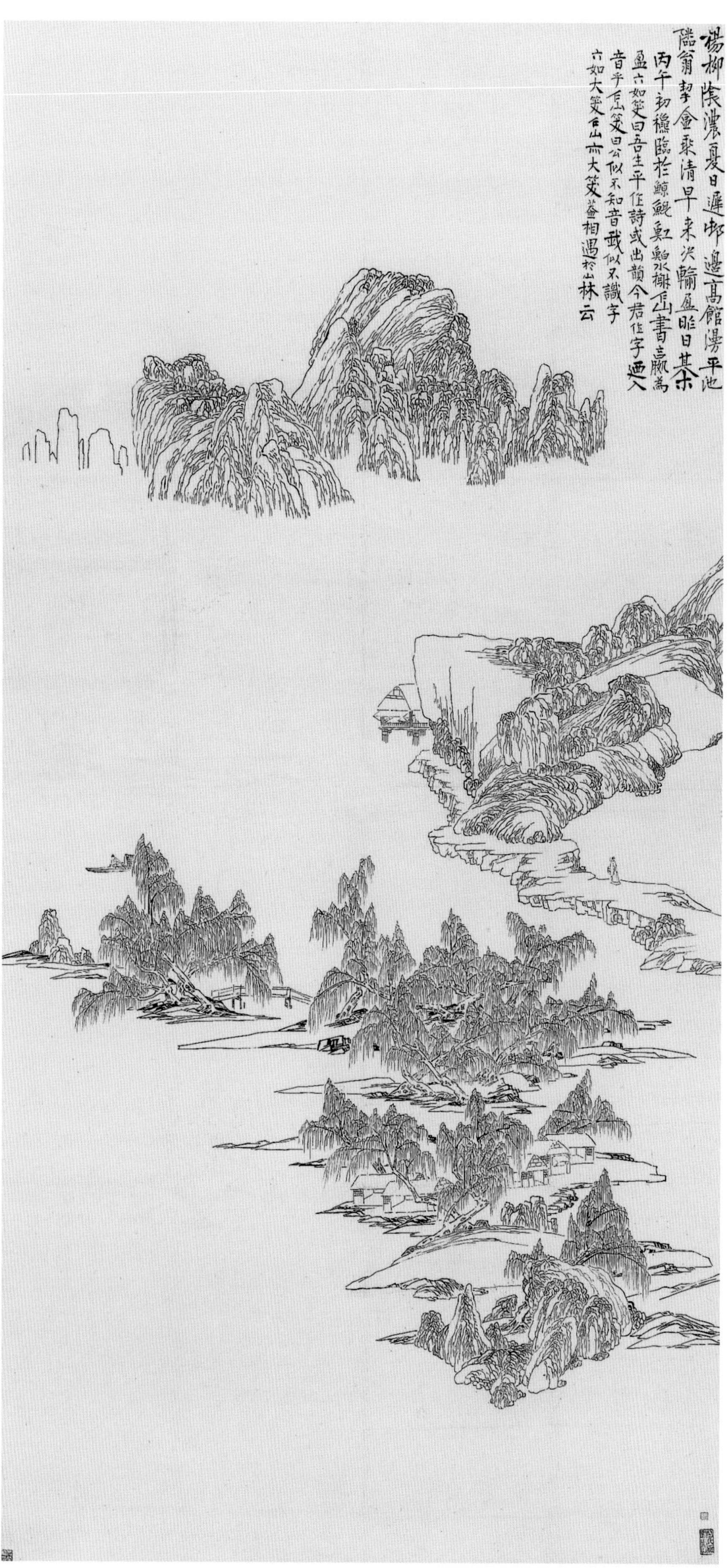

Figure 105 In *Landscape with Willow*. Hanging scroll, dated 1846, ink on paper, 257 x 119 cm. Reproduced by permission of the Art Museum of the Chinese University of Hong Kong from the collection of the Art Museum.

a character based on sound rather than on meaning may suggest something of the difficulty in exchanges between Cantonese and Mandarin speakers, who may write the same way but pronounce words so differently that misunderstandings were not uncommon. The disconnections in this painting, however, were not found in regional differences (it is an intimate exchange between friends) but rather the knowledge that this conversation could never have taken place.

Su Renshan forms a connection with Tang Yin through an unusual source. The poem cited at the beginning of the inscription comes from a painting by Tang Yin, reproduced in Wang Gai's *Jieziyuan huazhuan* 芥子園畫傳 (Mustard seed garden painting manual) (Fig. 106). It is possible that Su's knowledge of Tang Yin's painting came from the painting manual, as it is unlikely that he saw the real painting. But it may also be possible that Su exploits the printed manual by deliberately referencing the fragmented layout of the printed book's page. Su also paints with the distinctive unwavering line that mimics the printed line, but what is unusual about this painting is its size, and in this exaggerated form it heightens the graphic quality. In all, this is a painting about painting transmitted through the manual. The meeting of the two artists separated by time is claimed by Su Renshan to have taken place "amid mountains and streams," a standard trope for landscape painting. The self-revealing artifice of this meeting is therefore a poetic testimony for an object that was known for its reproduction value.

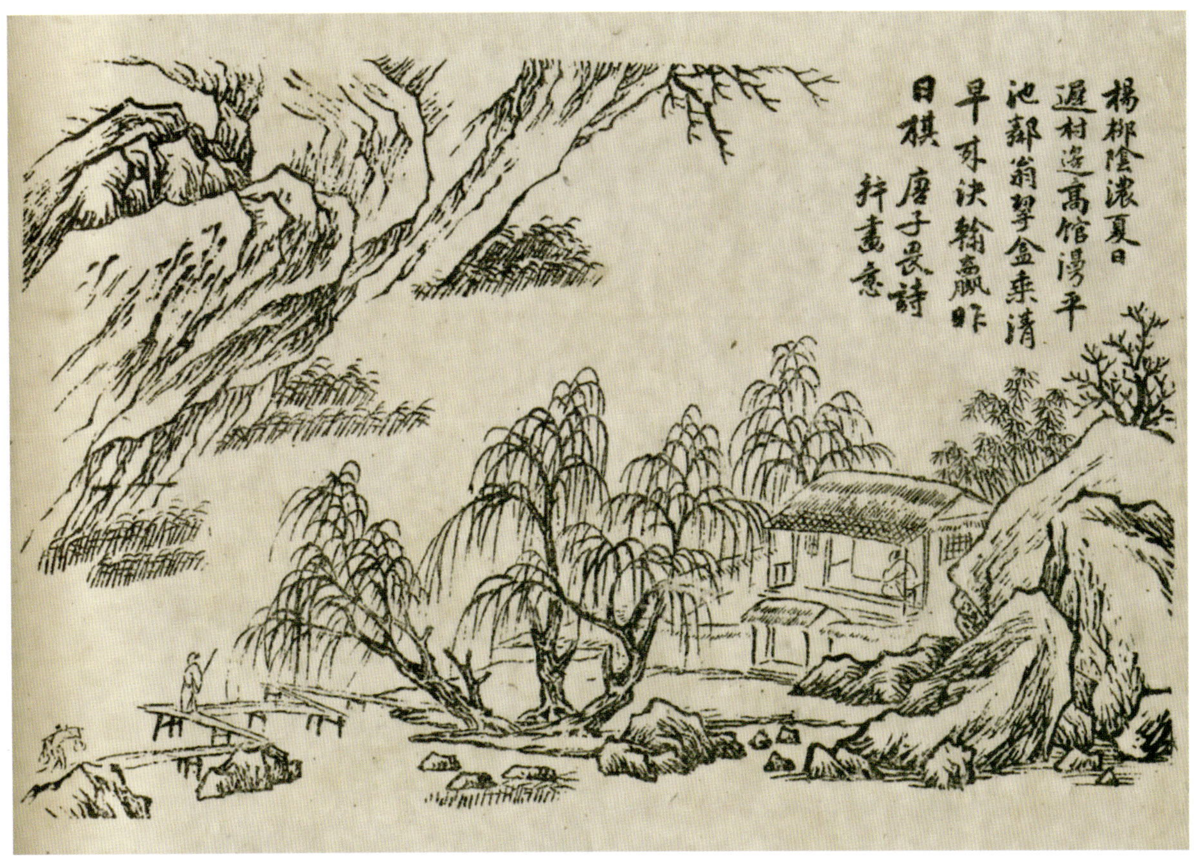

Figure 106 After Tang Yin, *Landscape and Poem.* Wang Gai, *Mustard Seed Garden Painting Manual.* Facsimile reproduction, vol. 1, *juan* 5 (on landscapes: hanging scroll format by master painters), 1b, 1977.

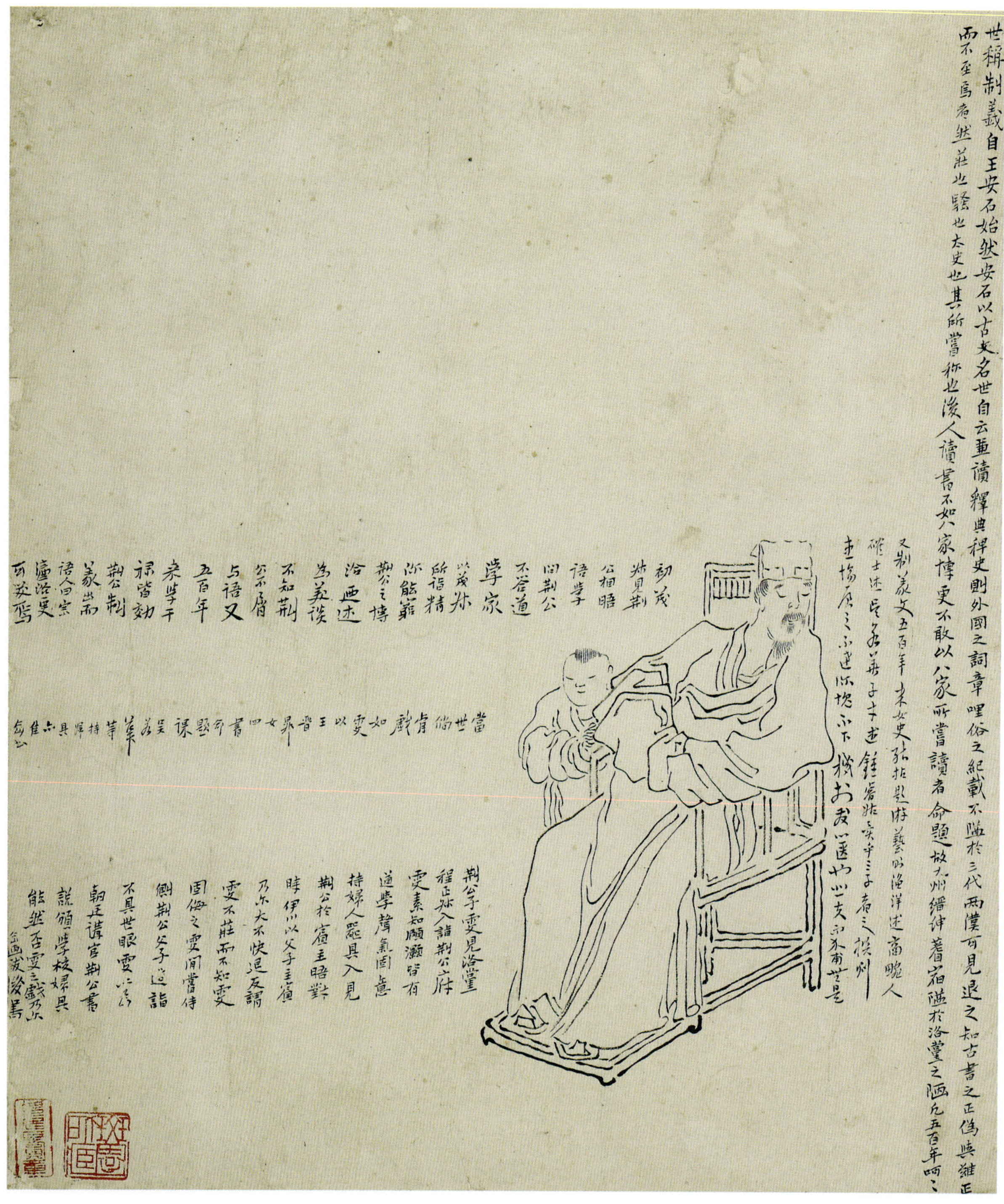

Figure 107 Su Renshan, *Portrait of Wang Anshi* in *Album of Figures*. Album of four leaves, 1847, ink on paper, 35 × 29 cm. Reproduced by permission of the Art Museum of the Chinese University of Hong Kong from the collection of the Art Museum.

Evidence of this painting-as-print is seen in an album-leaf portrait of Wang Anshi (王安石, 1021–86), a Song Dynasty prose writer and radical and controversial reformist (Fig. 107). Su uses a center-tipped brush for minimal fluctuation within the strokes. He avoids shading and color and exploits the juxtaposition of geometric forms to flatten the surface. Scholars have noted that this painting references the printed portraits by the Fujian artist Shangguan Zhou, whose works were popular in Guangdong, and consequently interpret the image as a reflection of regional taste and as a compensatory replica of an artist who had little means of seeing authentic artworks. However, this interpretation does not explain why Su Renshan insisted on maintaining the appearance of print. If we accept that Su was working against the normative structure of painting aesthetics, to him, the printed image vis-à-vis the ink brush painting bears a similar relationship to that between the novel and the Classics. Indeed, instead of suppressing the print aesthetic, Su revels in the graphic quality of lines and consequently takes it outside the usual aesthetic hierarchy that favors brush traces.

It can be argued that Su's desire to expand the sources that one reads as a means of going beyond the restrictive structure of classical learning was nonetheless a conceit rather than a pursuit. By producing paintings, Su demonstrated a greater interest in the strategy of mimicry than in concretizing his utopian idea by reaching out to a broader audience by producing actual prints. Moreover, his complex narratives and references suggest a readership familiar with canonical texts as well as vernacular stories, and sophisticated enough to understand how and what he was borrowing from the two. As seen in his *Portrait of Wang Anshi*, Su exploits the formal arrangement of inscriptions to assert his presence as the writer; he does not forego or hide his training as an erudite scholar. His "voice" or his presence underscores the

inscription through his placement of the text in two columns on the right and, more unusually, in horizontal bands on the left. This arrangement asserts a strong inscriptional presence, once again emphasizing the authority of the written word—or more precisely, the authority of Su Renshan's words. The lengthy inscription begins with praise for Wang and his unconventional training:

> Generations claim that the eight-legged essay began with Wang Anshi. But Anshi was famous for his *guwen* prose. He said himself that he also read works from the Buddhist canon and popular literature, as well as foreign poetry and prose and vernacular records. He did not restrict himself to the books from the Three Dynasties and the Two Hans. It can be seen that Han Yu could distinguish ancient texts from apocryphal ones and know which ones were admissible yet not penetrating. But *Zhuangzi*, Qu Yuan's *Li Sao*, and Sima Qian's *Records of the Grand Historian* are all works that he praised. Later scholars are not as erudite as the Eight Masters [of the Tang and Song], and they do not dare propose essay questions using phrases from the books read by the Eight Masters. Thus, the officials and venerable scholars of China have been confined by the secular world with the vulgar ways of the Cheng brothers for the last five hundred years. Ha ha![30]

Wang Anshi is famous for advocating a pseudo-welfare state, regulated wages, and pensions for elderly people and those who were unemployed.[31] Part of his scheme included education reform, such as new state schools, examinations, a fresh curriculum, and the establishment of scholar-officials, to support the political elite serving the state through the institutions of government.[32] In the eleventh century, questions were raised among the educated elite concerning the role of government in relation to society. By evoking Wang Anshi, Su was using historical figures to draw parallels with the current situations and pointing out how Wang's unusual reading habits had been forgotten by later scholars aspiring to or working in bureaucratic office. Indeed, training such as Wang's could only be seen in the literary activities of scholarly women who were not burdened by the civil examination curriculum.

> Over the last five hundred years of eight-legged essays, educated ladies were able to select titles [for questions] as an artistic leisure pursuit. Thus, Shang Wanren [商畹人] was a disciple of Wang Shizhen [王世貞], Wu Ruohua [吳若華] was a disciple of Shen Deqian [沈德潛], and Zhong Ruigu [鍾睿姑] was taught by Yuan Mei [袁枚].[33] How exceptional the three [female] masters' compositions were! One grieves that they could not reach the examination yard and feels deep shame! . . . Over the last five hundred years, students seeking official emolument have all followed the model of Wang's eight-legged essay, yet they go forth and tell people they are of the Qian and Luo schools. This is even more laughable. If people today could be as playful as [Wang] Wen [王雯], using the *Women's Four Books* by Wang Xiang [王晉昇] to set examination questions, and exhort the likes of Wu Ruohua to carry the "matron's tools" (broom), it would be a fine thing. Written by Renshan.[34]

The ending of his inscription was too abstruse, and he elaborated his thoughts by appending a section recalling a well-known anecdote of Wang Anshi's son, Wen (who reads the *Women's Four Books*), to explain why Wen carried a broom rather than a brush.

> Wang Anshi's son, Wen, saw Cheng Yi of the Luo School entering his father's home to pay a visit. Wen knew well that the Cheng bothers, Yi and Hao, were reputed to be Confucianists and deliberately carried a broom to meet them. When Wang formally received his guest, Cheng Yi thought that this was the way that the father and son received guests. He was most unhappy and retreated. He turned around and said that Wen was not correct in his conduct, but he did not realize that Wen had been deliberately insulting.
>
> Wen occasionally attended court. Although father and son both reached a level of attainment in their scholarship, they did not see things in a worldly fashion. Wen, too, lectured at court on administration. Wang Anshi's books and teachings were promulgated in schools, but how could

> the same be true of [the story of] the broom? Thus, this was only a joke of Wen. Renshan added this inscription later to the painting and its colophons.[35]

Although it would appear that Su is simply recalling a famous anecdote in his inscription, the details of his version differ from the original, and this deliberate misreading has been used to introduce an unusual degree of satire. Su alerts his readers to his intent by insisting that Wen, who had inappropriately greeted the conservative neo-Confucian scholar Cheng Yi, was merely playing a "joke." By calling attention to Wen's escapade as a deliberate ploy, Su engineers a sardonic tone as he himself becomes the instigator of a joke. Su distorts the story using lexical devices: Wang only had one son who reached maturity, Wang Pang (王雱, 1044–76). Su misnames Wang's son in his inscription as Wen (雯) by replacing the bottom component *fang* (方) from the character *pang* (雱) with the component *wen* (文). In so doing he has altered the name and possibly gender of Wang Pang. Wen is a character more commonly found in female names, and Su's cross-gendering adds to his twist of the anecdote, which had been circulating since the twelfth century. Wen's cross-dressing was hinted at in the earlier section of the inscription, as he had supposedly learned the *Women's Four Books* rather than the *Four Books*, which were standard classics for the Han male scholar. In the original anecdote, Wang Pang greeted his father and Cheng Yi while wearing a woman's hat; in Su's version, Wang Wen greets guests with a broom. By inserting a lexical clue that changes the gender, Su has also exploited the meaning and cultural authority of *wen* (文) as writing/culture, to set up a different confrontation, one between the broom (the matron's tool) and the brush (the scholar's tool). This brings his story back to the premise of female writers being as talented as male scholars.

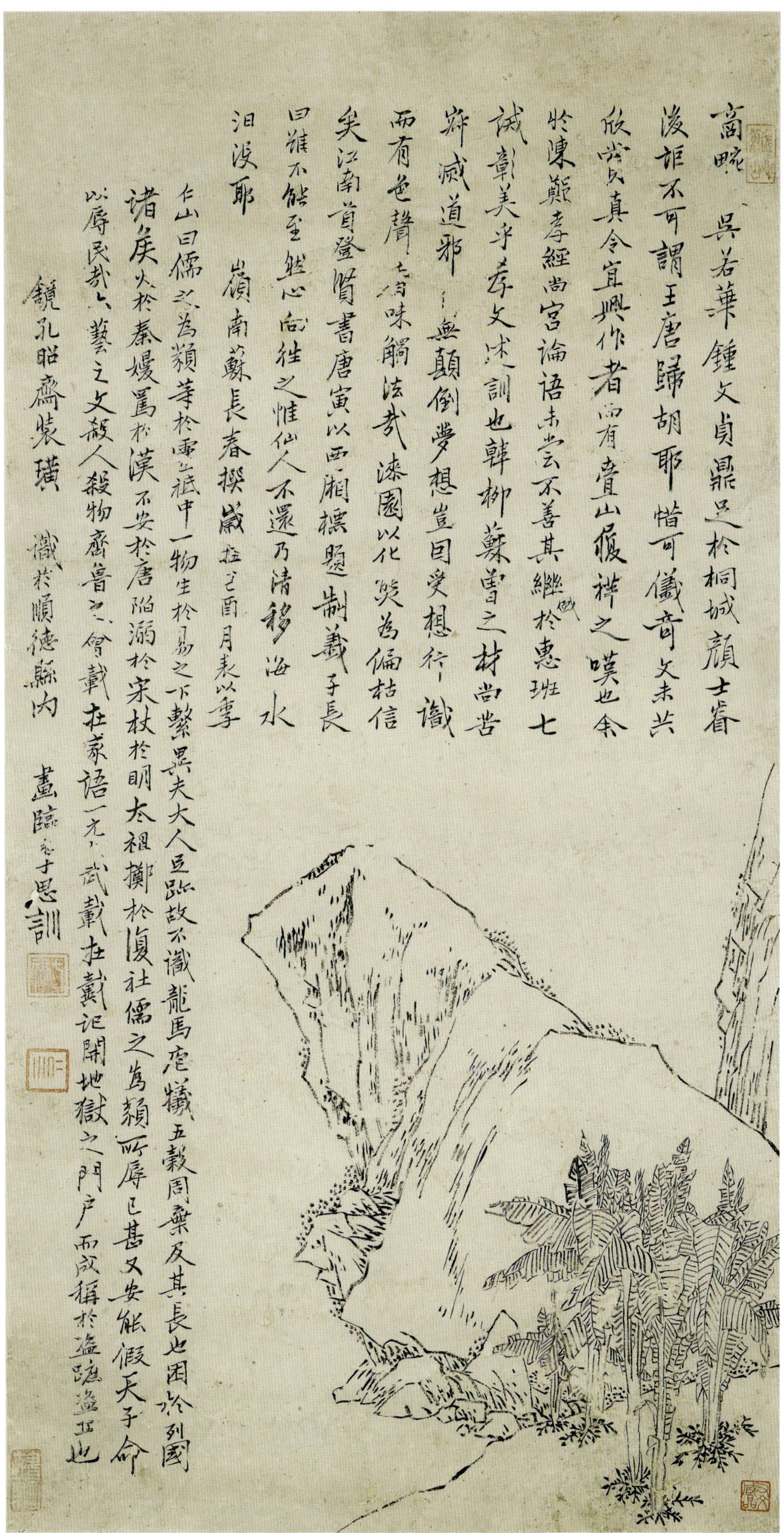

Figure 108 Su Renshan, *Landscape after Li Sixun.* Hanging scroll, 1850, ink on paper, 72 × 37 cm. Reproduced by permission of the Art Museum of the Chinese University of Hong Kong from the collection of the Art Museum.

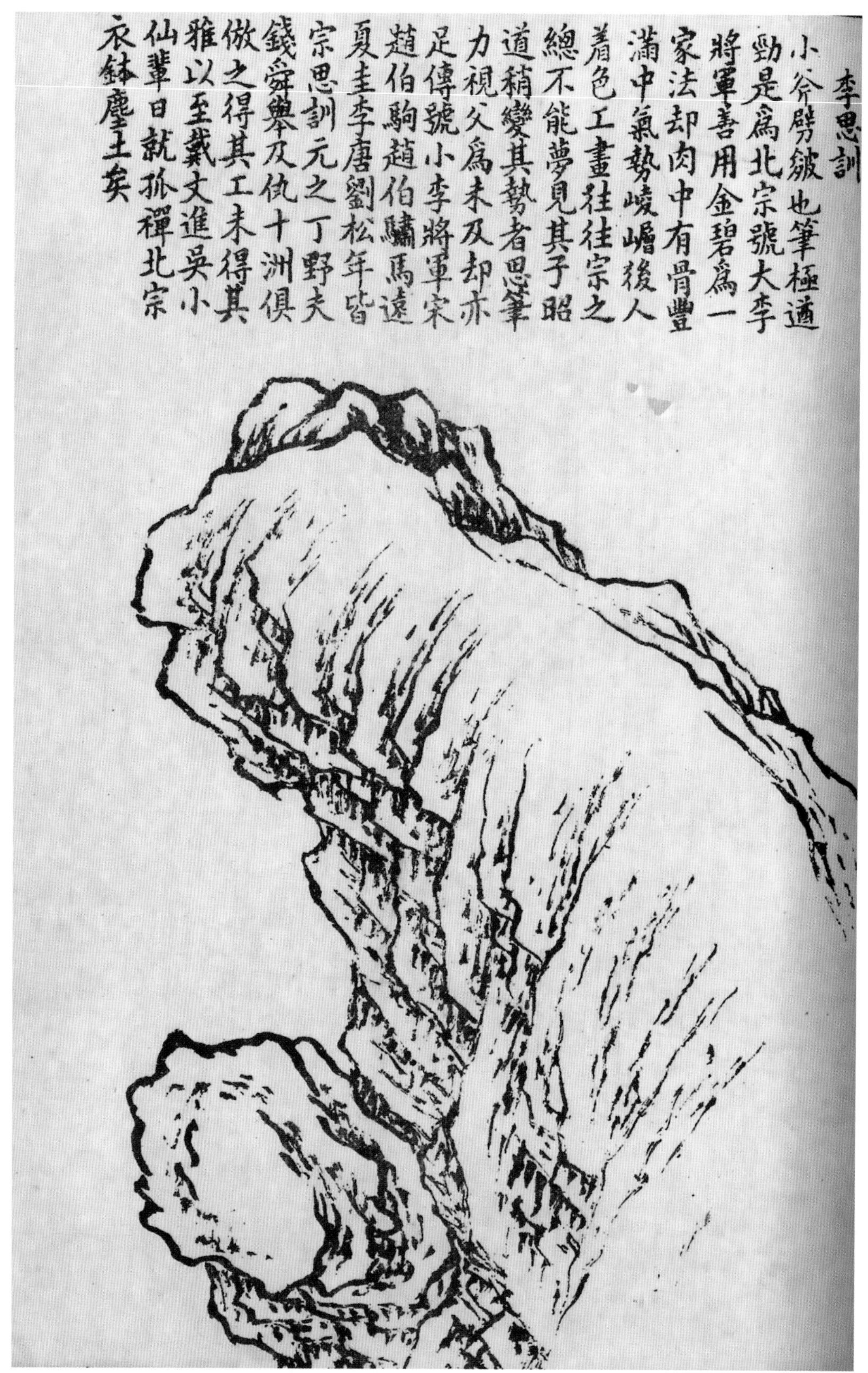

李思訓

小斧劈皴也筆極遒勁是爲北宗號大李將軍善用金碧爲一家法却肉中有骨豐滿中氣勢峻嶒後人著色工畫往往宗之總不能夢見其子昭道稍變其勢者思筆力視父爲未及却亦足傳號小李將軍宋趙伯駒趙伯驌馬遠夏圭李唐劉松年皆宗思訓元之丁野夫錢舜舉及仇十洲俱倣之得其工未得其雅以至戴文進吳小仙輩日就狐禪北宗衣鉢塵土矣

Figure 109 After Li Sixun, *Small Axe-Cut Stroke* by Wang Gai, *Mustard Seed Garden Painting Manual*. Facsimile reproduction, vol. 1, *juan* 3 (on rocks), 13a, 1977.

Last Painting, Final Words

I conclude, fittingly, with Su's final known painting, *Landscape after Li Sixun* (Fig. 108), executed while he was imprisoned in 1850. It captures many of the themes that have been raised so far: the influence of philology, women as alternative barometers of moral and intelligent community, the failure of the institution of learning, and Su's debt to the literary novel and the printed book. This painting is a delicate rendering of a landscape with light and careful brushwork that shows a direct borrowing of an image from *Mustard Seed Garden Painting Manual* (Fig. 109) of the late seventh-century artist Li Sixun's style. In the manual, Li's style is represented in a depiction of the rock surface. Su has taken Li's rock and turned it into a small mountain, creating a disjunction of scale with the original. Unlike in the other paintings, there are no figures to direct a narrative reading. However, he wraps his inscription in an inverted L-shape that creates a sharp corner as it bends around the negative space of the upper left-hand corner. In effect, combined with the ratio of the empty space to the rock-like mountain, he has created the appearance of a page taken from a painting manual. The imitation of a printed page brings Su's viewer into a world of words on a painting that should belong in a printed manual, and through this referentiality, his words mime the instructional authority of texts.

In contrast to the quiet landscape, in his inscription, Su vents some of his strongest feelings. It begins with a reference to the same three literary women cited in the Wang Anshi album leaf, naming them as leading female scholars, which allows him to ramble through famous incidents of transgression by male scholars in the second part of the inscription. Su is at his most virulent in his final words as he traces a history of how scholars have been scorned:

> I harbor no dreams of destruction. If I am able
> to perceive, reflect, act and make distinctions,

with my thoughts, conduct, and knowledge, why can't my senses compete against the law? Qiyuan [漆園 Zhuangzi] regarded the transformed bear as paralyzed. I believe! The most successful candidate in the Jiangnan provincial examination, Tang Yin, used the chapter titles of *Xixiangji* [西廂記 Romance of the western chambers] for his eight-legged essays.[36]

Sima Qian said, "Although one cannot reach the [peak of one's masters], nevertheless, their hearts continue forth."[37] Only the immortals have not returned. Can purity calm the choppy movements of the waves?

Renshan says: "Scholars as a group amount to one species amongst many sentient beings. They are born under the restraints of the *Book of Changes*. Confucius differed from Fuxi as he was not miraculously conceived.[38] Therefore, the scholars could not distinguish between the vigorous Fuxi on his mythical dragon-horse, and Zhou Qi, the differentiator of grains. And as he grew up, they [the scholars] were trapped in the various kingdoms of dukes and lords, suffered from the burning of the books during the Qin, the contemptuous scorn of Emperor Taizu of Han, they held precarious positions during the Tang, the scholars did not always thrive during the Song, they were flogged under Emperor Taizu of Ming, and they suffered through their associations with the Fushe [復社 Restoration Society]. Scholars as a group have been disgraced to the extreme; how can they falsely claim their instructions as that of the emperor and use it to disgrace the people?

The texts of the Six Arts kill people, and they kill things.[39] The meeting of Qi [Mencius] and Lu [Confucius] is recorded in *Jiayu* [家語]. The military might of King Wu is recorded in the *Liji*. The doors to Hell are opened and referred to as bandits Zhi and Qiu.[40]

Mounted at the Jingkongzhao Studio.[41] Recorded in Shunde. Painted in the style of Li Sixun.[42]

According to Su, the futility of the institutionalized Confucian teaching based on emulation has led to a cycle of history that has demonstrated over and over again the incompetence and shame of those who adhere to it. Moreover, the same books that are the backbone of China's moral intelligentsia also sanctioned the killing of people and animals in wars and sacrifices. But it is also a reference to the strong sentiments put forth by Dai Zhen (戴震, 1724–77): The philologist considered that the adherents of Cheng-Zhu Neo-Confucianism abused fundamental ideals of principle and accused them of killing people (以理殺人 *yili sha ren*).[43] Su Renshan uses Dai Zhen's accusation for his own argument of the hypocrisy of Confucian learning that endorsed violence, and as a result faced violence. Su Renshan ends his passionate plea by again referring to Chapter Twenty-nine of *Zhuangzi*. If frequency can be used as a gauge for the foundation of Su's frustrations against the hypocrisy of the Confucian class, Su's oft-cited comment that Robber Qiu opened the gate to Hell is his firmest critique. In 1850, when Su painted his last work, incarcerated in the local jail, the rebel group, the Red Turbans, was inciting violence in Guangzhou City. Beginning in Guangxi, the Taiping Rebels also went to war against the Qing, besieging towns and cities as they headed north to Nanjing, which became their capital.[44] For fourteen years, the Taiping Army fought and held back the imperial forces, but their rampage through China bore a heavy toll: Over twenty million lives are estimated to have been lost. Poignantly, as Su Renshan foregrounds an alternative history of failures, his angry last words prove to be prophetic.

Su's final painting is the deposit of the accumulated ideas, pictorial experiments, and sentiments of a man whose anger and frustrations led to his exile and later imprisonment. Historical events may account for his plea for the former glory of scholars, such as Wang Anshi, or for female talents who, because they were outside the education system, were as worthy of emulation as Wang Anshi. In order to present his thoughts, he veered towards the ambitions of writers who combined the vernacular with the literary, added commentaries to popular histories, and appealed to marginal spaces and types to convey personal sentiments and sociopolitical insights.

It is unclear whether Su ever viewed text and images as distinct genres with separate systems of presentations. Novels, as he himself stated, were, or at least should be, part of the intellectual and moral foundation of any scholar. He was a scholar, and, as such, the divide between words and pictures as traces of the author/painter, as with classical texts and popular tales, was nonexistent. But he was aware of how, through juxtapositions, the hermeneutics of brushwork with its long history of trace quality and inscriptional practices would be challenged. The excessiveness of his writing, the use of words as paintings, and the unusual compositions meant that he was not only exploring the stylistic quality of individual words (which would follow calligraphic traditions) but also giving his "blocks of words" (the text) imagistic properties. They can thus be seen as linguistic gestures that added an emotional or commanding tone to Su's narration. His pictorial image, meanwhile, increasingly took on the properties of print, accumulating into a candid mimicry of a printed page from a painting manual, a book of instructions accessible to all. However, if Su Renshan was a scholar who took on the dual role of a painter and a writer, it raises a question that cannot be answered: Who was his audience? His viewers or readers have left no inscriptions or colophons as was common practice with Chinese paintings. Were they too fearful to respond, or did they find his aggression too much? Or, perhaps this lack of inscriptional response is his most telling triumph because, for Su, the identity of the reader is less important than the act of reading.

Notes

An Introduction

1. Guangzhou or Guangzhou City refers to the city area where the administrative seat is located and where the Governor-General is based overseeing the two provinces of Guangdong and Guangxi. Canton, a term popularized by the foreign traders in the region, generally refers to Guangzhou City.

2. The title in this painting has been damaged. According to the Kyoto National Museum, taken from the Sumo Collection catalogue, it is referred to as *"A Celebration of Myriad Birds."* Previously, I have used the title "One Hundred Birds," in alignment with the Chinese translation of the title (百鳥萬歲). Although there are less than 100, the flock of swallows vis-à-vis the paired birds in the picture bears similar compositions with paintings belonging to this established genre. See Chapter Four for more examples of other paintings and further analysis of this unusual painting by Su Renshan.

3. In contrast, there is abundant research conducted by historians, particularly those interested in regional studies. A small example of works by scholars working on late imperial Guangdong includes the following: David Faure, "The Lineage as a Cultural Invention: The Case of the Pearl River Delta," *Modern China* vol. 15, no. 1 (January 1989), 4–37. "What Made Foshan a Town? The Evolution of Rural-Urban Identities in Ming-Qing China," *Late Imperial China* vol. 11, no. 2 (December 1990), 1–31. Liu Zhiwei, "Lineage on the Sands," in *Down to Earth: The Territorial Bond in South China*, edited by David Faure and Helen Siu (Stanford, CA: Stanford University Press, 1995), 21–43. Helen F. Siu, "Where were the Women? Rethinking Marriage Resistance and Regional Culture in South China," *Late Imperial China* vol. 11, no. 2 (1990), 32–62. Steven B. Miles, *The Sea of Learning: Mobility and Identity in Nineteenth-Century Guangzhou* (Cambridge, MA: Harvard University Asia Center, 2006). Maybo Ching, "Picturing Knowledge in a Late Qing Periodical, 1907–1911," *Journal of Modern Chinese History* vol. 1 (2007), 31–51.

4. I am deeply indebted to Zhuang Shen's study, *Cong baizhi dao baiyin: Qing mo Guangdong shuhua chuangzuo yu shoucang shi* 從白紙到白銀：清末廣東書畫創作與收藏史 (From paper to gold: A history of collecting painting and calligraphy in late Qing Guangdong), 2 vols (Taipei: Dongda tushu gongsi, 1997). The manuscript date of the catalogues for the five large art collections in Guangdong are, in chronological order: Wu Rongguang's *Xinchou xiao xia ji* 辛丑銷夏記 (1841); Ye Menglong's *Fengman lou shuhua lu* 風滿樓書畫錄 (ca. 1830); Pan Zhengwei's *Tingfanlou shuhua ji* 聽颿樓書畫記 (1843); Liang Tingnan's *Tenghuating shuhua ba* 藤花庭書畫拔 (1858); and Kong Guangtao's *Yuexuelou shuhua ji* 嶽雪樓書畫記 (1865). Other important research is by Xian Yuqing, "Guangdong zhi jiancang jia" 廣東之鑑藏家 (Connoisseurs and collectors from Guangdong) in *Guangdong wenwu* 廣東文物 (Cultural relics of Guangdong) (Hong Kong: Zhongguo wenhua xiejinhui, 1984, reprinted Shanghai shudian, 1990), *juan* 10, 982–996.

5. There are two exhibition catalogues that should be mentioned: Claudia Brown and Chou Ju-hsi, *Transcending Turmoil: Painting at the Close of China's Empire, 1796–1911* (Phoenix, AZ: Phoenix Art Museum, 1992); and Asian Art Museum of San Francisco, *Between the Thunder and the Rain: Chinese Paintings from the Opium War through the Cultural Revolution, 1840–1979* (San Francisco, CA: Asian Art Museum, 2000).

6. Klaas Ruitenbeek, *Discarding the Brush: Gao Qipei (1660–1737) and the Art of Chinese Finger Painting* (Amsterdam: Rijksmuseum, 1992).

7. Patricia Berger, *Empire of Brightness: Buddhist Art and Political Authority in Qing China* (Honolulu, HI: University of Hawaii Press, 2003).

8. Susan Naquin, *Temples and City Life, 1400–1900* (Berkeley, CA: University of California Press, 2000).

9. Richard Vinograd, *Boundaries of the Self: Chinese Portraits 1600–1900* (Cambridge: Cambridge University Press, 1992).

10. Jonathan Hay, *Shitao: Painting and Modernity in Early Qing China* (Cambridge: Cambridge University Press, 2001b).

11. Carlos Ginzburg, "Titian, Ovid and Erotic Illustrations," in *Clues, Myths and the Historical Method*, translated by John Tedeschi and Anne C. Tedeschi (Baltimore, MD: Johns Hopkins University Press, 1986). Deborah Poole, *Vision, Race and Modernity: A Visual Economy of the Andean Image World* (Princeton, NJ: Princeton University Press, 2007).

12. Since the late 1970s, the study of regional history of China in the West has been strongly influenced by the works of G. W. Skinner and his research on the macroregion. His regional history approach has focused on the environment, trade networks (in particular, market towns), and social ties as means of looking at the urbanization of China before the early 1890s and outside the imperial narrative. Skinner identified nine distinct regional systems that corresponded to the physical environment centered on the drainage basins with a set of core-periphery characteristics. The southeast macroregion is the best studied of the nine, providing a model for regional studies thereafter. G. W. Skinner, *The City in Late Imperial China* (Stanford, CA: Stanford University Press, 1977) was the third of three volumes on China's urban history. It is organized into three sections dealing with cities: the historical context, the spatial context, and as social systems. The impact of Skinner's work has been enormous, providing the foundation for work that looks at Chinese urban history, life, and networks. Susan Naquin and Evelyn Rawski, *Chinese Society in the Eighteenth Century* (New Haven, CT: Yale University Press, 1987) is an example of how Skinner's macroregion model has been used by other scholars. In art history, James Cahill and Jennifer Purtle have broadened the field with their scholarship on regionalism and painting; see James Cahill, *The Compelling Image: Nature and Style in Seventeenth-Century Chinese Painting* (Cambridge, MA: Harvard University Press, 1982), and Jennifer G. Purtle, "Placing Their Mark: An Art-Historical Geography of Min (Fukien) Painters of the Ming Dynasty, 1368–1644," Ph.D. thesis (Yale, 2001). Skinner's macroregion model has since become a pedagogical paradigm, but it is not without flaws. The approach tends to frame regionalism as a natural state, emphasizing the region's physical and environmental effect on society and urbanism, and downplaying the significance of diverse human activities as opposing agents in the construction of place and identity. For a critical examination of Skinner's work, see Carolyn Cartier, "Origins and Evolution of a Geographical Idea: The Macroregion in China," *Modern China* vol. 28, no. 1 (January 2002), 79–142; Martin Heijdra, "A Preliminary Note on Cultural Geography and Ming History," *Ming Studies* vol. 34 (July 1995), 151–175; and Rupert Hodder, *The Creation of Wealth in China* (London: Belhaven, 1995). Other scholars have taken different approaches to regionalism. See David Faure and Tao Tao Liu, eds., *Town and Country: Identity and Perception* (Basingstoke, UK: Macmillan, 2001) for a variety of essays that look beyond economic networks as the dominant structural force enforcing an ideal of the region as a cultural unity.

13. William T. Rowe, *Hankow: Commerce and Society in a Chinese City, 1796–1889* (Stanford, CA: Stanford University Press, 1984).

14. See Tobie Meyer-Fong's *Building Culture in Early Qing Yangzhou* (Stanford, CA: Stanford University Press, 2003) on how Yangzhou reinvented itself after the Qing victory in the mid-seventeenth century.

15. Meng Yue's *Shanghai and the Edges of Empire* (Minneapolis, MN: University of Minnesota, 2006) discusses the broader historical connections of Shanghai within an eighteenth-century Yangzhou, thus overturning conventional history that laps Shanghai's cosmopolitanism as a result of the West. By also tracing Yangzhou's impact on an early nineteenth-century Guangdong, I add an element of continuity. The interconnected dynamics of Yangzhou, Guangdong, and later Shanghai are further explored in the epilogue.

16. Steven B. Miles discusses the issues concerning cultural competition between the residents of the city center and the hinterlands throughout *The Sea of Learning: Mobility and Identity in Nineteenth-Century Guangzhou* (Cambridge, MA: Harvard University Asia Center, 2006).

17. The writing of the history of Guangdong art and collecting practices is still in its formative stage. One of the earliest comprehensive studies is Wang Zhaoyang's *Lingnanhua zhenglue* (Concise Record of Lingnan Painting) written in early twentieth century. In 1941, Xi Wuqing wrote an article on Guangzhou-based collectors, listing thirty collectors from the Ming and Qing Dynasties, of which nine were before the nineteenth century and only two from the Ming period: Li Shixing 李時行 (*jinshi* 1513) and Zhang Xuan 張萱 (*juren* 1557). See Xian Yuqing (1990), 982–996. Zhuang Shen (1997) examines various Guangdong-based collectors, their connoisseurship skills, and how their taste in art influenced Guangdong art. I have also examined the interrelationships and social networks of merchants and painters in an unpublished paper, "Windblown Whispers: Pan Zhengwei's Tingfan lou Art Collection and Its Impact on Early 19th Century Guangzhou."

18. Craig Clunas, *Pictures and Visuality in Early Modern China* (Princeton, NJ: Princeton University Press, 1997), 46–48.

19. Xian Baogan, *Foshan zhongyi xiangzhi* 佛山忠義鄉志 (Gazetteer of the loyal and righteous town of Foshan) (Foshan: Xiuzhi ju, 1923), *juan* 14, 7–8.

20. Shunde was a culturally vibrant area, boasting more native artists and scholars during the Qing Dynasty than any other area in Guangdong. Shunde was also a wealthy region with alluvial lands belonging to old landed families, some claiming a lineage dating to the Song period in the eleventh century, whose wealth came from mulberry cultivation and silk production. Therefore, Shunde was an area that straddled the two dominant worlds of local power in Guangzhou: one dominated in the south by the lineage clans and the other, in the north, by the China trade merchants.

21. It is important to recognize that this was not a new approach, and Su's heretical forebears include eighteenth-century Yangzhou eccentric artists such as Jin Nong, Luo Ping, and Li Shan. However, the field of Chinese art has yet to construct a coherent historical development, and Su Renshan's highly individualistic paintings sit uneasily within the current narrative that favors the elite *wen* practices of a closed circuit. It is only by examining Su's paintings as embodying the shared ethos of both circuits, and by acknowledging that this approach had precedents, that his paintings can make historical sense. More importantly for this project, by examining his works as a bridge between the two iconic circuits, what will emerge is a new social role of the artist that will be relevant to the development of modern Chinese art.

22. There is a long history of representations of sanctioned violence, whether religious, ritual, or martial; for example, scenes of Buddhist hells and paintings of conquering soldiers that are often used as a form of documenting history. This is a large topic that deserves further study. It has been suggested that representations of wars and other forms of violence ceased from the eleventh century. Alexander Soper suggested that paintings of battles were common themes during the Han period and continued to be made until the beginning of the Song Dynasty; see Barend J. ter Haar, "Rethinking 'Violence' in Chinese Society," in *Meanings of Violence: A Cross-Cultural Perspective*, edited by Goran Aijimer and Jos Abbink (Oxford: Berg, 2000), 135. However, there are many paintings of battles, hunting scenes, and portraits of military men produced after the tenth century. There are handscrolls of the Yuan nobles out hunting, large hanging scrolls of the Hongwu Emperor in the martial guise reminiscent of Guanggong, the God of War, and Castaglione's engravings of the Qianlong Emperor's battle victories, to name just a few examples. Representations of military successes were not confined to the courts. Gu Luo (1763–after 1837) and Qian Du (1763–1844) produced a joint work in 1835 entitled *Capturing Enemies in Mountain Range* (Lot 79, Sotheby's Hong Kong, Nov. 1998) that commemorated the success of General Li Zongchuan in his campaign against the barbarian rebels in Sichuan, 1833 (the date cited in the catalogue entry is erroneous).

23. The inscription is found on the painting, *Bodhidharma* in The Chinese University of Hong Kong Art Museum. See Chapter 2.

24. Su Renshan was included in the appendix of the new edition in 1961. Wang Zhaoyong was from Panyu, Guangzhou, and was editor of the 1918 *Panyu Gazetteer*. On Wang's contribution to the study of Guangdong and Macau see Peng Hailing, *Wang Zhaoyong yu jindai Yue Ao wenhua* 汪兆鏞與近代粵澳文化 (Wang Zhaoyung and the cultural history of modern Guangdong and Macau) (Guangzhou: Guangdong renmin chubanshe, 2004).

25. For a discussion on the connoisseurship of Su Renshan paintings, see Yeewan Koon, "Literati Iconoclasm: Violence and Estrangement in the Art of Su Renshan (1814–c.1850), Ph.D. thesis, Institute of Fine Arts, New York University, 2006.

26. Chu-Tsing Li, "Su Jen-shan (1814–1849), The Rediscovery and Reappraisal of a Tragic Cantonese Genius," *Oriental Art*, vol. IV (Winter 1970), 349–60; Pierre Ryckmans, *The Life and Work of Su Renshan: Rebel, Painter and Madman, 1814–1849*, translated by Angharad Pimpaneau (Paris: University of Paris, 1970); and Jian Youwen, *Huatan guaijie Su Renshan* 畫壇怪傑蘇仁山 (Su Jen-shan: Eccentric genius of Kwangtung: His life and art) (Hong Kong: Jianshi Mengjing shuwu, 1970).

27. There are, unfortunately, many dubious works in Jian Youwen's collection, and his analysis must be treated with a degree of caution.

28. Kao Mayching cites Huang Mozi's private manuscript on the artist in *The Art of Su Liupeng and Su Renshan* (Hong Kong: The Chinese University of Hong Kong Art Museum, 1990), 148.

29. Given that Su's artistic life ended early, the three stages of development are very short: before 1836, 1836–43, and 1843–50. Kao (1990), 157–164.

30. For further analysis of these two paintings, see Chapter Four.

31. Although I have differentiated copies from fakes as different modes of replications, there are overlaps between the two in that copies can be deliberate acts of forgery

that pose as an original; but to allow for the practice of copying as a legitimate form of learning, as a ritual act and as a referential homage, I have not differentiated the two.

32. There are many cases of scholars engaged in lively connoisseurship debates that are rooted in assessing authenticity based on these criteria, but oftentimes they are in conflict because they may prefer one method over the other. For an example, see Richard Barnhart et al., "The Tu Chin [Du Jin] Correspondence, 1994–95," *Kaikodo Journal,* vol. 5 (Autumn 1997), 8–45.

33. I would like to thank Jonathan Hay for his help in defining the issues involved in connoisseurship. He emphasized the importance of using artifactual connoisseurship and the "conceptual craft" of connoisseurship as forming a system of "checks and balances" that can help better identify the gradations of "authenticity" in painting.

34. Although the lack of textual data on Su Renshan prior to the twentieth century does not prove that his paintings did not circulate among collectors, it would suggest that, if they did, they were probably appreciated by a small and/or intimate group of people who did not engage in the more public (published) network of connoisseurs, collectors and patrons.

35. Clifford Geertz, *The Interpretation of Cultures* (New York: Basic Books, 1973), 29.

Chapter One

1. Shen Fu, *Six Records of a Floating Life*, translated by Leonard Pratt and Chiang Su-Hui (London: Penguin Books, 1983), 116.

2. Shen (1983), 118.

3. Without any data about rice prices in 1843 Guangdong, I am using an average price cited by Kenneth Pomeranz in *The Great Divergence: China, Europe and the Making of the Modern World Economy* (Princeton, NJ and Oxford: Princeton University Press, 2000), 319. This figure is comparable to Wang Yeh-chien's cost of rice in the Yangzi Delta, which in 1843 was 2.26 taels of silver; Wang Yen-chien, "Secular Trends of Rice Prices in the Yangzi Delta," in *Chinese History in Economic Perspectives,* edited by Thomas G. Rawski and Lillian M. Li (Berkeley, Los Angeles, and Oxford: University of California Press, 1992). Given that the price of rice was generally higher in the Yangzi Delta than in Guangdong, 2 taels per *shi* is a relative estimate. See Robert B. Marks, "Rice Prices, Food Supply, and Market Structure in Eighteenth-Century South China," *Late Imperial China,* vol. 12, no. 2 (December 1999), 64–116.

4. Guangzhou cheng (Guangzhou City), the name used since the fourteenth century to denote the city and capital of the prefecture, was seen as the heart of politics, trade, academia, and the arts. The city walls enclosed parts of Nanhai (南海) and Panyu (番禺) counties.

5. Susan Naquin and Evelyn Rawski, *Chinese Society in the Eighteenth Century* (New Haven, CT: Yale University Press, 1987), 181–183.

6. Miles (2006), 29. Shaoxing natives had the reputation of being legal experts, and many served as private secretaries in the Guangdong region.

7. Miles (2006), 42.

8. In her study on why and how Shanghai became a cosmopolitan center, Meng Yue considers the cultural requisites of pre-nineteenth-century Jiangnan cities and Guangzhou as the templates for Shanghai. For example, Suzhou had 100 presses, and Guangzhou had approximately two dozen. Suzhou and Guangzhou (with some overlaps) had about one-fifth of the scholars in the region that were listed in the prestigious *Chouren zhuan* 籌人傳 (Biographies of mathematicians and astronomers). See Meng Yue, *Shanghai and the Edges of Empire* (Minneapolis, MN: University of Minnesota Press, 2006), xiv–xviii.

9. Images of an exotic Guangdong can be seen in early writings such as the Han Dynasty text *Yiwu zhi* 夷物志 (Account of strange things) attributed to Yang Fu. The Tang Dynasty saw the publishing of *Lingbiao lu yi* 嶺表錄異 (Records of strange things beyond the mountains). See David Faure, *Emperor and Ancestor: State and Lineage in South China* (Stanford, CA: Stanford University Press, 2007), 18–24.

10. Poole (2007), 9–12.

11. Carlo Ginzburg differentiates between sacred and erotic images based on their efficacy. In the intentionally erotic images aimed at the private circuit of the elite, images were couched in a culturally and socially elevated code that excluded the uneducated masses. Ginzburg (1986), 77–95.

12. Clunas (1997), 46–48.

13. Miles (2006), 75–78.

14. Xiang Dongshan et al., *Guangzhou Yuexiu gu shuyuan gaiguan* 廣州越秀古書院概觀 (An overview study of academies in Yuexiu) (Guangzhou: Zhongshan daxue chubanshe, 2002).

15. See Tobie Meyer-Fong's *Building Culture in Early Qing Yangzhou* (Stanford, CA: Stanford University Press, 2003) on how Yangzhou reinvented itself after the Qing victory in the mid-seventeenth century.

16. Miles (2006), 42–54.

17. Liang Jiabin, *Guangdong shisan hang kao* 廣東十三行考 (An examination of Guangdong's thirteen cohongs) (Guangzhou: Guangdong renmin chubanshe, 1999), 259–269.

18. Liang Jiabin (1999).

19. Huang Qichen, *Mingqing Guangdong shangren* 明清廣東商人 (Guangdong merchants in the Ming and Qing Dynasties) (Guangzhou: Guangdong jingji chubanshe, 2002), 259–269.

20. Pan Yizeng, comp. *Panyu Panshi shilue* 番禺潘氏詩略 (Poems by the Pan Family of Panyu), manuscript,1894.

21. The eighteenth-century eccentric artist Zheng Xie (鄭燮, 1693–1765), in 1759, famously wrote, "A large hanging scroll costs six taels, a medium-size one is four, a small scroll costs two, couplets and streamers are one tael a pair, and albums and fans are half a tael each . . . gifts cause nothing but trouble, not to mention deferred payment that is most unreliable, like bad credit. Furthermore, my body gets tired in my old age; therefore, please excuse me from accompanying you gentlemen in unprofitable conversations." Ginger Cheng-chi Hsu, *A Bushel of Pearls: Painting for Sale in Eighteenth-Century Yangzhou* (Stanford, CA: Stanford University Press, 2001), 146. Zheng's price list can be seen as a reaction against the social obligations involved in painting patronage. His openness about the cost of making art can be seen as a form of eccentric rhetoric.

22. Zhuang Shen's study on collectors in Guangdong is an invaluable source for my study. However, his bias against the mercantile class can be seen throughout his work.

23. Li Bozhong, "Daoguang xiaotiao yu guiwei da shui" 道光蕭條與癸未大水 (The Daoguang depression and the 1823 Flood—economic decline, climatic cataclysm and the nineteenth-century crisis in Songjiang), *Journal of Social Sciences*, vol. 6, 173–178; and William T. Rowe, "Money, Economy and Polity in the Daoguang-era Paper Currency Debate," *Late Imperial China*, vol. 31, no. 2 (December 2010), 69–96.

24. As discussed, although the value of taels fluctuated in the Qing period, an estimated value of 2 taels would be approximately 2.5 *shi* of rice.

25. Estimates of average rice consumption range from 1.74 *shi* to 2.62 *shi*; I am following Robert B. Marks's figure of 2.17 as the average. Mark (1999), 77–78.

26. According to the preface to Wu's *nianpu* by the later scholar Ye Dehui (葉德輝, 1864–1927), Ruan Yuan was responsible for honing Wu's connoisseurship skills. There were four paintings in his catalogue on which Ruan had inscribed his comments. See Wu Rongguang, *Wu Rongguang zi ding nianpu* 吳榮光自訂年譜 (A chronological biography of Wu Rongguang) (Jiulong: Zhongshan tushu gongsi, 1971). However, according to Wu's *nianpu* and the inscriptions on his paintings, the person with whom Wu consulted the most was Weng Fanggang (翁訪綱, 1733–1813), another renowned scholar-official who was also based in Guangzhou

as Inspector of Education between 1764 and 1771. For more on Wu Rongguang's collecting habits and his relation with Weng, see Yeewan Koon, "Literati Iconoclasm: The Art of Su Renshan (1814–c.1850)," Ph.D. thesis, Institute of Fine Arts, New York University, 2006.

27. The two catalogues that Wu Rongguang emulated were *Gengzi xiaoxia ji* 庚子銷夏記 (Record of whiling away the summer in Gengzi Year) by Sun Chengze (孫承澤, 1592–1676) and *Jiangcun xiaoxia lu* 江村銷夏錄 (Jiangcun's records of whiling away the summer) by Gao Shiqi (高士奇, 1645–1704), both of whom were based in Beijing. Sun and Gao both traced the movement of paintings in the collection by looking at and referring to other catalogues, seals, and inscriptions, and both wrote in a straightforward manner.

28. Wu Rongguang (1971), 5.

29. Xie Lansheng was a Nanhai resident and an important scholar friend of the *cohong* merchants. Unlike Zhang Weiping, Xie's family had been long-term residents of this region.

30. According to Wu, the marriage took place in 1832; see Wu Rongguang (1971), 16.

31. Miles (2006), 36.

32. In celebration of this event, Pan Zhengheng commissioned Xie Lansheng to paint a picture of the studio.

33. Kao Mayching, ed., *The Art of Li Jian and Xie Lansheng* (Hong Kong and Guangzhou: Art Gallery, The Chinese University of Hong Kong and Guangzhou Art Gallery, 1993), 178.

34. For references to Li's professional art life, his opium addiction, and relation to the Xie family, see Kao Mayching (1993), 16, 23, and 34. Lantern painting was also a popular form of art in Guangdong. Of greater relevance were the famed Guangzhou lantern makers, many of whom, according to *Zhu Yue baqi zhi* 駐粵八旗誌 (Gazetteer of the eight bannermen in Guangdong), were from Bannermen families; see Liu Yangming, *Zhu Yue baqi zhi* (Shanghai: Shanghai guji chubanshe, 2002 reprint). Unfortunately, the ephemeral nature of lanterns has meant that we have little actual evidence of the types of imagery painted on them.

35. Kao Mayching (1993), 178.

36. Christina Chu, "An Overview of Li Jian's Painting," in *Chinese Painting under the Qianlong Emperor*, edited by Chou Ju-hsi and Claudia Brown, Phoebus 6, no. 2 (Tucson, AZ: Arizona State University Press, 1991), 302.

37. Nila Ann Baker, "Li Jian and Xie Lansheng as Painters of the Cantonese Scholar-Artist Tradition," in *The Art of Li Jian and Xie Lansheng*, edited by Kao Mayching (Hong Kong and Guangzhou: Art Gallery, The Chinese

University of Hong Kong and Guangzhou Art Gallery, 1993), 23.

38. This colophon was written on a Shitao painting in the Guangzhou Art Museum. 清湘繪事於南宗獨得奇氣，訾之者，目為野狐禪，殊非定論。實則於惲王外別樹一幟也。自謝裏甫太史以嗜痂之癖推波助浪耳。□者羣與耐和，一時奇價伯仲宋元。古畫賈視爲奇貨，遂於大江南北搜羅赴粵，故我粵藏此老筆迹最夥。Luo Tianchi was part of the tight network of Guangdong artists and scholars. Zhang Weiping designated Luo, Xie, Li, and another close friend, Zhang Ruzhi, as the Four Masters of Guangdong. Kao Mayching (1993), 175.

39. Shitao was friends with the poets Cheng Keze 程可則, Liang Peilan 梁佩蘭, and Qu Dajun 屈大均. See Li Chu-tsing, *Ming Qing Guangdong mingjia shanshui huazhan* 明清廣東名家山水畫展 (Catalogue of landscape paintings by Guangdong masters in the Ming and Qing dynasties) (Hong Kong: The Chinese University of Hong Kong Art Gallery, 1973), n.p. (Introduction, section 5). Xie Lansheng also commented on Li Jian's exhaustive copying of Shitao's work during his middle years in *Changxingxing zhai shuhua tiba* 常惺惺齋書畫題跋 (Inscriptions and colophons from paintings and calligraphy in the Changxingxing Studio) (Macau: Wenxin tushu gongsi, 1974), *juan* 2, n.p. See also Nila Ann Baker in Kao (1993), 22–23.

40. Kao Mayching (1933), 174.

41. It was one of the items listed in the *Yiwu zhi*. Faure (2007), 20.

42. The lychee was the second most popular theme in poems by Xuehaitang scholars, who also appropriated Su Shi's poem on the subject as part of a literary tradition.

43. Translation by Miles (2006), 140. Lin Botong's family originally came from Fujian and moved to Panyu several generations earlier.

44. 寫此羣山六月時，時時眼內餐之。正夫前世香山老；特作（去聲）南人為荔枝。正夫囑兒輩畫此，雲隱翁謝景卿題。二樵山人書字。

45. *Nanyue youji* 南粵遊記 (Record of travels in Nanyue) by Chen Huiyan (d.1856) and *Yuedong wen jian lu* 粵東聞見錄 (A record of things heard or seen in Yuedong) by Zhang Qu are some of the travelogues that devoted several chapters to local produce.

46. Ge Hong was an eclectic philosopher who dedicated his life to searching for physical immortality, which he thought was attainable through alchemy. He lived during China's tumultuous Period of Disunity (220–589), a time when alien-conqueror regimes ruled northern China, the cradle of Chinese civilization, while a series of weak, transplanted Chinese states occupied recently colonized southern China. These political conditions, along with the social chaos they engendered, no doubt gave rise to Ge Hong's ardent desire to establish order and permanency in both his spiritual and secular worlds. His most important contribution to Chinese philosophy was his attempt to reconcile an immortality-centered Daoism with Confucianism. Equally important, to establish political order, he also tried to reconcile Legalism with Confucianism. It was during his period of reclusion at Mount Luofu that Ge wrote his two-part magnum opus whose title bore his sobriquet: *Inner Chapters of the Master Who Embraces Simplicity* and the *Outer Chapters of the Master Who Embraces Simplicity*.

47. See Jonathan Hay, "Wen Zhengming, Stone Lake, and the Aesthetics of Disjunction," *Taiwan 2002 Conference on the History of Painting in East Asia*, 266–307.

48. The Hong Kong Chih Lo Lou Collection includes paintings from Pan Zhengwei's collection. For a brief history of collecting in Guangdong in the late nineteenth and twentieth centuries, see Raymond Tang Man Leung, "Collecting in Guangdong Epitomized by the Chih Lo Lou Collection," in *Nobility and Virtue: A Selection of Late Ming and Early Qing paintings and Calligraphies from the Chih Lo Lou Collection* (Hong Kong: Hong Kong Museum of Art, 2010), 52–61.

49. Relationships formed through marriage between rich merchants from outside Guangzhou to local elite families were common practice and discussed in greater detail by Miles (2006), 34.

50. Andreas Everard van Braam, *An Authentic Account of the Embassy of the Dutch East India Company, to the Court of the Emperor of China, in the years 1794 and 1795; Containing a Description of Several Parts of the Chinese Empire* (London: R. Philips, 1798), 297–324.

51. William Fane de Salis, *Reminiscences of Travels in China and India in 1848* (London: Waterlow & Sons, 1892), 12.

52. *The Canton Press*, August 19, 1938.

53. There are numerous writings of these two famous sites. See William C. Hunter, *Bits of Old China* (Taipei: Cheng-hua, reprinted 1966) and Osmond Tiffany, *The Canton Chinese or The American's Sojourn in the Celestial Empire* (Boston, MA: James Munroe, 1849).

54. Cited by Kee Il Choi, Jr., "Carl Gustav Ekeberg and the Invention of Chinese Export Painting," *The Magazine Antiques*, vol. 143, 429.

55. Catherine Stuer, "Reading the World's Landscape in Zhang Bao's Images of the Floating Raft," in *Rethinking Visual Narratives from Asia: Intercultural and Comparative Perspectives,* edited by Alexandra Green (Hong Kong: University of Hong Kong Press, 2013), 77–93.

56. Stuer (2013), 91–92. To add to Stuer's study, while little is known about Zhu Yingfang, he was one of the editors

of *Xiaowanjuan zhai shitie* 小萬卷齋試帖 (Poetry compositions for examinations from the Small Studio of Myriad Scrolls). Xiaowanjuan zhai is associated with the Anhui scholar Zhu Jian (朱珔, 1759–1850).

57. A set of paintings was acquired by the Victoria and Albert Museum, London, in 1898, and is believed to be the original drawings for Mason's book. For a more detailed discussion of this album in a cross-cultural context, see Yeewan Koon, "Narrating the City: Pu Qua and the Depiction of Street Life in Canton Trade Art," in *Qing Encounters: Artistic Exchanges between China and the West*, edited by Petra Chu (Los Angeles: Getty Publication), forthcoming.

58. Stacey Sloboda, "Picturing China: William Alexander and the Language of Chinoiserie," *British Art Journal*, vol. 9, no. 2, 451.

59. *Qua* is Pidgin English for "official" but became loosely used as a form of address for men, functioning similarly to "mister." Pidgin English was a language shared by nearly all who lived among the foreign *hongs* that mixed words from Portuguese, Indian, English, and various Chinese dialects, spelling them according to Chinese syntax. Sometimes names would be passed along to descendants, thus making it even harder to trace the actual Chinese identity of artists. However, more recent research has uncovered more information regarding the Chinese identity of these artists. The Chinese identity of Lamqua, the most famous of the export trade artists, may be Guan Qiaochang (1801–ca.1860).

60. I want to thank William Shang for bringing another variation of Pu Qua's album to my attention: *A Collection of Pig-tails* presented to a Francis Stretchen, dated Christmas 1858 in the Morrison Collection at the Toyo Bunko. Shang has noted the similarities of these images to Pu Qua's album and concluded that these may be another set of paintings based on or by Pu Qua's workshop.

61. Poole (2007), 132.

62. Ernest Gombrich has elaborated on this idea at length in his work on "Truth and Stereotype" as part of the process of art-making. However, his idea that "the starting point of a visual record is not knowledge but a guess conditioned by habit and tradition" can also be expanded to the viewer. This set schema then allows us to "sort out our impressions" so that with these filing aids we can "identify an object through inclusion or exclusion along any network of classes," almost like a game of Twenty Questions. See Ernest H. Gombrich, *Art and Illusion: A Study in the Psychology of Pictorial Representation* (London: Phaidon Press, 1986), 78–80.

63. Ju Lian served within the private secretariat office of Zhang Jingxiu in Guangxi, where he and his cousin studied with the Jiangnan artists Song Guangbao and Meng Jinyi. Zhang was famous for his Panyu gardens, and the cousins contributed to its fame by making detail paintings of flora and insects from the site. Wang Zongyan, *Guangdong shuhua zhengxian lu* (Macau: no publisher name, 1988), 99–201.

64. Tan San appeared to have been somewhat of a street celebrity; Ye Menglong also commissioned Jiang Lian to depict a portrait of him in 1831. See Wang Zongyan, (1988), 164.

65. Although there is a difference between the depiction of urban images and of rural customs, both purport to represent the ordinary. It was a genre that could trace its political support to the Song Dynasty with scholar-officials such as Su Shi (蘇軾, 1037–1101) who insisted that *su* (custom) reflected a country's morality, and the happiness of the people could be used as a measurement of the government's success. Moreover, Su Shi's political convictions carried over into his cultural world as he composed poems that celebrated vernacular phrasing and emphasized the beauty of the simplicity and practicality of rural living. The representations of local customs became embedded in this broader narrative of social responsibility, where the official class became the mediator between the emperor and the villager. Richard Barnhart, *Painters of the Great Ming: The Imperial Court and the Zhe School* (Dallas, TX: Dallas Museum of Art, 1993).

66. The comparison of the export art album and the printed version of *Taiping huanle tu* was first mentioned by Ming Wilson in "As True as Photographs: Chinese Paintings for the Western Market," *Orientations* (November 2000), vol. 31, no. 9.

67. An undated handscroll painting in the Roy and Marilyn Collection by Fang Xun entitled *Glimpses of the Duanwu Festival* shows a literary gathering at Jin Deyu's residence. The members of the gathering included Jin Deyu; Zhu Fang'ai (朱方藹, 1721–86), who was a prunus painter and wrote a treatise on the subject; Zhao Huaiyu (趙懷玉, 1747–1823), a compiler on the *Siku quanshu* imperial project; and Bao Tingbo (鮑廷博, 1728–1814), who came from a wealthy merchant family and was one of the best-known bibliophiles of the Qianlong period. See Chou Ju-hsi and Claudia Brown, *The Scent of Ink: The Roy and Marilyn Papp Collection of Chinese Painting* (Phoenix AZ: Phoenix Art Museum, 1989), catalogue entry 30.

68. Roslyn Lee Hammers, *Pictures of Tilling and Weaving: Art, Labor, and Technology in Song and Yuan China* (Hong Kong: Hong Kong University Press, 2011).

69. The 52-leaf album was commissioned sometime between 1712 and 1722. In 1712, the Kangxi Emperor

removed his second son, Yinreng, as successor to the throne and did not designate a replacement. This led to intense fighting, primarily between Yinzhi (third son), Yinzhen (fourth son), and Yinsi (fourteenth son). The former heir apparent was charged with immorality, sexual impropriety, and usurpation of power. The commissioning of the masquerade portrait of Yinzhen in the *Gengzhi tu* album can be seen as a clever ploy to present himself as a morally upright person who, with his wife, followed the gender codes of proper behavior: As a loyal subject, he would follow his father's commitment to a Qing state.

70. Laura Hostetler has convincingly argued for the role of pictorial ethnography in shaping an imperial vision of Qing universality as part of their imperialist programs. Laura Hostetler, *Ethnography and Cartography in Early Modern China* (Chicago, IL: Chicago University Press, 2001).

71. Emma Teng traces the development of travel and visuality to the late Ming, when long-distance travel became part of elite practice, and records that depended on the eyes were deemed more valuable than what one might hear, which was deemed hearsay. See Emma Jinhua Teng, *Taiwan's Imagined Geography: Chinese Colonial Travel Writing and Pictures, 1683–1895* (Cambridge, MA: Harvard University Asia Center, 2004), 22–24.

72. Ma Ya-chen, "Fengsu, difang yu diguo: Taiping huanle tu de zhizuo ji qi dui xihao zhi xiang de chengxian" 風俗、地方與帝國：太平歡樂圖的製作及其對熙皞之象的呈現 (Customs, provinces, and the empire: The making of *Taiping huanle tu* and its representation of "Peaceful Regime"), *National Central University Journal of Humanities*, vol. 45, 141–194.

73. Poole (2007), 132.

Chapter Two

1. Wang Zhaoyong, *Lingnan hua zhenglue* 嶺南畫徵略 (Summary of paintings from Lingnan) (Hong Kong: Commercial Press, 1961).

2. Miles (2006), 134–141.

3. David Faure, "The Lineage as a Cultural Invention: The Case of the Pearl River Delta," *Modern China*, vol. 15, no. 1 (January1989), 4–37.

4. Faure (2007), 219.

5. Faure (2007).

6. For samples of mid-nineteenth-century contracts of the Sands, see Patrick Mok, "Lineage and Elite Dominance in Late Imperial Chinese Society: A Case Study of Shunde County, Guangdong," M. Phil. thesis (University of Hong Kong, 1995), 61–62. As Mok has shown, there were terrible risks involved in buying reclaimed lands. Additional costs of building embankments and dikes to accelerate the process of reclamation were extremely high, and after the initial reclamation period, tax levies added to the financial burden.

7. Liu Zhiwei (1995), 21–43. See also Mok (1995).

8. Miles (2006), 46–54.

9. Miles (2006), 51–52.

10. Steven B. Miles, "Creating Zhu 'Jiujiang': Localism in Nineteenth-Century Guangdong," *T'oung Pao International Journal of Chinese Studies,* vol. 90, no. 4 (December 2004), 299–340.

11. Faure (2007), 193–217.

12. Faure (2007), 196.

13. Faure (2007), 202.

14. Translation by Kao (1990). The source is *Shunde xianzhi, juan* 3.

15. The preface to the genealogy is dated to 1856. However, Su Renshan is part of the Dongxi patriarch clan, whose details were included in an undated addendum. I would like to thank Professor Kao Mayching for her generosity in sharing the relevant pages of the genealogy.

16. There is no indication of which child was born to whom, and there is no information about whether the daughters were married or not.

17. The word *sui* (歲), meaning "years of age," is used for counting one's age, whereby newborns start at one year old, and at each passing of New Year, rather than the birthday, one year is added to the person's age. Two of the inscriptions have been recorded, but the whereabouts of the paintings on which they were written are unknown. The third appears on a self-portrait, a hanging scroll dated to 1842, and is the second of the three in chronological order. The earliest of the three inscriptions is recorded by Jian Youwen from a painting, now lost, *Landscape Painting after Wen Zhengming*; see Kao (1990), 151.

18. This translation is based on Kao Mayching's version in her catalogue, with some alterations, *The Art of Su Liupeng and Su Renshan,* 151. 余自少齡便雅嗜圖繪。及長，慕先生藻翰，而筆畊硯畹，歷年多矣。予生一齡，懼貓犬而多癇病。二齡，反則母膝而父與剃髮，便知毀譽焉。尚未能自言，何復知畫？三齡，母教食，乃食；母不命，雖左右與食，弗食。四齡，父教以區正叔《三字經》。至是始知書，亦不及畫。五齡、六齡，嗜寫字，遇門墻垣壁，無不學書。七齡、八齡，能畫山水景物，題句頗能道說景中意。九齡，出館就傅授經，日受經書數過，不暇計畫。十齡、十一齡，間以學誦之餘及畫。十二齡，而畫著閭里。十三齡，名動庠士。十四齡，出游羊城。十五齡，嗜臨盈尺漢隸。十六齡，學舉業。十七齡，嗜詩賦。十八齡，嗜理學。十九齡，赴督學試，不遇。廿齡，博覽策學。廿一齡，就傅兼習當代典禮。廿二齡，赴試，仍不遇。廿三齡，決志去試藝而畫，復辟嗜焉。廿四，適蒼梧。廿五，游桂林巖洞。廿七，始圖居室大倫。廿八，而侮言行多謬矣，故記之。時道光廿一，歲次辛丑，冬十月中旬二日，畫於仙城。

19. Kao suggests that he was based in Guangzhou for his studies, based on a set of paintings dated to 1831 in The Chinese University of Hong Kong Collection (no. 344 in *Guangdong shuhua lu*). However, the authenticity of this set of scrolls is in dispute and cannot be used conclusively to confirm Su's whereabouts. Another more plausibly authentic hanging scroll, dated 1833, was made in Guangzhou City, supposedly on his second visit (no. 345, The Chinese University of Hong Kong). As we know, he was in the city when he was thirteen or fourteen, and it is possible that he did not return to the city until he was twenty. Su may have studied in the neighboring town of Daliang in Shunde prefecture.

20. 山水吾人未了緣，贈君早作臨游仙。百年收拾須珍重；莫向當爐質酒錢。

21. See page 81 for Su Ruohu's inscription.

22. As these were provincial examinations held in Guangzhou, this would suggest that Su Renshan had already passed the first-level examinations.

23. Kao (1990), 153.

24. The gazetteer entry suggests that Su was there sometime during the Daoguang and Xianfeng reigns.

25. This river runs through Guangxi.

26. A similar line is found in Chapter Forty-two of *Jinghuayuan*, when the empress announces the holding of a special civil examination for female candidates. According to the decree, the empress states, "Today, the essence of grace is not only found in men" (今日靈秀不鍾於男子); Li Ruzhen, *Jinghuayuan* (Beijing: Beijing shi zhongguo shudian, reprinted 1985), 1. See also Chapter Four for discussion of *Jinghuayuan* in relation to Su Renshan's paintings.

27. 一痕山影淡如無。余四歲，受經於庭訓，十有六齡，出就外傅。至廿有一齡，成文藝儒業之事而歸。處篷篳挾策俯誦兩三年。試於督學，兩不遇。慨然思遠遊。適桂林，遍游巖洞。見其木香而烈，曰桂；其水清且淺，曰灘；其山峭而秀，其巖幽而潔，其洞玲然瓏然而通，深然森然而曲，兀然聳然而有象，陂然平然而可往可復。余欣然而喜曰：「其間必有得山水之秀者，鐘為偉人，為之容與。」久之而未有所遇。余退而思之曰：「天地之秀，不惟鍾於男子，必分鍾於婦人，其間必有淑善者。」而九十亦未之見，余不禁悄然而悲矣。

Although the painting is now lost, it had been recorded by Jian Youwen. See Jian (1970), 6.

28. Miles (2006), 242–243.

29. See Janice E. Stockard, *Daughters of the Canton Delta: Marriage Patterns and Economic Strategies in South China 1860–1930* (Stanford, CA: Stanford University Press, 1989).

30. Kao (1990), 153.

31. 自十三歲寫畫到廿三，於此十年，非不能成技藝，自以為志未得也。廿四游於外，廿五居家，廿六仍居家，廿七修業在書畫，廿八修業在儒書。今年廿九，將拋去書卷，囑家人諸弟為儒事，我則不暇當文几也。母號寒，妻啼饑，與韓愈同。但愈出而吾處，愈有常祿，吾無定所。此文章事業，悵悵無所之，不知天竟何如？命竟何如？此事非己所能操。武侯有云：「成敗利鈍非所逆睹。」得君且爾，□我布衣耶？仁山記。

32. Miles (2006), 72–74.

33. 韓愈焚膏孫映雪，未聞懶者留其名。爾懶豈自知，待我詳言之：官懶吏曹欺，將懶士卒離，母懶兒號寒，夫懶妻啼饑. Chen Xianzhang, *Chen Baisha ji* 陳白沙集 (Collection of Works by Chen Baisha) (Taipei: Taiwan shangwu yinshuguan, 1985).

34. I have come across only one other painting that mentions his siblings, *Physicians*, a handscroll dated 1847 in The Hong Kong Museum of Art.

35. The 1841 autobiographical inscription suggests that, when he was one year old, he suffered from convulsions that might have been epilepsy that eventually worsened and became dangerous to others. Ryckmans (1970), 30.

36. 蘇仁山，又名長春，吾邑杏壇鄉人。妙畫得於天趣。其族人禹田為余言，祖父時，仁山常至彼家，或住數日，或一兩月，襤褸亂頭，可飯可不飯。或從外來，人有方食過半者，取而噉之，少噉即告飽。入園摘得果子一二枚，即可代一飯。自少喜山水，十五歲強從人往桂林，樂而忘反。閱數年反，畫名大噪。然性介，特不喜與俗交。其父交遊太雜，往往代所游強仁山為作畫，仁山不以時應，或終不應。遂借他事報其不孝，繫之獄，久不得釋。無聊則以畫過日。六房吏及獄卒皆艷其畫，具紙墨，興到十紙不吝，有意索之不得也。獄牆頗淨，暇則遍畫之，無餘隙。縣尉見之，怒，立責手板，即命工圬而新之。人咸斥尉之焚琴煮鶴云。

37. James Cahill, *Pictures for Use and Pleasure: Vernacular Painting in High Qing China* (Berkeley, Los Angeles, and London: University of California Press, 2010), 1–6.

38. Rubie Watson, "The Named and the Nameless: Gender and Person in Chinese Society," *American Ethnologist*, vol. 13, no. 4 (November 1986), 619–631.

39. The character 潺 is pronounced *chan* in Mandarin, the character 虎 is pronounced *hu*, and the character 祥 is pronounced *xiang*.

40. Kao (1990), 129.

41. To give an idea of just how astonishingly high this number is, Su Liupeng (蘇六朋, ca. 1796–1862), a contemporary professional artist also from Shunde, had about thirty different names in a period of fifty years.

42. I am very grateful to Lisa Claypool for sharing her research on this painting, including her detailed translation of the inscriptions. The following footnotes (43–57) are taken from her research, and published in *China's Imperial Modern: The Painter's Craft,* edited by Lisa Claypool (Edmonton: University of Alberta Museum, 2012), 128–132.

43. A historical narrative dating to the tenth to fifth centuries BCE.

44. A chronicle of the history of the state of Lu (722–481 BCE) during the Spring and Autumn Period (770–476 BCE). At the time Su Renshan was writing, it was believed that Confucius was the author.

45. The *Zuo zhuan* 左傳 is a canonical commentary on the *Spring-Autumn Annals* (*Chunqiu* 春秋) attributed to Zuo Qiuming 左丘明 and dating to ca. 400 BCE.

46. Commentaries on the *Spring-Autumn Annals* dating to the Han Dynasty (206 BCE–220 CE).

47. See Chapter 29 of *Zhuangzi,* "Robber Zhi," in which the robber says to Confucius, "There's no robber worse than you. Why doesn't the world call you Robber Confucius instead of calling me Robber Zhi?"

48. An early chronicle of history dating to ca. 300 BCE.

49. A book of ancient history compiled by the Southern Song scholar Luo Mi 羅泌 (1131–89).

50. The home of Zhuanxu's grandmother Leizu, as somewhat ironically recorded in the first chapter of Sima Qian's *Records of the Historian.*

51. Zou was the name of a small state known in the Zhou Dynasty by the name of Zhu. It was granted by King Wu of Zhou to Cao Xie 曹挾, a direct lineal descendant of the Yellow Emperor through his grandson, the legendary Emperor Zhuanxu, the same ancestor that Su Renshan claims as his own.

52. One of the five legendary emperors.

53 A Daoist tract compiled by Xu Dao 徐道 and published in the Kangxi reign (1662–1723) of the Qing Dynasty.

54. In the *Classic of Mountains and Seas* (*Shanhaijing* 山海經), the Ruomu "Accord Tree" is one of three mysterious trees from the wild fields of the West, with a crimson trunk and flowers that shed light on the ground. The tree is also associated in the *Masters from Huainan* (*Huainanzi* 淮南子) with the story of the archer Houyi who shot down the suns that rest at night in the branches of the Ruomu tree in the west.

55. Zhu Rong, or "Blessed Heat," is the fire god, most famous for battling his own son, Gong Gong 共工, a water demon responsible for causing floods.

56. A lost classic mentioned in *Zuo zhuan.*

57. The translation is by Lisa Claypool: 西周末是王綱墜，國語能詳祖顓頊，魯史三隅能反者。左邱外傳時往復，公羊穀梁更何言，曆數候封盜丘哭，請讀竹書紀年者，曾不刪脩系益足。君不見老泉家譜無皇后，太史軒轅失所錄，丈不見長源路史寫西陵，後生文章火花回去。我來琴譜讀鄒者，注入譽妃笑當局，而今再讀神仙鑑，始信匡盧可青綠，帝高陽之苗裔兮。沉石作島登若木，祝融玉牒發其英，上溯三墳路史足。嶺南蘇長春吟稿。

58. Su Renshan often refers to Confucius as Robber Qiu, which comes from Chapter 29 of *Zhuangzi.* This reference is explained in greater details in Chapter Four.

59. Maram Epstein, *Competing Discourses: Orthodoxy, Authenticity, and Engendered Meanings in Late Imperial Chinese Fiction* (Cambridge, MA, and London: Harvard University Press, 2001), 156.

60. For later examples of the three-tone palette, see *Evening Clouds over a River* (1847, The Chinese University of Hong Kong), and *Grassy Path with Pine and Bamboo* (undated, Guangzhou Art Gallery).

61. I am indebted to Judith Zeitlin's research on the conceptual properties of writings, ghosts, and ghostliness. This is one of many of Professor Zeitlin's works that has been influential in my own studies; "Disappearing Verses: Writings on Walls and Anxieties of Loss," in *Writing and Materiality in China: Essays in Honor of Patrick Hanan* (Cambridge, MA: Harvard-Yenching Institute Monograph Series 58), 73–132.

62. Wu Hung, "On Rubbings: Their Materiality and Historicity," *Writing and Materiality in China: Essays in Honor of Patrick Hanan* (Cambridge, MA: Havard-Yenching Institute Monograph Series 58), 29–72.

63. Amy McNair argues for this point in her article, "Engraved Calligraphy in China: Recension and Reception," *The Art Bulletin,* vol. 77, no. 1 (March 1955), 106–114.

64. Li Tiaoyuan, *Yuedong biji, juan* 4 (Shanghai: Shanghai huiwentang shuju, reprinted 1922).

65. There is no painting by Tangdai with this title, but a hanging scroll painting, currently in the National Palace Museum entitled *Sundown over a Thousand Mountains* (千山落照), has a poem inscribed by Prince Hongli (later the Qianlong Emperor) that includes the line " 萬壑秋風起" and dates to 1732. It is unlikely that Su Renshan saw this painting, which was in the imperial collection, but this poem was recorded by Zhang Geng (張庚, 1685–1760) in *Records of Paintings in the Qing Dynasty* (清朝畫徵錄), published in 1735.

66. This line is taken from a well-known Tang poem "Yellow Crane Tower" by Cui Hao (崔顥, ca. 704–54). Lu

Yuansu did not compose this line, but her family was part of the Yellow Banner and her sobriquet was "crane cloud," thus obliquely referencing Cui Hao's famous poem.

67. 香績圖。唐岱嘗作《萬壑秋風起》山水，故添其像於羅漢傍。又盧元素亦嘗作「下人已乘黃鶴去」句，作畫菊，故併繪之；以同拈花微笑意云爾。仁山附十九觀音於後

68. There are no recorded paintings of this title by Tangdai. Tangdai, a Manchurian bannerman (Blue Banner), worked in the Qing court and was particularly active under the Kangxi and Qianlong Emperors. He also wrote a treatise on painting entitled *Huishi fawei* (On the Secret of Painting), in which he strongly advocated the orthodox tradition as passed on by his teacher, Wang Yuanqi. However, the book also noted the importance of natural light, angles, and perspectives, ideas that he probably gained from the Jesuit artists at the Qing court; see Chou Ju-hsi's "Tangdai: A Biographical Sketch," in *Chinese Painting under the Qianlong Emperor: Symposium Papers in Two Volumes*, edited by Chou Ju-hsi and Claudia Brown, Phoebus 6, no. 1 (Tempe, AZ: Arizona State University, 1991), 132–141.

69. Yuan Mei did venture to Guangdong, but there is no record, to date, of Lu Yuansu accompanying him.

70. The connection between Guangdong and Qing Bannermen was strengthened when Shang Kexi, a former Ming general, pledged allegiance to the Qing in 1633. Despite his involvement with the Rebellion of the Three Feudatories, Shang and his family were pardoned by the Kangxi Emperor, and they remained members of the Yellow Banner. By the eighteenth century, Guangzhou had the biggest congregation of bannermen garrison on a frontier town. Among the many bannermen in this region was Gao Bing, the grandson of the famous finger painter Gao Qipei (1660–1734). In 1771, Gao Bing wrote the *Manual of Finger Painting*, which was published in Guangdong, where he was based. It is perhaps not a coincidence that finger painting thrived in Guangdong around this time.

71. When the British first encountered Hong Kong, they mistook Aberdeen's name "Xiang Gang Village" as the name for the whole island. Aberdeen was renamed in 1845, after the Opium War and the Treaty of Nanjing.

72. Su Renshan also has a seal that reads Qizu, seventh patriarch, naming him as a follower of Huineng, the sixth patriarch of *Chan* Buddhism. See Kao (1990), 150.

Chapter Three

1. There are too many secondary sources on the Opium War to list. For an alternative viewpoint of historiography, Glenn Melancon considers the role of historians in writing about the Opium War, particularly from the British viewpoint, in *Britain's China Policy and the Opium Crisis: Balancing Drugs, Violence and National Honour, 1833–1840* (Aldershot: Ashgate, 2003), 133–141.

2. The introduction of opium to China is usually attributed to Arab traders along the Silk Road during the Tang Dynasty. One of the Chinese names for the poppy flower, *a-furong*, is believed to have derived from the Arabic word *af-yum*. It was considered a princely plant, serving the medicinal and aphrodisiac needs of the wealthy. In the sixteenth century, opium smoking became more commonplace as it was developed alongside tobacco smoking from South and Southeast Asia. It was cultivated locally in Sichuan, Fujian, and Shanxi. The increased sea trade also meant the increased availability of the drug. By the mid-eighteenth century, it was consumed in its unadulterated state and had become part of the cultural landscape of the imperial court, urban centers, and rural areas. Zheng Yangwen, *The Social Life of Opium* (New York: Cambridge University Press, 2005), 41–55.

3. The semantic variance of opium can also be used to map its social life. By the late nineteenth and twentieth centuries, opium was used as means of defining class and national identities and can be reflected in the names used to refer to the drug. Zheng (2005).

4. Shen (1983), 45–46.

5. Morphine, which affects the central nervous system, also induces drowsiness and can depress respiration. Another alkaloid in the latex of the poppy is codeine, which has one-seventh the biological activity of morphine.

6. Christina Chu (1991), 302.

7. Baker (1993), 23.

8. The calligraphy scroll is reproduced in Kao (1993), 118–223.

9. In the same year, Li composed a series of paintings and poems (Guangzhou Art Gallery), which included a poem with the line "The medicinal smoke separated [him] from the place of melancholy beyond the walls." Kao (1993), 128–129.

10. Estimates for the smuggling trade have varied. See Zheng (2005), 105–111.

11. My calculations are based on citations by Zheng of Rev. Dr Smith, who was later the Bishop of Hong Kong and traveled to Zhusan on a non-opium-smuggling ship that nonetheless carried 750 chests of opium as freight, each box weighing 200 pounds. The exchange rate for US dollars and sterling was roughly $4.85 dollars to the pound. The *Chinese Repository* reported that the estimated smuggling in 1845 was roughly 48,000 chests (exceeding the recorded amount), and each chest was worth approximately $700, making the total worth of the

smuggled trade \$33.6 million. Rev. Dr Smith estimated that 1,500 taels were exchanged for the transaction of 750 boxes. See Zheng (2005), 106–108, for smuggling trade figures.

12. Zheng (2005), 131–145.

13. There are numerous accounts of these incidents. See Auguste Borget, *Sketches of China and the Chinese* (London: Tilt and Bogue, 1842); William C. Hunter, *The "Fan Kwae" at Canton: Before Treaty Days* (Shanghai: Oriental Affairs, 1938); and the *Canton Register* (December 13, 1838 and February 27, 1839).

14. In 1849, Dai Xi lost favor after a report to the emperor on the forced entry of the British into Guangzhou City. Thereafter, he lived in retirement in the 1850s. Nonetheless, he was a devoted Qing subject, and when the Taipings attacked Hangzhou, his home city, he committed suicide.

15. 熬花作膏膏有毒。裝以陶坯吸以竹。精氣耗盡臟腑腐。漸剝爾肌銷爾肉。安用肉安用肌，髑髏之樂世人那得知。謂醉非醉夢非夢。奄奄待斃，其樂不可支。可以渴，此愛最難割。可以飢，此道最難離。昨聞南鄰誅死北鄰械。今日飽餐明日戒。Su Ruohu comp., *Mengxing furong ji, juan* 1 (1897). This is among the earliest compilation of writings on opium and the wars. This is the same Su Ruohu from Shunde who had inscribed Su Renshan's painting entitled *Bodhidharma*, discussed in Chapter Two, in which he talked about Su's imprisonment and his difficult relationship with his father.

16. In the *Chinese Repository* (May 1836–April 1837), there is a detailed description of an album by Sunqua of the downfall of the opium addict. The writer suggests that the album was similar to Hogarth's *Rake's Progress*. The comparison with Hogarth is a telling example of the moral undertones of a Victorian England that understands Sunqua's work of art as a form of social critique. The image of a sick, morally apprehensible China was reinforced as news of the possibility of war was being addressed in newspapers in England, and debates about Britain's role in supplying opium to China intensified. It captures the compulsion to associate national character with the physical properties of the body. Larissa Henrich's work on Lamqua's medical portraits for the American doctor Peter Parker offers further insight into how national character was associated with the body and pathology. A comparison of Lamqua's portrait of tumor patients who can be cured by surgery and Sunqua's opium addict suggest a more complex power dynamics of representation and perception. Henrich examines how, through increased circulation, these images changed from intimate pictures to concretize the perception of the "sick man of China" in the nineteenth century and circled back to China in the twentieth century, contributing to Lu Xun's own diagnosis of China's cultural pathology. Larissa N. Henrich, *The Afterlife of Images: Translating the Pathological Body between China and the West* (Chapel Hill, NC: Duke University Press, 2008).

17. Frederic Wakeman, Jr., *Strangers at the Gate: Social Disorder in South China, 1839–1861* (Berkeley and Los Angeles: University of California Press, reprinted 1997). This book is important for its focus on regional activities and, in particular, examining the roles of the lettered elite and academies in organizing factions and militia groups. See in particular 71–76 for how the militias at Sanyuanli were able to mobilize so quickly and the importance of local *she* (社) schools. Another useful source is Philip A. Kuhn's *Rebellion and Its Enemies in Late Imperial China: Militarization and Social Structure, 1796–1864* (Cambridge, MA: Harvard University Press, 1980). This book examines the militarization of nineteenth-century rural society, stressing the organizational, or even organic, similarities between orthodox and heterodox military groups. At a time when the government's professional armies were too decrepit to be effective against either external invasion or internal uprising, the government had little choice but to encourage the suppression of rebellion by locally organized militias.

18. Wakeman (1997), 11–29.

19. Wakeman (1997), 58.

20. Kuhn (1980), 54.

21. Translation by Wakeman (1997), 20; the original poem can be found in A-Ying, comp., *Yapian zhanzheng wenxue ji* 鴉片戰爭文學集 (A collection of writings on the Opium War), 2 vols. (Beijing: Guji chubanshe, 1957). The different colored banners represented the various groups of militia.

22. Jonathan D. Spence, *God's Chinese Son: The Taiping Heavenly Kingdom of Hong Xiuquan* (New York: W. W. Norton, 1996), 230.

23. The term *han jian* (漢奸) for traitors had been used indiscriminately prior to the Opium War. By 1823, it was used to refer to opium smugglers, and by the time of the Opium War, it came to designate the entire commercial establishment. Wakeman (1997), 49.

24. 洋煙之毒我中國也甚矣哉！有洋煙而逆夷之萌乃浸起矣，有逆夷而漢奸之孽且潛生矣，有漢奸而土賊之蠹又滋熾矣！患中於忽微，禍成於漸積，豈一朝一夕之故耶？我朝威德遐敷，人樂清晏者，垂二百年矣。歲在辛丑，蠢爾英夷，違禁犯順。狡逞戎心，一時內地漢奸，罔識同仇之義，反張助逆之謀，而萑苻土賊，更復所在跳梁，乘墉伏莽……吾鄉瀕海而居，舟舶往來，下通板沙，遠連洋面，屢奉憲諭，防禦加嚴。各士民同心敵愾，協力勸捐，計共得公費銀四百有奇。蓋保障之功，於是有賴焉！Tan Dihua et al., *Guangdong beike ji* (Guangdong: Guangdong gaodeng jiaoyu chubanshe, 2000), 418.

25. The details of the origins of any brotherhood are difficult to verify, but the political beginnings of *Tiandihui* has provided some insights. The group was formed in Fujian in the 1760s and was instrumental in the first Triad Rebellion, the Lin Shuangwen Uprising of 1787–88. David Ownby, *Brotherhoods and Secret Societies in Early and Mid-Qing China* (Stanford, CA: Stanford University Press, 1996), 55–81.

26. *Xiaodaohui* flourished in Taiwan during the 1770s and 1780s and was first set up by Chinese merchants to provide mutual aid and protection from local troops. Ownby (1996), 44.

27. Barend J. ter Haar provides extensive research on triad (Heaven and Earth Society) lore and rituals in his *Ritual and Mythology of the Chinese Triads* (Leiden, Boston, and Koln: Brill, 1998). He presents a convincing argument for the local dimension of these groups, in particular among Cantonese and Hakka communities where local languages played a big role in determining triad jargon. Although many of the rituals are supposedly secret, there was, as emphasized by ter Haar, a certain degree of local public knowledge, which was important for the effectiveness of the triads as a pressure group (458–462).

28. Ownby (1996), 3.

29. Ownby (1996), 159–161.

30. James M. Polachek, *The Inner Opium War* (Cambridge, MA: Harvard University Asia Center, 1992), 177–185.

31. There were many incidents, including violent skirmishes, but most were petitions, placards, and gatherings denouncing the British demands for entry. On December 7, 1842, a British subject got into an argument with a Chinese fruit seller and stabbed him to death. This led to further violence with an irate mob that burned and looted some of the foreign factories. Qiying had to pay a large indemnity and decapitate ten of the mob leaders to satisfy the foreign traders. Public agitation died soon afterwards, and, several months later, in July 1843, Qiying was confident that the excitement was over and announced that Guangdong would soon be opened to the West, but this again met with very strong objections. Qiying appealed to Pottinger, who agreed to postpone their entry.

32. For further information on the relationship of Qiying and foreign diplomats, see John King Fairbank, *Trade and Diplomacy on the China Coast: The Opening of the Treaty Ports, 1842–1854* (Cambridge, MA: Harvard University Press, 1969). I also discuss the relation of portraiture and diplomacy in "The Face of Diplomacy in Nineteenth-Century China: Qiying's Portrait Gifts,"

in *Narratives of Free Trade: The Commercial Cultures of US-Chinese Relations*, edited by Kendall Johnson (Hong Kong: Hong Kong University Press, 2011).

33. There are many examples of how the term "yi-ti-mi-te" was used in the correspondence from Qiying to Pottinger. For a case in point, see accession number FO 682/68/3 at the Public Records Office, National Archives, Kew, London.

34. Public Records Office, National Archives, Kew, London, accession number FO 17/68 (no. 74).

35. Wakeman (1997), 81.

36. I use the term "violence" in its modern sense: the threat or use of physical or symbolic acts with the intent to injure others or oneself. There are numerous studies on violence in China that discuss its terminology, and the moral, cultural, and sociopolitical implications in mainstream and subcultures: Charles Tilly and Barend J. ter Haar are two scholars who have produced a number of books and articles. In particular, see Charles Tilly et al., *The Rebellious Century, 1830–1930* (London: Dent, 1975); ter Haar (2000), 123–140, argues that violence was and is an intrinsic part of Chinese culture, even at elite levels; and Mark Edward Lewis, *Sanctioned Violence in Early China* (Albany, NY: State University of New York Press, 1990). I discuss the representation of violence and anger in Chapter Four.

37. Craig Clunas, *Empire of Great Brightness* (Honolulu, HI: University of Hawaii Press, 2007), 182–187.

38. The pictorial theme of blind men fighting deserves further study. My own background investigation traces Su Liupeng's roots to his predecessor Huang Shen, the eighteenth eccentric artist who also depicted images of blind men. More broadly, Su has a number of images of blind men with some that were intended as satires. On example is a handscroll painting, *Gathering of Blind Musicians*, in Guangzhou Museum. On this scroll, Su penned an inscription saying how he was once criticized for painting a scene of blind men appreciating antiques, and so instead he depicted a gathering of musicians instead.

39. This manual has been translated in Ruitenbeek (1992).

40. Finger painting continued into the twentieth century with artists including Gao Jianfu and Gao Qifeng of the Lingnan school who made finger paintings of hawks and tigers that carried a nationalist tone of a heroic China.

41. Jonathan Hay, "Luo Ping: The Encounter with the Interior Beyond," in *Eccentric Visions: The Worlds of Luo Ping (1733–1799)*, edited by Kim Karlsson (Zurich: Museum Rietberg, 2009), 104.

42. Shun Kwong-loi, "On Anger—An Experimental Essay in Confucian Moral Psychology," in *Zhu Xi Now: Contemporary Encounters with the Great Ultimate*,

edited by David Jones and He Jinli (Albany, NY: State University of New York, forthcoming).

43. Cathy Caruth in *Unclaimed Experience: Trauma, Narrative and History* (Baltimore, MD and London: Johns Hopkins University Press, 1996) examines how the effects of a trauma can manifest in forms not associated with the event. One of the characteristics of trauma is that it resists being spoken of, and while evidence is witnessed firsthand, it is through the construction of a narrative of what happened that a witness forms a picture of the trauma. In particular, Caruth focuses on the retrospective reconstruction in which the representational means is as important as what it being represented.

44. Rania Huntington, "Chaos, Memory, and Genre: Anecdotal Recollections of the Taiping Rebellion," *Chinese Literature: Essays, Articles, Reviews,* vol. 27 (December 2005), 59–91.

45. Huntington (2005), 64.

46. The lines recalled by Huang Peifeng from Meng Haoren are: 氣蒸雲夢澤，波撼岳陽城, from the poem, "Gazing at Dongting Lake, Presented to Prime Minister Zhang" (望洞庭湖贈張丞相). It has been suggested that Meng used this poem to gain a position, but it also reflects his ambivalence of serving at court. See, Alfreda Murck, *Poetry and Painting in Song China: The Subtle Art of Dissent* (Cambridge, MA: Harvard University Asia Center for the Harvard-Yenching Institute, 2000), 103–104.

47. Ibid.

48. 老病有孤舟，戎馬關山北，憑軒涕泗流。

49. 釣鰲歸去正長空，吹起晴霞一片。傑閣高寒烟(煙)霧杪，小試紫鸞仙管。萬木無聲，眾山皆響，咳唾從天半。元龍豪氣，怒濤飛上歌版。曾記烏帽青衫，銅琶鐵綽，正斜陽秋晚。猛拍闌干翻變徵，不怕海風吹斷。孤鶴盤雲，瘦蛟掀浪，聽我紅牙按。

50. A. C. Graham, *The Work of Lie-tz'u* (London: Paragon Book Gallery, 1960), 97–98.

51. Edward Schafer, *Vermilion Bird: T'ang Images of the South* (Berkeley and Los Angeles: University of California Press, 1967), 217.

52. There is a long history of heroic men, some of whom were later venerated as protectors, and as such were interwoven into imperial statecraft by having temples dedicated to them. These venerated men became the exemplar for later followers who identified with them. Zhang Weiping, the recipient of Dai Xi's painting and author of the Sanyuanli poem, eulogized the deaths of brave men who had died in the fight against the British. He composed an ode titled "Three Generals," in which he praised Chen Liansheng (陳聯陞), Chen Huacheng (陳化成), and Ge Yunfei (葛雲飛). Wang Zheng (王

拯), in his "Record of General Chen's Portrait," talks about General Chen's achievements and his untimely death: "Two portraits were commissioned, one was for the people of Wusong and to remain in a temple there, the other was to be given to Lian [Tinghuang, 練廷璜]. Lian received General Chen's corpse ten days after he died. According to Wang, General Chen's body looked as it had when he was alive. Thus, a portrait was made, and when those who knew the general saw it, all cried in grief… Alas! When the British barbarians attacked, soldiers were sent one after another to the sea for years. During the battle at Wusong, the people from the north and south of the Yangtze River all said that General Chen was a general of extreme valor who received a quick and untimely death in the defeat of Wusong… Today, we revere his portrait, sad in our anguish." See A-Ying (1957), 880.

53. A-Ying (1957), 793.

54. A-Ying (1957), 793–94.

55. Wang Zhaoyong (1961), *juan 10*, 2.

56. Beginning in the Tang Dynasty, painters such as Han Gan (韓幹, act. ca. 740–56) specialized in images of powerful horses, muscular steeds that symbolized the military strength of the dynasty and the authority of the Tang emperors. Also, beginning in the Tang Dynasty, paintings of emaciated horses came to symbolize neglected human beings, above all talented scholars who deserved, but often failed, to receive recognition and reward. These themes endured in various forms throughout the later history of Chinese painting. The scholar-painter Gong Kai (龔開, 1222–1307) painted his famous *Emaciated Horse* (Osaka Municipal Museum) after he witnessed the fall of the dynasty under which he was born. For many centuries, his depiction of an old gaunt horse was seen as a reflection of his own fate as a *yimin* and as a poignant representation of the ill-fated Song Dynasty, to which he remained loyal. No longer a powerful, confident animal, the horse symbolized China in decline.

57. Cited by Wakeman (1997), 176, from John Backhouse Papers, Duke University, translation of a Chinese proclamation, dated January 15, 1846 (Box 15, Folder 4).

58. A-Ying (1957), 191.

59. A-Ying (1957).

60. Marc Abramson, *Ethnic Identity in Tang China* (Philadelphia, PA: University of Pennsylvania Press, 2008), 89.

61. Translation by Stephen Owen. I have altered the translation of 胡 from Turk to barbarian. Stephen Owen, *An Anthology of Chinese Literature: Beginnings to 1911* (New York and London: W. W. Norton and Company, 1996), 428.

62. Owen (1996).

63. For details of the 1850–51 Shengguang Si Incident, see Ng Chin-keong, "Treaties, Politics, and the Limits of Local Diplomacy in Fuzhou in the Early 1850s," in *Power, and Identity in the Chinese World Order: Festschrift in Honor of Professor Wang Gungwu*, edited by Billy K. L. So et al. (Hong Kong: Hong Kong University Press, 2003), 239–268.

64. Translation by Ng Chin-keong, "Shooting Eagles: Lin Changyi's Agony in the Wake of the Opium War," in *Maritime Asia in Transition, 1750–1850*, edited by Wang Gangwu and Ng Chin-keong (Weisberg: Harrossowitz Verlag, 2004), 376–377. An abridged version of this can also be found in correspondence between the British vice-consul in Fuzhou, J. Walker, to the Governor of Hong Kong, Sir Samuel George Bonham, Foreign Office, Embassy and Consular Archives, China, FO 228/128, no. 56. The letter is dated December 10, 1851. 餘繪射鷹驅狼圖橫幅小照，題咏甚多。後又繪射鷹圖手卷，粵東長樂溫伊初孝廉（訓）題云：射鷹高墉絕技聞，海鷹何事劇翻翁。黃間白羽乘空發，雨血風毛墜地紛。爪嘴莫矜同勁鐵，乾坤從此靜妖氛。層樓海上雕弧影，已懾愁胡抉暮雲。

65. When Li Chengdong pledged allegiance to the Qing and took over Guangdong in 1646, resistance against the Manchu Qing court grew. By 1647, much of the Ming Loyalist army had been defeated, but in 1648, General Li defected form the Qing to become a Ming Loyalist. Thereafter, Guangdong suffered massive attacks from the Qing. A ten-month siege was held in 1650, followed by a five-day massacre. It was then that the Qing enforced the shaving of the hair to inform the most emblematic symbol of submission—the queue. This did not end Guangdong resistance that now included support from Zheng Chenggong in Taiwan. In order to cut off support from the Taiwan base, the Qing evacuated large areas of the Delta region including Dongguan, Zhang Mu's hometown. Opportunist bandits raided these areas, creating more havoc. Coupled with the increasing costs of grain, widespread famine in the region eventually wore down resistance. It was not until 1684, when the evacuation decree was rescinded, that signaled the end of Ming resistance. Faure (2007), 164–176.

66. Lydia Liu, *The Clash of Empires: The Invention of China in Modern World Making* (Cambridge, MA: Harvard University Press, 2004).

67. Liu (2004), 100.

68. This reference is cited by Liu (2004), 99–100. The original source is from the *Chinese Repository*, vol. 11, no. 6 (June 1842), 342.

69. Yeewan Koon, "Lives and Afterlives: Luo Ping's 'Guiqu tu,'" *Orientations*, vol. 40 (September 2009), 66–72.

70. The relevant part of Pan Shicheng's postscript reads:
又聞四裔有鬼國 其人夜遊而晝藏身
至如夜叉 羅刹國諸鬼窟 其鬼非鬼 皆在萬裏之重洋
鬼之始來開鬼市
糸集貨紛紜忺聽視
販布運以車與船
轉風火輪疾如駛 [……]
窺伺讒鬼𩲢佞魖鬼𩲢 鬼𩲢索索為鬼姦
窮鬼餓鬼齒門 齒門齧齧供鬼使
上不信天道 下無人理
始知非鬼而鬼 名鬼之為言詐而已。

71. There is a handscroll painting by Su Renshan entitled *Physicians*, dated 1847, in the Hong Kong Museum of Art. It has a long inscription of Su speaking of a time when he was young and suffered from a "fright" after falling down a ladder. His mother had to call in the doctors to cure him.

72. Ginger Hsu, "The Drunken Demon Queller Chung K'uei in Eighteenth Century Chinese Painting," *Taida Journal of Art History*, vol. 3 (1996), 145.

73. 昔或能文，今仍不武，所事紛紛竟臥忘。聊為戲，料名心未死，宦興偏長。徜徉小憩何妨，是息靜功夫快活方。儘精靈聚魅，聞聲驚走；乜邪多鬼，見影潛藏。

Chapter Four

1. This is a reference to Mencius, 12.7: "The five chiefs of the princes were sinners against the three kings. The princes of the present day are sinners against the five chiefs. The Great officers of the present day are sinners against the princes." James Legge, *The Chinese Classics Book VI, Part II* (London: Truber & Co., 1861–1872), 311. The chapter is part of an ongoing debate between Mencius and the philosopher Gaozi, in which Mencius discusses how these various personages were each in turn as guilty as their superiors.

2. Sima Qian cites a passage from Zhuangzi, Chapter 10, of the following lines: 彼竊鈎者誅，竊國者爲諸侯，諸侯之門而仁義存焉，則是非竊仁義聖知邪？ The translation of this reference is: "He who steals a belt buckle pays with his life; he who steals a state gets to be a feudal lord—and we all know that benevolence and righteousness are to be found at the gates of the feudal lords. Is this not the case of stealing benevolence and righteousness and the wisdom of sages?" Burton Watson, trans., *Chuang Tzu: Basic Writings* (New York: Columbia University Press, 1964), 110.

3. The story about Rangfu comes from *Gaoshi zhuan* (Records of eminent men) compiled by Huangfu Mi. It was recorded that, under the rulership of Yao, all was peaceful, and no harm came to the people. An elderly

man, who was over eighty years old, strikes the land in the middle of the road. A bystander exclaimed, "Oh dear! The virtue of Yao!" In response, Rang said: "I work when the sun is out and I rest when the sun is down. I dig a well for water, I toil in my fields for food; what does the virtue of the emperor have to do with me?" This story is also the subject of a prose-rhyme song in the Yuefu Collection entitled "The Song of Striking the Land" 擊壤歌; see *Lienü zhuan, Gaoshi zhuan*, emended by Liu Xiaodong (Shenyang: Liaoning jiaoyu chubanshe, 1988), *juan shang*, 2. "孤竹君" (Gentleman Guzhu [Solitary bamboo]) is the title of a melody in *Xilutang Qintong*. The introduction to the melody talks about a man of Jin (265–420) seeing an inscription on a grave that reads, "On the mound (tomb) there was a solitary bamboo; the wind blowing causes it to bend. Underneath is a centenarian, sleeping forever and not knowing dawn." It was called *Guzhu Jun*. The introduction does not mention Bo Yi or Shu Qi, but *Qinshu daquan* suggests that *Guzhu Jun* is an alternate title for the melody *Caiwei cao* 採薇操, which is a reference to Bo Yi and Shu Qi; see Zhu Changwen, *Qin shi*, edited by Palace Museum (Haikou: Hainan chubanshe, 2001), 5.

4. 豪傑則病民甚矣！蓋神農、后稷，其餘風不外耕織醫藥耳。詎若後世帝堯，乃竟單均刑儀，遂使世界成戕賊，良可憫也。至於湯武以兵為君，陶及姬公以刑設官，真使中原成地獄，求復成為飽食煖衣世界，尚可得耶？故軻此說，良為神農、稷棄之罪人矣。太史遷曰：竊□誅，竊國王侯之門，仁義存此。武周以暴易暴，乃開盜蹠盜丘之門戶，而帝堯單刑儀，舜任□陶誅四凶，俱屬草介百姓。此壤父辨帝力為無有，孤竹懷神農於□沒也。仁山識。

5. Paul Kjellberg, trans., "Selections from Zhuangzi," in *Readings in Classical Chinese Philosophy*, edited by Philip J. Ivanhoe and Bryan W. Van Norden (Indianapolis, IN: Hackett Publishing Company, Inc., 2005), 371–373.

6. Peter C. Perdue, "Nature and Nurture on Imperial China's Frontiers," *Modern Asian Studies*, vol. 43, no. 1, 2009, 245–267.

7. Perdue (2009).

8. Schafer (1967), 125.

9. 宓羲、孔子、女媧、熒惑像。此圖發明伏羲之道，與仲尼殊有生死之判也。伏羲明陰陽，法鬼神，以一畫開天，成象八卦，以木德王以風為性，謂之太皥。渾沌之民得見文明之世者，伏羲也。故首冠三墳。趙穿弒君，仲尼書之曰趙盾，傳曰：非趙盾也，趙穿也。而仲尼職在司寇，倒置是非。余曰：使地獄出天堂，伏羲以陰陽開文明之世也。使天堂為地獄，仲尼作《春秋》，而責備賢者也。周書無求備於一人，余於是並繪其像，而加一女媧者，宓羲之妹也；加一熒惑，

星宿之神也。伏羲之道行，則天柱尚可石補；仲尼之道行，則熒惑星現。

10. The idea that harmony is the state of centrality achieved by focus is the foundation of *Zhongyong*, a philosophical text attributed to Kong Ji (孔伋, 483–402 BCE), grandson of Confucius. It was incorporated into the *Record of Rites,* and it was included as part of Zhu Xi's (1130–1200) influential Four Books, together with *Analects of Confucius, Great Learning,* and *Mencius.*

11. See Roger Ames and David Hall, *Focusing the Familiar: A Translation and Philosophical Interpretation of the Zhongyong* (Honolulu, HI: University of Hawaii Press, 2001), 35–37.

12. Li Chengyang, "Zhongyong as Grand Harmony: An Alternative Reading to Ames and Hall's *Focusing the Familiar,*" *Dao* 3, no. 2, 173–188.

13. This ancient form was regaining importance in the eighteenth century as a component of philology. Su's interest in seal scripts is part of this interest in remote history, and he uses the aesthetics of an engraved past that could bear the moral weight of authenticity.

14. John Hay, "Values and History in Chinese Painting: The Hierarchal Evolution of Structure," *Res* vol. 7/8 (Spring 1984), 106.

15. Although there are hundreds of paintings with Lin Liang's signature, there is not a single dated document about his life, which is typical of many of the Ming court artists, for whom very little is recorded. However, the absence of any texts also suggests the marginal position of Guangdong.

16. Barnhart (1993), 15.

17. Hou-mei Sung, *Decoded Messages: The Symbolic Language of Chinese Animal Painting* (New Haven, CT and London: Yale University Press, 2009), 110–112.

18. The earliest record of a painting of cranes dates to the Tang Dynasty and has since evolved into a large repository of meanings that link the bird to the moral character of a person. In particular, this is seen in the "act" of the crane; preening (*limao*), wind-dancing (*wufeng*), and heaven-crying (*litian*) are acts that are embodied with values and human attributes. See Sung (2009), 40–44.

19. I am aware that the idea of a plague of locusts may also refer to biblical themes, which may add fuel to the speculations that Su was associated with the Taiping Rebels. Given that the Taiping Rebellion leader, Hong Xiuquan, who had a vision of himself as a son of god, and brother to Jesus, took his exams at the same time as Su Renshan, the two men may have met. Moreover, Su was active in Wuzhou where the first Taiping led rebel fight took place, and Su's position against Confucius, Confucian institutions, and the value of female scholarship (explored in the next chapter) offers tantalizing grounds

for this speculation. However, my search for stronger connections has yet to unveil stronger associations with the Taipings (largely through trying to trace social networks, or pictorial sentiments more directly engaged with Taiping ideology), and all possible suggestions, including this painting, if indeed it refers to locusts, are still too tenuous.

20. The phrase comes from the fourth chapter of the *Ji jiu pian*, written by Shi You (史遊, act. 48–33 BCE).

21. I want to thank Wang Cheng-hua for drawing this to my attention. Although images of single or paired locusts are common auspicious motifs, especially in Guangdong, a large group of locusts can only be seen as a sign of calamity. Perhaps related, the locust (*huangchong* 蝗蟲), is used as a rebus for *chongjing* (崇敬)—esteemed or respect, and therefore popular as motifs on auspicious work—these multiple plays of words and images that are almost, but not quite, alike add to the iconoclastic cleverness that we expect from Su Renshan.

22. Qiu Ying painted this theme in an album leaf from "Stories of People" (人物故事), undated, ink and color on silk, Palace Museum Beijing.

23. Translation from Jonathan Hay (2001b), 214.

24. Albums on the production of tea, silk, and ceramics were among the most popular form of export art. See Chapter One for further discussion on export trade art.

25. Clunas (1997) citing Song Lian (宋濂, 1310–81) discusses the differences between *hua* (painting) and *tu* (diagram), 108–109.

26. There are numerous stories of Jing Jiang of Lu, and they can be found in various ancient texts including the *Li ji* 禮記 (Book of rites), *Guoyu* 國語 (The discourses of the States), and *Han Shi waizhuan* 韓詩外傳 (The outer commentary to the Book of Songs by Master Han). The longest biography is found in the *Lienü zhuan* 列女傳 (Biographies of exemplary women), which is also the only place where this passage can be found. This translation, with some adaptation, is taken from Lisa A. Raphals, "A Woman Who Understood the Rites," in *Confucius and the Analects*, edited by Bryan W. Van Norden (Oxford: Oxford University Press, 2002), 277.

27. Francesca Bray, *Technology and Gender: Fabrics of Power in Late Imperial China* (Berkeley, CA: University of California Press, 1997), 256–257.

Chapter Five

1. 商畹□、吳若華、鍾文貞鼎足於桐城顏士睿後，詎不可謂王唐歸胡耶？惜可儀奇文未共欣賞，真令宜興作者而有疊□山履祥之嘆也。余於陳鄭孝經、尚宮論語，未嘗不善其繼盛於惠班七誡，彰美乎孝文述訓也。韓、柳、蘇、曾之材，尚苦寂滅道邪？

2. This is a reference to a famous line from Tao Qian's poem "Moving House, No. 1": 奇文共欣賞，疑義相與析, translated by Burton Watson (1964) as "Unusual writings we appreciate with one another, working out the difficult passages together." This poem refers to his move, after his retirement from court, to the rural south, where he was able to share his thoughts with like-minded friends.

3. Zhang Hongxing, "Re-reading Inscriptions in Chinese Scroll Painting: The Eleventh to the Fourteenth Centuries," *Art History* (December 2005), 606–625; Anne Burkass-Chasson, "Visual Hermeneutics and the Act of Turning the Leaf: A Genealogy of Liu Yuan's *Lingyan ge*," in *Printing and Book Culture in Late Imperial China*, edited by Cynthia Brokaw and Kai-wing Chow (Berkeley, CA: University of California Press, 2002), 371–416.

4. Epstein (2001), 156.

5. Stephen J. Roddy, *Literati Identity and Its Fictional Representations in Late Imperial China* (Stanford, CA: Stanford University Press, 1998).

6. Although the novel *Jinghuayuan* is often compared to *Honglou meng* because of its shared interest in talented females, literary contests, and garden imagery, Stephen Roddy argues that Li Ruzhen took his plot line from a lesser-known military romance novel, *Lu mudan* 綠牡丹 (The green peony, 1800), 282, ft. 6. Ellen Widmer, however, sees a closer relation with the famous late Ming novels *Shuihu zhuan* (Water margin) and *Xiyou ji* 西遊記 (Journey to the West): "Jinghua yuan: Where the Late Late Ming Meets the Early Late Qing," in *Dynastic Decline and Cultural Innovation: Late Ming and Late Qing*, edited by David Der-wei Wang and Shang Wei (Cambridge, MA: Harvard University Asia Studies Center, 2005), 264–295. I want to thank Dorothy Ko for bringing this article to my attention.

7. Wu Zetian is inspired to hold the examinations after being moved by the talents of her female subjects.

8. Roddy (1998), 175.

9. 五言八韻　擬崇山帖：御製黃維德，長孫風雅篇。馬玄玄太放，薛素素如仙。薄少君真富，郭貞順戍邊。王激源把臂，徐媛淺師前。晉代東山謝，宋遺精衛填。不妨許景樊，多染絳濤箋。楊太真誰識，宋楊妃似焉。胡笳同調者，王嬙幾人然。仁山稿并書。

10. Ibid.

11. Xue Susu appears to have gained her reputation when she went to Beijing in the 1590s. Aside from her martial abilities and literary talents, she was known to have been involved in political intrigues. Among her admirers were the artist and politician Dong Qichang, the connoisseur Pan Zhizeng, and Shen Dafu, whom she married.

See Daria Berg, "A Cultural Discourse on Xue Susu, a Courtesan in Late Ming China," *International Journal of Asian Studies,* vol. 6, no. 2 (2009), 171–200.

12. Liu Bang composed a song, *Song of the Great Wind,* after his victory over Xiang Yu: "A Great wind rises, clouds fly and scatter; With power over the four seas, I return to my homeland; Where shall I get brave warriors to safeguard the four quarters?"

13. 壽莊曰：……漢沛公非不知儒之陋劣，果於亡國之效者，但緣三尺劍，不能辨盜蹠與盜丘合傳爾。泣懷猛士不得已之辭，自呈本色爾。楚羽虞姬皆劍俠，知文辭，不曉仙策而棄安期生，故亦自盡不辱，以成本紀。故太史公一曰秦楚之際年月表，一曰項羽本紀。漢若無楚，則漢亦無秦。漢無秦，漢祚安在？漢無楚，漢篡安在？史公次楚於秦，次漢於楚矣。劍可戒哉？

14. Legend has it that the First Emperor of Qin had demanded that An Qisheng should give him one of his famous pills or else face death. An was uneasy with this request, but while deliberating the dilemma of whether to present the megalomaniac emperor with the pill, he met a wandering hermit who asked him why he could not differentiate good from bad. Thus resolved, he took the magical pill himself and became an immortal.

15. Translation by Burton Watson, *Records of the Grand Historian of China, translated from the Shih Chi of Ssu-ma Ch'ien,* 2 vols. (New York: Columbia University Press, 1961), 70–71.

16. Madeline Chu, "Journey into Desire: Monkey's Secular Experience in the Xiyoubu," *Journal of the American Oriental Society,* vol. 117 (October 1997), 654–664.

17. Stephen W. Durrant, *The Cloudy Mirror: Tension and Conflict in the Writings of Sima Qian* (New York: State University of New York Press, 1995), 123–143.

18. Ellen Widmer, *The Beauty and the Book: Women and Fiction in Nineteenth-Century China* (Cambridge, MA, and London: Harvard University Press, 2006).

19. James Cahill, "Paintings Done for Women in Ming-Qing China?" *Nan Nü,* vol. 8, no. 1, 2006, 1–54.

20. I have not been able to trace any Han steles with similar inscriptions but have found bronze mirrors with the phrase 五穀孰成; see Guo Yuhai, *Gugong zang jing* (Beijing: Zijincheng chubanshe, 1996), 32.

21. Clunas (1997), 53.

22. There are a number of extant texts published in Guangdong from the sixteenth century onwards about the worlds beyond the borders. Among them is *Hai lu* 海錄 (Record of seas), based on observations from Xie Qinggao (謝清高, 1765–1821), a young sailor who, after a sea mishap, ends up working on a foreign ship and as a result travels to many countries. Later, when he was thirty-one, he lost his eyesight and was abandoned by his captain in Macau. He regaled his new neighbors with stories of many foreign countries, describing the people and their strange customs. Later, Yang Bingnan (楊炳南, act. ca. early nineteenth century) turned Xie's stories into a book when it was published in Guangzhou in 1820—just before *Jinghuayuan* was published.

23. 戊申夏五，仲妹造廬閱帖，自秦漢逮宋，鮮許。惟岳麓書院石刻於右軍草法二則，大加嘆惋。至魯公文殊帖曰：「不如矣。」予遂指陳鐘王飛白，且以肅恭王閣帖示之。至衛李氏則曰：「百美圖。衛夫人邪？其書如此邪？」□而曰：「閨閣論詩有幾人？」及覽唐太宗於梅炎藻夏此段，稱賞彌洽，因道駢體文字，節述《百美圖序》一段，手擎布傘而去，如鷿鳥之乍飛也，惟女紅盡棄。

24. According to Dorothy Ko, women travelers took to the road for three reasons. First, wives, daughters and daughters-in-law followed the bureaucratic transfers of their husbands, fathers, and father-in-laws. Second, they traveled for pleasure, usually with families and other women. Third, women traveled for work. However, it was an activity that was considered a privilege because of the entourage required. Dorothy Ko, *Teachers of the Inner Chambers: Women and Culture in Seventeenth-century China* (Stanford, CA: Stanford University Press, 1994), 224.

25. Clunas (1997), 102–133.

26. An example is Tang Yin's *Tao Gu Presents a Poem,* undated hanging scroll, Shanghai Museum of Art.

27. The writing of self-as-other is a traditional rhetorical device using elaborate comparisons, metaphors, and tropes to concoct alternative figures, often of the past, as a form of self-expression and self-analysis. The device's openness allows for hypertextual readings that create multiple readings in colophons and inscriptions. Strong authorial presence requires viewers to acknowledge the artist as the principal voice, reducing possible responses.

28. Su Renshan's debt to the printed book has been examined by Kao Mayching, who traced the roots of some of his images to painting manuals and woodblock images, which she considered to be his primary source of training. Kao (1990), 156–157.

29. 楊柳陰濃夏日遲，村邊高館漫平池。鄰翁挈盒乘清早，來決輸盈昨日棋。丙午初秋臨於鯨鯢缸(魚白)水榭。仁山書「嬴」為「盈」，六如笑曰：「吾生平作詩或出韻，今君作字迺入音乎？」仁山笑曰：「公似不知音，我似不識字。」六如大笑，仁山亦大笑。蓋相遇於山林云。

30. 世稱制義自王安石始，然安石以古文名世，自云兼讀釋典稗史，則外國之詞章，哩俗之紀載，不隘於三代兩漢。可見退之知古書之正偽，與雖正

而不至焉者。然莊也、騷也、太史也，其所嘗稱
也。後人讀書不如八家博，更不敢以八家所嘗讀
者命題。故九州縉紳耆宿，隘於洛黨之陋凡五百
年。呵呵！

31. By the Northern Song, many peasants had become tenants or small freeholders. Laws such as those proposed by Wang Anshi were introduced to protect tenants; others that protected landholders were drafted as well. He implemented a series of reforms, the New Policies, most of which were attempts to reassert the state's control over a growing private economy. See Robert P. Hymes and Conrad Schirokauer, eds., *Ordering the World: Approaches to State and Society in Sung Dynasty China* (Berkeley, CA: University of California Press, 1997).

32. Peter Bol, "Government, Society, and State: On the Political Visions of Ssu-ma Kuang and Wang An-shih," in *Ordering the World: Approaches to State and Society in Sung Dynasty China*, edited by Robert P. Hymes and Conrad Schirokauer (Berkeley, CA: University of California Press, 1997), 190.

33. All three men were scholars who actively promoted female talents. Wang, a famous poet, organized a famous literary meeting (1657)—the Autumn Willow Poetry Association—and invited many female participants. Yuan Mei, admitted to the Hanlin Academy in 1739 but unsuccessful in his Manchu language test (1742), was subsequently appointed a magistrate. He concentrated on writing, particularly poetry. He was very active in fostering the talents of educated women, especially in his seventies. In 1796, he compiled an anthology of poems entitled *Suiyuan nüdizi shixuan* 隨園女弟子詩選 (Anthology of the female disciples of Harmony Garden) with works by twenty-eight female disciples. Shen Deqian, a contemporary of Yuan Mei and a Hanlin Academician, edited the compilation *Qingshi biecai* 清詩別裁 (Styles of Qing poetry, 1760), which included works by women. See Ellen Widmer and Kang-I Sun Chang, eds., *Writing Women in Late Imperial China* (Stanford, CA: Stanford University Press, 1997), 164–165.

34. 又制義文五百年來，女史能拈題游藝，則漁洋述
商畹人，確士述吳若華，子才述鍾睿姑。異乎三
子者之撰，則患瞶屋之不達，深愧不下機於發篋
也，悲夫，而介甫無是。初，茂叔見荊公，相晤
語學，問荊公不答。道學家以茂叔所詣精深，
能窮荊公之博洽，□述為美談，不知荊公不屑與
語。又五百年來，學干祿皆效荊公制義，出而語
人曰宗濂洛，更可笑焉。當世倘肯戲如雯，以王
晉昇女四書命題，課吳若華等持婦具，亦佳。仁
山書。

35. 荊公子雯見洛黨程正叔入詣荊公府，雯素知頤、
灝皆有道學聲氣，固意持婦人器具入見。荊公
於賓主晤對時，伊川以父子主賓乃爾，大不快，
退，反謂雯不莊，而不知雯固侮之。雯聞嘗侍
側，荊公父子造詣，不具世眼，雯亦為朝廷講
官。荊公書說頒學校，婦具能然否？雯之戲乃
爾。

36. *Xixiangji* is a famous Yuan dynasty drama piece by Wang Shifu set in the Tang dynasty. It was a popular lover story and there were many Ming dynasty illustrations of this story.

37. "然心向往之" is a quote taken from Chapter 47, *Biographies of Hereditary Households and Eminent Persons*, from *Records of the Grand Historian*. Sima Qian praises the talents of Confucius and says his followers must continue forth despite the demise of their eminent teacher. Although this famous quote by Sima Qian is used to urge scholars to continue to pursue knowledge, Su Renshan suggests that determination alone is not enough, as seen in the examples set by Yu, who became paralyzed, and Tang Yin who, despite or because of his witty intelligence, was rejected from officialdom.

38. Fuxi is said to have been conceived when his mother stepped into a giant footprint; see Anne Birrell, *Chinese Myths* (London: British Museum Press, 2000), 29.

39. The Six Arts was used to describe the six areas that the educated elite were expected to excel in: ritual, music, archery, charioteering, writing, and arithmetic. During the Han Dynasty, the Six Arts were reorganized around the Confucian classical texts. Subsequently, the Six Arts represented the orthodox canon of literati scholars.

40. The reference to Confucius as a bandit comes from Chapter Twenty-nine of Zhuangzi, which is the same chapter referring to the Yu as being paralyzed.

41. This painting was mounted at a local mounting shop. I have not been able to trace any references to this Shunde-based shop.

42. □無顛倒夢想，豈因受想行識，而有色聲香味
觸法哉？漆園以化熊為偏枯，信矣。江南首登賢
書，唐寅以西廂標題制義。子長曰：雖不能至，
然心向往之。惟仙人不還，乃清移海水洇沒耶？
嶺南蘇長春撰……仁山曰：儒之為類，等於靈
祇中一物，生於易之下繫，異乎大人足跡。故不
識龍馬庖犧五穀周棄及其長也，困於列國諸侯，
火於秦，嫚□於漢，不安於唐，陷溺於宋，杖於
明太祖，擲於復社。儒之為類，所辱已甚，又安
能假天子命以辱民哉？六藝之文，殺人殺物。齊
魯之會，載在家語，一元之武，載在戴記。開
地獄之門戶，而成稱於盜蹠盜丘也。鏡孔昭齋裝
璜。識於順德縣內。畫臨李思訓。

43. Dai Zhen's (戴震, 1724–77) famous accusation that moral principles killed people can be seen in the way that

late eighteen- and nineteenth-century scholars used the idea in their discussions and writings. Stephen Roddy discusses how, in the final chapters of *Rulin waishi*, one of the prominent themes was the problem in the exaltation of rituals and draws on Dai Zhen's famous words as part of his argument, 141. The late nineteenth-century scholar Tan Sitong (譚嗣同, 1865–98) also used this idea in his writing on benevolence (*Renxue* 仁學) and the moral dilemmas faced by Confucianized women in a patriarchal society. Benjamin Elman, "The Failures of Contemporary Chinese Intellectual History," *Eighteenth Century Studies*, vol. 43, no. 3, 2010, 377.

44. Hong Xiuquan (洪秀全, 1814–64), of Guangxi Province, led the Taiping Rebellion. He was influenced by Christian missionaries during his Guangzhou visits when he took (and failed) the civil examinations. One night, he had a vision that named him as the brother of Jesus sent to found the Heavenly Kingdom. See Spence (1996); Jian Youwen, *Qingshi Hong Xiuquan zaiji* 清史洪秀全載記 (Historical records of Hong Xiuquan) (Hong Kong: Jianshi Mengjin shuwu, 1967); Michael H. Franz et al., *The Taiping Rebellion: History and Documents* (Seattle, WA: University of Washington Press, 1966–71); and Kuhn (1980).

Bibliography

Archives

Manuscript Division, Library of Congress, Caleb Cushing Papers: Box 28–48.

Peter Parker Collection, Cushing/Whitney Medical Library, Yale University: Series 1, Folder 5, 6, 9, 11.

Peter Parker Collection, Cushing/Whitney Medical Library, Yale University: Series V, Objects including portraits and photographs of paintings by Lamqua.

Public Records Office, National Archives, Kew, London: FO 17/68 (no. 74).

Public Records Office, National Archives, Kew, London: FO 233/185.

Public Records Office, National Archives, Kew, London: FO 682/68/3.

Public Records Office, National Archives, Kew, London: FO 682/137/13.

Public Records Office, National Archives, Kew, London: FO 705/79.

Public Records Office, National Archives, Kew, London: FO 931/484.

Public Records Office, National Archives, Kew, London: FO 1048/13/19.

Public Records Office, National Archives, Kew, London: FO 1048/29/9.

Manuscripts, Books and Journals

Abramson, Marc. *Ethnic Identity in Tang China*. Philadelphia, PA: University of Pennsylvania Press, 2008.

Ames, Roger, and David Hall. *Focusing the Familiar: A Translation and Philosophical Interpretation of the Zhongyong*. Honolulu, HI: University of Hawaii Press, 2001.

Andrews, Julia F., and Kuiyi Shen. *A Century in Crisis: Modernity and Tradition in the Art of Twentieth-Century China*. New York: Henry N. Abrams, 1998.

Asian Art Museum of San Francisco. *Between the Thunder and the Rain: Chinese Paintings from the Opium War through the Cultural Revolution, 1840–1979*. San Francisco, CA: Asian Art Museum, 2000.

A-Ying, ed. *Yapian zhanzheng wenxue ji* 鴉片戰爭文學集 (A collection of writings on the Opium War). Beijing: Guji chubanshe, 1957.

Baker, Nila Ann. "Li Jian and Xie Lansheng as Painters of the Cantonese Scholar-Artist Tradition." In *The Art of Li Jian and Xie Lansheng*, edited by Kao Mayching. Hong Kong and Guangzhou: Art Gallery, The Chinese University of Hong Kong and Guangzhou Art Gallery, 1993.

Barnhart, Richard. *Painters of the Great Ming: The Imperial Court and the Zhe School*. Dallas, TX: Dallas Museum of Art, 1993.

Barnhart, Richard et al. "The Tu Chin [Du Jin] Correspondence, 1994–95," *Kaikodo Journal*, vol. 5, Autumn 1997, 8–45.

Berg, Daria. "A Cultural Discourse on Xue Susu, a Courtesan in Late Ming China," *International Journal of Asian Studies*, vol. 6, no. 2, 2009, 171–200.

Berger, Patricia. *Empire of Brightness: Buddhist Art and Political Authority in Qing China*. Honolulu, HI: University of Hawaii Press, 2003.

Bernhardt, Katherine. "A Ming-Qing Transition in Chinese Women's History?" In *Remapping China: Fissures in Historical Terrain*, edited by Gail Hershatter et al., 42–58. Stanford, CA: Stanford University Press, 1996.

Birrell, Anne. *Chinese Myths*. London: British Museum Press, 2000.

———. *Chinese Mythology: An Introduction*. Baltimore, MD and London: Johns Hopkins University Press, 1993.

Bol, Peter K. "Government, Society, and State: On the Political Visions of Ssu-ma Kuang and Wang An-shih." In *Ordering the World: Approaches to State and Society in Sung Dynasty China*, edited by Robert P. Hymes and Conrad Schirokauer, 128–192. Berkeley, CA: University of California Press, 1997.

———. *This Culture of Ours: Intellectual Transitions in T'ang and Sung China*. Stanford, CA: Stanford University Press, 1992.

Borget, Auguste. *Sketches of China and the Chinese*. London: Tilt and Bogue, 1842.

Bray, Francesca. *Technology and Gender: Fabrics of Power in Late Imperial China.* Berkeley, CA: University of California Press, 1997).

Brook, Timothy, and Bob Tadashi Wakabayashi, eds. *Opium Regimes: China, Britain and Japan, 1839–1952.* Berkeley, CA: University of California Press, 2000.

Brown, Claudia, and Ju-shi Chou. *Transcending Turmoil: Painting at the Close of China's Empire, 1796–1911.* Phoenix, AZ: Phoenix Art Museum, 1992.*The Elegant Brush: Chinese Painting under the Qianlong Emperor, 1735–1795.* Phoenix, AZ: Phoenix Art Museum, 1985.

———. *The Elegant Brush: Chinese Painting under the Qianlong Emperor, 1735–1795.* Phoenix, AZ: Phoenix Art Museum, 1985.

Buoye, Thomas. "From Patrimony to Commodity: Changing Concepts of Land and Social Conflict in Guangdong Province during the Qianlong Reign (1736–1795)," *Late Imperial China,* vol. 14, no. 2, December 1993, 33–59.

Burkass-Chasson, Anne. "Visual Hermeneutics and the Act of Turning the Leaf: A Genealogy of Liu Yuan's *Lingyan ge.*" In *Printing and Book Culture in Late Imperial China,* edited by Cynthia Brokaw and Kai-wing Chow, 371–416. Berkeley, CA: University of California Press, 2002.

Cahill, James. *Pictures for Use and Pleasure: Vernacular Painting in High Qing China.* Berkeley, Los Angeles, and London: University of California Press, 2010.

———. "Paintings Done for Women in Ming-Qing China?" *Nan Nü,* vol. 8, no. 1, 2006, 1–54.

———. *The Compelling Image: Nature and Style in Seventeenth-Century Chinese Painting.* Cambridge, MA: Harvard University Press, 1982.

Cai Pengyang. *Hua zhi siseng: Luo Ping Zhuan* 花之寺僧：羅聘傳 (A biography of Luo Ping, Monk of a Temple of Flowers). Shanghai: Shanghai renmin chubanshe, 2001.

The Canton Press (August 19, 1938).

Canton Register (December 13, 1838; February 27, 1839).

Carlitz, Katherine. "The Social Uses of Female Virtue in Late Ming Editions of *Lienu Zhuan,*" *Late Imperial China* vol. 12, no. 2, December 1991, 117–148.

Cartier, Carolyn. "Origins and Evolution of a Geographical Idea: The Macroregion in China," *Modern China* vol. 28, no. 1, January 2002, 79–142.

Caruth, Cathy. *Unclaimed Experience: Trauma, Narrative and History.* Baltimore, MD and London: Johns Hopkins University Press, 1996.

Chan, Helen. *A Catalogue of Chinese Painting in the Luis de Camões Museum, Macau.* Hong Kong: Centre of Asian Studies, University of Hong Kong, 1977.

Chang, Kang-I Sun, and Haun Saussy, eds. *Women Writers of Traditional China: An Anthology of Poetry and Criticism.* Stanford, CA: Stanford University Press, 1999.

Chen Huiyan. *Nanyue youji* 南越游記 (Record of travels in Nanyue). Guangdong, preface dated 1857.

Chen Xianzhang, *Chen Baisha ji* 陳白沙集 (Collection of works by Chen Baisha). Taipei: Taiwan shangwu yinshuguan, 1985.

Chinese Repository (May 1836–April 1837).

Ching, Maybo. "Literary, Ethnic, or Territorial? Definitions of Guangdong Culture in the Late Qing and Early Republic." In *Unity and Diversity: Local Cultures and Identities in China,* edited by David Faure and Tao Tao Liu. Hong Kong: Hong Kong University Press, 1996.

———. "Picturing Knowledge in a Late Qing Periodical, 1907–1911," *Journal of Modern Chinese History,* vol. 1, 2007, 31–51.

———. "Taste and Scent: The Culture of Chow and Flower among Canton Hong Merchants." Unpublished paper.

Choi, Kee Il, Jr. "Carl Gustav Ekeberg and the Invention of Chinese Export Painting," *The Magazine Antiques,* vol. 143, March 1998, 426–437.

Chou Ju-hsi. "Rubric and Art History: The Case of the Eight Eccentrics of Yangzhou," *Chinese Painting under the Qianlong Emperor.* Phoebus 6, no. 2. Tempe, AZ: Arizona State University Press, 1991, 329–350.

———. "Tangdai: A Biographical Sketch." In *Chinese Painting under the Qianlong Emperor: Symposium Papers in Two Volumes,* edited by Chou Ju-hsi and Claudia Brown. Phoebus 6, no. 1. Tempe, AZ: Arizona State University Press, 1991, 132–141.

Chou Ju-hsi, and Claudia Brown. *The Scent of Ink: The Roy and Marilyn Papp Collection of Chinese Painting.* Phoenix AZ: Phoenix Art Museum, 1989.

Chu, Christina. "An Overview of Li Jian's Painting." In *Chinese Painting under the Qianlong Emperor,* edited by Chou Ju-hsi and Claudia Brown. Phoebus 6, no. 2. Tempe, AZ: Arizona State University Press, 1991, 295–315.

Chu, Madeline. "Journey into Desire: Monkey's Secular Experience in the Xiyoubu," *Journal of the American Oriental Society,* vol. 117, 1997, 654–664.

Clapp, Anne de Coursey. *The Paintings of T'ang Yin.* Chicago and London: University of Chicago Press, 1991.

Claypool, Lisa, ed. *China's Imperial Modern: The Painter's Craft,* Edmonton: University of Alberta Museum, 2012.

Clunas, Craig. *Empire of Great Brightness.* Honolulu, HI: University of Hawaii Press, 2007.

———. *Pictures and Visuality in Early Modern China.* Princeton, NJ: Princeton University Press, 1997.

———. *Superfluous Things: Material Culture and Social Status in Early Modern China.* Urbana and Chicago, IL: University of Illinois Press, 1991.

———. *Chinese Export Watercolours.* London: Victoria and Albert Museum, 1984.

Conner, Patrick. *The Hongs of Canton: Western Merchants in South China (1700–1900), as seen in Chinese Export Art.* London: English Art Books, 2009.

———. "Lamqua, Western and Chinese Painter," *Arts of Asia,* March–April 1999, 46–62.

———. *George Chinnery, 1774–1852: Artist of India and the China Coast.* London: Antique Collectors' Club, 1993.

Crary, Jonathan. *Suspensions of Perception: Attention, Spectacle, and Modern Culture.* Cambridge, MA and London: MIT Press, 2001.

Dai Xi. *Fang Yue ji* 訪粵集 (Writings on travels to Yue). Manuscript, 1840.

de Salis, William Fane. *Reminiscences of Travels in China and India in 1848.* London: Waterlow & Sons, 1892.

Dikotter, Frank, Lars Laaman, and Zhou Xun. "Narcotic Culture: A Social History of Drug Consumption in China," *British Journal of Criminology,* vol. 42, 2002, 317–336.

Dong Qi and Xu Zhihao. *Taiping huanle tu.* Shanghai, Xuelin chubanshe, 2003 reprint.

Durrant, Stephen W. *The Cloudy Mirror: Tension and Conflict in the Writings of Sima Qian.* New York: State University of New York Press, 1995.

Elliot, Mark. "Bannermen and Townsmen: Ethnic Tension in Nineteenth-Century Jiangnan," *Late Imperial China,* vol. 11, no. 1, 1990, 36–74.

Elman, Benjamin A. "The Failures of Contemporary Chinese Intellectual History," *Eighteenth Century Studies,* vol. 43, no. 3, 2010, 371–391.

———. *A Cultural History of Civil Examinations in Late Imperial China.* Berkeley, CA: University of California Press, 2000.

Elman, Benjamin A., and Alexander Woodside, eds. *Education and Society in Late Imperial China, 1600–1900.* Berkeley, CA: University of California Press, 1994.

Eng, Robert Y. "Institutional and Secondary Landlordism in the Pearl River Delta, 1600–1949," *Modern China,* vol. 12, no. 1, 1996, 3–37.

Epstein, Maram. *Competing Discourses: Orthodoxy, Authenticity, and Engendered Meanings in Late Imperial Chinese Fiction.* Cambridge, MA and London: Harvard University Press, 2001.

Fairbank, John King. *Trade and Diplomacy on the China Coast: The Opening of the Treaty Ports, 1842–1854.* Cambridge, MA: Harvard University Press, 1969.

Faure, David. *Emperor and Ancestor: State and Lineage in South China.* Stanford, CA: Stanford University Press, 2007.

———. "What Made Foshan a Town? The Evolution of Rural-Urban Identities in Ming-Qing China," *Late Imperial China,* vol. 11, no. 2, December 1990, 1–31.

———. "The Lineage as a Cultural Invention: The Case of the Pearl River Delta," *Modern China,* vol. 15, no. 1, January 1989, 4–37.

Faure, David, and Helen Siu, eds. *Down to Earth: The Territorial Bond in South China.* Stanford, CA: Stanford University Press, 1995.

Faure, David, and Tao Tao Liu, eds. *Town and Country: Identity and Perception.* Basingstoke, UK: Macmillan, 2001.

Franz, Michael H. et al. *The Taiping Rebellion: History and Documents.* Seattle, WA: University of Washington Press, 1966–71.

Gamboni, Dario. *The Destruction of Art: Iconoclasm and Vandalism since the French Revolution.* London: Reaktion Books, 1997.

Geertz, Clifford. *The Interpretation of Cultures.* New York: Basic Books, 1973.

Ginzburg, Carlo. "Titian, Ovid and Erotic Illustrations." In *Clues, Myths and the Historical Method,* translated by John and Anne C. Tedeschi. Baltimore, MD: Johns Hopkins University Press, 1986, 77–95.

Gombrich, Ernest, H. *Art and Illusion: A Study in the Psychology of Pictorial Representation.* London: Phaidon Press, 1986.

Graham, A. C. *The Work of Lie-tz'u.* London: Paragon Book Gallery, 1960.

Gray, John Henry. *Walks in the City of Canton.* Hong Kong: De Souza & Co., 1875.

Guangdong Paintings of the Ming and Qing Periods. Hong Kong: Art Gallery, The Chinese University of Hong Kong, 1982.

Guangdong wenwu 廣東文物 (Cultural relics of Guangdong), 3 vols. Hong Kong: Zhongguo wenhua xiejinhui, 1941.

Guo Rucheng et al. *Shunde xianzhi* 順德縣志 (Shunde gazetteer), 36 *juan.* 1853 edition.

Guo Yuhai. *Gugong cang jing* 故宮藏鏡 (Glass in the Palace Museum). Beijing: Zijincheng chubanshe, 1996.

Haddad, John. *The Romance of China: Excursions to China in US Culture, 1776–1876.* New York: Columbia University Press, 2008.

Hamilton, Robyn. "The Pursuit of Fame: Luo Qilan (1775–1813?), and the Debates about Women and Talent in Eighteenth-Century Jiangnan," *Late Imperial China,* vol. 18, no. 1, 1997, 39–72.

Hammers, Roslyn Lee. *Pictures of Tilling and Weaving: Art, Labor, and Technology in Song and Yuan China.* Hong Kong: Hong Kong University Press, 2011.

Harrist, Robert E. Jr. *The Landscape of Words: Stone Inscriptions in Early and Medieval China.* Seattle: University of Washington Press, 2008.

———. "Connoisseurship: Seeing and Believing." In *Issues of Authenticity in Chinese Painting,* edited by Wen C. Fong and Judith G. Smith. New York: Metropolitan Museum of Art, 1999.

———. "Ch'ien Hsuan's *Pear Blossoms*: The Tradition of Flower Painting and Poetry from Sung to Yuan," *Metropolitan Museum Journal*, vol. 22, 1987, 53–70.

Hawkes, David, trans. *The Story of the Stone, also known as The Dream of the Red Chamber Vol. 2: The Crab-Flower Club.* London: Penguin Books, 1977.

Hay, John. "Subject, Nature, and Representation in Early Seventeenth-Century China." In *Proceedings of the Tung Ch'i-ch'ang International Symposium*, edited by Wai-ching Ho. Kansas City, MO: Nelson-Atkins Museum of Art, 1991.

———. "Surface and the Chinese Painter: The Discovery of Surface," *Archives of Asian Art*, vol. 38, 1985, 95–123.

———. "Values and History in Chinese Painting: The Hierarchal Evolution of Structure," *Res* vol. 7/8, Spring 1984, 102–136.

Hay, Jonathan. *Sensuous Surfaces: The Decorative Object in Early Modern China.* London: Reaktion, 2009.

———. "Luo Ping: The Encounter with the Interior Beyond." In *Eccentric Visions: The Worlds of Luo Ping (1733–1799)*, edited by Kim Karlsson. Zurich: Museum Rietberg, 2009.

———. "Wen Zhengming, Stone Lake, and the Aesthetics of Disjunction," *Taiwan 2002 Conference on the History of Painting in East Asia*, 266–307.

———. "Painting and the Built Environment in Late Nineteenth-Century Shanghai." In *Chinese Art: Modern Expressions*, edited by Maxwell Hearn and Judith G. Smith, 60–101. New York: Metropolitan Museum of Art, 2001a.

———. *Shitao: Painting and Modernity in Early Qing China.* Cambridge: Cambridge University Press, 2001b.

———. "Culture, Ethnicity, and Empire in the Work of Two Eighteenth-Century 'Eccentric' Artists," *Res: Anthropology and Aesthetics*, vol. 35, Spring 1999, 201–223.

———. "Painters and Publishers in Late Nineteenth-Century Shanghai." In *Art at the Close of China's Empire*, edited by Chou Ju-hsi. Phoebus Occasional Papers in Art History vol. 8, 1998, 134–189.

Hearn, Maxwell, and Judith G. Smith, eds. *Chinese Art: Modern Expressions.* New York: Metropolitan Museum of Art, 2001.

Heijdra, Martin. "A Preliminary Note on Cultural Geography and Ming History," *Ming Studies* vol. 34, July 1995, 151–175.

Heinrich, Larissa N. *The Afterlife of Images: Translating the Pathological Body between China and the West.* Chapel Hill, NC: Duke University Press, 2008.

———. "Handmaids to the Gospel: Lam Qua's Medical Portraiture." In *Tokens of Exchange: The Problem of Translation in Global Circulations*, edited by Lydia H. Liu, 239–276. Durham, NC and London: Duke University Press, 1999.

Hershatter, Gail et al., eds. *Remapping China: Fissures in Historical Terrain.* Stanford, CA: Stanford University Press, 1996.

Ho, Wai Kam et al. *Eight Dynasties of Chinese Painting.* Cleveland, OH: Cleveland Museum of Art, 1980.

Hodder, Rupert. *The Creation of Wealth in China.* London: Belhaven, 1995.

Hostetler, Laura. *Ethnography and Cartography in Early Modern China.* Chicago, IL: Chicago University Press, 2001.

Hsu, Ginger. "The Drunken Demon Queller Chung K'uei in Eighteenth-Century Chinese Painting," *Taida Journal of Art History*, vol. 3 (1996), 145.

Hsu, Ginger Cheng-chi. *A Bushel of Pearls: Painting for Sale in Eighteenth-Century Yangzhou.* Stanford, CA: Stanford University Press, 2001.

Hu Wenkai, ed. *Lidai funü zhuzuo kao* 歷代婦女著作考 (A survey of women's writings through the ages). Shanghai: Shanghai guji chubanshe, 1985.

Huang Foyi. *Guangzhou Cheng fangzhi* 廣州城坊志 (The historical geography of Guangzhou City). Guangzhou: Jinan daxue chubanshe, 1994.

Huang Mengtian. "Shunde er Su" 順德二蘇 (The two Sus of Shunde). In *Tan yi lu* 談藝錄 (Notes on literature and art). Hong Kong: Shanghai Book Co., 1973.

Huang Peifang. *Yue xiaoji* 粵小記 (Notes on Yue). Guangdong, preface dated 1832.

Huang Qichen. *Ming Qing Guangdong shangren* 明清廣東商人 (Guangdong merchants in the Ming and Qing Dynasties). Guangzhou: Guangdong jingji chubanshe, 2002.

Hunter, William C. *Bits of Old China.* Taipei: Cheng-hua, reprinted 1966.

———. *The "Fan Kwae" at Canton: Before Treaty Days.* Shanghai: Oriental Affairs, 1938.

Huntington, Rania. "Chaos, Memory, and Genre: Anecdotal Recollections of the Taiping Rebellion," *Chinese Literature: Essays, Articles, Reviews*, vol. 27, December 2005, 59–91.

Hymes, Robert P., and Conrad Schirokauer, eds. *Ordering the World: Approaches to State and Society in Sung Dynasty China.* Berkeley, CA: University of California Press, 1997.

Itier, M. Jules. *Journal d'un Voyage en Chine en 1843, 1844, 1845, 1846*, 2 vols. Paris: Chez Duvin et Fontaine, 1848.

Jian Youwen. "Guangdong shuhua jiancang ji" 廣東書畫鑑藏記 (Records of collectors and connoisseurs in

Guangdong), *Guangdong wenxian jikan* 廣東文獻季刊 (Guangdong literature quarterly), vol. 2, 1972, 11–32; vol. 3, 1973, 27–51; vol. 4, 1974, 16–19.

———. *Huatan guaijie Su Renshan* 畫壇怪傑蘇仁山, also entitled *Su Jen-shan: Eccentric Genius of Kwangtung: His Life and Art*. Hong Kong: Jianshi Mengjin shuwu, 1970.

———. *Qingshi Hong Xiuquan zaiji* 清史洪秀全載記 (Historical records of Hong Xiuquan). Hong Kong: Jianshi Mengjin shuwu, 1967.

Johnson, Kendall, ed. *Narratives of Free Trade: The Commercial Cultures of US-Chinese Relations*. Hong Kong: Hong Kong University Press, 2011.

Kao Mayching, ed. *The Art of Li Jian and Xie Lansheng*. Hong Kong and Guangzhou: Art Gallery, The Chinese University of Hong Kong and Guangzhou Art Gallery, 1993.

———. *The Art of Su Liupeng and Su Renshan*. Hong Kong and Guangzhou: Art Gallery, The Chinese University of Hong Kong and Guangzhou Art Gallery, 1990.

———. *Paintings of the Ming and Qing Dynasties from the Guangzhou Art Gallery*. Hong Kong and Guangzhou: Art Gallery, The Chinese University of Hong Kong and Guangzhou Art Gallery, 1986.

Karlsson, Kim, ed. *Eccentric Visions: The Worlds of Luo Ping (1733–1799)*. Zurich: Museum Rietberg, 2009.

Kjellberg, Paul, trans. "Selections from Zhuangzi." In *Readings in Classical Chinese Philosophy*, edited by Philip J. Ivanhoe and Bryan W. Van Norden. Indianapolis, IN: Hackett Publishing Company, Inc., 2005, 207–254.

Ko, Dorothy. *Teachers of the Inner Chambers: Women and Culture in Seventeenth-Century China*. Stanford, CA: Stanford University Press, 1994.

Koon, Yeewan. "The Art of Tales: Qing Novels and Paintings by Su Renshan (1814–c.1850). In *Rethinking Visual Narratives from Asia: Intercultural and Cpmarative Perspectives*, edited by Alexandra Green. Hong Kong: Hong Kong University Press, 2012, 61–75.

———. "The Face of Diplomacy in Nineteenth-Century China: Qiying's Portrait Gifts." In *Narratives of Free Trade: The Commercial Cultures of US-Chinese Relations*, edited by Kendall Johnson. Hong Kong: Hong Kong University Press, 2011, 131–148.

———. "Lives and Afterlives: Luo Ping's 'Guiqu tu,'" *Orientations* 40, September 2009, 66–72.

———. "Luo Ping and Guiqu tu." Exhibition catalogue article in *Eccentric Visions: The Worlds of Luo Ping (1733–1799)*, edited by Kim Karlsson et al. (Zurich: Rietberg Museum of Art, 2009).

———. "Literati Iconoclasm: Violence and Estrangement in the Art of Su Renshan (1814–c.1850). Ph.D. thesis, Institute of Fine Arts, New York University, 2006.

———. "Windblown Whispers: Pan Zhengwei's Tingfan lou Art Collection and Its Impact on Early 19th Century Guangzhou." Unpublished paper.

———. "Narrating the City: Pu Qua and the Depiction of Street Life in Canton Trade Art." In *Qing Encounters: Artistic Exchanges between China and the West*, edited by Petra Chu. Los Angeles: Getty Publication, forthcoming.

Kuhn, Philip A. *Rebellion and Its Enemies in Late Imperial China: Militarization and Social Structure, 1796–1864*. Cambridge, MA: Harvard University Press, 1980.

Kwangtung Paintings by Kwangtung Masters during the Ming and Ch'ing Periods. Hong Kong: Art Gallery, The Chinese University of Hong Kong, 1973.

Laing, Ellen Johnston. "Chinese Palace-Style Poetry and the Depiction of A Palace Lady," *Art Bulletin* vol. 72, no. 2, June 1990, 285–295.

———. "Wives, Daughters, and Lovers: Three Ming Dynasty Women Painters." In *Views from a Jade Terrace: Chinese Women Artists 1300–1912*, edited by Marsha Weidner. Indianapolis, IN: Indianapolis Museum of Art, 1988.

Lee, Chi-kwong. *Su Renshan*. Guangzhou: Lingnan meishu chubanshe, 2011.

Lee, Hui-shu. "The Domain of Empress Yang (1162–1233): Art, Gender and Politics at the Late Southern Song Court." Ph.D thesis, Yale University, 1994.

Legge, James. *The Chinese Classics Book VI, Part II*. London: Truber & Co., 1861–1872.

———. *Li Chi: Book of Rites. An Encyclopedia of Ancient Ceremonial Usages, Religious Creeds, and Social Institutions*. New York: University Books, 1967.

Leung, Raymond Tang Man. "Collecting in Guangdong Epitomized by the Chih Lo Lou Collection." In *Nobility and Virtue: A Selection of Late Ming and Early Qing Paintings and Calligraphies from the Chih Lo Lou Collection*, exhibition catalogue. Hong Kong: Hong Kong Museum of Art, 2010, 52–61.

Lewis, Mark Edward. *Sanctioned Violence in Early China*. Albany, NY: State University of New York Press, 1990.

Leys, Simon. *The Analects of Confucius*. New York and London: W. W. Norton & Co., 1997.

Li Bozhong. "Daoguang xiaotiao yu guiwei daishui" 道光蕭條與癸未大水 (The Daoguang depression and the 1823 flood—economic decline, climatic cataclysm and the nineteenth-century crisis in Songjiang), *Journal of Social Sciences*, vol. 6, 2007, 173–178.

Li Chengyang. "Zhongyong as Grand Harmony: An Alternative Reading to Ames and Hall's *Focusing the Familiar*," *Dao* 3, no. 2, 173–188.

Li Chu-tsing. *Ming Qing Guangdong mingjia shanshui huazhan* 明清廣東名家山水畫展 (Catalogue of landscape paintings by Guangdong masters in the Ming and Qing dynasties). Hong Kong: The Chinese University of Hong Kong Art Gallery, 1973.

———. "Su Renshan (1814–1849), The Rediscovery and Reappraisal of a Tragic Cantonese Genius," *Oriental Art*, vol. IV, Winter 1970.

Li Ruzhen. *Jinghuayuan* 鏡花緣 (Flowers in the mirror). Beijing: Beijing shi zhongguo shudian, reprint 1985.

Li Tiaoyuan. *Yuedong biji* 粵東筆記 (Jottings on Yuedong). Shanghai: Shanghai huiwentang shuju, reprinted 1922.

Li Yuchun. "Su Liupeng de fengcai hua," 蘇六朋的諷刺畫 (Satirical paintings by Su Liupeng), *Lingnan wenshi* 嶺南文史 (History and literature from Lingnan), vol. 1, 1985, 157–158.

Liang Jiabin. *Guangdong shisan hang kao* 廣東十三行考 (An examination of Guangdong's thirteen cohongs). Guangzhou: Guangdong renmin chubanshe, 1999, 259–269.

Liang Qichao. *Wang Anshi zhuan* 王安石傳 (A biography of Wang Anshi). Haikou: Hainan chubanshe, 2001.

Lienü zhuan, Gaoshi zhuan 列女傳，高士傳 (Biographies of exemplary women, biographies of sages and hermits). Emended by Liu Xiaodong. Shenyang: Liaoning jiaoyu chubanshe, 1988.

Little, Stephen. "Early Chinese Painting at the Art Institute of Chicago," *Art Institute of Chicago Museum Studies*, vol. 22, no. 1, 1996, 36–53.

Liu, Lydia. *The Clash of Empires: The Invention of China in Modern World Making*. Cambridge, MA: Harvard University Press, 2004.

Liu, Lydia H., ed. *Tokens of Exchange: The Problem of Translation in Global Circulations*. Durham, NC and London: Duke University Press, 1999.

Liu Yangming. *Zhu Yue baqi zhi* 駐粵八旗誌 (Gazatteer of the eight bannermen in Guangdong). Shanghai: Shanghai guji chushuban, 2002 reprint.

Liu Zhiwei. "Lineage on the Sands." In *Down to Earth: The Territorial Bond in South China*, edited by David Faure and Helen Siu, 21–43. Stanford, CA: Stanford University Press, 1995.

Ma Ya-chen. "Fengsu, difang yu diguo: Taiping Huanle tu de zhizuo ji qi dui xihao zhi xiang de chengxian" 風俗、地方與帝國：太平歡樂圖的製作及其對熙皞之象的呈現 (Customs, provinces, and the empire: The making of *Taiping huanle tu* and its representation of "Peaceful Regime"), *National Central University Journal of Humanities*, vol. 45, January 2011, 141–194.

Madancy, Joyce. *The Troublesome Legacy of Commissioner Lin: The Opium Trade and Opium Suppression in Fujian, 1820s to 1920s*. Cambridge, MA: Harvard University Press, 2003.

Malcolm, Howard. *Travels in South-Eastern Asia: Embracing Hindustan, Malaya, Siam, and China*. Philadelphia, PA: American Baptist Publication Society, 1853.

Mann, Susan. *Precious Records: Women in China's Long Eighteenth Century*. Stanford, CA: Stanford University Press, 1997.

———. "The Education of Daughters in the Mid-Ch'ing Period." In *Education and Society in Late Imperial China, 1600–1900*, edited by Benjamin A. Elman and Alexander Woodside, 19–49. Stanford, CA: Stanford University Press, 1994.

———. "'Fuxue' by Zhang Xuecheng (1738–1801): China's First History of Women's Culture," *Late Imperial China*, vol. 13, no. 1, 40–63.

Marks, Robert B. "Rice Prices, Food Supply, and Market Structure in Eighteenth-Century South China," *Late Imperial China*, vol. 12, no. 2, December 1999, 64–116.

———. *Tigers, Rice, Silk and Silt: Environment and Economy in Late Imperial South China*. New York: Cambridge University Press, 1998.

McMahon, Keith. *The Fall of the God of Money: Opium Smoking in Nineteenth-Century China*. Lanham, MD: Rowan and Littlefield Publishers, 2002.

———. "Opium and Sexuality in Late Qing Fiction," *Nan Nü: Men, Women, and Gender in Early and Imperial China* vol. 2, no. 1, 2000, 129–179.

McNair, Amy. "Engraved Calligraphy in China: Recension and Reception," *The Art Bulletin*, vol. 77, no. 1, March 1955, 106–114.

Melancon, Glenn. *Britain's China Policy and the Opium Crisis: Balancing Drugs, Violence and National Honour, 1833–1840*. Aldershot, UK: Ashgate, 2003.

Meng Yue. *Shanghai and the Edges of Empire*. Minneapolis, MN: University of Minnesota Press, 2006.

Meyer-Fong, Tobie. *Building Culture in Early Qing Yangzhou*. Stanford, CA: Stanford University Press, 2003.

Miles, Steven, B. *The Sea of Learning: Mobility and Identity in Nineteenth-Century Guangzhou*. Cambridge, MA: Harvard University Asia Center, 2006.

———. "Creating Zhu 'Jiujiang': Localism in Nineteenth-Century Guangdong," *T'oung Pao International Journal of Chinese Studies*, vol. 90, no. 4, December 2004, 299–340.

———. "Local matters: Lineage, Scholarship and the Xuehaitang Academy in the Construction of Regional Identities in South China." Ph.D. thesis, University of Washington, 2000.

———. "Merchant and/as Literati in Early Nineteenth-Century Guangzhou: A View from the Xie Lansheng Diary." Unpublished paper.

Miyazaki, Ichisada. *China's Examination Hell: The Civil Service Examinations of Imperial China*, translated by Conrad Schriokauer. New York and Tokyo: Weatherhill, 1963.

Mok Kin Wai Patrick. "Lineage and Elite Dominance in Late Imperial Chinese Society: A Case Study of Shunde County, Guangdong." M.Phil. thesis, University of Hong Kong, 1995.

Morton, Dianne Lorell. "Paintings as Social Rhetoric: Wei-Jin Themes in Ming Dynasty Illustrations and Inscriptions." Ph.D. thesis, University of Kansas, 2003.

Murck, Alfreda. *Poetry and Painting in Song China: The Subtle Art of Dissent*. Cambridge, MA: Harvard University Asia Center for the Harvard-Yenching Institute, 2000.

Murray, Dian H. *Pirates of the South China Coast*. Stanford, CA: Stanford University Press, 1987.

Naquin, Susan. *Temples and City Life, 1400–1900*. Berkeley, CA: University of California Press, 2000.

Naquin, Susan, and Evelyn Rawski. *Chinese Society in the Eighteenth Century*. New Haven, CT: Yale University Press, 1987.

Ng Chin-keong, trans. "Shooting Eagles: Lin Changyi's Agony in the Wake of the Opium War." In *Maritime Asia in Transition, 1750–1850*, edited by Wang Gangwu and Ng Chin-keong. Weisberg: Harrossowitz Verlag, 2004.

——. "Treaties, Politics, and the Limits of Local Diplomacy in Fuzhou in the Early 1850s." In *Power and Identity in the Chinese World Order: Festschrift in Honor of Professor Wang Gungwu*, edited by Billy K. L. So et al., 239–268 (Hong Kong: Hong Kong University Press, 2003).

Nienhauser, William H. Jr., ed. *The Indiana Companion to Traditional Chinese Literature*. Bloomington, IN: Indiana University Press, 1986.

Owen, Stephen. *An Anthology of Chinese Literature: Beginnings to 1911*. New York and London: W. W. Norton and Company, 1996.

Ownby, David. *Brotherhoods and Secret Societies in Early and Mid-Qing China*. Stanford, CA: Stanford University Press, 1996.

Pan Shangji. *Nanhai xianzhi*, 44 *juan* 南海縣志 (Nanhai gazetteer). 1835 edition.

Pan Shicheng. *Haishan xianguan congshu* 海山仙館叢書 (Collectaneum of works from Haishan xianguan), manuscript, 1849.

Pan Yizeng, comp. *Panyu Panshi shilue* 番禺潘氏詩略 (Poems by the Pan family of Panyu), manuscript 1894.

Pease, Jonathan Otis. "From the Wellsweep to the Shallow Skiff: Life and Poetry of Wang Anshi, 1021–1086." Ph.D. thesis, University of Washington, 1993.

Peng Hailing. *Wang Zhaoyong yu jindai Yue Ao wenhua* 汪兆鏞與近代粵澳文化 (Wang Zhaoyong and modern culture of Guangdong and Macao). Guangzhou: Guangdong renmin chubanshe, 2004.

Perdue, Peter C. "Nature and Nurture on Imperial China's Frontiers," *Modern Asian Studies*, vol. 43, no. 1, 2009, 245–267.

Polachek, James. *The Inner Opium War*. Cambridge, MA: Harvard University Asia Center, 1992.

Pomeranz, Kenneth. *The Great Divergence: China, Europe and the Making of the Modern World Economy*. Princeton, NJ and Oxford: Princeton University Press, 2000.

Poole, Deborah. *Vision, Race and Modernity: A Visual Economy of the Andean Image World*. Princeton, NJ: Princeton University Press, 2007.

Powers, Martin. "'Humanity and Universals' in Sung Dynasty Painting." In *Arts of the Song and Yuan*, edited by Maxwell Hearn and Judith G. Smith. New York: Metropolitan Museum of Art, 1996.

Purtle, Jennifer G. "Placing Their Mark: An Art-Historical Geography of Min (Fukien) Painters of the Ming Dynasty, 1368–1644." Ph.D. thesis, Yale University, 2001.

Qian Ma. *Feminist Utopian Discourse in Eighteenth-Century Chinese and English Fiction: A Cross-Cultural Comparison*. Hampshire, UK: Ashgate Publishing Ltd., 2004.

Raphals, Lisa A. "A Woman Who Understood the Rites." In *Confucius and the Analects*, edited by Bryan W. Van Norden, 275–302. Oxford: Oxford University Press, 2002.

Rankin, Mary Barkus. "Managed by the People: Officials, Gentry, and the Foshan Charitable Granary, 1795–1845," *Late Imperial China*, vol. 15, no. 2, December 1994, 1–52.

Red Pine. *The Heart Sutra: The Womb of Buddhas*. Washington, DC: Shoemaker and Hoard, 2004.

Roddy, Stephen J. *Literati Identity and Its Fictional Representations in Late Imperial China*. Stanford, CA: Stanford University Press, 1998.

Ropp, Paul. "Between Two Worlds: Women in Shen Fu's *Six Chapters of a Floating Life*." In *Women and Literature in China*, edited by Anna Gerstlacher. Bochum: Studienverlag Brockmeyer, 1985.

——. *Dissent in Early Modern China: Ju-lin wai-shih and Ch'ing Social Criticism*. Ann Arbor, MI: University of Michigan Press, 1981.

Rowe, William, T. "Money, Economy and Polity in the Daoguang-era Paper Currency Debate," *Late Imperial China*, vol. 31, no. 2, December 2010, 69–96.

——. "Women and the Family in Mid-Qing Social Thought: The Case of Chen Hongmou," *Late Imperial China*, vol. 13, no. 2, December 1992, 1–41.

——. *Hankow: Conflict and Community in a Chinese City, 1796–1895*. Stanford, CA: Stanford University Press, 1989.

Ruitenbeek, Klaas. *Discarding the Brush: Gao Qipei (1660–1734) and the Art of Chinese Finger Painting*. Amsterdam: Rijksmuseum, 1992.

Ryckmans, Pierre. *The Life and Work of Su Renshan: Rebel, Painter and Madman 1814–c.1849*, translated by Angharad Pimpaneau. Paris and Hong Kong: University of Paris, 1970.

Ryor, Kathleen. "Fleshy Desires and Bodily Depravations: The Somatic Dimensions of Xu Wei's Flower Paintings." In *Body and Face in Chinese Visual Culture*, edited by Wu

Hung and Katherine R. Tsiang, 121–146. Cambridge, MA and London: Harvard University Press, 2005.

Schafer, Edward. *Vermilion Bird: T'ang Images of the South.* Berkeley and Los Angeles, CA: University of California Press, 1967.

Screech, Timon. *The Western Scientific Gaze and Popular Imagery in Later Edo Japan: The Heart within the Lens.* Cambridge: Cambridge University Press, 1996.

Shangguan Zhou. *Wanxiaotang huazhuan* 晚笑堂畫傳 (Painting record of Wanxiao Hall). Beijing: Zhongguo shudian, reprinted 1984.

Shen Fu. *Six Records of a Floating Life*, translated by Leonard Pratt and Chiang Su-Hui. London: Penguin Books, 1983.

Shih Heng-ching. *A Comprehensive Commentary on the Heart Sutra.* San Francisco, CA: Numata Center for Buddhist Translation and Research, 2001.

Shih Shou-chien. "Wen Zhengming and the Effects of Popular Culture." In *Taiwan 2002 Conference on the History of Painting in East Asia.* Taipei: National Taiwan University, 2002, 308–322.

Shun Kwong-loi. "On Anger: An Experimental Essay in Confucian Moral Psychology." In *Zhu Xi Now: Contemporary Encounters with the Great Ultimate*, edited by David Jones and He Jinli. Albany, NY: State University of New York, forthcoming.

Siu, Helen F. "Where were the Women? Rethinking Marriage Resistance and Regional Culture in South China." *Late Imperial China*, vol. 11, no. 2, 1990, 32–62.

Skinner, G. W. *The City in Late Imperial China.* Stanford, CA: Stanford University Press, 1977.

Sloboda, Stacey. "Picturing China: William Alexander and the Language of Chinoiserie," *British Art Journal*, vol. 9, no. 2, 28–36.

Spence, Jonathan D. *God's Chinese Son: The Taiping Heavenly Kingdom of Hong Xiuquan.* New York: W. W. Norton, 1996.

———. *Chinese Roundabout: Essays in History and Culture.* New York: W. W. Norton, 1992.

Stockard, Janice E. *Daughters of the Canton Delta: Marriage Patterns and Economic Strategies in South China, 1860–1930.* Stanford, CA: Stanford University Press, 1989.

Stuer, Catherine. "Reading the World's Landscape in Zhang Bao's Images of the Floating Raft." In *Rethinking Visual Narratives from Asia: Intercultural and Comparative Perspectives*, edited by Alexandra Green. Hong Kong: Hong Kong University Press, 2013, 77–94.

Su Liupeng. Hong Kong: City Hall Museum and Art Gallery, 1965.

Su Renshan. Hong Kong: City Hall Museum and Art Gallery, 1966.

Su Ruohu, comp. *Mengxing furong ji* 夢醒芙蓉記 (Awakening from the hibiscus dream). Manuscript, 1897.

Sung, Hou-mei. *Decoded Messages: The Symbolic Language of Chinese Animal Painting.* New Haven, CT and London: Yale University Press, 2009.

Tan Dihua et al. *Guangdong beike ji* 廣東碑刻集 (Collection of stele engravings from Guangdong). Guangdong: Guangdong gaodeng jiaoyu chubanshe, 2000.

———. *Guangdong lishi wenti lunwen ji* 廣東歷史問題論文集 (Collection of essays on Guangdong history). Taipei: Daohe chubanshe, 1993.

Teng, Emma Jinhua. *Taiwan's Imagined Geography: Chinese Colonial Travel Writing and Pictures, 1683–1895.* Cambridge, MA: Harvard University Asia Center, 2004.

ter Haar, Barend J. "Rethinking 'Violence' in Chinese Society." In *Meanings of Violence: A Cross-Cultural Perspective*, edited by Goran Aijimer and Jos Abbink, 123–140. Oxford: Berg, 2000.

———. *Ritual and Mythology of the Chinese Triads.* Leiden, Boston, and Koln: Brill, 1998.

Tiffany, Osmond. *The Canton Chinese or The American's Sojourn in the Celestial Empire.* Boston, MA: James Munroe, 1849.

Tilly, Charles et al. *The Rebellious Century, 1830–1930.* London: Dent, 1975.

Topley, Majorie. "Marriage Resistance in Rural Kwangtung." In *Studies in Chinese Society*, edited by Arthur P. Wolf, 247–268. Stanford, CA: Stanford University Press, 1978.

Tsin, Michael. *Nation, Governance, and Modernity in China: Canton, 1900–1927.* Berkeley, CA: University of California Press, 1999.

van Braam, Andreas Everard. *An Authentic Account of the Embassy of the Dutch East India Company, to the Court of the Emperor of China, in the years 1794 and 1795: Containing a Description of Several parts of the Chinese Empire.* London: R. Philips, 1798.

van Gulik, Robert. *The Lore of the Chinese Lute: An Essay in Ch'in Ideology.* Tokyo: Sophia University, 1940.

Van Norden, Bryan W., ed. *Confucius and the Analects.* Oxford: Oxford University Press, 2002.

Vinograd, Richard. "Relocations: Spaces of Chinese Visual Modernity." In *Chinese Art: Modern Expressions*, edited by Maxwell Hearn and Judith G. Smith, 162–181. New York: Metropolitan Museum of Art, 2001.

———. *Boundaries of the Self: Chinese Portraits, 1600–1900.* Cambridge: Cambridge University Press, 1992.

———. "Family Properties: Personal Context and Cultural Pattern in Wang Meng's Pien Mountains of A.D. 1366," *Ars Orientalis*, vol. 13, 1982, 1–29.

Wakeman, Frederic, Jr. *Strangers at the Gate: Social Disorder in South China, 1839–1861.* Berkeley and Los Angeles, CA: University of California Press, reprinted 1997.

Wakeman, Frederic, Jr., and Carolyn Grant, eds. *Conflict and Control in Late Imperial China.* Berkeley, CA: University of California, 1975.

Waley, Arthur. *Yuan Mei: Eighteenth-Century Chinese Poet.* New York: Grove Press, 1956.

Wan Qingli. *Bing fei shuailuo de bai nian: shijiu shiji Zhongguo huihua shi* 並非衰落的百年：十九世紀中國繪畫史 (The century was not declining in art: A history of nineteenth-century Chinese painting). Taipei: Xiongshi tushu gufen youxian gongsi, 2005.

Wang, David, and Shang Wei, eds. *Dynastic Decline and Cultural Innovation: Late Ming and Late Qing.* Cambridge, MA: Harvard University Asia Studies Center, 2005.

Wang Gai. *Yuanban yingyin Jieziyuan huazhuan. Chu, er, san ji.* 原版影印芥子園傳。初，二，三集。 (Mustard seed garden painting manual. Facsimile copy of three volumes). Shanghai: Tian bao, 19—.

Wang Rongpei et al. *The Complete Works of Tao Yuanming.* Changsha: Hunan Publishing House, 2003.

Wang Yen-chien. "Secular Trends of Rice Prices in the Yangzi Delta." In *Chinese History in Economic Perspectives,* edited by Thomas G. Rawski and Lillian M. Li. Berkeley, Los Angeles, and Oxford: University of California Press, 1992.

Wang Zhaoyong, *Lingnan hua zhenglue* 嶺南畫徵略 (Summary of paintings from Lingnan). Hong Kong: Commercial Press, 1961.

Wang Zongyan. *Guangdong shuhua zhengxian lu* 廣東書畫徵獻錄 (Record of painting and calligraphy in Guangdong). Macau: no publisher name, 1988.

Watson, Burton, trans. *Chuang Tzu: Basic Writings.* New York: Columbia University Press, 1964.

———. *Records of the Grand Historian of China, translated from the Shih Chi of Ssu-ma Ch'ien,* 2 vols. New York: Columbia University Press, 1961.

Watson, Rubie. "The Named and the Nameless: Gender and Person in Chinese Society," *American Ethnologist,* vol. 13, no. 4 (November 1986), 619–631.

Weidner, Marsha, ed. *Latter Days of the Law: Images of Chinese Buddhism 850–1850.* Lawrence, KS: Spencer Museum of Art, 1994.

———. *Views from a Jade Terrace: Chinese Women Artists 1300–1912.* Indianapolis, IN: Indianapolis Museum of Art, 1988.

Widmer, Ellen. *The Beauty and the Book: Women and Fiction in Nineteenth-Century China.* Cambridge, MA and London: Harvard East Asian Monographs, 2006.

———. "Jinghua yuan: Where the Late Late Ming Meets the Early Late Qing." In *Dynastic Decline and Cultural Innovation: Late Ming and Late Qing,* edited by David Wang and Shang Wei, 264–295. Cambridge, MA: Harvard University Asia Studies Center, 2005.

Widmer, Ellen, and Kang-I Sun Chang, eds. *Writing Women in Late Imperial China.* Stanford, CA: Stanford University Press, 1997.

Wilheim, Helmut. *Change: Eight Lectures on the I Ching, translated from the German by Cary Baynes.* New York: Pantheon Books, Bollingen Series, 1960.

Wilson, Ming. "As True as Photographs: Chinese Paintings for the Western Market." *Orientations,* vol. 31, no. 9, November 2000.

Wu Hung. "On Rubbings: Their Materiality and Historicity." In *Writing and Materiality in China: Essays in Honor of Patrick Hanan.* Cambridge, MA: Havard-Yenching Institute Monograph Series 58 (2003), 29–72.

———. *The Double Screen Medium and Representation in Chinese Painting.* London: Reaktion Books, 1996.

Wu Peiyi. *The Confucian's Progress: Autobiographical Writings in Traditional China.* Princeton, NJ: Princeton University Press, 1990.

Wu Rongguang. *Wu Rongguang ziding nianpu* 吳榮光自訂年譜 (A chronological biography of Wu Rongguang). Jiulong: Zhongshan tushu gongsi, 1971.

Xian Baogan et al., *Foshan zhongyi xiangzhi* 佛山忠義鄉志 (Gazetteer of the loyal and righteous town of Foshan). Foshan: Xiuzhi ju, 1923.

Xian Yuqing, "Guangdong zhi jiancang jia" 廣東之鑑藏家 (Connoisseurs and collectors from Guangdong), *juan* 10. In *Guangdong wenwu* 廣東文物 (Cultural relics of Guangdong), 982–996. Hong Kong: Zhongguo wenhua xiejinhui, 1984, reprinted Shanghai shudian, 1990.

Xiang Dongshan et al. *Guangzhou Yuexiu gu shuyuan gaiguan* 廣州越秀古書院概觀 (An overview study of academies in Yuexiu, Guangzhou). Guangzhou: Zhongshan daxue chubanshe, 2002.

Xie Wenyong. *Guangdong huaren lu* 廣東畫人錄 (Record of artists from Guangdong). Guangzhou: Lingnan meishu chubanshe, 1986.

Yang Boda, ed. *Tributes From Guangdong to the Qing Court; Jointly Presented by the Palace Museum, Beijing and the Art Gallery, The Chinese University of Hong Kong.* Hong Kong: Art Gallery, The Chinese University of Hong Kong, 1987.

Yang Chunqiu, ed. *Xinyi Kongzi jiayu* 新譯孔子家語 (New Translations of the Analects). Taipei: Sanmin shuju, 1996.

Zeitlin, Judith. "Disappearing Verses: Writings on Walls and Anxieties of Loss." In *Writing and Materiality in China: Essays in Honor of Patrick Hanan,* 73–132. Cambridge, MA: Harvard-Yenching Institute Monograph Series 58, 2003.

Zhang Hongxing, "Re-reading Inscriptions in Chinese Scroll Painting: The Eleventh to the Fourteenth Centuries," *Art History,* December 2005, 606–625.

Zhang Pengzhou. *Xue Tao shi jian* 薛濤詩箋 (Poems by Xue Tao). Chengdu: Sichuan renmin chubanshe, 1981.

Zhang Qu, ed. *Yuedong wen jian lu* 粵東聞見錄 (A record of things heard and seen in Yuedong). Guangzhou: Guangdong gaodeng jiaoyu chubanshe, 1990 reprint. This edition also includes a reprint of Chen Huiyan's *Nanyue youji*.

Zhang Weiping. *Huajia xiantan* 花甲閒談 (Idle talks of the elderly). Manuscript 1839.

Zheng Yangwen. *The Social Life of Opium*. New York: Cambridge University Press, 2005.

———. "The Social Life of Opium in China 1483–1999," *Modern Asian Studies*, vol. 37, 2003, 1–39.

Zhongguo jin bai nian huihua zhanlan xuanji 中國近百年繪畫展覽選集 (Exhibition of modern Chinese painting in the past 100 years). Beijing: Wenwu chubanshe, 1959.

Zhou Zhuojie. *Mazu* 媽祖. Beijing: Tuanjie chubanshe, 1999.

Zhu Changwen. *Qin shi* 琴史 (History of the *qin* zither). Edited by Palace Museum. Haikou: Hainan chubanshe, 2001.

Zhuang Shen. *Cong baizhi dao baiyin: Qing mo Guangdong shuhua chuangzuo yu shoucang shi* 從白紙到白銀：清末廣東書畫創作與收藏史 (From paper to gold: A history of collecting painting and calligraphy in late Qing Guangdong), 2 vols. Taipei: Dongda tushu gongsi, 1997.

Zhuo Chengyuan, ed. *Zhongguo funü renming cidian* 中國婦女人名詞典 (Dictionary of famous women in China). Shijiazhuang: Hebei kexue jishu chubanshe, 1991.

Index